D1595738

America's Unending
Civil War

America's Unending Civil War

The Enduring Conflict from Jamestown through to Recent Elections

William R. Nester

FRONTLINE BOOKS

First published in Great Britain in 2024 by
Frontline Books
An imprint of Pen & Sword Books Limited
Yorkshire – Philadelphia

ISBN 978 1 39908 118 4

Typeset by Mac Style
Printed in the UK by CPI Group (UK) Ltd, Croydon, CR0 4YY.

Pen & Sword Books Limited incorporates the imprints of After
the Battle, Atlas, Archaeology, Aviation, Discovery, Family History,
Fiction, History, Maritime, Military, Military Classics, Politics,
Select, Transport, True Crime, Air World, Frontline Publishing, Leo
Cooper, Remember When, Seaforth Publishing, The Praetorian Press,
Wharncliffe Local History, Wharncliffe Transport, Wharncliffe True
Crime and White Owl.

For a complete list of Pen & Sword titles please contact

PEN & SWORD BOOKS LIMITED
47 Church Street, Barnsley, South Yorkshire, S70 2AS, England
E-mail: enquiries@pen-and-sword.co.uk
Website: www.pen-and-sword.co.uk
or
PEN AND SWORD BOOKS
1950 Lawrence Rd, Havertown, PA 19083, USA
E-mail: uspen-and-sword@casematepublishers.com
Website: www.penandswordbooks.com

Contents

Acknowledgements

I would like to express my deep gratitude and pleasure at having had yet another opportunity to work with the outstanding editorial team of Alison Flowers, Lisa Hoosan, John Grehan, and Martin Mace, who were always as kind as they were professional. I am especially grateful to Alison for her meticulous editing of my book.

List of Tables

Introduction

"The past is never dead. It's not even past."

William Faulkner

aulkner was a wise man. His insight is certainly true of America's Civil War. Whether Americans realize it or not, they are still fighting many of the Civil War's issues that stretch back to the first settlement and will persist until the end of time.

The Civil War was America's Iliad leading from and to Odysseys. The war itself was an Iliad of brilliant generals like Grant, Sherman, and Sheridan for the Union, and Lee, Jackson, and Forrest for the Confederacy; epic battles like Gettysburg and Chickamauga, sieges like Vicksburg and Petersburg, and naval combats like the *Monitor* versus the *Merrimack* and *Kearsarge* versus the *Alabama*. Although most military campaigns were east of the Mississippi River, fighting nearly spanned the continent: a Confederate army invaded New Mexico; California volunteers occupied forts across the West as regular soldiers were withdrawn east, and often skirmished with local tribes; General James Carleton led 2,350 men across 900 miles of mostly desert from Los Angeles to El Paso, and fought Apaches along the way; rebels from Canada raided St Albans, Vermont. Meanwhile Confederate warships hunted and destroyed scores of American merchant and whaling vessels on churning seas around the world.

It was America's most horrific war with more dead than all others combined. At least 618,222 troops, 360,222 Union and 260,000 Confederate, died, and possibly around 750,000 soldiers and civilians from combat and disease during four years of war.[1] Battle and accidents maimed hundreds of thousands of men. The war destroyed hundreds of millions of dollars' worth of businesses, railroads, barns, factories, warehouses, stations, crops, bridges, courthouses, livestock, and homes across swaths of the South and elsewhere, with entire cities gutted like Richmond, Atlanta, Jackson, Chambersburg, and Columbia. Of 31 million Americans, 2.1 million northerners and 880,000 southerners donned uniforms. An astonishing three of four southern men of military age fought three of ten northern men. Among survivors, countless veterans as well as civilians with ruined lives suffered what is now called post-traumatic stress disorder that mingled sorrow, lassitude, and rage, while tens of thousands of amputees struggled to find work with many begging on street corners.

Fortunately, Abraham Lincoln was America's president. Lincoln was a brilliant politician, statesman, strategist, and humanist; his wisdom, wit, and eloquence inspired Americans then and ever since. His leadership culminated with the Confederacy's destruction and slavery's abolition. Atop those stunning achievements, he also helped initiate the Homestead Act, land grant colleges, modern banking system, and transcontinental railroad. Tragically, an assassin murdered Lincoln just days after Lee surrendered his army to Grant at Appomattox, effectively ending the war.

An Odyssey led to and from the Civil War. It began in 1607 with the Jamestown settlement followed a dozen years later when colonists purchased the first shipload of African slaves. Although slavery was the Civil War's core cause, there were related chronic conflicts over the nature of government, citizenship, liberty, property, voting, equality, wealth, race, identity, crime, justice, power, and history from the nation's origins. Over the first seventeen decades, American liberalism and nationalism developed, leading to the war for independence then the Constitution and early republic. Thereafter crises erupted over whether new states should allow or forbid slavery, "Bloody Kansas," the Supreme Court's Dred Scott decision, John Brown's attempt to incite a slave rebellion at Harpers Ferry, the 1860 election with Lincoln's victory, the secession of slave states, formation of the Confederacy, and attack on Fort Sumter. Nearly as divisive an Odyssey followed the Civil War that spanned Reconstruction, the Ku Klux Klan, Jim Crow, the civil rights movement, election of the first black president, battles over Civil War and other historical monuments, and recently the 2020 election with its stark choice between candidates, beliefs, policies, and visions for America.

Indeed, an attempted insurrection marred the 2020 election. President Donald Trump refused to accept his overwhelming defeat and called on his followers to prevent Congress from certifying the Electoral College vote on January 6, 2021. A mob of 20,000 Trumpians swarmed around the Capitol, many waving Confederate flags, and around 2,000 broke in to vandalize that symbol of American democracy before police expelled them. Fortunately, the members of Congress fled to safety before the rioters could assault them and that night reconvened to certify the election results. That horrifying scene of anarchy and terrorism recalled a similar attempt to destroy America's electoral process 160 years earlier. On February 13, 1861, a pro-Confederacy mob threatened to prevent the certification of Abraham Lincoln's victory. That time, General Winfield Scott ringed the Capitol with troops armed with Springfield rifles bristling with bayonets, and the mob dispersed.

For all the preceding reasons, the Civil War fascinates Americans like no other war in their history. Millions are "buffs" who devour Civil War books and explore battlefields. Many got hooked when they were kids on some family or school trip to a site. Among buffs, two groups stand out. Academic and amateur scholars alike eagerly meet at scores of annual conferences and over 200 Civil War Round Tables across the nation to discuss and debate their cherished latest findings. Reenactors gather around campfires or charge across fields in mock battles. The hardcore among them eat the same wretched food and abstain from bathing and shaving just like the men who actually fought a century and a half ago.[2]

What explains America's Civil War?[3] The beginning was clear enough. Starting with South Carolina on December 20, 1860, legislatures or conventions in one southern slave state after another voted to secede from the United States. On February 8, 1861, delegations met in Montgomery, Alabama to form the Confederate States of America. On April 14, Confederate artillery began bombarding Fort Sumter, garrisoned by American troops in Charleston Bay. That sparked a war that lasted 4 years, caused 750,000 deaths, and resulted in the destruction of both the Confederacy and slavery.

That begs the question, why did eleven states eventually band together to rebel against the United States? President Jefferson Davis began an answer when he said: "If the Confederacy falls, there should be written on its tombstone, Died of a Theory."[4] That theory justified the enslavement of blacks by whites as a natural right and duty of a superior race over an inferior race that morally and economically elevated both races. Slavocrats pointed to Bible passages that called on masters to care for their slaves and for slaves to obey their masters. That right was so fundamental that proponents had to fight by any means any attempt to abolish or even limit it.

Slavocrats increasingly faced and felt threatened by a contrary theory that slavery was morally wrong and should be abolished. That theory was perhaps best expressed in America's Declaration of Independence with the line: "We hold these truths to be self-evident, that all men are created equal; that they are endowed by their Creator with certain unalienable rights; and that among these are life, liberty, and the pursuit of happiness." Increasing numbers of Americans wanted to realize that ideal for all people in the United States. One by one, the northern states abolished slavery for themselves and, with the 1787 Northwest Ordinance, banned slavery in territory north of the Ohio River that would eventually be populated and transformed into states.

For decades preceding the rebellion, demagogue politicians and newspaper editors, then called fire-eaters, condemned "Yankee" financiers for dominating the South's economy and abolitionists for trying to free their slaves. In doing so, slavocrats martyrized themselves and scapegoated despised northerners. Slavocrats reacted in rage and paranoia to Abraham Lincoln's election to the White House in November 1860. Although Lincoln's Republican Party accepted slavery where it then existed, it was committed to preventing its spread to new territories and future states out West. But that was the excuse that slavocrats wielded to justify their rebellion. Charleston socialite Mary Chesnut explained: "We are divorced, North from South, because we hated each other so."[5]

Three of four southern men of military age fought in that war even though only one of four were slaveowners. Indeed, the 4 million slaves amidst millions of hardscrabble farmers and laborers actually depressed their wages. Why would men fight for a system of slavery that actually worsened their own poverty? With 22 years old the average enlistment age, peer pressure, especially from young women, and a chance to prove one's manhood were the most powerful motives, along with a lifetime of hearing about states' rights and identity with one's state rather than the nation.

Ironically, slavery both caused the war and contributed to the South's defeat. Slavocracy, like communism, nurtured the seeds of its own eventual destruction. One reason for this was philosophical. The practice violated the fundamental principles of natural law and America's Declaration of Independence with most Americans deploring that hypocrisy. Another was psychological. To varying degrees, most people prefer freedom to subjection, enterprise to exploitation. The third and most critical was economic. Slavocracy condemned the South to a mostly stagnant agrarian economy when modern warfare demanded sophisticated mass finance, manufacturing, transportation, and communications. After forming and declaring independence, the Confederacy initiated a war against the United States without the material power to win it.

However, none of that made the Confederacy's defeat inevitable. Leaders and luck, good and bad, shape human events often in unexpected ways. After Lincoln, no man was more responsible for crushing the rebellion than Ulysses Grant who captured three armies. How would the war have unfolded and ended had a bullet killed Grant at, say, Belmont in November 1861?

America's Unending Civil War: The Enduring Conflict from Jamestown through Recent Elections is unique among thousands of books on the subject as it explores the Civil War over four centuries of the nation's history from its inception to the latest headlines.

Part I

Conflicts and Violence, 1607–1860

Chapter 1

Colonists and Slaves

One-hundred-sixty-eight years separated Jamestown's founding in 1607 and the battles of Lexington and Concord in 1775.[1] During that time, what became the United States underwent extraordinary transformations in values, institutions, and identities. Originally, the colonists were authoritarian, not libertarian, communitarian, not individualistic, theocratic, not freethinking, elitist, not pluralist, and English, not American. Gradually, that changed. By 1775, most colonists identified themselves as Americans, cherished an array of civil rights, and had quasi-republican governments with elected assemblies and governors appointed by the king; Connecticut and Rhode Island voters actually elected their own governors. Property qualifications for voting and running for office varied among the colonies and were confined to white males 21 years and older. Most Americans were the "middling sort" who owned their own homes and farms or businesses. Of course, slaves and common laborers were mostly poor. Nonetheless, the average American was far wealthier and less taxed than the average Briton.

American nationalism developed naturally. The vast Atlantic Ocean separated the colonists from the mother country. Each generation born in what became thirteen colonies increasingly saw themselves as Americans. A series of wars with the neighboring French and Spanish empires and their Indians allies reinforced American identity. The Americans largely fought all those wars except the last on their own.

The British did send over large armies and navies for the war that erupted in 1754. Ironically, the fighting began when Lieutenant Colonel George Washington ordered his men to encircle and fire on a French patrol in disputed territory. What began as the latest struggle between the rival British and French empires eventually involved the other European powers and campaigns in North America, Europe, the West Indies, India, West Africa, Argentina, the Philippines, and the seas connecting those lands. The fighting in North America ended in 1760 with the conquest of Canada by British armies with large contingents of American troops. The fighting ended in Europe in 1763 with the Treaty of Paris. Under that treaty, the French ceded Canada and its lands east of the Mississippi River to Britain, and its land west of the Mississippi along with New Orleans to Spain.

That latest war and especially its aftermath swelled American nationalism. Most British officers sneered at their American counterparts like Washington, wounding their pride. Then from 1763 to 1775, King George III and Parliament imposed a series of taxes and restrictions on the colonists and ever more troops to enforce them. The excuse was the need to pay for Britain's national debt that doubled during the war. Yet many British leaders feared that America's swelling population, prosperity, and nationalism would lead colonial leaders to demand more autonomy and eventually outright independence. They thought they could smother that with more hard power. Instead, they enflamed it.

The colonists split among loyalists who obeyed, moderates who protested, and radicals who committed violence against British officials and officers who upheld the repressive measures. The acts of moderate and radical patriots succeeded in forcing Britain's government to rescind the 1765 Stamp Act and 1767 Townsend Acts. Then in 1770, Parliament enacted the Tea Act with a tax and monopoly for the East India Company to sell tea in the colonies. In December 1773, a group of radicals swarmed aboard three vessels packed with tea and dumped it in Boston Harbor. London sought to make an example of Massachusetts by imposing martial law, suspending its general assembly, doubling the number of redcoats in Boston, and shutting off Boston's trade for all products except food and firewood until the colonists paid for the destroyed tea.

That provoked moderates and radicals in the other colonies to unite with Massachusetts in protest. In September and October 1775, representatives met in the First Continental Congress at Philadelphia and issued a petition that called on Britain's government to respect American rights. They planned to reconvene in May 1775.

General Thomas Gage was Massachusetts's military governor headquartered in Boston. Learning of a munitions depot in Concord 20 miles west, he sent a thousand redcoats to capture it. Word of that approaching force caused militia companies across the region to muster and march to intercept it. At dawn on April 19, 1775, the British column marched into Lexington where the town's military company deployed on the common. When someone fired a shot, the British opened fire then charged, routing the company. That "shot heard round the world" began a war that resulted in America's independence.

Extraordinary individuals led the extraordinary liberal and nationalist transformations in the American colonies from 1607 to 1775. No one alone exemplified them but two did. John Smith was in the governing council that founded Virginia and took over, when starvation, disease, and Indian attacks threatened to destroy the colony. Smith's enterprise, courage, decisiveness, curiosity, vision, pragmatism, and adventurous spirit not only saved Virginia but became core American characteristics. Benjamin Franklin's long life spanned most of the eighteenth century and exemplified the Age of Enlightenment values of reason, science, humanism, and liberalism. His Americanism blossomed during a decade in London as a lobbyist for Pennsylvania and several other colonies. He returned to Philadelphia as Congress convened in May 1775. He was instrumental in nurturing America's Declaration of Independence in 1776, France's alliance with the United States in 1778, and the Constitution in 1787.

Slavery is likely as old as humanity. Anthropologists and historians find slavery in virtually all premodern societies around the world.[2] Europeans did not invent African slavery. From 30 to 60 percent of sub-Saharan Africa's population were slaves when the trans-Atlantic trade began.[3] What Europeans did was buy from, and thus expand, the existing continental network. The guns and chains that Europeans exchanged for slaves empowered African kings and chiefs to launch more expeditions that netted more slaves.

The Spaniards initiated the triangular trans-Atlantic trade that exchanged manufactured goods for African slaves, then exchanged the slaves for colonial products like sugar and tobacco that they exchanged in Europe for more manufactured goods. Eventually the Portuguese, Dutch, English, French, and Americans developed their own triangular trans-Atlantic trade systems. The best estimate is that over 4 centuries from 1451 to 1870, Africans sold Europeans around 9,391,100 slaves of whom at least 1 in 10 perished along with 1 in 20 sailors during 54,200 voyages to the New World.[4] Slaves referred to that harsh voyage as "the middle passage."

Slavery in what became the United States originated when a Dutch sea captain sold twenty slaves to Virginians in 1619.[5] The purchasers treated the Africans as indentured servants and released them after seven years with 50 acres of land for each because the colony then had no slave laws. Gradually, more Africans were sold as servants in Virginia and other colonies. In 1641, Massachusetts was the first colony to legalize and regulate slavery with its Body of Liberties. One by one the other colonies enacted similar laws with Virginia's in 1661.

From 1619 to 1770, 122,735 African slaves were officially brought to the 13 colonies, although likely thousands more arrived unrecorded.[6] Slavery's relative economic importance, and thus its political, social, and cultural importance, varied considerably among the colonies. The portion of slaves to the population was greater the further south one journeyed. Slaves were about 2.6 percent of New England's population, 6 percent of the mid-Atlantic colonies, and 40 percent of the southern colonies. By 1770, blacks numbered 459,822 of 2,148,076 people.[7] A free black population emerged as owners manumitted their slaves. Overall, about one of ten people of African descent were free, and three of five in New York and other ports.

Chapter 2

The Early Republic

The American Revolution unfolded through two phases.[1] Americans won independence in the first and formed a less imperfect union in the second. The first took eight years and ended decisively. The second also took eight years but twenty-four decades later remains a work of mostly progress.

The fighting that began at Lexington on April 19, 1775, resulted in an American victory. Ever more militia companies converged, fought the redcoats at Concord, then harassed them as they retreated to Boston. They then besieged the British in Boston. Militia regiments from other New England colonies joined the siege. Congress appointed George Washington to command that growing army. The delegates sent an "olive branch petition" to George III, assuring him of their loyalty and requesting the withdrawal of British troops. The king replied by declaring the colonies in rebellion.

Washington was able to force the British army to abandon Boston in March 1776. Elsewhere, British governors and redcoats fled American troops and governments. Word arrived that the king had rejected any compromise and instead condemned them as rebels. Congress declared independence on July 4, 1776. In justifying that act, Thomas Jefferson drafted and the other Congressmen refined the document that eloquently and rofoundly expressed the philosophy of natural law and rights:

> We hold these truths to be self-evident; that all men are created equal; that they are endowed with their creator with certain unalienable rights; that among these are life, liberty and the pursuit of happiness; that to secure these rights, governments are instituted among men, deriving their just powers from the consent of the governed; that whenever any form of government becomes destructive of those ends, it is the right of the people to alter or abolish it, and to institute new government.

For nearly two and a half centuries since those lines were penned, Americans have struggled over what they mean and who should enjoy them.

American victory in its war for independence was not inevitable. Two forces were critical to how and when the Americans won independence. One was George Washington whose indomitable character kept the American army together for eight years of war despite more defeats than victories and a chronic lack of enough munitions, arms, provisions, and other equipment. The other was the American capture of a British army at Saratoga in September 1777 that encouraged France to openly ally with the United States against Britain. A French fleet bottled up a British army at Yorktown and a French army joined the American army led by Washington in forcing the British army to surrender in October 1781. Britain formally granted the United States independence with the Treaty of Paris, signed on September 3, 1783.

With independence, America's leaders turned to the next great challenge, framing a government that fulfilled the Declaration of Independence's ideals. The existing Congress was a confederation of thirteen sovereign states. Each state had one vote on all issues with unanimity required for any resolution or law. Congress had no powers of taxation and limited power to impose trade tariffs for revenue. In 1787, Congress did agree that a convention could suggest a more efficient government.

Representatives from twelve of the thirteen states met at Philadelphia from May to September. During that time, they debated, compromised, devised, and revised a constitution. They soon agreed to ground sovereignty ultimately in "the people" who would manifest it through the national government. Thus in ratifying the Constitution, the states surrendered their sovereignty to that new government. They also agreed to spread power among the executive, legislative, and judicial branches so that none was superior and they had to work together. For weeks, they argued over how to distribute legislative power among states with greatly varying populations. They finally decided on a bicameral Congress in which states had equal power in the Senate with two members each while each state's members in the House of Representative was proportional to its population. What would become a controversial decision was to make the president indirectly elected by an electoral college based on the states.

It took longer to forge the government's six great duties. The preamble reads: "We the People of the United States, in Order to form a more perfect Union, establish Justices, ensure domestic Tranquility, provide for the common defense, promote the General Welfare, and ensure the Blessing of Liberty for ourselves and our Posterity, do ordain and establish this Constitution of the United States of America." Ever since Americans have debated just how to realize each of those goals.

The final great issue was slavery.[2] The 1790 census counted 3,929,000 people including 757,000 blacks of whom slaves were nine of ten.[3] Although the population was split nearly equally between 1,968,000 northerners and 1,961,000 southerners, among blacks, 67,000 lived in the North and 690,000 in the South. Although nearly one of five Americans was enslaved, the words "slave" and "slavery" are mentioned nowhere in the Constitution. The framers were too ashamed explicitly to insert them. However, in opaque language the Constitution upheld slavery in three ways. First, slaves were counted as three-fifths of a human when determining the allocation of representatives. Second, slaves who escaped to another state had be returned to their masters. Third, the United States could not abolish its international slave trade before 1808.

After approving the Constitution, the Convention sent copies to each state government for ratification. In late 1788, the ratification was completed and the states held elections. The first Congress convened on March 4 and George Washington took the oath as the first president on April 30, 1789. The most important issue for the new government was to amend the Constitution with an explicit list of Rights for all Americans. Ten amendments defining that Bill of Rights were ratified by December 15, 1791. And ever since Americans have debated the meaning and assertion of those rights.

Alexander Hamilton and Thomas Jefferson had conflicting visions for America's economic future.[4] Hamilton wanted to transform the United States into an increasingly powerful, diversified, urban, middle-class economy fueled by inventors, entrepreneurs, financiers, manufacturers, and merchants. Government policies that promoted financial stability, infrastructure, innovation, education, and exports were critical to that transformation. High tariffs protected infant American industries from cheap foreign goods that could destroy them while providing government revenues to invest in infrastructure that promoted economic development. A United States Bank would be a joint venture between the Federal government and private investors to maintain a stable currency, keep inflation low, and give low-interest loans to entrepreneurs. Jefferson wanted to keep America's economy largely agrarian, the products of which would be exchanged for European manufactured goods. For that, low tariffs kept import prices low. He adamantly opposed a national bank.

Their differences did not end there. Hamilton favored a muscular problem-solving national government while Jefferson sought a weak national government with most power in the states. For defense, Hamilton called for an army and navy large enough to deter foreign or domestic threats and swiftly expanded to defeat them should deterrence fail. Jefferson wanted a military confined to state militia and gunboats in ports. Although both men considered slavery morally wrong, Hamilton opposed slavery's expansion and hoped for its eventual extinction while Jefferson saw equal evils in blacks enslaved or free.

As for the Constitution, Hamilton explained that it empowered the Federal government to do anything that it did not expressly forbid, while Jefferson insisted that the Federal government could only do what it specifically enumerated. Which view was correct? The Federalist Papers were 85 essays, of which Hamilton penned 51, James Madison 29, and John Jay 5 to explain the Constitution and so build support for its ratification. All three men had attended the Convention, with Madison's role in drafting the Constitution's key tenets so crucial that later he was dubbed its "father." All three then espoused a muscular problem-solving Federal government. Jefferson did not attend the Convention, as he was then minister to France.

Those rival views grounded rival political parties. Hamiltonism inspired the Federalists, Whigs, and Republicans while Jeffersonism inspired the Republican-Democrats and then the Democrats.

The Federalist Party lasted only from 1790 to 1800 then disappeared for three decades before its reincarnation as the Whig Party, which lasted from 1832 to 1852 before its reincarnation as the Republican Party in 1854. Jeffersonians shed the Republican part of their name to celebrate themselves as Democrats and politically dominate the early nineteenth century.

The prevalence of Jeffersonism and the Democratic Party does not reflect the practical effects of the rival philosophies. By that measure, America's economy develops with Hamiltonian policies and distorts with Jeffersonian policies. The policies that Treasury Secretary Hamilton implemented transformed the economy from a vicious cycle of depression, poverty, debt, trade deficits, and joblessness into an expanding middle class, exports, manufacturing, and hard money. The policies that Presidents Jefferson, James Madison, and Andrew Jackson imposed devastated the economy. Jefferson's 1807 trade embargo provoked a depression, high joblessness, and bankruptcies. The elimination of the First United States Bank by Madison in 1811 and the Second United States Bank by Jackson in 1836, unleashed speculation, inflation, bankruptcies, and depression. Atop this, Madison and a Democratic Congress declared war against Britain in June 1812. The War of 1812 was disastrous for the United States. Americans endured horrific death, destruction, and debt for no practical gain of territory or compensation from Britain. Yet, voters did not penalize the Democratic Party but instead enthusiastically supported it for a couple of generations through what became known as the "Era of Good Feelings" and the "Jacksonian Era."

So what explains that vast discrepancy between the political popularity and economic performance of the two philosophies and the parties that conveyed them? Human nature is one critical cause. Feelings and prejudices dominate most people's perceptions and here one outlook was far more appealing. Jeffersonism and its cousin Jacksonism were populist movements that claimed to uplift "the people," and most people fervently believed that. Atop that was the Federalist

Party's self-destruction at the national level by the 1800 election. Mingled organization, philosophical, and political reasons explain that. Hamilton failed to develop a party organization that extended to grass-roots voters in every state. It was a party that espoused policies that championed financers, shippers, innovators, and manufacturers but gave nothing specific to small businesses, farmers and slaveowners. President John Adams dealt the party's deathblow by pushing through a Federalist-dominated Congress the Alien and Sedition Acts whereby his administration prosecuted Democratic newspaper editors who criticized him.

Henry Clay resurrected Hamiltonism and the Federalist Party with his "American System" and Whig Party from 1832.[5] Yet Clay failed in each of his three presidential runs. Three presidents – John Quincy Adams and Whigs William Henry Harrison and Zachery Taylor – did espouse Hamiltonian ideas but failed to implement any of them; Adams mostly because of Democratic opposition and Whigs Harrison and Taylor because they died shortly after taking office.

Chapter 3

The Industrial Revolution

An industrial revolution transformed the United States during the nineteenth century's first half despite the prevailing Jeffersonian and Jacksonian hostility or indifference to it.[1] A number of innovators and entrepreneurs initiated that revolution, and that ingenuity was mostly Yankee. The first was Eli Whitney who, in 1793, invented the cotton gin that separated seeds from fiber. That device revolutionized cotton production on southern slave plantations and thus the textile industries in New England and Britain. Francis Lowell spent two years in Britain studying mass manufacturing techniques then, in 1814, established a factory with partners Patrick Jackson and Nathan Appleton in Waltham, Massachusetts. Lowell died in 1817. Jackson and Appleton founded what became the factory town of Lowell on the Merrimack River in 1821. Other entrepreneurs like Samuel Slater opened their own textile factories. Arial Bragg devised machinery and techniques to mass-produce shoes. Cincinnati entrepreneurs devised a factory system for transforming pigs into brine-barreled pork, hides for leather, lard for soap and lubricants, bones for buttons, bristles for brushes, intestines for sausages, and chops and bacon for the table. Some inventions made farming much more productive like Cyrus McCormick's reaper in 1831 and John Deere's plow in 1837. Precision tools mass-produced parts so refined that they were interchangeable.

Although America's industrial revolution began a couple of generations after Britain's and emulated it, at least one American industry surpassed its British rival – firearms. During the late 1830s, Samuel Colt developed first a five-shot then a six-shot revolver that he mass-produced at a factory outside Hartford, Connecticut. In the 1840s, the invention of percussion caps replaced the unreliable flintlock system for firing. In 1855, Springfield's arsenal began producing the .58 caliber rifle that used a Minnie ball, a cone-shaped bullet. Britain produced an improved copy of the Springfield at a factory in Enfield. Springfield's 1861 model incorporated those and other improvements.

Far-sighted state governments enacted their own Hamiltonian policies. The most ambitious and lucrative was New York's 363-mile long Erie Canal that linked the Hudson River and Lake Erie.[2] Governor Dewitt Clinton rallied a majority in the state's legislature to underwrite the project. The construction began on July 4, 1817 and ended eight years later with the first transit on

October 26, 1825. The canal included eighty-three locks with the highest 675ft above sea level. The economic result was as extraordinary as the engineering. Tolls paid the construction cost within nine years. New York City boomed with the population soaring from 122,000 in 1820 to 813,669 in 1860. The canal transformed several towns along the route into cities like Syracuse, Rochester, and Buffalo along with Cleveland and Toledo on Lake Erie. That inspired other northern states like Pennsylvania, Maryland, Ohio, and Illinois to build their own canals although with more modest results.

Steam power fueled a transportation revolution that accelerated the industrial revolution.[3] In 1807, after years of development, Robert Fulton launched a steamboat on the Hudson River at New York City that reached Albany 140 miles and 32 hours later. Within a decade, steamboats churned all the nation's navigable rivers and traversed the Atlantic Ocean. Meanwhile, British entrepreneurs developed railroads and steam-powered locomotives in the 1810s and 1820s. America's network began in 1828 with the Baltimore and Ohio Railroad and by 1861 a score or so companies had built 31,256 miles of track, including 21,973 northern and 9,283 southern miles.[4] Prices for goods plummeted with mass production and transportation in a united national market. An increasingly sophisticated banking system financed the related transportation and industrial revolutions.[5]

Then there was the telecommunication revolution. On May 24, 1844, Samuel Morse, an inventor and painter, sat in the Supreme Court chamber surrounded by leading officials, and tapped a coded message into a black device on the desk before him. A wire connected that device to a similar one on a desk where his assistant sat surrounded by officials in Baltimore 45 miles away. The message was "What hath God wrought?" The assistant received the message and tapped it back. By 1860, telegraph wires linked cites across the eastern United States.

Economic growth and development differ. Growth merely measures economic expansion. Development involves both the creation and distribution of wealth so that ever more people enjoy higher standards of material living and emotional quality of life. Decade after decade, the northern states developed while the southern states merely grew.[6]

The northern economy diversified as its middle class expanded in numbers and wealth, and became better educated. Between 1800 and 1860, its share of farmers fell from 70 percent to 40 percent while the south's share stagnated at 80 percent. In 1860, 1 of 4 northerners and 1 of 10 southerners lived in cities with more than 2,500 people. Innovations and the wealth they create and distribute was almost exclusively a northern phenomenon. From 1790 to 1860, 93 percent of 143 key innovations came from northern states and half from New England.

By 1860, the northern states held 80 percent of the nation's manufacturing output while the four border states accounted for half of the South's 20 percent. Of 128,000 manufacturing firms, 110,000 were in the North and 18,000 were in the eleven states that would form the Confederacy. Southern states exported 70 percent of their cotton, mostly to Britain, sold 25 percent to northerners, and retained only 5 percent for their own factories.[7]

Meanwhile, the South largely stagnated in overlapping slavocrat and quasi-feudal economic, social, and political systems with a tiny rich elite, a small middle class of merchants, lawyers, doctors, and other professionals, a large class of hardscrabble white farmers and laborers, and slaves living mostly a subsistence existence. On paper, the average white southerner was twice as wealthy as the average northerner, but that was a mirage. That greater wealth was grounded on land and slaves owned mostly by the elite. By 1860, only one of four white southerners owned any slaves while the wealthiest 5 percent of free adult males owned 53 percent of the economy and the poorest half owned merely 1 percent.[8] Southerners complained that they depended on northern finance and factories but had only themselves, or specifically slavery, to blame for that.

Chapter 4

The Old South

Slavery was at once the Old South's source of pride and shame, profit and poverty.[1] Native boosters insisted that their region was a land of moonlight and magnolias, honorable masters and happy slaves. Northerners who journeyed through the South were appalled by what they witnessed. New York Senator William Seward took prolonged trips to Virginia in 1835, 1840, and 1857, and found an "exhausted soil, old and decaying towns, wretchedly neglected roads, and ... an absence of enterprise and improvement ... Such has been the effect of slavery." Visitors contrasted poverty-stricken white southerners with the North's enterprising workers, artisans, and merchants. Vermont Senator Jacob Collamer concluded that most of the South's whites "are depressed, poor, impoverished, degraded in caste, because labor is degraded."[2]

Most of the South's wealth was measured by the value of the slaves and the crops they produced. The Lower South produced most of the nation's cotton, rice, and sugar, while the Upper South produced most of its tobacco. As the South's economy slowly diversified, the share of slaveholders fell from 36 percent in 1836 to 26 percent in 1860. Wealth, however, concentrated. Of landowners, those with slaves averaged $25,000 or fourteen times more wealth than non-slaveholders with $1,800 in 1860. In stark contrast, about four of ten whites were tenant farmers annually subsisting on a few hundred dollars. Around 16 percent of southerners worked outside of agriculture compared with 60 percent of northerners. Immigrants split 90 percent for the North and 10 percent for the South. A few cities sporadically dotted the South including Baltimore, Richmond, Charleston, Savannah, Atlanta, Mobile, Nashville, Memphis, and New Orleans that prospered by being ports or rail hubs.[3]

Of the South's 4 million blacks, about 94 percent or 3,740,000 were slaves. Among them around 75 percent worked crops with 55 percent in cotton, 10 percent tobacco, 10 percent sugar, rice, or hemp, and 5 percent other crops or livestock. Of the other 25 percent, about half were house servants and the other half worked in factories, mines, transportation, construction, or lumbering.[4] Among the South's 186,000 free blacks, some owned slaves. That was most common in Louisiana where one black master boasted 152 chattel. Among South Carolina's slaveholding elite was William Ellison who held 63 slaves on his 800-acre plantation.[5] Many free men were mulattoes manumitted by their white fathers. From 1620 to 1850, 7.7 percent of slaves were mulattoes.[6]

Cotton was dubbed "king" for dominating the South's economy.[7] Two types of cotton prevailed. Sea island or long-staple cotton grew best only in the wet soil of the Carolina and Georgia coastal regions which limited production. Short-staple or green-seed cotton grew best in the humid black soils of the region stretching from western Georgia to eastern Texas. That potentially vast production was limited by the difficulty in separating the fibers from the seeds or boll, a tedious, time-consuming process by hand. A simple but profound invention resolved that problem. Eli Whitney helped spark a revolution in cotton production and thus wealth for slaveholders when he invented the cotton gin in 1793. The gin was a relatively simple device, easily replicated, that extracted cottonseeds from fiber fifty times faster than by hand.

Cotton prices and production soared. America's share of global cotton production skyrocketed from 9 percent in 1801 to 68 percent in 1860; 75 percent was exported. Cotton production is labor intensive and grueling. Few people would voluntarily choose to work in cotton fields. Slaves filled that labor void. The price of slaves rose with the demand for them whether or not they produced cotton. The 1808 laws that outlawed the importation of foreign slaves limited the supply to reproduction by native-born slaves.

As in most industries, cotton producers represented a production pyramid. About half averaged a hundred acres worked by half a dozen or so slaves worth $3,000. About one in three averaged several hundred acres and a score of slaves worth $10,000. Finally, atop the pyramid was King Cotton's aristocracy of a couple thousand planters that averaged a thousand acres and a hundred slaves worth $100,000; about one in ten producers enjoyed this status. The distribution of slaves shifted over the decades. The Upper South, especially Maryland and Virginia sold its surplus slaves to the Lower South. From 1790 to 1860, the Upper South's slave population actually declined by 700,000 and its share of the total number from 60 percent to 18 percent while the Lower South's swelled from 21 percent to 55 percent.[8]

Masters treated house and field slaves differently. House slaves were status symbols adorned with fine clothes, good food, comfortable housing, and refined manners. Field slaves received minimal food, clothing, and shelter. However, punishments for infractions varied less with lashings liberally administered to deter others. States and most owners did not recognize slave marriages so couples and their children could be split up among different masters. Most states outlawed teaching slaves to read and write.

The South had a quasi-feudal economy and thus society.[9] That socioeconomic pyramid was a tough climb for enterprising whites with few reaching the top; free blacks had their own parallel even steeper pyramid. Slavery depressed wages for working class white farmers and laborers.[10] The South's elite created a culture grounded on notions of honor that trickled down through the classes. A gentleman's honor must be defended at all costs, including death. Dueling was a common if outlawed practice among eighteenth-century gentlemen. During the nineteenth century, dueling gradually died out among northerners but persisted among southerners up to the Civil War, although it was increasingly rare.[11] On one level the southern rebellion and war against the United States was an epic affair of insulted honor.

William Tecumseh Sherman, who had lived in parts of the region before the war, described the cultural mindset that produced rebel cavalry leaders:

> The young bloods of the South; sons of planters, lawyers about towns, good billiard players, and sportsmen, men who never did work and never will. War suits them, and the rascals are brave and good riders, bold to rashness ... They hate Yankees ... and don't bother their brains about the past, present, or future ... they are the most dangerous set of men that this war has turned loose on the world.[12]

As for education, the elite tutored its young, objected to paying for public schools for lower class whites, and outlawed teaching slaves to read, write, and do sums. The number of academies for boys and girls met the demand for those who could afford them. Each state had one or more colleges and military schools mostly filled with students from rich families.

Women held an exalted place in southern high society.[13] Ideally, chivalric southern gentlemen esteemed and protected southern belles throughout their lives. A belle should exemplify virtue, charm, and loyalty to her husband, children, and state. Mary Chesnut revealed that "our women are soft and sweet – low toned, indolent, graceful, quiescent."[14] As with other aristocracies, the South's slaveholders tended to marry among themselves. A girl's father decided whether the whispered declarations of love between her and her beau led to marriage. Suitors had to make a formal appeal to the patriarch.

The actual life of most white women of slaveholding families, especially on plantations, fell short of that ideal. The household mistress was responsible for the behavior of any attached slaves 24 hours a day. She had to manage their tasks and punish them if they failed to fulfill them. That included not just daily cooking and cleaning but season spells of making candles and soaps. Husbands granted their wives an allowance to cover household expenses. Planation mistresses complained most about the scarcity of white female friends and their slaves' laziness and impudence. As for her slaves, Sarah Gayle despaired that: "Indulgence has ruined them – they are idle yet full of complaints, easy to take offense at the slightest admonition which they frequently merit."[15]

There were often darker secrets involving sex that many women refused to admit to themselves let alone to others. One was venereal disease related to their husbands' infidelity. Historian Catherine Clinton found that: "The recipe books of southern plantation mistresses are full of concoctions to cure gonorrhea. Venereal disease plagued plantation society."[16] As for infidelity, straying husbands usually enjoyed it with the most easily available female or, in some cases, male, slaves.

States outlawed sex between blacks and whites but the enforcement varied. Black men accused of having had sex with white women were usually hanged whether it was consensual or rape. White men could freely seduce or rape their female slaves and often succumbed to being seduced. The result was a growing population of mulattoes living among their white half siblings. A female slave who bore her master's child usually fared better than those who did not. Mary Chesnut was disgusted by being "surrounded by prostitutes" with the result that husbands "live all in one house with their wives and their concubines, and the mulattoes one sees in every family exactly resemble their white children – and every lady tells you who is the father of all the mulatto children in everybody's household but" her own which "she seems to think drop from the clouds."[17]

Slavocrats devised elaborate arguments to justify slavery and asserted them through impassioned speeches in Congress and state capitols, through newspaper editorials and essays in publications like *De Bow's Review* and the *Southern Literary Messenger*, and "scholarly" books.[18] They pointed to biblical passages whereby God or Jesus called on slaveholders to be good to their slaves and on slaves to obey their masters. They insisted that slavery was good for blacks, arguing that their chattel lacked the intellectual and moral ability to be free and govern themselves, and, like children, could only be paternalistically cared for by their masters in return for serving them. As Senator John Calhoun of South Carolina put it: "In the present state of civilization, where two races of different origin, and distinguished by color, and other physical differences, as well as intellectual, are brought together, the relation now existing in the slaveholding States between the two, is instead of an evil, a good – a positive good."[19] In their respective books *Types of Mankind* (1854) and *Indigenous Races of the Earth* (1857), Josiah Nott and George Glidden argued that blacks were an inferior species that could and should be enslaved to benefit themselves and their masters. Charles Fitzhugh penned the most extended defenses of slavery in his books, *Sociology for the South, or the Failure of Free Society* in 1854 and *Cannibals All!, or Slaves without Masters* in 1857. He argued that slaves lived more comfortable, secure lives than northern factory workers and laborers. By his reckoning: "about nineteen out of twenty individuals have 'a natural and inalienable right' to be taken care of and protected … in other words have a natural and inalienable right to be slaves. The one in twenty are as clearly born or educated or in some way fitted for command and liberty." Thus did he espouse: "Liberty for the few – Slavery, in every form, for the mass!"[20]

Those willing to concede some qualms about slavery's morality also insisted that it was a necessary evil to prevent a worse one if slaves were liberated. Thomas Jefferson metaphorically expressed that dilemma: "We have the wolf by the ears, and we can neither hold him nor safely let him go. Justice is in one scale, and self-preservation is in the other."[21] Some slavocrats tried to reassure those troubled by slavery that it would gradually fade away.

Slaves resisted their masters mostly through passive aggressiveness. They worked as slowly as possible, misplaced or broke tools, played dumb, feigned pregnancies, exaggerated, and lied. A few resorted to violence, poisoning their masters or burning their homes. Murders of masters by their slaves were actually quite rare. Historian William Freehling found that: "Between 1834 and 1861, 31 cases involving blacks allegedly murdering whites came to the highest courts of Mississippi, Alabama, and Louisiana. Sixteen cases – over 50% – of the convictions were overturned."[22]

The ultimate terror that slaveowners harbored was being butchered by their chattel. A series of aborted or actual revolts stoked those fears, including in New York City in 1712 and 1741, at Stono, South Carolina in 1739, and New Orleans in 1811, and those led by Gabriel Prosser in Richmond in 1800, Denmark Vessey in Charleston in 1822, and Nat Turner in Virginia in 1831. Turner's was the bloodiest; he and his followers murdered fifty-seven whites, including forty-six women and children, before militia finally killed or captured them.

Slavery was legal in fifteen states in 1860. In varying degrees and ways, the cotton revolution helped transform the southwest territories into seven new slave states including Louisiana in 1812, Mississippi in 1817, Alabama in 1819, Missouri in 1820, Arkansas in 1836, and Florida and Texas in 1845. The Constitution's three-fifths clause gave slave states disproportionate political power by partly counting slaves with the white population for representatives in Congress. In 1790, the southern states had 40 percent of the nation's population and 47 percent of its representatives and Electoral College.[23] That was a key reason why more southerners than northerners won the White House before 1861.

Slavocrats did not hesitate to assert that power.[24] They provoked crises in 1820 and 1850 to maintain the balance between slave and free states. Slavocrat power in Congress was so great that in 1836, they imposed a "gag rule" that prevented any submission and discussion of abolitionist petitions it received; clerks piled them in a storage room. Atop that, congressional slavocrats imposed censorship rules for the postal system that outlawed any mailing of abolitionist literature. Massachusetts Representative John Quincy Adams and Kentucky Senator Henry Clay led the opposition to those rules and were able to rescind the gag rule in 1844.

Senator John Calhoun was the most outspoken defender of such rules, arguing that they shielded slaveholders from: "a war of religious and political fanaticism ... waged not against our lives but against our character. The object is to humble and debase us in our estimation, and that of the world."[25] Of course, Calhoun was absolutely right. Abolitionists wanted to expose slaveholders to their own immorality and hypocrisy. But nearly all slaveholders reacted in rage not reflection and projected their own vilest behavior on their accusers. They rejected any notion that they morally debased themselves by holding, debasing, and humbling slaves.

The Slavocrat gag and censorship rules grossly violated the Constitution's tenets on congressional duties and citizen First Amendment rights of free speech, press, and petition. Ironically, that empowered rather than quelled the abolitionist movement. Abolitionist ranks and actions swelled. The free speech gag provoked abolitionists to collect and send more petitions with the number rising from 32 in 1836 to 107 in 1840. In 1838 alone, the petitions presented to Congress contained more than 400,000 signatures.[26]

The Constitution vaguely and the 1793 Fugitive Slave Law explicitly granted slaveowners the right to pursue and capture escaped slaves in other states with the aid of local authorities. The 1850 Fugitive Slave Act required federal marshals to aid slaveowners in capturing their chattel, empowered them to deputize any citizen to aid that effort, fined them a thousand dollars if they refused to do so, and forced the federal government to pay any expenses. During the following decade, Federal officials helped return 416 slaves to their masters and freed only 16.[27]

Some slavocrats sought to expand slavery by conquering Latin American countries and imposing the institution there. Known as "filibusters," John Quitman and Narciso Lopez failed in their attempts to conquer Cuba as did William Walker's brief takeover of Nicaragua during the 1850s; Cuban and Nicaraguan authorities eventually captured and executed Lopez, Walker, and scores of their followers. Slavocrat lobbyists pressured the Democratic administrations of Franklin Pierce and James Buchannan to expand American slavery by acquiring Cuba.[28]

Known as "fire-eaters," radical Slavocrats insisted that the Constitution was a mere pact among sovereign states, an elaborate version of the Articles of Confederation that it replaced. State sovereignty meant each state could "nullify" or refuse to comply with any federal law or Constitution tenet, secede from the Union, and even war against the United States if its government violated its sovereignty. Slavery was the God-given right of whites to enslave blacks for their mutual well-being. South Carolina was a hotbed of fire-eaters including John Calhoun, Robert Barnwell Rhett, James Hammond, Edmund Ruffin, and Robert Hayne. Of them, Senator John Calhoun presented the most elaborate arguments for "nullification."

Chapter 5

Abolitionism

From slavery's origins in America, some people condemned it as evil and called for its abolition.[1] Those that did gradually rose in number and share of the population although they remained a minority even when the Civil War erupted. Quakers were the colonial era's most numerous abolitionists with John Woolman and Anthony Benezet prominent voices during the mid-eighteenth century. The early republic's leading abolitionists were Benjamin Franklin, Alexander Hamilton, and John Jay. They established the Pennsylvania Abolition Society with Franklin its president in 1784. Hamilton and Jay created the New York Manumission Society in 1785; Jay was its first president even though he was a slaveholder. Their next step was to form the American Convention for Promoting the Abolition of Slavery and Improving the Condition of the African Race in 1794. Early black abolitionists included freemen William Hamilton of New York and Richard Allen of Philadelphia.

Abolitionists scored some limited victories. Pennsylvania was the first state that partly abolished slavery. Its 1780 constitution liberated slaves born after that year but retained slaves then living for the rest of their lives. Rhode Island passed a similar law in 1784. Elsewhere, the gap between initiating and completing emancipation for Connecticut was 1790 and 1848, for New York 1799 and 1827, and for New Jersey 1804 and 1860. In contrast, Massachusetts, New Hampshire, and Vermont liberated their relatively miniscule slave populations immediately.

The Federal government took measures to limit slavery within the United States. The Northwest Ordinance 1787 forbad slavery in the territory that eventually yielded the states of Ohio, Indiana, Illinois, Michigan, and Wisconsin. Congress passed a law forbidding the importation of foreign slaves from 1808. Although thereafter smugglers brought a trickle of slaves into the country, conception caused most of the slave population's steady rise.

The American Colonization Society was founded in 1816 by Henry Clay seconded by James Monroe, John Marshall, and James Madison, all slaveholders.[2] In 1819, the Society received a Congressional grant of $100,000 with which they purchased land in west Africa that they called Liberia and eventually transported 13,000 free blacks there. Virtually all free blacks opposed colonization and instead called for equal racial rights and opportunities in the United States.

Abolitionism came of age from the 1820s as ever more voices joined to form an increasingly powerful chorus against slavery.[3] They promoted their cause through publications, speeches, petitions to Congress and state assemblies, protests, the Underground Railroad, and the legal defense of escaped slaves recaptured in northern cities.

Most were male. John Rankin made his home on a hilltop above Ripley, Ohio, a prominent station on the Underground Railroad visible to escapees across the Ohio River in Kentucky. He called for abolition in his 1826 tract, *Letters on American Slavery*. Kentucky's legislature offered $3,000 for his apprehension but no one ever collected. David Walker was a black abolitionist most famous for his 1829 pamphlet, "An Appeal to the Colored Citizens of the World" that called on slaves violently to overthrow their masters. The brothers Arthur and Lewis Tappan were wealthy evangelicals who underwrote the New York Anti-Slavery Society in 1832, the American Anti-Slavery Society in 1833, and the American and Foreign Anti-Slave Society in 1840. Theodore Weld offered the most systematic condemnations of slavery through his books. His 1837 *The Bible Against Slavery* countered slavocrats who justified slavery by passages from scripture with conflicting scriptural passages. His 1839 *American Slavery as It Is* chronicled the institution's cruelties. He wrote that book in collaboration with his wife Angelina Grimké Weld. James Birney was an Alabama plantation owner who freed his slaves in 1833, then migrated north where he founded the abolitionist Liberty Party and ran for president in 1840 and 1844. *New York Tribune* editor Horace Greely condemned the institution: "Enslave a man and you destroy his ambition, his enterprise, his capacity. In the constitution of human nature, the desire of bettering one's condition is the mainspring of effort."[4]

Depending on one's point of view, William Lloyd Garrison was the most famous or infamous abolitionist.[5] In 1831, he founded the newspaper *The Liberator* that promoted abolition with editorials and stories of slavery's horrors. He and other leading abolitionists created the New England Anti-Slavery Society in 1832 then transformed it into the American Anti-Slavery Society in 1833. By 1838, they had 1,350 affiliates with 250,000 members or nearly 2 percent of the nation's population.[6] Georgia's legislature issued a $5,000 reward for Garrison's arrest and rendition for trial. In 1840, the Tappans and other moderate abolitionists broke with Garrison to form the American and Foreign Anti-Slavery Society.

Abolitionism was among the first political causes that progressive women openly embraced.[7] Female abolitionist leaders included Angelina and Sarah Grimké, Lydia Maria Childs, and former slaves Harriet Tubman and Sojourner Truth. The Grimké sisters were born into a slaveholding Charleston family, came to detest slavery, and as young women migrated to Philadelphia to join the abolitionist movement then give lectures of the evils of slavery throughout the Northeast. Childs' 1836 pamphlet, "Appeal in Favor of That Class of Americans Called Africans," was acclaimed for its powerful abolitionist argument.

Some female abolitionists were immigrants appalled by slavery. Among the pioneers of early nineteenth-century abolitionism was Frances Wright, a free-spirited, progressive, and adventurous British woman far ahead of her time. She visited the United States in 1820 and lived there several years from 1824. She had an idealized view of the nation that she explained in her 1820 book, *Views of Society and Manners in America*. Only slavery marred her adopted country but she had a solution for that which she explained in her 1825 "Plan for the Gradual Abolition of Slavery in the United States without Danger of Loss to the Citizens of the South." At Nashoba, Tennessee, she founded a plantation with nine slaves that she hoped would be a model for her ideals. Her enterprise failed and she returned to Britain in 1828. Fanny Kemble was another British woman repulsed by slavery after she married Pierce Butler who owned a Georgia cotton plantation.

Abolitionists argued that freeing slaves would benefit not just blacks but most poverty-stricken white southerners whose wages, enterprise, skills, and learning slavery depressed. Hinton Helper elaborated that idea in his 1857 book, *The Impending Crisis of the South*. George Weston argued that, "to destroy slavery is not to destroy the South, but to change its social organization for the better." A Cincinnati *Gazette* editorial insisted that abolition would lead to the "introduction upon Southern Territory of the northern system of life." Horace Greeley's New York *Tribune* asserted that southern mass poverty could transform eventually into mass prosperity only "by the abolition of slavery and the cessation of slaveholding and the slave trade, followed by an immigration of Northern capitalists, manufacturers, and merchants."[8]

The number of abolitionist groups and members grew slowly to around sixty with perhaps several thousand members before 1836. Most northerners may have disapproved of slavery but accepted its faraway southern existence. Then in 1836, slavocrats in Congress imposed the gag rule on receiving abolition petitions. In doing so, slavocrats unwittingly spotlighted the slavery issue magnified by their nefarious power to forbid its discussion. That shifted the consciousness of countless thoughtful, moral northerners. Within a year, the number of groups soared to about 300 with 100,000 members, and the number of petitions to Congress to about 300 with 40,000 signatures.[9]

The Supreme Court's 1841 ruling on *United States versus Schooner Amistad* boosted the abolitionist cause. The *Amistad* was a Spanish ship sailing with a load of slaves who revolted, murdered all the crew except the navigator, and ordered him to sail them back to Africa. Instead, he sailed for the United States, was intercepted by an American warship, and brought to port. The ship's owners sued for the return of their vessel and slaves. Abolitionists employed lawyers to defend the right of the slaves to liberate themselves in international waters. They won that case but the owners appealed. John Quincy Adams defended the slaves when the case appeared before the Supreme Court. He grounded his defense on the Declaration of Independence's core principles. Although the justices rejected that argument, they did uphold the earlier decision. The freemen were returned to Africa.

The most successful abolitionist effort was the Underground Railroad, an expanding network of homes whose proprietors sheltered escaped slaves on their way to freedom in northern cities or Canada.[10] The network began among slave communities across the south that communicated, visited, and hid one another. Just across the free state border, John Rankin in Ripley Ohio, William Still in Philadelphia, and Thomas Garrett in Wilmington, Delaware were key leaders in organizing safe houses leading north. Among the 100,000 or so slaves that fled through the Underground Railroad was Harriet Tubman. Rather than blend into a free black community, Tubman made several trips back to the South to shepherd as many as seventy slaves to liberty in the North. She later recalled: "I was the conductor of the Underground Railroad for eight years and I can say what most conductors can't say – I never ran my train off the track and I never lost a passenger."[11]

Despite all these efforts, relatively few antebellum Americans embraced abolitionism even if many thought slavery was morally wrong. Perhaps the best indicator was the 1840 election for which abolitionist James Birney formed the Liberty Party and ran as its presidential candidate. He won 6,747 votes or 0.3 percent of 2,411,808 cast that year and 62,103 or 2.3 percent of 2,703,659 cast four years later. That was the fate of several other abolitionist parties including the Free Soil Party founded in 1848 to stop slavery's spread rather than abolish it.[12]

Most northerners wanted nothing to do with blacks let alone the Underground Railroad. They condemned abolitionists for worsening regional and political animosities. Among the most outspoken was Catherine Beecher, Harriet's sister, who made that argument in her 1837 *Essay on Slavery and Abolitionism, with Reference to the Duty of American Females*.

Black men lost the right to vote in Connecticut in 1818, Rhode Island in 1822, North Carolina in 1835, and Pennsylvania in 1838, and the right to migrate to Indiana and Iowa in 1851, and to Illinois in 1853. By 1860, only two states – Massachusetts and New Hampshire – recognized blacks as citizens with full legal rights; two states – New York and New Jersey – granted them partial civil rights; while slave state North Carolina allowed free blacks limited legal rights.

Even in northern cities, slavocrats opposed and at times terrorized abolitionists.[13] On July 4, 1834 in New York City, abolitionists tried publicly to celebrate the seventh anniversary of the state's outlawing of slavery. A mob attacked the celebrants, and for three days beat blacks and white sympathizers and vandalized sixty of their businesses, homes, and churches. Elijah Lovejoy had an abolitionist printing press in Alton, Illinois. A mob destroyed his press three times before murdering him in November 1837. A mob overran an abolitionist meeting at Pennsylvania Hall in Philadelphia, beat participants, and burned the building to the ground in 1838. A mob attacked black protesters and burned their meeting places at Smith's Hall and the Second African Presbyterian Church in 1842. A mob attacked an abolitionist meeting in Utica in 1845. A mob destroyed the press for Cassius Clay's abolitionist *True American* newspaper and he barely escaped with his life in Lexington, Kentucky in 1845, then destroyed the press for his *Examiner* newspaper and beat him at Louisville in 1849.

The legal power of slavecatchers to pursue, apprehend, and return to slavery escapees appalled and infuriated abolitionists. Before 1860, that was the fate of around 400 slaves. Pressured by abolitionists, legislators in ever more states enacted laws that granted escaped slaves equal legal protection including the rights of habeas corpus, appearing before a jury, and testifying in court.

Abolitionism was among many related progressive causes and outlooks championed by many northern intellectuals from the 1820s through the 1850s and eventually called the American Renaissance. Transcendentalism was a philosophy developed chiefly by Ralph Waldo Emerson and Henry David Thoreau that combined elements of deism, romanticism, humanism, liberalism, and the sublimity of nature. Transcendentalism reflected and shaped the Hudson River school of painters like Thomas Cole, Asher Durand, and Frederick Church. Brilliant novelists and poets like James Fenimore Cooper, Herman Melville, Walt Whitman, Edgar Allen Poe, and Nathaniel Hawthorne explored a variety of themes. Elizabeth Cady Stanton and Lucretia Mott organized at Seneca Falls, New York a convention attended by a hundred women and men that called for equal political rights in 1848. Unitarianism emerged as a protestant sect that upheld Jesus as a solely human model of brotherly love and charity for the poor, oppressed, and outcasts. But slavery remained the nation's most contentious issue.

Frederick Douglass was the late nineteenth century's leading black abolitionist and civil rights advocate.[14] He was born a slave on Maryland's eastern shore in 1818, but escaped in 1838. He began his public career as an abolitionist, with a speech at the African Methodist Episcopal Church in New Bedford, Massachusetts in 1839. He expressed his views by founding and editing the newspapers *North Star, Frederick Douglass's Paper, Douglass's Monthly*, and the *New National Era*. His *Narrative in Life of Frederick Douglass, an American Slave* appeared in 1845.[15]

Douglass provides insights into the psychological power of masters over their slaves. He noted that masters were so determined to keep their slaves dependent and ignorant that few let them know their birthdays or their fathers if they were mulattoes. Masters even tried to "part children from their mothers at a very early age … and the child is placed under the care of an old woman, too old for field labor … to hinder the development of the child's affection for its mother, and to blunt and destroy the natural affection of the mother for the child." Defiant and even innocent slaves suffered violence from their masters: "To be accused was to be convicted, and to be convicted was to be punished." A mulatto child often faced extra cruelty from the master's wife "who is ever disposed to find fault with them … she is never better pleased when she sees them under the lash … The master is frequently compelled to sell this class of his slaves, out of deference to his white wife." Douglass was rarely whipped but often suffered from "hunger and cold." As for food and clothing, slaves received "as their monthly allowance … eight pounds of pork, or its equivalent of fish, and one bushel of corn meal … [and] yearly … two coarse linen shirts, one pair of linen trousers … one jacket, one pair of trousers for winter … one pair of stockings, and one pair of shoes." Slaves vented their sorrow and rage through song: "They would sometimes sing the most pathetic sentiment in the most rapturous voice, and the most rapturous sentiment in the most pathetic tone … Those songs still follow me, to deepen my hatred of slavery." Yet, despite the cruelties they suffer, many "think their own masters are better than the masters of other slaves … Indeed, it is not uncommon for slaves even to fall out among themselves and quarrel … about the relative goodness of their masters … They seem to think that the greatness of their masters was transferable to them." Most slaves did enjoy a vacation from Christmas to New Year when they "engaged in such sports and merriment as playing ball, wrestling, running foot-races, fiddling, dancing, and drinking whiskey." Thus did masters, by wielding an array of carrots and sticks, act on the maxim that "to make a contented slave, it is necessary to make a thoughtless one … and … annihilate the power of reason. … he must be made to feel that slavery is right."[16]

Douglass observed that slavery's harshness varied: "A city slave is almost a freeman, compared to a slave on a plantation. He is much better fed and clothed, and enjoys privileges altogether unknown to the slave on the plantation … Every city slaveholder is anxious to have it known that he feeds his slaves well." For seven years, he was a house slave for a "kind and tender-hearted" Baltimore women for whom "slavery proved as injurious to her as it did to me." He learned to read and write by "making friends of all the little white boys whom I met in the street" and trading bread for lessons. He found himself "much better off than many of the poor children in our neighborhood." Yet, despite those advantages, Douglass "often myself regretting my own existence, and wishing myself dead … but for the hope of being free … I should have killed myself."

His worst suffering came after being sold to a new master who brutalized him for his intelligence and free spirit: "Mr. Covey succeeded in breaking me. I was broken in body, soul, and spirit. My natural elasticity was crushed, my intellect languished, the disposition to read departed, the cheerful spark that had lingered about my eye died."[17]

Douglass informs the reader that: "You have seen how a man was made a slave; you shall see how a slave was made a man." Rather than submit to the latest beating, he fought back and beat up Covey. That might have gotten him publicly whipped but the master was so ashamed that he never again committed violence against him. Douglass finally escaped by taking a series of trains and ferries from Baltimore to New Bedford; no one pursued or challenged him along his route to freedom or thereafter. Living conditions in the North astonished him:

I had somehow imbibed the opinion that, in the absence of slaves, there could be no wealth, and very little refinement … knowing nothing of the ease, luxury, pomp, and grandeur of southern slaveholders … Everything looked clean, new, and beautiful … The people looked more able, stronger, healthier, and happier … But the most interesting thing … was the condition of the colored people … living in finer houses and … enjoying more of the comforts of life than average of slaveholders.[18]

By the Civil War, Douglass had become the most prominent black leader. Lincoln welcomed him for talks at the White House several times. Douglass recalled their first encounter:

Happily for me, there was no vain pomp and ceremony about him. I was never more quickly or more completely put at ease in the presence of a great man than in that of Abraham Lincoln … Proceeding to tell him who I was and what I was doing, he promptly but kindly, stopped me, saying: 'I know who you are, Mr. Douglass … Sit down, I am glad to see you.'[19]

Chapter 6

Manifest Destiny

From the beginning, most Americans have considered themselves an exceptional people with values, institutions, enterprise, liberties, and opportunities to develop one's self and nation superior to all other nations yet open to immigrants who sought to become Americans. In 1630, Massachusetts Governor John Winthrop expressed that belief in a sermon, describing their community as a "city on a hill" for all of humanity to admire and emulate. Much later, President Thomas Jefferson spoke of America as an "empire of liberty" that had the right and duty to expand across the continent and beyond. In 1845, John O'Sullivan, the *Democratic Review*'s publisher, coined the term "manifest destiny" to express that same mission.[1]

The United States was born in a war that asserted sovereignty over an expanse of eastern North America. Under the 1783 Treaty of Paris, Britain recognized the United States as a sovereign state with boundaries on the Atlantic Ocean eastward, the Mississippi River westward, the 31st Parallel southward, and midway through the Great Lakes of Superior, Huron, Erie, Ontario, and then eastward from the upper St Lawrence River with a northern bulge for Maine. The Appalachian Mountains split the country between the original states eastward and a few clusters of settlements westward.

Slavery inevitably entangled with the nation's territorial expansion.[2] Congress passed ordinances or laws in 1787 and 1790 that established rules for transforming the Northwest and Southwest territory, respectively, divided by the Ohio River, into states. The process was the same for each. When a region's population exceeded 5,000, they could vote to establish a territorial government with a governor, assembly, and non-voting representative in Congress; when a territory's population exceeded 60,000, they could vote to make themselves a state. Slavery was the only difference between the ordinances, with it illegal in the Northwest and legal in the Southwest. The Northwest Territory was eventually carved into the free states of Ohio, Indiana, Illinois, Michigan, and Wisconsin, and the Southwest Territory into the slave states of Kentucky, Tennessee, Alabama, and Mississippi.

Manifest destiny meant that virtually any frontier boundary was temporary. The United States expanded in a series of steps westward across the continent in treaties with neighboring foreign powers. The first major expansion took place in 1803, when Thomas Jefferson's administration negotiated a treaty with Napoleon whereby the United States paid $15 million for New Orleans and the Louisiana Territory that then was the Mississippi River's western watershed extending to the Rocky Mountains. Jefferson dispatched an expedition led by Captains Meriwether Lewis and William Clark to explore a stretch of that territory and then beyond all the way to the Pacific Ocean and back. In 1814, the Treaty of Ghent ending the 1812 War with Britain resulted in no new territory for the United States but simply reacknowledged what it already held. In 1819, James Monroe's administration signed the Adams-Onís Treaty whereby Spain granted East and West Florida to the United States. In 1823, Monroe issued what was soon called the Monroe Doctrine that essentially declared the western hemisphere an American sphere of interest and warned the European powers to keep out. Under the 1842 Webster-Ashburton Treaty, John Tyler's administration negotiated with Britain the present boundary of Maine with Canada. James Polk's administration negotiated a treaty with Britain for America's takeover of the Pacific Northwest in 1846.

Until this point, the White House peacefully negotiated treaties to acquire new territory, although to settle it the Americans fought wars that defeated and disposed the tribes living there. To varying degrees, each acquisition was preceded by a mostly peaceful conquest as ever more Americans infiltrated and settled in that foreign territory, starting with trappers, hunters, and traders, and then homesteaders. Britain was forced to cede the Northwest to the United States because by 1846 Americans outnumbered British there by ten to one. Nowhere was that process more decisive than in Texas.

After Mexico won independence from Spain in 1821, the government opened Texas to immigrants. Thousands of Americans, mostly southerners and many slaveowners, flocked to Texas for its free land, ignoring laws that forbad slavery and required them to be Catholic. By 1835, Americans outnumbered Mexicans in Texas by six to one. When President Antonio Lopez de Santa Anna suspended the 1824 liberal constitution and asserted dictatorial powers, the Texans revolted and declared independence on March 2, 1836. Santa Anna led an army into Texas and massacred rebels at Goliad and the Alamo at San Antonio in mid-March. General Sam Houston and his Texans defeated Santa Anna at San Jacinto on April 27, and forced him to sign a treaty recognizing Texan independence. Mexico's Congress refused to ratify that treaty and viewed Texas as a rebellious province.

Mexico severed diplomatic relations with the United States after it annexed Texas on March 1, 1845, and declared war after President Polk sent an army led by General Zachery Taylor to the Rio Grande to assert that acquisition in April 1846. A Mexican army crossed the Rio Grande and attacked Taylor's army. The United States declared war against Mexico on May 12. Over the next year and a half, American armies invaded various Mexican regions and one under General Winfield Scott captured Mexico City. American settlers in New Mexico and California aided the American army in conquering those provinces.

Under the Treaty of Guadaloupe Hidalgo, the United States paid Mexico $15 million directly and $3.5 million indirectly by paying debts it owed American investors in exchange for Mexico's recognition of the acquisition of Texas and cession of the provinces of New Mexico and California. In 1853, the United States paid Mexico $10 million for a wedge of land south of the Gila River. That Gadsden Purchase was the final acquisition of territory that would eventually number forty-eight states.

Each acquisition from 1803 to 1853 provoked controversy over whether to allow or forbid slavery. The result was a series of political crises and compromises. Slavocrats feared that non-slave states would exceed slave states in number and population so that politically they would exploit their majorities in the Senate and House of Representatives to abolish slavery across the United States. Populations of the non-slave northern states expanded faster because their diverse open economies attracted immigrants. The number of representatives from the North in Congress expanded after each ten-year census and reallocation of seats. If slavocrats could not prevent that, they could demand that new states be admitted split between free and slave to maintain a power balance in the Senate. The 1820 Compromise, brokered by Representative Henry Clay of Kentucky, brought in Maine as a free state and Missouri as a slave state, and thereafter free states would be made from territory north and slave states from territory south of a line extending west from Missouri's southern boundary.[3]

That 1820 compromise and subsequent deals embittered both radical slavocrats and abolitionists. Slavocrats demanded and abolitionists opposed slavery in the new territories. Amidst the Mexican War, David Wilmot, a first-term Pennsylvania Democrat, provoked a political uproar when he presented an amendment to a war appropriations bill on August 8, 1846. He proposed: "that as an express and fundamental condition of the acquisition of any territory from the Republic of Mexico … neither slavery nor involuntary servitude shall ever exist in any part of said territory."[4] The House passed and the Senate killed what was called the Wilmot Proviso. That provoked slavocrats to demand enormous territorial spoils from Mexico with some insisting that the United States possess the entire country.

That issue reached boiling point after the United States won title from Mexico to the Southwest with the Treaty of Guadalupe Hidalgo. That vast expanse of territory would be carved into states as regions surpassed the 60,000-population threshold. Thanks to its gold rush, California's population soared to 100,000 by 1850 and its territorial assembly sent a statehood petition to Congress. On January 29, 1850, Senator Henry Clay offered a package of resolutions to appease slavocrats and abolitionists.[5] The first made California a free state. The second rejected the Texas claim of a border with New Mexico on the Rio Grande River but compensated disappointed Texans by the Federal assumption of the state's huge debt. The third abolished the slave trade but not slavery in Washington City. Tenets let voters in Utah and New Mexico determine the status of slavery in their territories. Tenets strengthened the fugitive slave law and denied congressional authority over the interstate slave trade. Illinois Senator Stephen Douglas negotiated the remaining compromises that enabled passage of the bundle of bills. Slavocrats condemned the abolition of Washington's slave trade and California's entrance as a free state. For abolitionists, the most egregious compromise was strengthening the Fugitive Slave Act that emboldened masters to pursue escapees.

When President Lincoln received Harriet Beecher Stowe at the White House in 1862, he reputedly exclaimed: "So you are the little woman who wrote the book that started this great war?"[6] He referred to her best-selling novel, *Uncle Tom's Cabin*, whose tale of abused slaves, cruel masters, painful deaths, and daring escapes swelled abolitionist ranks and provoked harsh slavocrat criticism of the book and author. That was her exact intention.

Stowe was the daughter of Lyman Beecher, a charismatic evangelical preacher whose pet cause was temperance.[7] Harriet learned about slavery while observing and questioning blacks in Cincinnati where she lived for eighteen years and during travels to Kentucky and other southern states. She married Calvin Stowe, a theology professor, in 1836. In 1850, he received a teaching post at Bowdoin College in Brunswick, Maine, where she penned her novel while mothering seven children. She was a prolific author with *Uncle Tom's Cabin* the best known of her thirty fiction and non-fiction books.

She wrote *Uncle Tom's Cabin* in response to the 1850 Fugitive Slave Act that boosted the legal power of masters to recapture fleeing slaves. She vowed that her novel would "make the whole nation feel what an accursed thing slavery is."[8] The story involves the successful escape of two slaves, Elisa and George, from the cruel overseer Simon Legree, who in vengeance murders Uncle Tom, another slave. An abolitionist newspaper initially published the novel as a series in 1851, then it became a bestseller after it appeared as a book in 1852. Over the next decade, more than 2 million Americans bought copies and it retains the best-selling record as a portion of the American population when it was published.

The novel transformed hundreds of thousands of mostly northerners into abolitionists and provoked hundreds of petitions demanding the end of slavery to Congress. It enraged slavocrats and inspired a dozen or so southern writers to pen novels extolling the virtues of slavery and happy slaves devoted to their masters. Bestsellers included Seth Eastman's *Aunt Philiss's Cabin, or Southern Life as It Is* (1852) and J.W. Page's *Uncle Robin in his Cabin in Virginia and Uncle Tom without one in Boston* (1853); similar slave characters populated many of William Simms's earlier novels like his *The Yamasee* of 1835 and the *Wigwam and the Cabin* of 1845.[9] Like countless southerners, planation mistress Mary Chesnut was haunted and obsessed with *Uncle Tom's Cabin*. She condemned the novel's stereotypes of slaves and slaveowners: "Think of these holy New Englanders, forced to have a negro village walk through their homes whenever they saw fit ... [and] have a swarm of blacks about them as children under their care – not as Mrs. Stowe paints them, but the hard, unpleasant, unromantic, undeveloped savage Africans." For all that, she and many fellow slaveowners "hate slavery worse than Mrs. Stowe."[10] To that, Mrs Stowe would likely have retorted that Mrs Chesnut could easily free herself from that burden by freeing her slaves, but of course would never do so because the privileges and wealth extracted from them far exceeded their foibles.

Democratic Senator Stephen Douglas sponsored the Kansas Nebraska Act that passed in May 1854. Animated by the notion of "popular sovereignty," the law established the territories of Kansas and Nebraska, and let the voters of each determine whether to legalize or outlaw slavery. In doing so, that law ended the 1820 Compromise that split the nation westward from Missouri's southern border with slavery permitted southward and freedom guaranteed northward.

With virtually no slaves, Nebraska's future as a free state was assured while Kansas was literally up for grabs.[11] After losing the congressional fight for Kansas as a free state, New York Senator William Seward warned slavocrats that: "We will engage in competition for the virgin soil of Kansas, and God give the victory to the side which is stronger in numbers as it is in right."[12] Free soilers formed the New England Emigrant Aid Company to help organize and finance groups of settlers to Kansas. Free soilers outnumbered but did not outgun slavocrat settlers in Kansas. Free soil and slavocrat militants became respectively known as Jayhawkers and Border Ruffians.

Slavocrats intended literally to fight for Kansas. Missouri Senator David Atkinson reassured Mississippi Senator Jefferson Davis that: "We will be compelled to shoot, burn, & hang, but the thing will soon be over."[13] Atkinson and his fellow Border Ruffians would eventually resort to violence but first they just threatened it. A *New York Tribune* reporter vividly described the typical ruffian: "Imagine a fellow, tall, slim, but athletic, with yellow corn complexion, hairy faced, with a dirty flannel shirt, red or blue or green; a pair of ... dark-colored pants ... a leather belt, in which a dirty-handled bowie knife is stuck ... an eye slightly whiskey-red and teeth the color of a walnut."[14]

President Franklin Pierce named Andrew Reeder Kansas's governor. Reeder scheduled the election for the territory's representative to Congress for November 29, 1854. The week before the election, Atkinson led a thousand armed men into Kansas to intimidate potential voters and pack the polls with false ballots. The slavocrat candidate "won." Atkinson and his gang invaded Kansas again to skew the vote for the territorial assembly on March 30, 1855. Although there were only 2,900 qualified voters in Kansas, 6,900 votes were counted. The result was thirty-six slavocrats and three free soilers took seats at the capital, then at Lecompton. The slavocrats drafted a constitution that legalized slavery and sent it to Congress for ratification. Congress would eventually return the constitution for Kansas voters to approve in a referendum.

When Reeder protested the fake votes, Atkinson pressured Pierce to replace him with outspoken slavocrat Wilson Shannon. The new governor enforced an assembly law that outlawed any anti-slavery speech with jail-time and onerous fines, made aiding an escaped slave a capital crime, and forced all inhabitants to take an oath to uphold this law.

Free soilers held a convention at Topeka in October 1855 and drafted a constitution that outlawed slavery in the territory. In November 1855, a slavocrat murdered a free soiler, the first of numerous killings. In December, free soilers approved the draft constitution by 1,731 to 46 votes. On January 15, 1856, they elected Charles Robinson their governor and on March 4 sent a petition requesting statehood to Congress.

Lawrence was free Kansas's front-line town. In November 1855, Atkinson led 1,500 ruffians across the border to confront 1,000 free soilers prepared to defend Lawrence. To his credit, Shannon talked Atkinson and his followers into going home. On May 21, 1856, when 800 ruffians again invaded Lawrence, Shannon was away and the free soilers did not resist. The slavocrats destroyed the two newspaper printing presses, burned Governor Robinson's home and the Free State Hotel, looted businesses, then gleefully rode back to Missouri.

John Brown was a radical abolitionist who believed in fighting slavocrat violence with violence. He was deadset to avenge those Ruffian invasions and the previous murders of five free soilers. On May 24, 1856, he led seven followers to Pottawatomie Creek and murdered five slavocrats. Subsequently, over 200 men died violently in the fighting between Jayhawkers and Ruffians.

Congress deadlocked over Kansas as the House and Senate respectively backed the Topeka and Lecompton constitutions. Mutual loathing and rage soared between congressional slavocrats and free soilers. On May 22, 1856, the day after the sack of Lawrence, Massachusetts Senator Charles Sumner made a speech condemning slavocrats in Kansas and elsewhere. Two days later, South Carolina Congressman Preston Brooks savagely beat Sumner with a cane while he was seated at his desk. Sumner needed months to recover while Brooks was never arrested for nearly murdering him, but was simply censured by a majority in the House of Representatives. Brooks became a hero for most southerners and a villain for most northerners.

When Shannon resigned, Pierce replaced him with John Geary, a Democrat who had been an engineer officer during the Mexican War, and San Francisco's mayor. Geary was able to end the violence by October 1856. Yet in March 1857, he resigned, exhausted by slavocrat machinations. Newly inaugurated President James Buchannan replaced him with Robert Walker, a Mississippi Democrat. In September 1857, Walker convened a constitutional convention at Lecompton which slavocrats dominated as free soilers boycotted it. That caused Walker to call for a new territorial election that he promised would be fair. He kept his promise by throwing out all the fraudulent slavocrat votes. That gave free soilers an assembly majority.

A territorial referendum on the Lecompton constitution was held on December 21, 1857. Free soilers boycotted the referendum. The vote was 6,143 to 589 for ratification. An investigation by Governor Walker found blatant voter fraud and he declared void those thousands of ballots. Free soilers held their own referendum on the Lecompton constitution on January 4, 1858, and rejected it by 10,226 to 138. Nonetheless, Buchannan sent the Lecompton constitution to Congress for its approval. Walker resigned in protest. Buchannan replaced him with James Denver. The Senate approved the Lecompton constitution by 33 to 25 votes while the House of Representatives rejected it by 120 to 112. Free soilers held a second vote over whether or not to accept the Lecompton constitution on August 2, 1858, with 11,300 against and 1,788 for. Denver informed the White House that the overwhelming majority of Kansas settlers had spoken and should be heard. Despite those overwhelming rejections, Buchannan clung to the Lecompton constitution. The deadly standoff in Kansas ground on.

Like a phoenix, the Republican Party rose from the wreckage of an array of parties like the Whig, Free Soil, American, Liberty, and Know Nothing that promoted versions of Hamiltonism.[15] The first official Republican Party appeared at a convention at Jackson, Michigan on July 6, 1854. News of that inspired like-minded men elsewhere to form their own clubs and join an expanding network. Popular support for the Republican Party was limited to northern free states and had virtually no open adherents in slave states. As for slavery, from the beginning Republicans split between mostly moderates who wanted to limit its expansion to the western territories and a minority of outspoken radical abolitionists. They began running candidates in local, state, and national elections, and won ever more seats from the prevailing Democrats. The most farsighted among them eyed winning the White House in November 1856.

The Democrats held their convention at Cincinnati, Ohio from June 2 to 6. Four candidates, all northerners, vied for the nomination, sitting President Franklin Pierce and Senators Stephen Douglas of Illinois, James Buchannan of Pennsylvania, and Lewis Cass of Michigan. Buchannan won on the eighteenth ballot. Senator John Breckinridge of Kentucky was his vice-presidential running mate.

The Republican Party convened at Philadelphia from June 17 to 19. They nominated John Fremont their presidential candidate and William Dayton, a New Jersey politician, his running mate.[16] Fremont was a national hero who had led five exploration expeditions across the West, played a critical role in conquering California during the Mexican War, and was one of California's first senators. The Republican Party platform championed the Declaration of Independence's principles and condemned slavery as "a relic of barbarism" that Congress had "the right and duty" to block from the territories while accepting it where it currently existed. The campaign slogan was "Free Soil, Free Speech, Free Men, Fremont!" An unofficial but increasingly popular slogan was "Fremont and Our Jessie," as for the first and last time for a long time, a wife appeared alongside her husband on the campaign trial.

The 1856 presidential election became a three-way race when the American Party nominated former president Millard Fillmore. Slavocrats rigged state elections against Fremont mostly by keeping his name off ballots. Fremont received no votes in Alabama, Arkansas, Florida, Georgia, Louisiana, Mississippi, Missouri, North Carolina, South Carolina, Tennessee, and Texas, and only 1,194 collectively from Delaware, Kentucky, Maryland, and Virginia. In the final tally, Buchannan won with 1,836,072 popular votes, and 174 electoral votes from 19 states; Fremont was second with 1,342,345 and 114 from 11 states; and Fillmore was last with 873,053 and 8 from 1 state. Buchannan would grossly mishandle the eventual secession of the slave states.

Dred Scott was a slave whose master, an army surgeon named John Emerson, had taken him to military posts in Illinois and Minnesota before returning to St Louis.[17] When Emerson died in 1843, his will gave his property, including Scott, to his wife, and designated his brother-in-law, John Sanford, to execute his estate. On April 6, 1846, Scott sued for his freedom in Missouri's circuit court at St Louis. He grounded his defense on his previous residence in a free state and territory, and the principle "once free, always free." After the suit was dismissed on a technicality, he won a retrial and the jury ruled in his favor in

1847. Sanford appealed and Missouri's supreme court overruled the lower court's decision on March 22, 1852. Scott first appealed to the United States circuit court that upheld Missouri's supreme court ruling, then appealed to the Supreme Court in 1856. The case was known as *Dred Scott v. John F.A. Sandford* because a clerk misspelled Sanford's name.

The Supreme Court's chief justice was Roger Taney, who President Andrew Jackson chose to replace John Marshall when he died in 1836. As Jackson's attorney general, Taney had zealously advocated slavery and state sovereignty, and condemned abolitionists and the Bank of the United States. As for free blacks, in 1832 he called them "a degraded class" that "exercise no political influence" and the "privileges they are allowed to enjoy, are accorded to them as a matter of kindness and benevolence rather than of right ... They were not looked upon as citizens by the contracting parties who formed the Constitution."[18] Those attitudes determined his rulings on any cases involving slavery.

The Supreme Court ruled seven to two against Scott on March 6, 1857. Taney wrote the fifty-five-page majority opinion that asserted three key principles. First, free and enslaved blacks alike could never be citizens and thus Scott had no standing to sue. Second, the 1787 Northwest Ordinance granted neither citizenship nor freedom to blacks living in that region. Finally, the 1820 Missouri Compromise that split the territories westward from Missouri's southern border between slavery below and freedom above was unconstitutional.

Slavocrats cheered while an array of Republicans, abolitionists, and legal experts condemned that ruling.[19] In his dissent, Justice Benjamin Curtis argued that blacks could be citizens with equal rights with whites, and cited five states where that was currently true. He also argued that the Constitution empowers Congress to determine the rules governing federal territories including whether freedom or slavery would prevail. Fifteen years earlier, Ohio politician Salmon Chase articulated a riposte to the "logic" behind Taney's future ruling: "The Constitution found slavery and left it a State institution – the creature and dependent of State law – wholly local in its existence and character. It does not make it a national institution."[20] The civil rights promoted by the Constitution apply to all people in federal jurisdictions including territories or states that embrace those rights. Thus, that liberates any slave who reaches a federal jurisdiction or free state.

Scott had endured eleven years of grueling legal struggle culminating with the Supreme Court's decision. Then, in May 1857, moral if not legal justice appeared when a sympathizer purchased then freed Scott and his wife.

John Brown was a radical abolitionist who believed that violence and even murder was justified to end slavery.[21] He first achieved notoriety after he led a gang in Kansas that butchered five slavocrats at Pottawatomie Creek in 1856. He concocted a plot to incite a slave revolt against their masters that he envisioned spreading across the South. That revolt's epicenter would be Harpers Ferry, Virginia, whose United States army arsenal's firearms he intended to seize and distribute to slaves. The Secret Six were rich Bostonians who underwrote Brown's scheme with $500 and guns. Brown tried to enlist Frederick Douglass in his scheme, but Douglass declined, dubious of its prospects and fearful it could worsen the plight of slaves. Harriet Tubman turned him down for the same reasons.

Brown's latest gang included sixteen white men, of whom three were his sons, five free blacks, one manumitted slave, and one fugitive slave. Over a week, they gathered and planned at a Maryland farmhouse half a dozen miles north of Harpers Ferry. Several of them would not join the attack because either they stayed behind to guard the farm or Brown dispatched them to gather intelligence. On the night of October 16, 1859, Brown and eighteen followers seized the arsenal from its single watchman. A few of them captured Lewis Washington, George Washington's grandnephew, at his nearby home and brought him to the arsenal.

Word of the seizure swiftly spread. The following morning, Harpers Ferry's militia mobilized and besieged the arsenal, firing at glimpses of rebels within. President James Buchannan ordered Lieutenant Colonel Robert E. Lee and Captain Jeb Stuart to lead an eighty-eight-man marine company to Harpers Ferry. They arrived on the evening of October 17. The troops stormed the building and quickly subdued the rebels. In all, 10 raiders were killed, 7 captured, and 5 escaped; 1 marine was killed and 1 wounded; 8 militia wounded; and 6 civilians killed and 9 wounded. Ironically, the first person Brown's gang murdered was a free black who worked for the railroad. Washington was freed, unharmed.

Brown was among those captured. He was tried in the court at nearby Charles Town; found guilty of murder, inciting a slave revolt, and treason against the state of Virginia; and hanged on December 2, 1859. The other six captured were also found guilty and hanged over the next several months. John Wilkes Booth was among those who gleefully watched Brown hang.

The Harpers Ferry raid further enflamed and split the nation.[22] For slavocrats, what Brown intended was their worst nightmare. Abolitionists backed Brown's aim but divided over whether his means was justified. Horace Greeley, Herman Melville, Henry David Thoreau, Ralph Waldo Emerson, Walt Whitman, John Greenleaf Whittier, and Julia Ward Howe were the most prominent writers who lauded Brown. Although Abraham Lincoln denounced Brown, his hatred for slavery swelled.[23]

Chapter 7

Lincoln and the 1860 Election

No man overcame greater hardships to become president than Abraham Lincoln.[1] He was born into abject poverty on February 9, 1809. He lived in a series of log cabins on hardscrabble farms in Kentucky, Indiana, and Illinois. He suffered his mother's death when he was 9 years old. He endured an abusive father threatened by his intelligence and desire to improve himself. His stepmother nurtured him with affection and books. He hated farming and tried to become a merchant. He made two trading voyages all the way from Illinois to New Orleans poling flatboats piled with farm goods to sell. Witnessing the public auction of a mulatto girl changed his life as from then he hated slavery to his last breath: "If slavery is not wrong, nothing is wrong."[2] He elaborated that view:

> When the white man governs himself, that is self-government; but when he governs himself and also governs another man … that is despotism. If the Negro is a man, why then my ancient faith teaches me that 'all men are created equal,' and that there can be no moral right in connection with one man making a slave of another.[3]

During another trading trip, this time on the Sangamon River in 1831, his flatboat ran aground at New Salem. He liked the village and decided to stay. He studied law amidst odd jobs like clerking a general store and splitting fence rails. He devoured any books or newspapers that he got his hands on, and joined a debating club. He won his first election to be his militia company's captain in 1832 during Black Hawk's War, but he and his men never came close to skirmish. That fall he lost his first election campaign to be an Illinois assemblyman.

Politically Lincoln backed the Whig Party that espoused a Hamiltonian agenda of a national bank; public schools; protective tariffs to promote manufacturing; public investments in roads, canals, and railroads; and tolerating slavery where it existed but opposing its spread to the western territories. Whig Party leader Henry Clay was his model statesman. Lincoln won election as an Illinois state assemblyman in 1834. He moved to Springfield, the state capital, in 1837, and passed the bar on March 1. He had two fleeting law partners before an enduring one with William Herndon who later wrote a biography of him. After four terms as an assemblyman, he won a race for the House of Representatives in 1846. He served for only one term during which his most noted stands included denouncing America's war with Mexico, backing the Wilmot Proviso that forbad slavery in any lands taken from Mexico, and calling for abolishing the slave trade but not slavery in Washington. Back in Springfield, he developed a successful law practice representing business corporations and common citizens alike, winning more cases than he lost.

Romantically, he loved two women. His first was Ann Rutledge but typhoid killed her and his grief nearly drove him to suicide. His second was Mary Todd, a friend of his best friend, Joshua Speed. She was a vivacious, petulant, spoiled, extravagant, and academy schooled offspring of a rich slaveholding family from Lexington, Kentucky. Their wedding was scheduled for January 1, 1841 but he panicked and failed to appear. Somehow, he reknit the relationship and they married on November 4, 1842. They eventually had four sons that he adored and spoiled, and deeply mourned the early deaths of two of them.

Herndon wrote a striking description of Lincoln's appearance and character:

When standing erect, he was six feet four inches high. He was lean in flesh and ungainly in figure. Aside from the sad, painted look due to habitual melancholy, his face ... had no fixed expression. He was thin through the chest, and ... slightly stoop-shouldered ... At first he was very awkward, and it seemed a real labor to adjust himself ... When he began speaking, his voice was shrill, piping, and unpleasant ... He never sawed the air ... as some orators do. He never acted for stage effect ... His style was clear, tense, and compact. In argument he was logical, demonstrative, and fair.[4]

Melancholy naturally afflicted him, pulling him between exhilaration and the abyss. Self-doubts and indecision plagued him. He was acutely aware of his lack of formal schooling and ignorance of countless subjects. He could be idle, whiling away his time bantering with others rather than working. He tried to stave off all that by swapping humorous stories, often with a moral. He was perhaps America's most existential president, at once assertive and fatalistic: "I claim not to have controlled events, but confess plainly that events have controlled me."[5]

The Bible and Shakespeare most influenced Lincoln as a writer and orator. He wrote brilliant speeches, insightful letters, and quite good poems.[6] He was among those rare geniuses capable of thinking beyond conventions and connecting far-flung ideas. In his 1863 State of the Union address, he explained: "The dogmas of the quiet past are inadequate to the stormy present. The occasion is piled high with difficulty, and we must rise to the occasion. As our case is new, so we must think anew and act anew. We must disenthrall ourselves and then we shall save our country."[7] He tried to exemplify republican virtues in his public and private life. In his first election campaign he reassured voters that: "Every man is said to have his peculiar ambition ... I have no other so great as that of being truly esteemed by my fellow men, by rendering myself worthy of their esteem."[8] He understood the power of public opinion in a democracy and sought to win most voters by inspiring them to embrace progressive views: "In this age and in this country, public sentiment is everything. With it, nothing can fail; against it, nothing can succeed. Whoever molds public sentiment, goes deeper than he who enacts statutes, or pronounces judicial decisions."[9]

The Declaration of Independence expressed Lincoln's core political values and he called for Americans to fulfill its principles: "If we do this, we shall not only have saved the Union, but we shall have so saved it as to make and to keep it forever worthy of the saving. We shall have so saved it that the succeeding millions of free, happy people, the world over, shall rise up and call us blessed to the latest generation."[10] Government's purpose was to help people realize those ends, "to elevate the condition of men – to lift artificial weights from all shoulders; to clear the paths of laudable pursuit for all; to afford all an unfettered start, and a fair chance in the race of life."[11]

Lincoln believed that no one should be above the law, but those with the most power should most uphold and exemplify the law: "Let every American, every lover of liberty ... swear by the blood of the Revolution never to violate ... the laws of the country, and never to tolerate their violation by others."[12] He elaborated the threat in a message to Congress on July 4, 1861:

> This issue embraces more than the fate of the United States. It presents to the whole family of man the question whether a constitutional republic or democracy – a government of the people by the same people – can or cannot maintain its territorial integrity against its own domestic foes. It presents the question whether discontented individuals ... can always upon pretenses made ... break up their government, and thus ... put an end to free government upon the earth. If forces us to ask: 'Is there, in all republics, this inherent and fatal weakness?' 'Must a government, of necessity, be too strong for the liberties of its own people, or too weak to maintain its own existence?'[13]

He gave his most extended view of the Constitution, government policies, and slavery during his Cooper Union speech on February 27, 1860.[14] He argued that the federal government had the power and duty to regulate the territories, including forbidding slavery, and had already done so through a variety of laws.

He expressed his opposition to slavery in principle, opposition to its extension to the territories, and toleration where it already existed. His concluding words succinctly expressed his core value: "Let us have faith that right makes might, and in that that let us to the end do our duty as we understand it."[15]

As for religion, Lincoln was essentially a deist like George Washington, Alexander Hamilton, and Thomas Jefferson. He believed in a higher power mostly indifferent to humanity, yet occasionally, God, also called Providence, might interfere in worldly affairs in often perplexing ways. He explained:

> The will of God prevails. In great contests each party claims to act in accordance with the will of God. Both may be, and one must be, wrong. God cannot be for and against the same thing at the same time. In the present civil war, it is quite possible that God's purpose is something different from the purpose of either party.[16]

When the Whig Party died in 1852, Lincoln first affiliated with the Free Soil Party then the Republican Party when it emerged in 1854. He was appalled by slavocrat attempts to impose slavery in Kansas, the string of murders, and Lawrence's looting and burning. He campaigned for John Fremont, the Republican Party's presidential nominee in 1856.

Lincoln aspired to displace Stephen Douglas, a Democrat, as one of Illinois's senators in Washington. The Republican Party nominated him to run against Douglas on June 16, 1858. In his acceptance speech, he famously declared:

> 'A house divided against itself cannot stand.' I believe this government cannot endure permanently half slave and half free. I do not expect the Union to be dissolved ... but I do expect it will cease to be divided. It will become all one thing, or the other. Either the proponents of slavery will arrest the further spread of it, and place it ... in the course of ultimate extinction, or its advocates shall push it forward till it shall become alike lawfully in all the states.[17]

Lincoln challenged Douglas to a debate in each of the state's seven congressional districts, which Douglas accepted.[18] They dueled at Ottawa on August 21, Freeport on August 27, Jonesboro on September 15, Charleston on September 18, Galesburg on October 7, Quincy on October 23, and Alton on October 15. Douglas enjoyed a vast financial if not moral edge over Lincoln. He was wealthy and George McClellan, then the Illinois Central Railroad's vice president, lent him a private car with which he traveled the state, making whistle-stop speeches in between the debates. Lincoln paid regular tickets from site to site.

Slavery and relations between whites and blacks was the key issue they debated. They both espoused a racist view of America. For Douglas: "This Government is founded on the white basis. It is made by the white man for the white man, to be administered by white men ... I am opposed to Negro equality. Preserve the purity of our Government as well as the purity of our race; no amalgamation, political or otherwise, with inferior races!"[19] Lincoln denied charges that he would grant blacks political, economic, and social equality with whites. He at once condemned and tolerated slavery where it was then legal, but would prevent its expansion to the western territories. He believed that the Declaration of Independence's expression of natural rights like life, liberty, and the pursuit of happiness extended to blacks as well as whites. He insisted that he was merely echoing the founding fathers' views.

The Illinois assembly election was held on January 5, 1859. The Republicans won the popular vote with 244,242 or 53.6 percent to 211,124 or 46.4 percent for the Democrats. However, because the Democrats had previously gerrymandered the districts, they won majorities in both houses, with 40 to 35 representatives and 14 to 11 senators. The members voted on party lines for the United States Senate seat with 54 for Douglas and 46 for Lincoln.

Although that defeat naturally disappointed Lincoln, he soon resumed his politicking. He would make an extraordinary comeback. Two years and two months later, he would enter the White House as the sixteenth president.

No American election was more divisive than that of 1860 when four major candidates vied for the presidency.[20] The Democratic Party held their presidential nomination convention at Charleston, South Carolina from April 23 to May 3. The party deadlocked bitterly between northern and southern delegates who respectively backed senators Stephen Douglas of Illinois and John Breckinridge of Kentucky; although Douglas won a majority, he failed to surpass the two-thirds needed for the nomination. They reconvened at Baltimore from June 18 to 28, when Douglas finally garnered two-thirds of the votes. The slavocrat Democrats walked out and in another hall nominated Breckinridge. Meanwhile, the newly founded Constitutional Union Party selected Tennessee Senator John Bell during a convention at Baltimore on May 10.

The Republican Party's convention began at Chicago on May 16. The leading candidates included William Seward of New York, Salmon Chase of Ohio, Simon Cameron of Pennsylvania, Edward Bates of Missouri, and Abraham Lincoln of Illinois. All those men except Lincoln had lengthy political resumes with some having served as governors and federal senators. Seward was the odds-on favorite with an array of elected posts culminating with a dozen years as a senator from New York. Yet many moderate Republicans feared that his at times outspoken attacks on slavery could cost them the election. For instance, two years earlier Seward triumphantly declared that abolitionism posed an existential dilemma for slavery: "You know, and I know, that a revolution has begun. I know and all the world knows that revolutions never go backward."[21]

Lincoln was the most prominent second choice to Seward. He did not attend but waited at Springfield. He was an unlikely candidate. His national political experience was limited to one term in the House of Representatives. He had achieved national fame as a brilliant orator with his speeches during the seven debates with Douglas in 1858 and his Cooper Union address in February 1860, which was mass-printed and distributed. Beyond that, his only advantage was being the favorite son of the state that hosted the convention. His campaign manager, David Davis, celebrated Lincoln's hardscrabble farm roots by popularizing him as the "rail-splitter," and tried to cut deals with the other candidates to back him. In the first round, Seward won a plurality with 173 votes to Lincoln's second place with 102. One by one the other candidates threw their support to Lincoln who won on the third ballot with 233. His running mate for vice president was Senator Hannibal Hamlin of Maine.

Republican leaders carefully designed the party's platform to appeal to the widest array of voters and reassure slavocrats that they advocated not slavery's abolition but only preventing its spread to the new territories. The platform also called for a protective tariff for manufacturers, investments in roads, ports, and bridges, a homestead act to open the western territories for settlers, and a transcontinental railroad dynamically to bind the nation's Pacific and Atlantic shores. To drum up support, Wide Awake clubs were Republican Party auxiliaries of mostly young men who paraded in the evenings with torches, drums, and fence rails. They also protected polling places to deter voting fraud.

Slavocrats viewed slavery as the election's core issue. They were terrified that somehow abolitionists would capture Congress and the White House then strip them of their wealth, privilege, and status. The rhetoric of some northern politicians stoked that paranoia. For instance, Wisconsin Republicans undercut their party's national campaign by publicly issuing this challenge: "Slaveholders of America, I appeal to you. Are you really in earnest when you speak of perpetuating slavery? ... You stand against a hopeful world, alone against a great century, fighting your hopeless fight ... against the onward march of civilization."[22]

The November 6 election split regionally with Lincoln and Douglas vying for the North, and Breckinridge and Bell for the South. In the final tally, Lincoln received 1,865,908 votes or 39.8 percent and 180 electoral votes from 18 states; Douglas 1,386,202 votes or 29.5 percent and 12 electoral votes from 1 state; Breckinridge 848,019 votes or 18.1 percent and 72 electoral votes from 11 states; and Bell 590,901 votes or 12.6 percent and 39 electoral votes from 3 states. Lincoln was the president-elect of a country that would soon be torn asunder.

Part II

The Civil War, 1861–5

Chapter 8

Enemy Nations

Slavocrat fire-eaters across the South reacted to Lincoln's election by calling for secession.[1] Starting with South Carolina, one state after another held a convention and voted to leave the United States. South Carolina's delegates voted 169 to 0 to do so on December 20, 1860, followed by Mississippi by 84 to 15 on January 9, 1861, Florida by 62 to 7 on January 10, Alabama by 61 to 39 on January 11, Georgia by 208 to 98 on January 19, Louisiana by 113 to 17 on January 26, and Texas by 166 to 8 on February 2. Although only South Carolina's vote was unanimous, the other states averaged four of five voters in favor. Only Texas submitted its secession declaration as a referendum to voters; Texans approved by three to one opposed.

Was secession constitutional? Secessionists justified their act by claiming that their states retained their sovereignty as independent countries when they ratified the Constitution and joined the United States. In fact, nothing in the Constitution refers to secession or state sovereignty but instead locates sovereignty in the Federal government. In other words, the states transferred sovereignty to the United States when they ratified the Constitution. Those states that declared secession committed an unconstitutional and illegal act. As for the Federal government's sovereignty, ultimately it is rooted in the Constitution's first three words, "We the people."

Protecting slavery was the core and often sole reason each state seceded. Vice President Alexander Stephens explained that the Confederacy's principles and practices diametrically opposed those of the United States: "Our new government is founded upon exactly the opposite ideals ... that the negro is not equal to the white man; that slavery is his natural and moral condition. This ... government ... is the first, in the history of the world, based upon this great ... truth."[2] Mississippi's secessionists declared: "Our position is thoroughly identified with the institution of slavery ... A blow at slavery is a blow at commerce and civilization." Texas's echoed that justification: "We hold as undeniable truths that the governments of the various States and of the Confederacy itself, were established exclusively by the white race ... That in this free government all white men are entitled to equal political and civil rights; that the servitude of the African race ... is mutually beneficial."[3] And so it went from one rebel state to the next.

The eventual secession of eleven states and formation of the Confederacy was as unprecedented as it was unconstitutional. However, two previous times states had taken steps toward secession. The first came in 1814 amidst the War of 1812 when the New England states sent delegates to a convention at Hartford, Connecticut to discuss breaking away from the United States. Nothing came of the meeting. In 1832, South Carolina's legislature and governor voted to "nullify" their state's compliance with a bill that raised tariff rates and threatened to secede if the Federal government tried to enforce that law. That provoked a crisis. President Andrew Jackson condemned nullification and secession as "treason," got Congress to increase military spending, and moved Federal revenue collection for Charleston offshore. Meanwhile, Henry Clay sponsored the Distribution Bill that cut tariffs and distributed the revenues more widely to the states. Angry at being upstaged, Jackson vetoed that bill yet included most of the same concessions in a Compromise Bill sponsored by his Congressional allies. Although South Carolina accepted that deal, its assertion of nullification and threat of secession established a powerful political if not legal precedent.[4]

As secession unfolded, President James Buchannan did nothing to discourage let alone prevent that. Instead, he cocooned in the White House, abjectly telling visitors that, "I am the last president of the United States."[5]

After the election, Congressional Republicans and moderate Democrats tried to dilute the swelling secessionist movement then entice back the breakaway states with concessions. On December 4, the House established the Committee of Thirty-Three devoted to easing tensions and finding compromises. After South Carolina seceded, the Senate formed their own committee. On December 18, Senator John Crittenden, a Kentucky slaveowner, presented a bill with a bundle of six constitutional amendments and four resolutions, the most important of which guaranteed slavery in the states; reinstituted the Missouri Compromise line between slave and free states in the western territories; continued slavery in Washington City as long as Virginia and Maryland opposed its abolition; forbad any Federal regulation of the interstate slave trade; and compensated slaveholders whose slaves escaped to freedom in the North. That bill never left the committee for a floor vote. Radical Republicans argued that it conceded too much while secessionists were deadset to establish their own nation founded on the principle of slavocracy.

Thirty-eight delegates of those seven breakaway states met in a convention at Montgomery, Alabama on February 4.[6] Their first step was to declare themselves a provisional Congress then hastily draft a provisional constitution that they approved on February 8. They established the Confederate States of America and elected Jefferson Davis and Alexander Stephens its president and vice president on February 9. On February 18, Davis took the oath and was inaugurated. Congress then refined the constitution from February 28 to March 11, approved it by 137 to 21 votes, and sent it to the states for ratification. Within a month, all seven states ratified it.

The Confederate constitution differed significantly from America's Constitution. The only similarity was the legislative branch. The Confederate Congress had a popularly elected House of Representatives and a Senate elected by state legislatures; with all eleven seceded states and exiled governments from Border States there were 105 representatives and 26 senators. Yet, unlike America's Congress, the Confederacy's had no power to raise taxes or tariffs for internal improvements, and proposed laws could only address one subject. The constitution could be more easily amended with two-thirds votes of both Congressional houses and two-thirds of the states; under America's constitution amendments passed only after three-fourths of the states voted in favor. An even bigger departure was the executive. Congress elected the president and vice president who served six-year non-renewable terms. The Confederate president was more powerful than the American president; he could line-item veto bills while his cabinet secretaries held seats in Congress. Another difference was sovereignty that America's constitution grounded in "the people" protected by the Federal government. The Confederate constitution's opening words were: "We the people of the Confederate States, each acting in its sovereign character."

A nation-state's most obvious symbol is its flag. The Confederacy had three versions of its national flag and one combat flag.[7] The most familiar flag with two intersecting diagonal blue lines with thirteen stars against a red field is actually the battle flag adopted first by the Army of Northern Virginia then other armies and state regiments. The first national flag consisted of two horizontal red strips embracing one white strip, with an upper left corner blue field with a circle of seven stars from March 4 to May 21, 1861, nine stars from May 21 to July 2, 1861, eleven stars from July 2 to November 28, 1861, and thirteen stars from November 28 to May 1, 1863. The thirteen stars included eleven states and seceded and two states – Missouri and Kentucky – with governments in exile that claimed to be representative, although each had formal state governments that did not secede. The next flag consisted of the battle flag in the upper left corner of a white field from May 1, 1863 to March 4, 1865 when a red vertical strip was added to the right side.

Jefferson Davis appeared to be an excellent choice for the Confederacy's president. He was a West Point graduate, Mexican War hero, United States representative then senator from Mississippi, secretary of war, and, most vitally, fierce advocate of slavery's expansion.[8] On June 3, 1808, he was born the tenth child of a humble eastern Kentucky family that emigrated to Louisiana then Mississippi and eventually transformed themselves into wealthy plantation owners. He was highly educated for his day, studying at Transylvania College before transferring to West Point. He was a fun-loving cadet who racked up demerits and nearly got dismissed for a drunken escapade with his friends. He could also be sharp-tongued and defiant. In 1835, a court martial charged and eventually acquitted him of insubordination. He graduated twenty-third in a thirty-four cadet class.

His first army stint lasted seven years through a series of posts. During that time, his most notable experience was falling in love with his commanding officer's daughter, Knox Taylor. His future father-in-law gave him a tough choice. Colonel Zachery Taylor would only let him marry his daughter if he resigned his commission and became a prosperous planter. He put love before duty. Tragically, malaria killed Knox and debilitated Davis three months after their wedding. He did acquire a Mississippi plantation, Brierfield, whose acres and slaves he expanded. When he was 36, he fell in love with and married a Natchez girl, Varina, eighteen years younger.

He was a loving husband to Varina and their six children, and loyal to his friends. Yet most strangers and political rivals found him aloof, calculating, condescending, and thin-skinned with a prickly easily offended sense of honor. He was a workaholic who rarely delegated authority. Texas Governor Sam Houston condemned him as "ambitious as Lucifer and cold as a lizard."[9] With his tall, emaciated frame, gaunt goateed face, high cheekbones, thin lips, and stern expression, Davis resembled Uncle Sam. Chronic ulcers, neuralgia, and insomnia plagued him; an infection clouded his left eye. Despite those demerits of character and appearance, he was an astute politician.

Davis won an election to become a Mississippi representative to Congress in 1845. When the Mexican War erupted, he raised a regiment of volunteers and courageously led them under General Taylor's command. His tactics at the battle of Buena Vista were critical to the American victory. After the war, the governor appointed him to a Senate seat when its holder died. He was among the Senate's most zealous slavocrats, calling for its unimpeded expansion across the United States, especially the newly conquered territories. He resigned to run for governor but lost that race. President Franklin Pierce appointed him secretary of war. He won back a Senate seat in 1857. He was in session on January 21, 1861, when he learned that his state had seceded. He promptly resigned and returned to his family at Brierfield. On February 10, 1860, he received a telegram from the Confederate Congress congratulating him for being unanimously elected president. He hurried to Montgomery where, on February 18, he was inaugurated president of the Confederate States of America.

Davis put together a cabinet that initially included Leroy Walker of Alabama as war secretary, Stephen Mallory of Florida as navy secretary, Judah Benjamin of Louisiana as attorney general, Christopher Memminger of South Carolina as treasury secretary, and John Reagan of Texas as postmaster general. Only Mallory and Reagan kept their positions through the war. The biggest turnover was in the war department whose secretaries included Walker from February 25 to September 16, 1861; Benjamin Judah from then to March 24, 1862; George Randolph from then to November 11, 1862; James Seddon from then to February 6, 1865; and John Breckinridge from then to May 10, 1865.

Despite his military experience as a West Point graduate, Mexican War veteran, Senate committee member, and secretary of war President Davis was at best a mediocre commander in chief.[10] He had a poor grasp of grand strategy. As bad, his astringent character caused a falling out with each war secretary and most of his generals, especially Joe Johnston, although he did have polite relations with Robert Lee. Randolph explained the frustrations of having to work under Davis, who he blasted for indecision, incompetence, an inability to distinguish "important and unimportant matters," and lacking "practical knowledge of the workings of our military system in the field and frequently mars it by theories which he has had no opportunity to correct by personal observation and in which he will not permit amendment from the experience of others."[11]

The Confederate philosophy of slavocracy, states' rights, and minimal government was ultimately self-defeating.[12] The state governments tended to hoard their troops and supplies, and competed with each other for more of each. Yet, with minimal powers, neither they nor the Confederate government could mobilize all the potential men and materiel that they desperately needed. Fears of slave flight or revolt worsened steadily as more white men went to the front and President Lincoln issued his Emancipation Proclamation.

To his credit, from the beginning Davis had no illusions about how onerous the Confederacy's war for independence would be. During a dinner party that included Mary Chesnut in June 1861, he:

Laughed at our faith in our own powers ... We think every Southerner equal to three Yankees at least .... he thinks it will be a long war. That floored me at once. It has been too long for me already. Then he said before the end came, we would have many a bitter experience. He said only fools doubted the courage of the Yankees or their willingness to fight when they saw fit. And how we have stung their pride – we have roused them till they will fight like devils.[13]

Abraham Lincoln had to wait in worsening impatience and frustration the four months between his election and inauguration as one state after another seceded then formed the Confederate States of America and raised an army against the United States. He vented his dismay in a speech at Cleveland en route to Washington:

> I think the crisis … is altogether an artificial one … What they do who seek to destroy the Union is altogether artificial. What is happening to hurt them? Have they not all their rights now as they ever have had? Do they not have their fugitive slaves returned now as ever? Have they not the same Constitution that they have lived under for seventy-odd years?[14]

Four days earlier, Lincoln expressed his personal angst during his farewell address in Springfield:

> My Friends, no one not in my situation can appreciate my sadness in parting. To this place and the kindness of these people, I owe everything. Here I have lived a quarter of a century, and have passed from a young to an old man. Here my children have been born, and one is buried. I now leave, not knowing when or whether ever I may return, with a task before me greater than that which rested upon Washington.

He then asked for their prayers so that the "Divine Being" could assist him.[15]

During the interim before the White House, Lincoln formed his cabinet. Historian Doris Kearns Goodwin called his picks a "team of rivals" since among them were several that Lincoln had beaten for the nomination.[16] In doing so, he hoped to diminish them as potential critics and foes by welcoming them inside the political tent rather than shunning them beyond. He also sought an array of moderate and radical voices to mull and play off against each other. He chose William Seward, a New York governor and senator, as Secretary of State; Simon Cameron, a Pennsylvania senator, as Secretary of War, Salmon Chase, an Ohio senator and governor, as Secretary of the Treasury; Edward Bates, a former congressman and current judge, as Attorney General; Gideon Welles, the *Hartford Evening Press*'s editor, as Secretary of the Navy; Caleb Smith, an Indiana congressman, as Secretary of the Interior; and Montgomery Blair, the United States Solicitor, as Postmaster General.

During his presidency, he made several changes. The first came on January 20, 1862, when he had Cameron resign after a series of Congressional committees and journalists revealed Cameron's corruption involving kickbacks for business contracts. Lincoln at once let off Cameron easy and exiled him by making him ambassador to Russia. Edwin Staunton, Buchanan's attorney general, took his place. Another came on September 24, 1864, when he accepted Blair's resignation as part of a deal whereby Blair's enemy John Fremont agreed not to run as a third-party presidential candidate. He replaced Blair with William Dennison, a former Ohio governor. He dealt with Salmon Chase's criticisms of him behind his back and maneuvers to become the Republican Party's presidential nominee in 1864 by elevating him to the Supreme Court's chief justice after Roger Taney died, and replacing him with Senator William Fessenden of Maine on June 30, 1864. Conservative Edward Bates resigned on November 24, 1864, disgruntled with black emancipation and soldiers; Lincoln replaced him as attorney general with his friend and Radical Republican Joshua Speed.

Lincoln was inaugurated president on March 4, 1861. In his address, he boiled down the dispute to two crucial differences of opinion. One was over secession that Lincoln condemned:

I hold that, in contemplation of universal law and of the Constitution, the Union of these States is perpetual … No State upon its own mere motion, can lawfully get out of the Union, that resolves and ordinances to that effect are legally void; and that acts of violence within any State or States, against the authority of the United States, are insurrectionary or revolutionary.

The other was over slavery where Lincoln was more conciliatory: "One section of our country believes slavery is right and ought to be extended, while the other believes it is wrong and ought not to be extended. This is the only substantial dispute." He ended with his haunting plea:

We are not enemies, but friends. We must not be enemies. Though passion may have strained, it must not break our bonds of affection. The mystic cords of memory, stretching from every battlefield and patriot grave to every living heart and hearth stone all over this broad land, will yet swell the chorus of the Union when against touched, as surely they will be, by the better angels of our nature.[17]

Lincoln's appeal to reason and patriotism failed to sway a single secessionist mind. Zealotry and paranoia drove the slavocrats to break away and nothing but being crushed in war would force them back into the United States.

The rebel states swiftly confiscated any federal property within their respective territories with five exceptions, Fort Pickens at Pensacola, Fort Taylor at Key West, Fort Jefferson at Garden Key in Dry Tortugas, Fort Monroe at Virginia's

Peninsula tip, and Fort Sumter at Charleston. Four of the five would remain in federal hands throughout the war.

Major Robert Anderson commanded Fort Sumter's 125-man garrison. General Winfield Scott, the army's commanding general, dispatched the unarmed merchant ship *Star of the West* packed with supplies and 200 reinforcements to Fort Sumter. On January 9, 1861, rebel batteries fired on the vessel as it approached the bay and one shot struck it, causing the captain to sail away to safety. Among Jefferson Davis's first acts as president was to send a three-man commission to Washington to demand the surrender of the forts and to commission Pierre Beauregard a general and command of troops and batteries massing at Charleston.

Lincoln favored holding rather than ceding the forts but wanted the cabinet's support.[18] On March 15, he gathered his department chiefs and asked their advice. Only Treasury Secretary Chase and Postmaster General Blair backed him. He tried to build a consensus for resistance before reconvening his cabinet on March 29. This time, more appeared to favor taking a stand.

Lincoln received a memo from Seward on April 1 that initially he must have hoped was an April Fool's prank. In his "Some Thoughts for the President's Consideration," Seward actually advocated provoking Britain, France, or some other European nation to war to reunite the United States against a common enemy. Lincoln immediately saw that Seward's proposal would actually realize the Confederacy's fervent hope to receive recognition, aid, and alliance with as many of Europe's great powers as possible with Britain and France leading the list. The utter absurdity of such a serious suggestion from such an esteemed political leader as Seward at first stunned and then transformed Lincoln. He had entered the White House and picked a team of rivals with trepidation and awe. He now recognized that his own inherent wisdom and instinct were superior to whatever greater wealth and education his colleagues could claim. He would be his own man.

Lincoln authorized a flotilla of supply ships guarded by the warship USS *Powhatan* to steam for Fort Sumter, then let South Carolina Governor Francis Pickens and the press know his intention. Davis ordered Beauregard to capture Fort Sumter before the vessels arrived. On April 11, Beauregard sent Anderson a surrender demand. Anderson refused. On April 12, the rebel batteries opened fire on Fort Sumter. Over the next 34 hours, most of the 4,000 rounds hit the fort, although not a defender was killed. Mary Chesnut was among the Charlestonians watching the bombardment: "The women were wild, there on the rooftop. Prayers from the women, imprecations from the men, and then a shell would light up the scene."[19] Anderson surrendered Fort Sumter on April

14. The next day, Lincoln called for 75,000 volunteers for ninety days' military service to help repress the rebellion.

The Confederates had committed treason by seceding then starting a war against the United States. Yet that inspired rather than discouraged slavocrats elsewhere. Four more states seceded, Virginia on April 17, Arkansas on May 6, North Carolina on May 20, and Tennessee on June 8. Virginia's government seized the American arsenal with 15,000 rifles and tons of ammunition at Harpers Ferry the same day it seceded.

The Confederate Congress approved on May 21, an invitation from Virginia's government to move its capital from Montgomery, Alabama to Richmond, Virginia, just a hundred miles due south of Washington. The Confederate government would officially open in Richmond on July 20.

Word of that decision provoked Unionist politicians and newspaper editors to urge the Lincoln administration to prevent that from happening. Horace Greeley's *New York Tribune* captured that zeal with its headline "Forward to Richmond!"

Chapter 9

Strategies

Strategy is about getting to or from battlefields while tactics is what commanders do on battlefields. The shared goals of strategy and tactics are destroying the enemy's material and morale capacity to resist by the decisive, relentless assertion of both hard or physical and soft or psychological power. That is best achieved in a fast-paced campaign that maneuvers then masses against the enemy's most vulnerable points, especially its supply lines. A venerable maxim guides offensive strategies and tactics: attack where the enemy is weak and distract where it is strong. The defense maxim is to anticipate and counter your enemy, while striking where he is most vulnerable.

Technologies implement strategies and tactics. Two recent technologies revolutionized warfare's speed and scale, steam engines for transportation and the telegraph for communications. Steamboats and steam locomotives conveyed large amounts of troops and supplies in a day further than they could walk or be carried by wagon in two weeks. Railroads were especially critical to both sides. A core strategy was protecting one's own network while launching raids that devastated the other's. The telegraph rendered communications nearly instantaneous. Of course, each technology had its limits. Railroads were expensive, time-consuming to build, and easily wrecked. Telegraph wires could be strung relatively easily among planted posts but were easily cut. Atop those technologies were countless that boosted mass-production that enabled armies and navies to be supplied on increasingly grander scales.[1]

The North and South had asymmetrical grand strategies.[2] The United States had to crush the rebellion by destroying all rebel armies, state governments, military supplies, and morale, an effort that would take years. Commanding General Winfield Scott had a strategy for that, dubbed the Anaconda Plan, which involved the navy's systematic blockade of the South's coast and capture of key coastal and river cities, while Federal armies overwhelmed rebel armies in one region after another. The Confederacy's grand strategy was clear and simple enough. The rebels won as long as their armies staved off Union offensives, while daring ship captains smuggled in enough vital war supplies to fill the South's near void of industry, and field commanders tried to live off the enemy's rifles, munitions, foodstuffs, and other supplies gleaned from victorious sieges, battles, and raids. Those dueling strategies reflected the asymmetrical powers and interests of the United States and the Confederacy. Confederates wanted independence and Americans wanted reunion. To assert their respective ends, the United States enjoyed a huge advantage over the Confederacy by virtually every measure of hard physical power.

Of America's 31,443,321 people in 1860, two-thirds or 22,339,989 lived in the 25 states that would stay loyal while the 11 future rebel states included 5,449,462 whites, 3,521,110 slaves, and 132,760 free blacks. There were 3.5 times more white males from 18 to 40 years old in the North than the South. Eventually, the Union would widen that military manpower lead by enlisting black soldiers. As for manufacturing, in 1859, America had 140,433 factories with 1,311,000 workers of which the North had about 110,000 factories with 1,200,000 workers while the South had 18,000 factories with 110,000 workers. In all, nine-tenths of America's manufacturing was in the North, including "97 percent of firearms, 94 percent of textiles, 93 percent of pig iron, and 90 percent of footwear."[3] Nonetheless, the Union did not make everything it needed for war. Perhaps the most crucial import was saltpeter that mixed with charcoal and sulfur made gunpowder. Most of the world's supply came from British India. To transport people and goods America had 31,256 miles of railroad track, including 21,973 northern and 9,283 southern miles in 1861. A network of 50,000 miles of telegraph wires crisscrossed the nation; over four years, the Union's Military Telegraph Corps added 15,000 more miles.[4]

Railroads were critical to victory. The North not only had more than twice as many miles of track as the South to supply its armies but enjoyed related critical advantages. All production of locomotives, cars, track, and spare parts was in the North and that production expanded faster than Confederate raiders could destroy it behind enemy lines as Union armies advanced further south on southern railroads. Likewise, the Confederates had increasing trouble repairing their own locomotives, cars, and tracks as they wore out. Another problem in both regions was the lack of a standard gage, although it was worse in the South. The result was long delays as supplies were exchanged between trains where different gauges met. Then there was the problem of fuel, with coal more efficient than wood, abundant in the North and scarce in the South.

During the war, the Confederacy filled its demand for war goods by three ways. The most vital was Richmond's effective nationalization and expansion of most production:

By the end of 1862 the output of the eight government-owned armories reached 170,000 cartridges and 1,000 field-artillery rounds of ammunition daily and 155,000 pounds of lead monthly. Altogether, the Augusta works turned out 2,750,000 pounds of gunpowder during the conflict. By the end of 1864, the Niter and Mining Bureau had nearly a million cubic feet of niter beds in operation, fulfilling at least the bulk of all saltpeter needs.[5]

The most important industrial complexes were the Tredegar ironworks in Richmond, Cumberland ironworks in Clarksville, Tennessee, a cannon factory at Selma, Alabama, and a gunpowder mill in Augusta, Georgia. Smuggling and capture supplemented the South's industrial production. Nonetheless, some key shortages undercut overall production. For example, limited sources of pig iron in the South straitjacketed Tredegar's production to one-third its prewar level when it could buy ample and inexpensive northern sources. Yet, although military supplies dwindled over four years, the authors of *Why the South Lost the Civil War* made the critical point that "no Confederate army lost a major engagement because of the lack of arms, munitions, or other essential supplies."[6]

The South enjoyed advantages that reduced the North's overwhelming material dominance. To conquer the South, the North faced three related challenges – strategic consumption, exterior lines, and a steep attacker-to-defender ratio.

The strategic consumption dilemma is nearly inevitable for an invader. The further one advances, the more troops must be hived off to protect supply lines, while the enemy withdraws on its own supply line, increasing in strength with more troops earlier deployed. Historian James McPherson detailed the enormous logistical challenges: "A Union army operating in enemy territory averaged one wagon for every forty men and one horse or mule (including cavalry and artillery horses) for every two or three men. A campaigning army of 100,000 men therefore required 2,500 supply wagons and at least 35,000 animals, and consumed 600 tons of supplies each day."[7] In addition, an invader had to commandeer and defend supply depots of warehouses, repair shops, stables, and pastures a few days' march apart.

One risky way to finesse that dilemma is to minimize one's own supplies and live off the enemy as much as possible. That "exhaustion" war strategy demands steady movement from region to region, relentlessly pursuing the enemy and leaving behind looted and burned farms, mills, and warehouses, and destroyed railroads.[8] The risk comes if the enemy blocks one's advance and thus access to more supplies.

Fortunately, for the American cause, a few generals like Ulysses Grant, William Sherman, and Phil Sheridan waged "total war" by ruthlessly and ceaselessly seeking to destroy enemy armies and the logistics that sustained them. Sherman explained that strategy: "We must keep the war South until they are not only ruined, exhausted, but humbled in pride and spirit."[9] He had an answer to those who condemned his total war strategy: "if the people raise a cry against my barbarity and cruelty, I will answer that war is war, and not popularity-seeking. If they want peace, they and their relatives must stop the war."[10]

Another Southern edge was interior lines or the ability as defenders to shift forces by road and rail from one front to another to mass against the worst threats. The Confederates fully exploited this advantage and were much more adept at concentrating their forces for decisive battles. In a study of twenty-five large battles, Confederate forces averaged 78 percent the size of Union forces at their fronts even though overall they were only 56 percent or slightly more than half as large.[11]

Finally, the greater the number of attackers against defenders in open ground, the more likely they will win. Tactics and technologies are inseparable. During the preceding age of muskets with an effective range of a couple score yards, attackers generally needed a three-to-one ratio to overwhelm defenders. The recent introduction of rifles with a killing range of a couple hundred yards rendered mass attacks nearly suicidal, especially if breastworks, stonewalls, sunken roads, or entrenchments protected the defenders. To win campaigns and battles, northern generals had to outmaneuver rebel armies deployed in nearly invincible positions and launch attacks where enemy troops were scarcest.[12]

A pedagogical problem plagued the Union war effort. A fatal flaw afflicted many West Point graduates, although it was hardly their own fault. The military academy trained young men to be engineers not combat officers or generals. The result was a methodical, scientific approach to war exemplified by Generals George McClellan, Don Buell, William Rosecrans, and Henry Halleck that emphasized capturing cities rather than armies. Indeed, those generals avoided combat if they could. Buell explained that: "The object is not to fight great battles, and storm impregnable fortifications, but by demonstrations and maneuvering to prevent the enemy from concentrating his scattered forces."[13] That, of course, is a strategy to avoid one's own defeat rather than defeat the enemy and so played into Confederate hands.

Most southern generals were immune to that West Point engineering orientation no matter how high or low their graduation rank. One clear regional difference among West Point graduates was that northerners were far better students than southerners: 40 percent of northern generals and 25 percent of southerners were in the top 25 percent of their class, while 23 percent of southerners and 6 percent of northerners were in the bottom 25 percent.[14] Fortunately, for the Confederacy, no apparent correlation existed between being a good student and a good general. Indeed, the opposite may have true as daredevil southern generals tended to trounce their by-the-book former northern classmates. Of course, Lee was among the war's most brilliant generals and ranked second in his class.

That was not the only burden that West Point's curriculum may have imposed on students. West Point graduates studied the campaigns of Napoleon and other great generals. From 1824 to 1871, Dennis Mahan taught tactics based on lessons drawn from *Traite des Grands Operations Militaire* by Antoine Henri Jomini, who fought first for and then against Napoleon; Mahan wrote nine books on engineering and tactics. Three other American officers wrote books that influenced many of the officers who later fought in the Civil War, Henry Halleck with *Elements of Military Art and Science* (1846), William Hardee with his *Rifle and Light Infantry Tactics* (1855), and Pierre Beauregard with *Principles and Maxims of the Art of War* (1863). Theory and practice often conflict. Although all three commanded armies during the war, none rank among the greatest generals.

Studying Napoleon's campaigns should have inspired the strategy of annihilating the enemy among graduates, although only a few generals pursued that like Lee and Grant. Emulating Napoleon's tactics was disastrous. Tragically, the tactics taught at West Point and other military academies lagged technological changes. Warfare was murderous enough when massed troops fired at each other with relatively short-range, inaccurate muskets. But now, armies fought with mass-produced rifles whose thick barrels with an inner groove were accurate at least four times further than muskets with their smoothbore barrels.

Rifles drastically diminished cavalry's role in battle from central to peripheral. During the musket age, infantry might get off an inaccurate volley against charging horsemen and so could be ridden over. Troops best protected themselves against cavalry by densely packing themselves in squares bristling with bayoneted muskets, with the first-row kneeling. Now rifle-armed infantry could begin firing volleys at horsemen a couple hundred yards away and decimate them before they got close.

Cavalry still had a vital strategic role to play in reconnaissance and raids. The South enjoyed an enormous advantage in cavalry commanders, with Nathan Bedford Forrest, James E.B. (Jeb) Stuart, John Morgan, Joe Wheeler, and Wade Hampton the most brilliant. Of the fifty-six cavalry officers before the war, thirty served with the South during the Civil War.[15] The best pre-war incubator of Confederate cavalry commanders was Albert Sidney Johnston's 1st Dragoons. Rebel raids deep behind enemy lines destroyed supply depots, burned railroad bridges, killed and captured enemy soldiers, and, most vitally, tied down tens of thousands of troops that otherwise would swell the armies trying to crush Confederate armies. For instance, in 1863 alone, 13,000 rebel raiders diverted 51,000 Federals guarding strategic rear echelon sites in northern Mississippi and western Tennessee, and 15,000 rebels 56,000 Federals in eastern Tennessee and Kentucky.[16]

The Union and Confederacy each boasted three generals who understood and brilliantly waged war, northerners Ulysses Grant, William Sherman, and Philip Sheridan, and southerners Robert Lee, Thomas Jackson, and Bedford Forrest. Yet, even the two greatest, Grant and Lee, ordered disastrous attacks that they later deeply regretted, the former at Vicksburg and Cold Harbor, the latter at Malvern Hill and Gettysburg.

Of course, the United States eventually crushed the Confederacy. That victory was not preordained. Many interrelated reasons led to it with leadership and numbers or soft and hard power most critical. Inseparable from that as with all human affairs is luck. Had a stray bullet killed Grant at, say, Belmont, the war might have ended quite differently.

Naval power was a key Union advantage over the Confederacy, and their respective strategies reflected that gap.[17] When the war began, the American navy numbered 90 warships manned by 7,500 sailors, although only 44 were immediately ready for action; the rest had to be refurbished, supplied, and manned. Navy Secretary Gideon Welles steadily expanded the fleet to 264 vessels by the end of 1861 and 671 vessels manned by 51,000 sailors when the war ended.[18]

Union naval strategy had five key elements: blockading the South's ports, transporting troops and supplies at sea and along navigable rivers, bombarding forts, destroying any rebel warships, and, most importantly, conducting joint operations with the army to capture ports and forts. The blockade was especially challenging given the Confederacy's 3,500 miles of coastline, ten large ports, and 180 river mouths, bays, and inlets. Although President Lincoln declared a blockade on April 19, 1861, the American navy would only slowly implement that over the next four years. The blockade reduced but never eliminated smugglers. That only happened after Union forces captured a port.[19]

The Confederacy faced the same daunting disparity in naval power in 1861 that the United States did in 1775, and initially tried to surmount it with the same strategy of deploying smugglers, navy warships, and privateers. Confederate Navy Secretary Stephen Mallory was well qualified for that position. As a senator from Florida, he had chaired the naval affairs committee. He cobbled together a Confederate navy by arming merchant ships and eventually by purchasing British-made warships to raid American shipping on the high seas. He also authorized the construction of ironclad warships, mines, then called torpedoes, and eventually a submarine to protect southern ports against the blockade. Mines were free-floating or cabled; detonated on contact or by an operator that generated an electric charge to a wire connected to the mine. Mines sank seven Union ironclads and twenty-two wooden vessels, and damaged fourteen other ships. By various means, Mallory eventually mustered around 150 warships including 50 ironclads in the Confederate navy.

Privateering was the most controversial strategy. On April 17, 1861, President Davis announced that he would issue letters of marque to privateers to raid Union shipping. Learning of that act, two days later President Lincoln declared that those who attacked American shipping would be treated as pirates, in other words hanged. Davis warned that if he did so, a corresponding number of Union prisoners would be drawn by lot and executed. When American warships captured the privateer *Savannah* in June, its thirteen-man crew was charged with piracy. Davis announced that thirteen Union soldiers had been randomly selected to suffer the same fate. The jury split in a mistrial. Rather than hold another trial, Lincoln agreed to hold the crew as regular war prisoners. Thus, did Davis decisively beat Lincoln in their battle of wills and greatly enhance the Confederacy's naval power as privateer crews sailed without fear of being executed if caught.

British Prime Minister Henry John Temple, Viscount Palmerston turned a deaf ear to the protests of American diplomats and a blind eye to Liverpool shipyards that were building warships for the Confederate navy. In doing so, Palmerston tolerated the blatant violation of a British law, the Foreign Enlistment Act that forbad such construction. James Bulloch, the Confederacy's agent in Liverpool, conceived a way to finesse that law. He had the warships and their cannons steamed separately to the Bahamas where a crew waited in a deserted cay. The crew boarded the warship then transferred the cannons from the accompanying transport vessel.

The CSS *Florida* was the Confederate navy's first warship via that channel and was commissioned on August 17, 1862. Under Captains John Maffitt, Joseph Barney, and Charles Morris, the *Florida* captured thirty-eight American merchant ships; two of those prizes became the CSS *Tacony* and CSS *Clarence* that took twenty-three vessels. Captain Napoleon Collins of the USS *Wachusett* captured *Florida* at Bahia, Brazil on October 6, 1864. The next warship Bulloch purchased was the CSS *Alabama*, commissioned on August 24, 1864. The *Alabama*'s career did not last as long but racked up far more prizes than the *Florida*. Over twenty-two months under Captain Raphael Semmes the *Alabama* destroyed sixty-four American ships before the USS *Kearsarge*, under Captain John Winslow, caught up to her off Cherbourg, France on June 19, 1864. Semmes accepted Winslow's challenge to a duel. The epic combat lasted just an hour before the *Kearsarge* sank the *Alabama*, although Semmes and most of his crew escaped to shelter aboard a nearby British vessel. Two other Confederate warships were the *Sumter* and *Shenandoah* that respectively took eighteen and thirty-eight prizes. Overall, rebel raiders captured around 250 American vessels, inflicted around $15.5 million of immediate losses, and caused insurance rates for American shipping to soar.[20]

Smuggling was an essential and lucrative element of the Confederacy's war effort. Cotton prices in foreign markets skyrocketed to as much as ten times their prewar value. In all, smugglers exported 500,000 cotton bales and imported 1,000,000 shoe pairs, 500,000 rifles, and 1,000 tons of gunpowder. By 1864, captains earned as much as $5,000 in hard coin for a round trip with lesser officers pocketing from $700 to $3,500, and sailors $250. The main foreign smuggling nests were Havana, Nassau, and Bermuda. The ideal smuggling vessel was shallow draft, low horizon, grey painted, and burned smokeless anthracite coal to power its steam engine. Smugglers made over 8,000 voyages during the war's 4 years, although most were intercoastal among the rebel states. Of the 1,300 voyages to or from foreign markets, 1,000 succeeded. The odds of evasion diminished as the blockade thickened, with nine of ten slipping through in 1861 and one of two in 1865. Charleston and Wilmington held out until February 1865, during which 87 percent of steamships and 81 percent of sailing ships evaded capture.[21] In February 1864, the Confederate Congress passed a law that required smuggling vessels to reserve half their cargo space for official shipments.

The American blockade eventually included around 450 warships with 150 on duty at any one time that patrolled or controlled virtually the entire 3,500 miles of rebel coastline.[22] The blockade was split among Atlantic and Gulf fleets, each with numerous squadrons that operated along specific ports and estuaries. Vessels rotated between patrols and returned to homeports for repairs and resupply. Blockade vessels were usually deployed in echelon with smaller warships near shore and larger warships further out. Signal flares shot skyward alerted blockaders to approaching smugglers. The average blockade vessel sighted a smuggler every three or four weeks and captured one or two a year. A prize crew was put aboard and the vessel sailed or steamed to the nearest friendly port where it and its cargo were sold. Blockade crews split the prize money from any captured vessels with captains taking 70 percent, lower officers smaller takes, and 16 percent spread among common sailors. Captured smugglers went to prison camps. As for the blockade's effectiveness, one historian found "the number of prizes brought in during the war was 1,149 of which 210 were steamers. There were also 355 vessels burned, sunk, driven on shores, or otherwise destroyed, of which 85 were steamers, making a total of 1,504 vessels."[23]

The blockade severely straightjacketed southern trade. For instance, the southern states exported 10,000,000 cotton bales during the 3 years before the war but only 500,000 during the war's last 3 years. British purchases of southern cotton in 1862 plummeted to 3 percent of prewar levels as importers rapidly shifted to Egypt and India. Cotton bales piled up in warehouses and production steadily dropped as farmers grew more food crops. Inflation skyrocketed with a Confederate dollar worth a penny by the war's end.[24]

Wars, of course, cost money as well as lives. Raising money is a critical element of hard power for waging war. There are three sources: taxes, loans, and prints. Here the United States enjoyed a vast edge over the Confederacy. Although Washington and Richmond used all three methods, they did so with starkly different shares, efficiency, and results. Overall, Washington and Richmond borrowed money to cover two-thirds and two-fifths, respectively, of all their expenses. By October 1864, Federal revenue included 62 percent from bonds, 21 percent from taxes, 13 percent from paper money, and 5 percent from other sources, while Confederate revenues included 60 percent paper money, 30 percent from bonds, 5 percent from taxes, and 5 percent from other sources.[25]

The Union war effort cost $3.2 billion for a daily average of around $1 million over four years. To pay for that, the White House and Congress constructed a modern financial and revenue system through a series of laws.[26] After Congress reconvened on July 4, 1861, its financial committees worked closely with Treasury Secretary Chase to raise money including $20 million in taxes on the states and sale of $250 million government bonds. Congress passed three bills that raised tariffs from an average 17 percent and 21 percent on durable goods to an average 38 percent and 48 percent on durable goods between 1861 and 1865. That garnered $345 million for the treasury and boosted American manufacturing. Congress enacted the nation's first income tax on August 4, 1861; the initial tax was 3 percent on incomes starting at $800. The Legal Tender Act, passed on February 25, 1862, created $150 million worth of America's first official paper currency, dubbed the "greenback" for its color. Congress authorized more releases until $450 million worth of greenbacks circulated by the war's end. That money could be used for all but two transactions: only gold coins were accepted as payments on import tariffs and bond interests. The Internal Revenue Act, passed on July 1, 1862, established within the Treasury Department a Bureau of Internal Revenue to collect an array of taxes for products and practices including tobacco and liquor that affected most men; on carriages, yachts, jewelry, and billiard tables that affected the rich; on business licenses, dividends, and interest. The income tax began at 3 percent for those between $600 and $10,000, then rose to 5 percent. The inheritance tax was 1 percent for estates worth $1,000 or more.

War	Dollars Then	2011 Dollars
World War II	$296,000,000,000	$4,104,000,000,000
Iraq	$715,000,000,000	$786,000,000,000
Vietnam	$111,000,000,000	$738,000,000,000
Korea	$30,000,000,000	$341,000,000,000
World War I	$20,000,000,000	$334,000,000,000
Afghanistan	$297,000,000,000	$321,000,000,000
Persian Gulf	$61,000,000,000	$102,000,000,000
Civil War	$3,000,000,000	$59,000,000,000
Spanish American	$283,000,000	$9,000,000,000
American Revolutionary	$101,000,000	$2,400,000,000
Mexican	$71,000,000	$2,300,000,000
1812	$90,000,000	$1,500,000,000

Table 9.1: Top Twelve American Wars by Financial Costs.[27]

The Banking Act that Lincoln signed into law on February 25, 1863, empowered the Treasury Department to issue charters to banks in return for their requirement to buy treasury bonds equal to 33 percent of their assets and issue "greenback" banknotes equal to 90 percent of their assets. The Federal government competed with state governments for chartering banks. Washington won that battle in 1865 by imposing a 10 percent tax on state banknotes. That forced state banks to seek federal charters and the number of greenbacks skyrocketed while state notes plummeted. There were 66 federal and 1,466 state banks in 1863 and 1,294 federal and 349 state banks in 1865. Despite the rise in revenues, they fell further behind the national debt that skyrocketed from $64,884,000 and $2.06 per person in 1860 to $2,677,929,000 or $75.01 by 1865.[28]

The Confederacy faced far worse financial problems. Like Congress during America's independence war, Richmond covered most of its worsening budget deficits with printed money that caused ever more devastating inflation.[29] During four years of war, prices rose 80 percent in the Union and 9,211 percent in the Confederacy.[30]

The Confederate Congress provoked protests in April 1863 with a law that required every farm to give one-tenth of its crops to the state. The Treasury and War Departments jointly enforced that law by eventually deploying 1,440 appraisers and 2,945 agents across the country that collected $5 million worth of crops.[31] Yet, Richmond had no alternative. Taxing incomes was ephemeral because the amount of hard money circulating in the South was small to begin with and soon disappeared as people hoarded it amidst soaring prices. Tariffs were just an erratic source of revenue. Tariffs depend on trade. The Union blockade steadily picked off more ships sailing to or from southern ports.

International diplomacy was critical to each side's war effort. The Confederacy wanted diplomatic recognition, trade, financial aid, and military alliances with as many foreign countries as possible, with Britain and France topping the list. The Union wanted to prevent all that.[32]

Queen Victoria issued a proclamation of British neutrality on May 13, 1861. In doing so, Britain recognized the Confederacy as co-equal with the Union as a legitimate power. Eventually, all the European states issued similar declarations. Yet Britain and other states hesitated openly to aid let alone ally with the rebels. The Confederacy faced a diplomatic dilemma similar to what the United States faced in its independence war against Britain nine decades earlier. Foreign nations would only massively aid and ally with the Confederacy if they inflicted a decisive defeat on the United States by, for instance, capturing Washington or an entire Union army. But without aid and an alliance, the rebel armies were unlikely to achieve that. That did not stop General Robert Lee from trying, but the Army of the Potomac defeated both his attempts to invade and win a decisive victory in the north, at Antietam in September 1862 and at Gettysburg in July 1863. Had Lee won either battle, Prime Minister Henry Temple, Viscount Palmerston was prepared to ally Britain with the Confederacy. After Antietam, he explained that, "we must continue merely to be lookers on till the war shall have taken a more decided turn."[33]

Confederates believed their diplomatic ace was what they called "king cotton." Textile mills in Britain, France, and other industrializing countries depended on southern cotton. The hope was that as the Union blockade reduced the volume and raised the price of cotton the pressure would grow on those countries eventually to side with the South. That did not happen.

The British were torn between their geopolitical and geoeconomic interests on one side and humanitarian interests on the other. Geopolitically, having America's rising economic and military power literally split between warring separate countries boosted British power. Atop that the textile industry was literally and figuratively the British economy's engine of growth. Textile production depended on imports of cotton from southern plantations. The number of southern cotton bales exported to Britain was 2,580,700 in 1860, 1,841,600 in 1861, 72,000 in 1862, 132,000 in 1863, 198,000 in 1864, and 462,000 in 1865. Although Britain made up some of that void with cotton imports from Turkey, Egypt, India, and Brazil, the plummet in supplies caused prices to soar and eventually three-quarters of textile workers either were fired or worked part-time.[34]

Yet, Britain depended on more than just American cotton that fed its textile machines. Britain was not self-sufficient in food production and depended on grain and meat from northern states to help feed its population. From 1859 to 1862, American exports of wheat flour to Britain soared from 250,000 tons to 5,000,000 tons while exports of salted pork doubled and wool tripled.[35] If London broke diplomatic relations let alone warred against the United States, Washington would immediately retaliate by embargoing grain and meat, thus provoking a food crisis.

Then, there were moral considerations. Many Britons including some prominent politicians, hated slavery and thus the Confederacy. Britain had led the world in 1808 by abolishing its international slave trade and in 1833 by abolishing slavery in its colonies. Countless Britons took pride in that. President Lincoln nurtured that sentiment by signing on July 11, 1862, a treaty that Secretary of State Seward negotiated with British ambassador Richard Lyons to suppress the slave trade that let the Royal Navy search suspected American vessels.

If Britain had an interest in avoiding war with the United States, a crisis in late 1861 nearly provoked one. President Davis dispatched two diplomats, James Mason to London and John Slidell to Paris, with the mission to gain aid, recognition, and alliance. They sailed from Charleston to Havana where they transferred to the British vessel *Trent* bound for London. Learning of their mission, Captain Charles Wilkes of the USS *San Jacinto* intercepted the *Trent* and sent aboard marines to arrest Slidell and Mason with their diplomatic documents on November 8.

Word of Wilkes' act enraged Prime Minster Palmerston and his cabinet. They reacted by sending 10,000 troops to Canada and embargoing sales of saltpeter, a critical gunpowder ingredient, to the United States until the Lincoln administration apologized and released the diplomats. Lincoln complied, quipping, "One war at a time." The crisis passed.

The United States had a different conflict with France. In 1863, Emperor Napoleon III sent 35,000 troops into Mexico to oust President Benito Juarez and replace him with Ferdinand Maximilian and Carlotta as puppet monarchs. The Lincoln administration supported Juarez and opposed French imperialism but could do nothing more than protest. In July 1862, Confederate Ambassador John Slidell tried to entice Napoleon III into an alliance in exchange for several hundred thousand cotton bales. The emperor declined that offer. In Washington, the fear was that the French might try to reconquer the territory that the United States won from Mexico in 1848. That was an unrealistic fear. Maximilian's regime faced a worsening rebellion led by Juarez that steadily reduced the territory controlled by the French army.

Russia was the only great power that openly tilted toward the United States. The Russians had fought the British, French, Austrians, and Turks during the Crimean War from 1853 to 1856, and welcomed American trade during those years. They were currently engaged in a cold war with Britain later called the Great Game as each's empire expanded toward the other in Central Asia. They wanted a strong United States to counter and distract British imperialism in the North America, the Caribbean, and beyond.

Abraham Lincoln proved to be an outstanding commander in chief.[36] Critical reasons for that were his profound understanding of human nature and drive to explore all dimensions of a problem to determine how best to overcome it. Although he had no formal training, his brilliant mind soon understood the essential art and science of war. He played devil's advocate with his advisors to provoke debates over strategy. He borrowed and devoured books on military history from the Library of Congress. He spent hours each day at the telegraph office reading the latest reports.

Lincoln clearly understood each side's grand strategy: "I state my general idea of this war to be that we have greater numbers, and the enemy has the greater facility of concentrating forces upon points of collision; that we must fail unless we can find some way of making our advantage an over-match of his; and that this can only be done by menacing him with superior forces at different points at the same time; so that we can safely attack ... and if he weakens one to strengthen the other, forbear to attack the strengthened one, but seize and hold the weakened one."[37]

Lincoln had a knack for explaining a strategy's potential flaws or attributes with colorful analogies. For instance, he critiqued General Joseph Hooker's planned spring 1863 offensive with this analogy:

I would not take any risk of being entangled upon the river like an ox jumped half over a fence and liable to be torn by dogs from the rear without a fair chance to gore one way or kick the other. If Lee would come to my side of the river, I would keep on the same side, and fight him on the defensive.[38]

General Ulysses Grant's spring 1864 plan had each regional commander relentlessly attack the nearest and largest rebel force while he went after Lee. Lincoln aptly compared Grant's order for simultaneous offensives to that of a butcher and his assistants: "Those not skinning can hold a leg."

Lincoln found two military advisors especially helpful. The first was Winfield Scott who commanded the army when he became president.[39] Although little known today, he ranks among America's greatest generals. He was an outstanding regimental colonel in the 1812 War when he drilled and inspired his troops to outfight the redcoats before them at the battles of Chippewa and Lundy Lane. During the Mexican War, he led the army that hit the beach near Vera Cruz, took that city, then, in conquistador Hernando Cortez's boot steps, fought their way over the mountains into the valley of Mexico City, where they won a string of victories and captured the capital. He certainly looked the part with his 6ft 5in height, immaculate dress, and fierce expression. Unfortunately, by 1861, an array of ills plagued him like dropsy, arthritis, vertigo, gout, obesity, and aches from old battle wounds; he often dozed during meetings with his staff and even the president. He retired on November 1, 1861.

After Fort Sumter, Scott became the Lincoln administration's Casandra. He warned those who naively believed that Union troops would crush the rebellion in a few months that instead it would take years, a million or more troops, several hundred warships, and vast amounts of money, death, and destruction to pay for it. During a cabinet meeting on June 29, he advocated what would be called the Anaconda Plan of steadily expanding the navy to blockade rebel ports and dominate navigable rivers, and armies to overwhelm rebel troops before them in the systematic conquest of the Confederacy. Eventually, that was exactly the strategy that Lincoln embraced. It took the humiliating defeat at Bull Run in July to shatter the delusion that the war would be short. But until then the mindset "on to Richmond!" dominated the cabinet, Congress, and northern public.

General Henry Halleck eventually became Lincoln's closest military advisor after being appointed general-in-chief on July 23, 1862. Lincoln retained Halleck in that role after he replaced him with General Ulysses Grant on March 9, 1864. Halleck was highly intelligent and knowledgeable, yet he excelled at the theory rather than practice of war. His book, *The Elements of Military Art and Science*, was a distillation of European theorists, especially Henri Jomini and Karl Clausewitz who had fought in the Napoleonic Wars. His fellow officers called him "Old Brains." Although his official title was general-in-chief, his actual role was chief of staff. He and his twenty-three staff officers provided Lincoln and Stanton information, proposed policies, and implemented decisions. Halleck explained his role as being "simply a military advisor to the Secretary of War and the President and must obey and carry out what they decide."[40] Lincoln used Halleck as a political shield as well as an advisor. He had Halleck sign all orders, fire incompetent generals and lower ranking officers, and take the blame for failures.

Lincoln did not hesitate to criticize Halleck's methodical approach to strategy that emphasized capturing cities rather than armies. He argued that:

to attempt to fight the enemy slowly back in his entrenchments at Richmond ... is an idea I have been trying to repudiate for some time ... I have constantly desired the Army of the Potomac to make Lee's army, and not Richmond, its objective ... If our army cannot fall upon the enemy and hurt him where he is, it ... can gain nothing by attempting to follow him over a succession of entrenched lines into a fortified city.[41]

Just because Lincoln was commander-in-chief did not mean he was obeyed. For instance, on January 27, 1862, he instructed all field commanders to prepare to attack the nearest large rebel for on February 22, pointedly Washington's birthday. None fulfilled that order. No general defied not just his suggestions but clear orders more than General George McClellan who Lincoln had named general of the Army of the Potomac on July 22, 1861 and general in chief on November 1, 1861. He would endure McClellan's insubordination along with his arrogance until finally cashiering him on November 5, 1862.

If Lincoln proved to be a more able strategist that most of his generals, he also exceeded in diplomatic savvy his secretary of state. In April 1861, he gingerly dismissed Seward's plan to provoke war with Britain and France with his deluded claim that it would reunite the nation. In May 1861, Seward showed Lincoln a letter that he wanted America's ambassador to Britain, Charles Francis Adams, to read to Foreign Secretary John Russell. Seward's words were essentially an ultimatum for Britain not to interfere in American affairs. Lincoln realized that made war with Britain more rather than less likely. He insisted that Seward order Adams not to reveal the dispatch to Russell or anyone else, but simply convey the administration's hope that the British government let the Americans resolve their divisions without foreign interference. To Seward's credit, he recognized Lincoln's superior wisdom in these and other critical issues, moderated his views, and became the president's closest civilian advisor.

Chapter 10

The 1861 Campaigns

Four Border States with 420,000 slaves – Missouri, Kentucky, Maryland, and Delaware – were so split between slavocrats and unionists that they did not secede. Of those four, only Delaware was solidly unionist since only 1.6 percent of the population were slaves. The other three states had much larger slave populations, 9.7 percent of Missouri's, 12.7 percent of Maryland's, and 19.5 percent of Kentucky's.[1]

For now, Maryland was the most critical of those states because Washington City and the District of Columbia north of the Potomac River were imbedded within it. Should Maryland secede, Washington would be an island in the rebel sea. John Merryman, a slavocrat and militia company commander, led his men to burn bridges and rip down telegraph wires to isolate Washington. Violence erupted in Baltimore on April 19, when a mob attacked the 6th Massachusetts as it marched across town from the north train station, where the troops arrived, to the south station where they would board for Washington. In the fighting, the soldiers killed nineteen rioters before driving off the rest, while four among them died.

Lincoln suspended habeas corpus for Maryland on April 27, and had Merryman and his men arrested along with twenty-seven state legislators; regular rail service was not restored until May 13. The Constitution grants the federal government the power to suspend habeas corpus in time of rebellion or invasion. However, that clause appears in Article I that defines congressional powers. Lincoln justified his act as a constitutional expedient while Congress was out of session. Two years later, the Supreme Court upheld Lincoln's argument by a five to four vote in the 1863 *Prize Cases*. For now, vitally, Maryland appeared secure.

Congress reconvened on July 4. Lincoln won Congressional approval of all his emergency measures except habeas corpus's suspension despite his long reasoned argument with this climax:

And this issue embraces more than the fate of the United States. It presents to the whole family of man the question whether a constitutional republic or democracy – a government of the people by the same people – can or cannot maintain its territorial integrity against its own domestic foes. It presents the question whether discontented individuals … can … on any

... pretenses ... break up their government, and ... put an end to free government upon the earth. It forces us to ask: 'Is there, in all republics, this inherent and fatal weakness?' 'Must a government, of necessity, be too strong for the liberties of its own people, or too weak to maintain its own existence?'[2]

Those poignant words have ever since echoed when America faced domestic extremists and violence, most recently the failed coup on January 6, 2021.

Two sets of armies faced each other in northern Virginia in July 1861. General Irwin McDonnell commanded 35,000 troops camped south of the Potomac River from Washington. There were 20,000 Confederates led by General Pierre Beauregard 20 miles southwest around Manassas Junction. In the Shenandoah Valley, General Robert Patterson and 15,000 Union troops were at Harpers Ferry while General Joseph Johnston and 11,000 Confederates were 30 miles southwest at Winchester.

The ninety-day enlistments of the volunteers would soon expire. Ever more northern newspapers published editorials urging the president "Forward to Richmond!" Lincoln pressured McDowell to devise a plan for both armies to attack their immediate enemies. McDowell pleaded for more time to train his troops. Lincoln famously replied: "You are all green, it is true, but they are green also; you are all green alike."[3]

McDowell devised a plan whereby he marched against Beauregard's western flank while Patterson moved against Johnston's eastern flank, thus keeping the rebel armies apart and attacking them with superior numbers. On July 16, McDowell began his offensive but Patterson failed to move, intimidated by threatening cavalry led by General Jeb Stuart. Johnston seized that chance to quick-march his troops to Strasburg where they boarded trains bound for Manassas Junction. The combined rebel army formed behind meandering Bull Run Creek. On July 21, each commander launched an attack against the other's left flank. The fighting seesawed. The turning point came when General Thomas Jackson's brigade on Henry Hill repelled a Federal attack. Beauregard ordered a counterattack that routed the Union army. McDowell finally rallied his army at Centreville a dozen miles south of Washington. The Confederates inflicted 2,708 casualties while suffering 1,982.

William Sherman, then a colonel commanding a regiment, explained what went wrong:

It was one of the best planned battles of the war, but was one of the worst fought. Our men had been told so often ... that all they had to do was to make a bold appearance, and the rebels would run … We had good organization, good men but no cohesion, no real discipline, no respect for authority, and no real knowledge of war. Both armies were fairly defeated, and whichever had stood fast, the other would have run.[4]

That other was the Union army.

The battle shattered the delusion held by countless northerners that the war would be short and easily won. On July 2, Lincoln signed a bill that authorized him to raise 300,000 troops with three-year enlistments. That step was vital for the northern cause. In Bull Run's aftermath, Lincoln signed another order that seemed sensible at the time but proved increasingly problematic.

President Lincoln replaced McDowell with George McClellan to command the demoralized army before Washington on July 22. McClellan had an impressive resume.[5] He was second in his West Point class of 1848, served on General Scott's staff in Mexico then at several western posts, taught at West Point for three years, and was a liaison officer during the Crimean War. In 1857, he resigned to become chief engineer then vice president of the Illinois Central Railroad then in 1860 president of the Ohio and Mississippi Railroad.

Lincoln initially appointed him to command the Department of the Ohio headquartered at Cincinnati. McClellan began a slow advance into western Virginia along the Baltimore and Ohio railroad and with 3,000 troops trounced 900 rebels at Philippi on June 3. One of his subordinates, General William Rosecrans with 2,000 troops routed 1,300 rebels at Rich Mountain, capturing 555 of them while suffering only 12 dead and 49 wounded on July 11. McClellan claimed that victory even though he was nowhere near the battle. Nonetheless, he had presided over a successful campaign and that was good enough for Lincoln.

When Winfield Scott resigned as the army's commander on November 1, Lincoln appointed McClellan to take his place. He did so hoping McClellan would devise and implement a grand strategy to crush the rebellion. That hope was terribly misplaced. On that and other crucial issues, McClellan would continually frustrate Lincoln with his incompetence and indecisiveness that lost campaigns.[6] Compounding his failures, McClellan mercilessly snubbed and insulted Lincoln, who he despised, calling him 'a well-meaning "baboon" behind his back.[7] McClellan was a narcissist obsessed with being adored and obeyed. He hogged credit for any success and blamed others for any failure. For his part, Lincoln was a paragon of patience and humility. He was sincere when he said: "I will hold McClellan's horse if he will only bring us success."[8]

McClellan massed ever more troops until he had 120,000 troops by October 1861, yet he refused to march what he called the Army of the Potomac against

General Beauregard whose Army of Northern Virginia had only 45,000 troops. He claimed that the rebel army actually had 150,000 troops and would soon attack him. That was wishful thinking on McClellan's part. He loved all the pomp and power of being a general but combat terrified him.

The first battle fought by part of the army under his command was a disaster. On October 21, General Charles Stone led his brigade across the Potomac at Ball's Bluff after reports that a Confederate brigade under General Nathan Evans had evacuated nearby Leesburg. That report was false. The rebels attacked and routed the federals, including 1,002 casualties while suffering 155. Among the Union dead was Colonel Edward Baker, a former senator from Oregon and friend of Lincoln's. McClellan castigated Stone for the rout and continued to reject all entreaties by Lincoln to launch an offensive against the rebel army at Manassas.

Missouri faced a crisis.[9] During the 1860 election, unionist and secessionist candidates received 110,000 and 30,000 respective votes. The trouble was that unionists did not gain state power commensurate with their votes. Governor Claiborne Jackson, militia commander General Sterling Price, and most legislators at the capital in Jefferson City, along with most militiamen across the state, were secessionists. One reason for the discrepancy in power was that most unionists lived in St Louis while secessionists dominated rural counties with large slave populations. Yet, slavery was not as pervasive in Missouri as in the lower South. Only one in eight families held slaves compared with one of four among the Confederate states, while only one of ten people were blacks of whom 98 percent were slaves.

In St Louis, Captain Nathaniel Lyon acted decisively to secure the United States arsenal against around 700 pro-rebel militiamen at Camp Jackson.[10] He secretly had 6,000 rifles in the arsenal sent across the Mississippi River to safety in Illinois. Then, on May 11, he had his troops surround Camp Jackson, disarm the militiamen, and march them for internment in the arsenal where they would be paroled. A secessionist mob gathered, hemmed in the column, and demanded the militiamen be freed. One among them fired a shot that wounded an officer. The troops opened fire, killing twenty-eight as the rest fled. The following day, the prisoners received formal parole and were released. Elated at Lyon's decisive acts, Lincoln promoted him to brigadier general and sent him reinforcements.

Lyon split his command, marched half to Springfield and packed the rest with himself on steamboats bound for Jefferson City. Jackson, Price, and the militia fled to Boonville on the Missouri River before Lyon and his men arrived on June 15. Lyon routed them on June 17. The 4,000 Confederates retreated southward. Colonel Franz Sigel with 1,100 troops caught up and routed them at Carthage on July 5. The rebels fled to Cowskin Prairie just above the Arkansas border, where reinforcements swelled their ranks. Thus did Lyon secure most of Missouri for the Union. Meanwhile, Lincoln named General John Fremont commander of the Western Department with its headquarters at St Louis. After arriving on July 25, Fremont massed reinforcements at St Louis rather than feed them to Lyon who had gathered 5,500 troops at Springfield.

Lyon faced a crisis. His supply line stretched 200 miles to St Louis and his troops' ninety-day enlistments were expiring. Scouts reported that Sterling Price and 13,000 Confederate troops had advanced 10 miles near Wilson Creek. Rather than withdraw, Lyon split his force and struck the rebel army from north and south on August 10. The initial assault caught the Confederates by surprise but they stood their ground and eventually their superior numbers forced the Federals to retreat. The Union and Confederate armies suffered 1,317 and 1,230 casualties, respectively; Lyon was among the dead. Sigel took command and withdrew to Rolla a hundred miles northeast on the road to St Louis. Price did not follow but instead advanced north to Lexington on the Missouri River, where he captured a 3,500-man Union garrison on September 20.

All along, Fremont remained ensconced in a St Louis mansion, ignoring requests from Lincoln to join forces with Sigel and pursue Price. Instead, on August 30, he provoked a political crisis by declaring martial law and proclaiming freedom for the slaves of Missouri's rebels. Fearing that would tilt the precarious political deadlock between slavocrats and unionists in favor of joining the Confederacy, Lincoln ordered Fremont to rescind the proclamation.

Fremont began a slow advance with 40,000 troops toward Springfield where Price had withdrawn. Lincoln sent General David Hunter with orders to replace Fremont if he failed to win a battle by November 2. The deadline passed. On November 9, Lincoln appointed General Henry Halleck commander of the Missouri Department with Hunter the field commander. Meanwhile, Price withdrew to Fayetteville in northwest Arkansas. Hunter did not pursue.

The Union won the war when and how it did largely because of two men – Abraham Lincoln and Ulysses Grant. Lincoln's brilliant leadership mobilized the United States for war and oversaw the grand strategy. It was Grant who decisively defeated the Confederacy in a series of campaigns that captured rebel armies at Fort Donelson in 1862, at Vicksburg in 1863, and, finally, at Appomattox in April 1865.[11]

Ample irony lies behind Grant's stunning feats. With extreme reluctance, he went to West Point, served in various posts, and fought in first the Mexican War and then the Civil War. In his brilliant *Memoirs,* he admitted: "A military life had no charms for me, and I had not the faintest idea of staying in the army even if I should graduate."[12] He abhorred war: "It is at all times a sad and cruel business. I hate war with all my heart, and nothing but imperative duty could induce me to engage in its work or witness its horrors."[13]

Grant was a naturally gifted commander. He explained: "the art of war is simple enough: find out where your enemy is, get at him as soon as you can, and strike him as hard as you can, and keep moving on."[14] He disdained theories and theorists: "There are no fixed laws of war which are not subject to the conditions of the country, the climate, and the habits of the people. The laws of a successful war in one generation would insure defeat in another." He observed that generals usually "failed because they worked out everything by rule.... Unfortunately for their plans, the rebels would be thinking about something else... If men make war in slavish observation of rules, they will fail." General Sherman lauded Grant as "the greatest soldier of our time if not all time. He fixes in his mind what is the true objective and abandons all minor ones. If his plan goes wrong he is never disconcerted but promptly devises a new one and is sure to win in the end."[15]

Grant hid his brilliance behind a humble introversion. One of his aides, Charles Dana, called him:

> The most modest, the most disinterested, and the most honest man I ever knew, with a temper that nothing could disturb, and a judgment that was judicial in its comprehensiveness and wisdom. Not a great man, except morally, not an original or brilliant man, but sincere, thoughtful, deep, and gifted with courage that never faltered ... a simple-hearted, unaffected, unpretending hero.[16]

A bulldog commitment to fulfilling a mission was among the vital attributes of his character and generalship. He explained his determination "when I started to go anywhere, or to do anything, not to turn back, or stop until the thing was done."[17] Beyond war, the calm, firm way he controlled the most spirited horses revealed his inner strength; he holds West Point's record for the highest steeple jump. Yet another key attribute was his ability to analyze the character and so predict the likely behavior of others.

Grant graduated from West Point twenty-first of thirty-nine students in 1843. He displayed his courage at the Mexican War battles of Monterey, Cerro Gordo, Molino del Rey, and San Cosme. His two exhilarating years of war divided nine others posted at dreary remote forts. His Achilles heel was alcohol that easily rendered him shamefully drunk. Boredom and despair at being away from his beloved wife and children drove him occasionally to binge drink. In 1854, he resigned after a disgraceful spree at Fort Humboldt in northern California. For the next seven years, he failed at a series of ventures including farming, land speculating, rent collecting, and store clerking. At one point, he cut firewood and carted it for sale in St Louis.

Grant was tending his father's store in Galena, Illinois, when the Civil War began. Two politicians decisively propelled the revival of his military career. Illinois Governor Richard Yates awarded Grant a colonel's commission and command of the 21st Illinois regiment on June 16, 1861. Then Elihu Washburne, an influential Illinois congressman, talked Lincoln into issuing Grant one of four brigadier generalship allocated to Illinois on August 5.

Grant learned a priceless lesson while commanding his brigade posted at Ironton, Missouri. He was ordered to march and attack a nearby rebel force. His anxiety soared as he led his troops to the site only to discover that they had disappeared. He concluded that the enemy "had been as much afraid of me as I had been of him.... From that event to the close of the war I never experienced trepidation upon confronting an enemy."[18]

Grant's brigade was transferred to defend Cairo, Illinois, at the strategic confluence of the Ohio and Mississippi Rivers. Grant did not intend to sit tight. Rebel forces straddled the Mississippi River just a dozen miles downstream, 10,000 troops under General Leonidas Polk at Columbus, Kentucky and 2,700 under General Gideon Pillow at Belmont, Missouri. After Polk took over Columbus on September 4, Grant dispatched General Charles Smith with 2,500 troops to occupy Paducah, Kentucky, just below the Tennessee River's mouth on the Ohio River.

Grant devised a plan whereby he attacked Belmont while Smith distracted Polk with an advance but not assault on well-fortified Columbus. On November 7, 1861, he packed his 3,114 troops in transports and steamed downstream preceded by 2 gunboats. As the gunboats bombarded Columbus, Grant landed his troops and routed the rebels at Belmont. Unfortunately, three events combined to turn that initial victory into a retreat. Smith never arrived before Columbus. Rebel batteries at Columbus drove off the gunboats. Many of his troops scattered to loot the rebel camp. That let Polk send 3,000 reinforcements to Pillow who counterattacked and drove off the Federals, inflicting 607 casualties while suffering 641. Tactically, Grant lost that battle but boosted his skills and confidence. He was the last man to embark on the transport.

Chapter 11

Soldiers

The slave-state secession, formation of the Confederacy, and war against the United States split America's army officer corps as thoroughly as it had the nation. The army had 1,105 officers when South Carolina seceded. Of that, 279 retired, 239 of them immediately joined the Confederate army, and another 31 subsequently joined. Of around 900 West Point graduates who were civilians, 114 donned blue and 99 grey uniforms. Of 184 officers from the 4 border slave states that remained in the United States, 128 fought for the North, 49 fought for the South, and 9 stayed home. Of 286 southern active-duty officers, 191 became Confederate officers, 80 remained in the Union army, and 14 resigned.[1] The South boasted 8 military colleges with the most esteemed the Virginia Military Institute (VMI) at Lexington, Virginia, and the Citadel at Charleston, South Carolina. Virtually all those graduates fought for the Confederacy, including 1,781 of 1,902 VMI graduates.[2] The navy experienced a similar split as 373 of 1,554 officers resigned, although unlike rebel army officers, few would find a berth in what became the Confederate navy.[3]

Mobilizing armies and navies on ever grander scales demanded increasingly sophisticated administrations to man, train, supply, transport, arm, and lead them.[4] Each side met that challenge in different ways. General Emory Upton ironically noted the "contrary principles" whereby each side mobilized troops for war, with Washington emphasizing states' rights and Richmond nationalism: "The Government sought to save the Union by fighting as a Confederacy; the Confederates sought to destroy it by fighting as a nation." Washington "recognized the states, appealed to them for troops, adhered to voluntary enlistments, gave the governors power to appoint all commissioned officers and encouraged them to organize new regiments." Richmond "abandoned State sovereignty, appealed directly to the people, took away from them the power to appoint commissioned officers, vested their appointment in the Confederate President, refused to organize war regiments, abandoned voluntary enlistments, and, adopting the republican principle that every citizen owes his country military service, called into the army every white man between ages of 18 and 35."[5] Those characterizations are exaggerated.

Similarities exceeded differences. Each side spilt the country into regional departments whose boundaries, numbers, and names often changed. By 1864, the Union had nineteen departments each with a commander. The general-in-chief's role was to coordinate strategies and logistics among the departments, an increasingly arduous task. The Confederacy emulated the War Department's organization with Adjutant General, Engineer, Medical, Ordnance, Paymaster, Quartermaster, Subsistence, and Topographical bureaus. The Adjutant General was the Secretary of War's assistant. The Inspector General tried to ensure that each bureau's officials fulfilled their respective duties.

One critical difference was how each side ran its railroads. Lincoln understood their vital importance. On January 31, 1862, he signed a law that authorized the president to nationalize and operate under military control the railroads and telegraphs. On February 4, he formally took over the railroads. On February 11, he appointed David McCallum, manager of the New York and Erie Railroad, the director of the United States Military Railroads. On April 22, he commissioned renowned engineer Herman Haupt to head the Military Railroads' Construction Corps. He commissioned McCallum a major general and Haupt a brigadier general. They brilliantly ran the expanding network of railroads and trains, managing traffic surges, and rapidly repairing damaged tracks, bridges, and tunnels. The Confederates had no equivalent of the organization or leaders.

The paper strength of regiments for both sides was a thousand men split among hundred-man companies along with a command staff. Over time, replacements failed to replenish ranks depleted by death, disablement, and desertion so the actual strength of regiments steadily diminished. Usually, four or five regiments were grouped into a brigade, two or three brigades into a division, two or three divisions into a corps, and two to six corps into an army. Artillery batteries usually included six cannons and a hundred or so gunners and teamsters.

At each level, commanders had a staff. Colonels led regiments assisted by a lieutenant colonel, a major, an adjutant who was the colonel's secretary, a quartermaster, a surgeon, an assistant surgeon, and a chaplain. A captain, a first lieutenant, and a second lieutenant commanded each company. Brigades, divisions, corps, and armies had increasingly elaborate command staffs. Army commanders had a staff split among those in charge of personnel, logistics, ordnance, intelligence, operations, and engineering presided over by a chief.

Embedded in the Union army's organization was a severe flaw in recruitment and promotion. Rather than replenish existing regiments with new recruits, the Union army formed more regiments. For General William Sherman that was:

The greatest mistake made in our Civil War [because] when a regiment became reduced by ... service, instead of being filled up at the bottom, and the vacancies among the officers filled from the best non-commissioned officers ... the habit was to raise new regiments, with new colonels, captains, and men, leaving the old experienced battalions to dwindle away to mere skeleton organizations. I believe that five hundred men added to an old and experienced regiment were more valuable than a thousand men in the form of a new regiment.[6]

Each side's president appointed generals with his senate's approval.[7] Abraham Lincoln and Jefferson Davis respectively picked 126 and 89 generals in 1861, and 583 and 425 over all four years. As for rank, Lincoln named Ulysses Grant lieutenant general, 17 major generals in the regular army, and 122 major generals of volunteers, while Davis named 8 lieutenant generals, and 72 major generals. One thing both armies shared was that West Pointers dominated army commands. By one count of "the sixty biggest battles, West Point graduates commanded both armies in fifty-five, and in the remaining five a West Pointer commanded one of the opposing armies."[8] Yet, even among graduates from West Point and other military academies, few were ready for high command; many grew into the position while others made a mess of it.

Then there were the political generals with little or no military experience, chosen to placate their states where they were prominent politicians. Here Davis actually appointed a greater portion of political generals than did Lincoln, 50 percent to 35 percent during the war. In 1861 alone, Lincoln and Davis issued 44 and 45 political appointments, respectively. Naturally, it was more challenging for politicians to master generalship than professional officers. Yet, most politicians had a natural charisma, confidence, and courage to lead even if they were initially ignorant of such essentials as drill, tactics, and logistics. Professionals mostly scorned amateurs. General Henry Halleck lamented that was "little better than murder to give important command to such men as [Nathaniel] Banks, [Benjamin] Butler, [John] McClernand, and [Lew] Wallace," with the first two prominent politicians from Massachusetts and the latter two respectively from Illinois and Indiana.[9]

The power of politicians forced many West Point graduates to seek their own patrons. The Civil War careers of Ulysses Grant and William Sherman might have been obscure and the Union victory unlikely without their respective patronage from Elihu Washburne, who chaired the House Military Affairs Committee, and older brother John Sherman, who chaired the Senate Finance Committee.

During the war, the average age for generals diminished from 43.6 and 44.8, respectively, for North and South in 1861 to a uniform 42.5 years in 1865. What effect the greater prudence and knowledge of older over younger men as generals had on the war is impossible to determine. Nearly all the major generals on each side were college graduates, with half from West Point; of the twenty highest-ranking Union generals only two were not, while only Nathan Forrest had that distinction among the twenty-highest ranking Confederate generals.

As for officers below generals in volunteer state regiments, governors appointed the colonels, lieutenant colonels, and majors; and soldiers elected their lieutenants and captains. Lincoln appointed all officers for regular regiments. Each side soon established officer boards to determine each officer's fitness and weed out those deemed inept. Eventually, both Washington and Richmond abolished elections and instead appointed all officers.

Those reforms alleviated but hardly eliminated incompetent commanders at all levels. To maintain a fragile political coalition between the Republican Party and the northern Democratic Party, Lincoln had to appoint as generals a number of "favored sons" who proved to be deficient such as Benjamin Butler, Nathaniel Banks, Daniel Sickles, and John McClernand. Of course, a number of West Point graduates were just as bad including George McClelland, Ambrose Burnside, and Joseph Hooker.

So, what makes a good general? Certainly, a general's vital attributes are partly identical to any soldier – courage, endurance, and obedience. They are also identical to any leader to be inspiring, decisive, prudent, knowledgeable, and adaptive.

Around 2,000,000 and 880,000 men respectively served in the Union and Confederate armies. The Union army was far more diverse with one of four or around 500,000 foreign born and one of ten or around 180,000 black soldiers. The exact figures will never be known given gaps in the records and multiple enlistments by many men. The average recruit for each side was single, protestant, 22 years old, 135lb, and 5ft 7in tall. Initially, Washington and Richmond had no trouble recruiting as northern and southern men and often boys enlisted freely and zealously. That initial rush to war soon dissipated amidst the war's tedium and horrors. Death from disease and combat along with desertion depleted both sides faster than new recruits could be enticed to replace them. As enthusiasm for the war and volunteers waned, both sides eventually resorted to a draft. If mingled patriotism, peer pressure, and desire to prove one's manhood initially inspired recruits, fighting alongside and not wanting to let down one's comrades became the most powerful motive.[10]

The Union had two recruitment advantages. One was that the North's military age population was three times that of the South, and would swell with immigrants during the war. Another was that when the war opened, the United States already had an army and the Confederacy did not. The American army numbered 1,105 officers and 15,259 soldiers. They were organized in ten infantry regiments, four artillery regiments, two cavalry regiments, and two dragoon regiments. No regiment was deployed in the same place. Instead, the 197 companies were scattered across the country with 179 manning 79 forts west and 18 forts east of the Mississippi River.[11] While officers could resign and about one-third did to join the Confederacy, soldiers had to serve out their enlistments.

President Lincoln asked for 75,000 volunteers for 3 months' service on April 13, for an additional 42,034 soldiers and 18,000 sailors for 3 years' service on May 3, and for 300,000 more volunteers for 3-year enlistments on July 2, 1861. As an enticement, the War Department would pay upfront $25 of the $100 honorable discharge bonus. On July 17, Congress passed a Militia Law that required all able-bodied men from 18 to 45 years old to enlist in their local regiment and empowered the president to require states to provide their militia regiments for nine months. On August 4, the War Department called on the states for 300,000 militia apportioned according to their respective populations. By the year's end, Union army ranks expanded with 421,000 volunteers but only 87,588 militia.[12]

The Union faced a crisis in 1863, as enlistments in thirty-eight two-year and ninety-two nine-month regiments would expire within six months. With Lincoln's urging, Congress established conscription with the Enrollment Act enacted on March 3, 1863. The law designated two categories of potential draftees, Class 1 of single and married men from 20 to 35 years old and Class 2 of married men older than 35, with the former drafted before the latter. The country was divided among 185 districts where draft boards compiled lists of those eligible and provost marshals supervised both the selection and collection of draftees. Each man's name was placed in a hopper, and picked by lottery.

Occupations	US Sanitary Commission Statistics	Comparison with 1860 US Census Bureau Occupation Share of Total Workforce
Farmer/Farm Laborer	47.5%	42.9%
Skilled Laborer	25.1%	24.9%
Unskilled Laborer	15.9%	16.7%
White Collar/Commercial	5.1%	10.1%
Professional	3.2%	3.5%
Miscellaneous/Unknown	3.2%	2.0%

Table 11.1: Livelihoods of Union Soldiers.[13]

The first draft was held in July 1863 with 20 percent of each district's names drawn. Astonishingly, only 9,881 men from 292,221 names drawn actually served. When that first draft was combined with drafts in March, July, and

December 1864, of 776,000 names selected, a stunning 522,000 were dismissed for physical, mental, or hardship reasons like being their family's sole financial support; 161,000 "failed to report" by fleeing where they could not be easily found; 86,724 paid the $300 commutation fee which generated $26,366,315.17 for the treasury; 74,000 found substitutes; and only 46,000 or 7 percent of the total joined the ranks. That still netted 120,000 soldiers for the Union army, most resigned if not enthusiastic about their fate.[14]

Critics denounced the draft as unfairly promoting "a rich man's war and poor man's fight." Wealthy men could pay the commutation fee or a substitute or bribe draft officers to declare them unfit for various reasons. Although that is true, in reality plenty of wealthy men volunteered or accepted the draft while 800,000 volunteers reenlisted. Historian James McPherson argues that the "half-billion dollars paid in bounties … represented … a transfer of wealth from rich to poor … By 1864, a canny recruit could pyramid local, regional, and national bounties into grants of $1,000 or more."[15]

Livelihoods among Union soldiers varied considerably with some groups overrepresented, others underrepresented, and some proportional. For instance, nearly half or 47.5 percent were farmers or farm laborers although they composed only 42.9 percent of the population, while white collar or commercial workers filled only 5.1 percent of the ranks, half their 10.0 percent share of all workers. Other categories like skilled laborers, unskilled laborers, professionals, and miscellaneous served as shares nearly equal to their shares of all workers. That speaks well for the men of that era who nearly all fulfilled their patriotic duty.

Of the Union army, 94 percent were volunteers and only 6 percent were draftees. What motivated Union volunteers?[16] As with all issues, Lincoln had a profound understanding of the complex reasons why men either join or avoid military service:

At the beginning of the war, and ever since, a variety of motives pressing some in one direction and some in the other, would be presented to the mind of each man physically fit for a soldier, upon the combined effect of which motives he would, or would not, voluntarily enter the service. Among these motives would be patriotism, political bias, ambition, personal courage, love of adventure, want of employment, and convenience, or the opposites of some of these.[17]

The Confederate Congress called 100,000 volunteers for 12-month stints on March 6 and another 100,000 for 3-year stints on April 29, and 400,000 more troops on August 8, 1861. Confederate soldiers would be clad in gray jackets and trousers with white shirts. All rebel regiments were raised by states. Cavalry and artillerymen had to provide their own horses.

In December 1861, Richmond hoped to convince one-year recruits to reenlist by offering a $50 bonus and sixty-day furlough. That proved inadequate. On April 16, 1862, the Confederate Congress enacted a draft for all able-bodied men from 18 to 35 years old and extended all one-year enlistments to three years. A draftee could pay a substitute to take his place. Some men became adept at pocketing a payoff, joining a regiment, deserting, taking another payment, and so on. The draft did boast Confederate ranks in 1862 from 325,000 to 450,000 troops, which with 75,000 men lost from various causes represented 200,000 more soldiers.[18]

Occupations	Soldiers	1860 Census
Planters, Farmers, and Farm Laborers	61.5%	57.5%
Skilled Laborers	14.1%	15.7%
Unskilled Laborers	8.5%	12.7%
White Collar/Commercial	7.0%	8.3%
Professional	5.2%	5.0%
Miscellaneous	3.7%	0.8%

Table 11.2: Livelihoods of Confederate Soldiers[19]

That was not enough. On September 27, 1862, Richmond raised the top draft age from 35 to 45 but exempted anyone who owned twenty or more slaves. That prompted widespread muttering about a rich man's war and poor man's fight. In February 1864, the top age rose to 50 years and the bottom to 15. Two subsequent Exemption Acts designated categories not eligible for the draft including government officials, college professors, teachers with more than twenty pupils, industrial workers, miners, and other skilled workers. Draftees could evade service by paying the government $500 or paying someone to take their place at a mutually agreed upon price. Davis appointed Colonel John Preston to head the Conscription Bureau and later promoted him to general. Eventually the Conscription Bureau had 2,813 personnel. Although 78.9 percent of those who served volunteered, 81,993 or 10.9 percent were draftees and 76,206 or 10.2 percent volunteered induced by the draft.[20]

In the Confederate army, planters, farmers, and farm laborers were overrepresented as workforce shares, unskilled and miscellaneous workers were underrepresented, and the other categories were proportional. What motivated southerners to fight? When asked, one captured Virginia private spoke for countless comrades when he replied, "I'm fighting because you're down here."[21]

Colored troops as they were known were critical to the Union victory.[22] Eventually, one of ten Federal soldiers was black and one of five died during the war. The official army number was 178,892 including 7,122 non-commissioned and 100 commissioned officers; about 10,000 blacks served in the navy. They fought in 16 battles and 410 skirmishes, and suffered 68,178 casualties including 2,751 killed in combat.[23] Germs killed ten black soldiers for every one in combat compared with two for one among white troops; overall one of twelve white and one of five black troops perished from disease.[24]

The legal authority for colored troops came on July 17, 1862, when Congress passed the Militia Act that empowered the president to enlist blacks "in any military or naval service for which they may be found competent." Actually, blacks had continually served alongside white sailors in the navy since the country's founding. Despite that authorization, the War Department did not establish the Bureau for Colored Troops to oversee the recruitment of officers and soldiers until May 1863.

Initially, black regiments were deployed in garrisons behind the lines to free white regiments for the front. But gradually, ever more black regiments were used for combat. Two fears initially limited black regiments to garrisons. One was the belief that blacks were not as courageous as whites and would skedaddle when the shooting started. Black troops disproved that fear after they finally got a chance to fight. The other fear was humanitarian. The Confederacy warned it would re-enslave captured black soldiers and put on trial their officers.

Lincoln posed this argument to skeptics about emancipation and the ability of blacks to fight:

You say you will not fight to free Negroes. Some of them seem willing to fight for you, but no matter ... I thought that in your struggle for the Union, to whatever extent the Negroes should cease helping the enemy, to that extent it weakened the enemy in his resistance to you ... I thought that whatever Negroes can be got to do as soldiers leaves just so much less for white soldiers to do in saving the Union.... Negroes, like other people, act upon motives. Why should they do anything for us if we will do nothing for them? If they stake their lives for us they must be prompted by the strongest motive, even the promise of freedom. And the promise being made, must be kept.

He recognized the enormous pride that black veterans would cherish: "there will be ... black men who can remember that with silent tongue and clenched teeth and steady eye and well-poised bayonet, they have helped mankind on to this great consummation."[25]

Blatant discrimination shadowed black troops who monthly received only $10, $3 less than white troops. Frederick Douglass met with President Lincoln to protest that discrepancy. Lincoln greeted Douglass with a warm smile, handshake, and invitation to sit. He then listened carefully to Douglass's argument before agreeing to close that pay gap. He got Congress to do so by law.

The Confederate Congress reacted to the Union's recruitment of black troops with a law that condemned "to death or slavery every negro taken to arms, and every white officer who commands negro troops."[26] The worst rebel massacres of surrendered blacks came at Fort Pillow, Olustee, Poison Spring, the Crater, and Plymouth. A Union sergeant recalled the horrific scene he viewed after the Confederates overran Plymouth, North Carolina, garrisoned by black troops:

> All the negroes found in blue uniforms or with any outward marks of a Union soldier upon him was killed. I saw some taken into the woods and hung. Others I saw stripped of their clothing … stood upon the bank of the river … and then they were shot – Still others were killed by having their brains beaten out by the butt end of the muskets in the hands of the Rebels.[27]

Word of such atrocities appalled Lincoln. On July 30, 1863, he issued this public order: "For every soldier of the United States killed in violation of the laws of war, a rebel soldier shall be executed, and for every one enslaved or sold into slavery, a revel soldier shall be placed at hard labor on the public works." That was a well-meaning bluff that he prayed would deter the Confederates. Privately he told War Secretary Stanton that, "blood cannot restore blood, and government should not act for revenge."[28] To his sorrow, reports of more sporadic atrocities reached him. He did not order any Confederate prisoners executed as a deterrent.

Late in the war, Confederate civilian and military leaders debated whether to enlist blacks as soldiers. On January 2, 1864, General Patrick Cleburne initiated that debate by circulating a memorandum among his fellow generals. He noted the dilemma and irony "that slavery, from being one of our chief sources of strength at the commencement of the war has now become, in a military point of view, one of our chief sources of weakness."[29] Indeed, the notion of mustering black soldiers posed a stunning dilemma and irony for a slavocracy that President Davis captured in February 1865: "We are reduced to choosing whether the negroes shall fight for or against us."[30] On February 18, Lee supported enlisting blacks: "The negroes, under proper circumstances, will make efficient soldiers. I think we could at least do as well with them as the enemy ... Those who are employed should be freed."[31] Congress took up the issue, debated, and eventually voted for a slave conscription law that Davis signed on March 13. The bill authorized drafting 300,000 slaves from 18 to 45 years old for 3 years' service with compensation to the owners but no promise of future liberty. That changed on March 23, when Davis issued General Order Number 14 stating that: "No slave will be accepted as a recruit unless with his own consent and with the approbation of his master by a written instrument conferring ... the rights of a freedman."[32]

That law's practical result was negligible. In Richmond, white officers formed two companies and deployed them at Petersburg. Other than that, elsewhere and earlier in the war one regiment did briefly serve the Confederacy although it never saw combat. The 1st Louisiana Native Guard was composed of free blacks from New Orleans.

For philosophical and practical reasons, most slaveowners fiercely opposed black Confederate troops. General Howell Cobb feared that: "If slaves will make good soldiers, our whole theory of slavery is wrong." General Robert Toombs predicted that: "the worst calamity that could befall us would be to gain our independence by the valor of our slaves ... The day the Army of Virginia allows a negro regiment to enter their lines as soldiers they will be degraded, ruined, and disgraced."[33]

The greater the morale among soldiers, the more courageous they perform in battle and the fewer malinger or desert when they have a chance.[34] Morale depends on a myriad of forces. Leadership is crucial. Depending on circumstances, a leader must display an appropriate mix of bravery, justice, endurance, humor, flexibility, and firmness. That includes both noncommissioned officers like sergeants and corporals who eat and sleep with the soldiers and commissioned officers who do so separately. Men can endure dismal food, cold, heat, mosquitos, and other deprivations if their leaders uncomplainingly do the same. Uniforms, regulations, and daily training in marching and maneuver dissolve individuals into something greater than themselves.

Steady supplies of provisions, munitions, and equipment are crucial to sustaining morale. Each soldier annually received a new uniform and was expected to sew or patch his clothes as needed. Shoes, however, had to be replaced when they wore out, which could be within weeks on campaign. The Union army tried to maintain a ratio of one wagon for fifty men or a wartime company. That wagon contained tents, shovels, saws, axes, cooking equipment, barrels of flour, salt pork, and water, and, during combat, often haversacks and blanket rolls. Sutlers supplied soldiers with extras. One chronic cancer on morale was what passed for food. The rations of salt beef and pork, and hardtack, a kind of wheat cracker, were not just bland and innutritious, but were often rancid and filled with maggots.

Symbols can boost morale. The bravest men volunteered to be color guards for the regimental and national flags with the names of battles stitched on them. General Joe Hooker elevated the Army of the Potomac's pride by giving each corps a badge like a cloverleaf or cross which each man sewed on his uniform. The idea was to promote identity and friendly rivalry among the corps. In battle, Union soldiers huzzahed and Confederate soldiers rebel yelled to boost their own courage and diminish the enemy's. Rewarding exemplary courage inspired more of it. On July 12, 1862, Abraham Lincoln signed a law that established the Congressional Medal of Honor. During the Civil War, 1,522 soldiers received that highest award for exemplary courage.

Most of the North's firearms and cannons were made at Springfield, Massachusetts, and Cold Springs, New York, respectively, although dozens of other manufacturers elsewhere received contracts. Cannons are easier to care for than firearms that rust quickly from moisture or black powder residue. Soldiers need an hour or so to dismantle and carefully dry or clean each part of their rifle and then reassemble it. Central to training was making each man highly proficient in firing and caring for his weapon.

The standard rifles that infantrymen on each side shouldered were different makes but nearly identical designs, with the North's .58 caliber Springfield and the South's British-made .577 caliber Enfield, although rebels captured tens of thousands of Springfields during the war. A well-trained soldier could fire three shots a minute. As for sidearms, officers holstered a .44 caliber Colt 1860 model. Union cavalrymen enjoyed greater firepower than Confederate horsemen. Although both sides carried six-shot pistols, Union cavalry initially also had single-shot breech-loading .52 caliber Sharps carbines. The firepower of Union cavalry skyrocketed from 1863 when they began hoisting .52 caliber seven-shot Spencer carbines.

The standard cannon was a 12-pounder named for the ball's weight. Cannons also fired conical shells with fuses whose lengths were cut to explode overhead enemy forces depending on how far away they were. Canister and grape shot were sacks of smaller balls fired at charging infantry with devastating shotgun like effects. The North also deployed a rifled 10-pounder cannon named after its developer, Captain Robert Parrott. Parrott guns fired shells further at higher velocities that were especially effective against fortifications. Well-trained cannon crews could fire two shots a minute. Yet, rifles diminished the effectiveness of cannons. Artillerymen tried to stay beyond rifle range to avoid being picked off by snipers. Cannons inflicted more casualties in the previous age of short-range muskets because they could be wheeled much closer to the enemy before opening fire.

Battle terrified some men and exhilarated others, but regardless, was relatively rare. Tedium was nearly round the clock endless day after day. Soldiers tried to break that monotony with gambling at dice or greasy cards, wrestling, boxing, and baseball matches, and tale-swapping. Prostitutes temporarily relieved the aching passions and tensions of some men. Fraternization with the enemy was forbidden but at times violated. Soldiers on picket duty on quiet fronts often established informal truces with the other side. When their officers were far away, they would meet to chat, trade, laugh, and lament the war.

Music boosted morale. Drummers beat rhythms for the men to march or rally. Buglers issued a variety of calls for action in camp and battle. Most evenings Union regimental bands serenaded the troops with patriotic songs like "The Star Spangled Banner," "America, My Country Tis of Thee," "Hail Columbia," and "Battle Cry of Freedom." In its February 1862 issue, the *Atlantic Monthly* published Julia Ward Howe's poem "Battle Hymn of the Republic" that became the North's unofficial anthem when sung to the tune of the popular soldier song "John Brown's Body." Ironically, northerner Dan Emmet actually composed the song "Dixie" that became the South's unofficial anthem. Other favorite Confederate patriotic songs included "The Bonnie Blue Flag" and "Yellow Rose of Texas."

Soldiers tended to prefer songs that evoked homesickness, melancholy, and hatred of the war. Off duty, most companies had a man with a battered banjo, fiddle, or guitar who could pluck tunes and plenty of eager accompanying voices. Both sides sang such favorites as "When This Cruel War Is Over," "Weeping, Sad, and Lonely," "Tenting on the Old Campground," "Bear This Gently to my Mother," "Yes, I Would the War Were Over," "Brother, Will You Come Back?" "Tell Me, Is My Father Coming Back?," "Lorena," "The Dew Is on the Blossom," "The Girl I Left Behind Me," "Aura Lea," "Wayfaring Stranger," "Amazing Grace," and "Home, Sweet Home." Many were Stephen Foster songs like "I Dream of Jeannie with the Light Brown Hair," "Oh! Susanna," and "The Old Folks at Home." The most prolific songwriter was George Root with over 2,000 including "God Bless Our Brave Volunteers," "Just Before Battle Mother," "The Prisoner's Hope," "The Empty Chair," and "Battle Cry of Freedom." During the Peninsula campaign, musically inclined General Daniel Butterfield composed the haunting melody "Taps" that nightly signaled lights out for the troops but also a final farewell to the freshly buried dead.

Nine of ten northern and eight of ten southern soldiers could read and write. Letters between soldiers and their distant loved ones usually boosted morale, unless they brought troubling or tragic news. Second Lieutenant Charles Brewster of the 10th Massachusetts wrote his mother that:

> It is the little common place incidents of everyday life at home which we like to read. It is nothing to the inhabitants of Northampton that the beans are up in the old garden at home ... but to me, way off here in the swamps and woods, frying in the sun, or soaking in the rain, it is a very important thing indeed. You do not realize how everything that savors of home relishes with us.[35]

Soldiers tended to read and reread their cherished letters until they wore them out. Knowing their letters would be shared spurred writers to be as eloquent and profound as possible.

The horrors of war, tedium of camp, and longing for loved ones caused an enormous number of men to risk severe punishment by skedaddling. An astonishing 201,397 Union soldiers deserted or about one of ten of which around 80,000 were arrested but only 141 chronic escapees were executed. The 103,400 Confederate troops that fled was a slightly larger portion.[36]

Combat is a soldier's ultimate purpose.[37] For that, he must be trained to obey orders without hesitation and kill mercilessly. Neither comes easily to most men. The survival instinct makes flight as sensible as fight depending on circumstances. Likewise, most men are leery of killing others and even as soldiers at least initially do so with reluctance, regret, and guilt.

Training partly involves desensitizing men to killing a dehumanized enemy. That did not prevent plenty of men from deliberately firing high or not at all. For instance, at Gettysburg alone, over 24,000 unfired rifles were found after the battle.[38] Yet, the experience of chronic combat, death, and destruction swiftly hardens most men. Union soldier Edwin Spoffold explained: "The man who shot him fell dead by my rifle. I felt bad at first when I saw what I had done, but it soon passed off, and as I had done my duty and was not the aggressor, I was soon able to fire again and again." Biblically, the desire for vengeance can shift one's mindset from "thou shall not kill" to "an eye for an eye." Witnessing the death or maiming of one's comrades can provoke survivors into frenzies of righteous slaughter. Confederate artillery officer Osmun Latrobe gleefully recalled: "I rode over the battlefield, and enjoyed the sight of hundreds of dead Yankees. Saw much of the work I had done in the way of severed limbs, decapitated bodies, and mutilated remains of all kinds. Doing my soul good. Would that they whole Union army were as such, and I had had my hand in it." Combat and even killing can be exhilarating. Union officer John De Forest admitted that, "to fire at a person who is firing at you is somehow wonderfully consolatory and sustaining; more than that, it is exciting and produces in you the so-called joy of battle."[39]

Most combat involved prolonged firefights supported by cannon fire with hand-to-hand combat rare. One survey of Union wounded found that firearms inflicted 94 percent followed by artillery for 5.5 percent and bayonets merely 0.4 percent.[40] The reason was that rifles stretched the ground where mass slaughter could begin.

General Sherman explained how topography determined tactics:

We were generally in a wooded country, and ... the men generally fought in strong skirmish lines, taking advantage of the shape of ground and every cover. We were generally assailants, and in wooded and broken countries the defensive always had an advantage ... for they were always ready, had cover, and always knew the ground to their immediate front; whereas we, as assailants, had to grope our way over unknown ground, and generally found a cleared field or prepared entanglements that held us for a time under a ... withering fire.

At rare times, "the lines did become comingled" and "the men fought individually in every possible style, more frequently with the musket clubbed than with the bayonet." The woods also covered the enemy's retreat, as "we often did not realize that ... till he was already miles away." Literally, a few steps can determine the difference between a successful and failed attack:

When a regiment is deployed as skirmishers, and crosses an open field or woods under heavy fire, if each man runs forward from tree to tree, or stump to stump, and yet preserves a good alignment, it gives great confidence to the men ... for they always keep their eyes well to the right or left, and watch their comrades; but when some few hold back, stick too close or too long to a comfortable log, it often stops the line and defeats the whole object.[41]

Sherman described initially being routed by a wild assault led by General Nathan Forrest:

The enemy's cavalry came down boldly at a charge led by General Forrest ... breaking through our line of skirmishers; when the regiment of infantry, without cause, broke, threw away their muskets, and fled ... As the regiment ... broke, Dickey's Cavalry began to discharge their carbines, and fell into disorder. I instantly sent orders to the rear for the brigade to form line of battle ... The broken infantry and cavalry rallied on this line, and, as the enemy's cavalry came to it, our cavalry charged and drove them from the field ... we found fifteen of our men dead, and about twenty-five wounded. I sent for wagons and had all the wounded carried back to camp, and caused the dead to be buried.[42]

Union Colonel Lewis Dayton recalled his part in the battle of Chickasaw Bluffs:

I overtook the rear of the advance about two or three hundred feet up the gentle slope, and was astonished to find how small a force was making the attack ... A heavy artillery and infantry fire was going on all this time. While making my way along the column, from which there were very few falling back, a shell burst near me, and the concussion confused me at the time and left me with a headache for several months. When I got my wits about me again I found a good many coming back but the main part ... was compact and keeping up the fight ... When our men fell back, very few ran but came slowly and sullenly, far more angry than frightened.[43]

A Virginia soldier observed a battle's horrific remnants "with a man's hand here & his body laying off to one side & men with their heads shot off & eyes & hips & bowels shot out & the wounded wet & freezing & some instances downing in the hole of water that gathered around them in the row of corn."[44]

Ambrose Bierce fought through the war and some of its fiercest battles including Shiloh, Stones River, Chickamauga, Chattanooga, Kennesaw Mountain, and Nashville. He was among countless men intoxicated by combat: "I cannot look over a landscape without noting the advantages ... for attack or defense ... I never hear a rifle-shot without a thrill in my veins. I never catch the peculiar odor of gunpowder without having visions of the dead and dying." He recalled a typical moral dilemma he and his men faced:

I had halted my platoon to await the slower movement of the line – a Federal sergeant ... lay face upward, taking in his breath in convulsive, rattling snorts, and blowing it out in sputters of froth which crawled creamily down his cheeks ... A bullet had clipped a groove in his skull ... from this the brain protruded ... dropping off in flakes and streams ... One of my men ... asked if he should put his bayonet through him ... I thought not, it was unusual and too many were looking.[45]

An extraordinary number of soldiers became prisoners, 419,568, and many died in captivity. Conditions in prisoner of war camps were abysmal on both sides. Overall, 15.5 percent or 30,218 of 194,743 prisoners in southern camps died compared with 12.1 percent or 25,979 of 214,865 prisoners in northern camps.[46] Dysentery, typhoid, and scurvy steadily killed with death spikes inflicted by smallpox plagues. That carnage reflected both the difficulty and disinterest of authorities properly to care for ever more inmates. The camps were last on a priority list and often got rancid food rejected by others.

The war's most infamous prison was Andersonville, formally called Fort Sumter and sited near Amicus, Georgia.[47] The camp was a rectangular stockade of 16 acres of bare ground with a languid creek through the middle. The men had no shelter from the scorching summer sun and the stream was a worsening sewer. Of 45,000 prisoners, 29 percent or 12,912 died from disease and starvation; those who survived the war were skeletal. After the war, Union officials arrested, tried, and executed its commandant, Major Henry Wirz, for war crimes. The prison in Salisbury, North Carolina, actually had a higher death rate of 34 percent although its commandant escaped prosecution. Union camps were not as bad. Every Union camp had wooden barracks for prisoners except one where they lived in tents. That helped reduce the death rate. Elmira was the Union's worst prison where one of four prisoners died.[48]

The American and Confederate government agreed to a formal exchange cartel on July 22, 1862. Each side paroled prisoners who promised they would not rejoin their regiments until they received notice of being formally exchanged. Of course, many men broke their promise and returned to the fight. Grant paroled the 30,000 soldiers he captured at Vicksburg then later learned that many of them had rejoined without formal exchange. Another problem was that thousands of men surrendered hoping to be paroled and sent home. That, of course, was a gamble since most ended up in a wretched camp and many died there.

Even those who survived endured incessant malnutrition, squalor, stench, and mind-numbing boredom. Lethargy and resignation dulled most men. Some plotted incessantly to escape. The most famous Confederate escape was that of cavalry General John Morgan and six of his officers from the Ohio State Penitentiary on November 27, 1863. They did so by chipping an opening into an airshaft that got them to a wall then descending with a sheet rope. After being feted as a hero and time with his wife, Morgan resumed his destructive raids behind Union lines. The greatest Union escape was 109 officers from Richmond's Libby Prison via a 57ft tunnel they had dug before February 9, 1864; authorities soon recaptured 48 escapees but 61 reached safety behind Union lines, often aided by slaves along the way.

Learning of the abysmal conditions in Richmond's Libby prison, General Ulysses Grant was determined to liberate the inmates. On February 28, 1865, he sent General Judson Kilpatrick and 3,500 cavalry cantering toward the rebel capital. Tragically, that proved to be a mission impossible. Rebel soldiers repulsed Kilpatrick and his troopers 2 miles from Richmond.

The Union use of black troops complicated the parole and exchange process. The Confederates not only refused to release black troops but re-enslaved escapees. Grant insisted that: "No distinction whatever will be made in the exchange between white and colored prisoners ... Non-acquiescence by the Confederate authorities ... will be regarded as a refusal on their part to agree to the further exchange of prisoners."[49] After the Confederate government refused to concede, President Lincoln suspended exchanges. Given the Confederacy's worse manpower shortage, that suspension hurt the rebel cause far more than the United States.

Lee proposed a resumption of the exchanges in October 1864. Grant replied that he would do so if blacks were treated equally with whites. Lee refused, insisting that: "negroes belonging to our citizens are not considered subjects of exchange and were not included in my proposition."[50] Desperate, President Davis finally yielded in January 1865. Exchanges resumed but too late to liberate many prisoners, let alone replenish rebel regiments.

Far more men died from illness or wounds than combat.[51] Germs then were a theory unproven until the microscope's invention later that century. Meanwhile, typhus, dysentery, measles, smallpox, meningitis, yellow fever, and malaria festered, sickened, and killed in squalid camps, hospitals, and prisons. Atop that, syphilis and gonorrhea afflicted those who frequented prostitutes. The stench of rotting flesh and feces was horrific and pervasive.

Some "cures" may have been worse than the wounds. Calomel is a mercury compound applied to wounds that might kill some pathogens but can kill the patient with too large a dose and rot one's gums in lesser amounts. Mercury also loosened constipated bowels. At least mercury was not addictive. Doctors prescribed opium for dysentery and morphine for pain, thus addicting thousands of veterans.

In battle, a regiment's surgeon selected a sheltered area behind the lines to set up a field station where he and the assistant surgeon would take care of the wounded brought in by the band's musicians dispatched with litters to the front. The Minnie balls fired by rifles shattered bones that rendered them useless and usually gangrenous. Amputation was essential for saving that life. Surgeons sawed off hands, feet, arms, and legs and tossed the limbs on growing piles. Wounded Civil War soldiers that suffered surgery had one advantage over those of previous wars. Ether and chloroform existed to put them out while morphine lessened their pain.

Compounding the carnage was the failure of doctors and nurses to keep up with skyrocketing wounds and diseases. In 1860, there were forty medical schools, thirty-two in the North and eight in the South. Nearly all the graduates went into private practice. Throughout the war, medical schools kept graduating students who medical examining boards either certified or rejected as doctors but the supply fell further behind the demand. The Confederacy not only endured dwindling numbers of trained doctors for soaring patients but the blockade also crimped supplies of opium, morphine, and quinine. Samuel Moore was the Confederacy's surgeon general for most of the war.

The American army's Medical Department included a surgeon general, four surgeons, and six assistant surgeons in 1861. Each regiment had a surgeon and an assistant surgeon. The Confederate army had a similar Medical Bureau but doctors were optional for regiments. Both sides requisitioned large buildings like warehouses and hotels as hospitals then supplemented them by building their own facilities. Outside Richmond, the Confederacy built the world's largest hospital, Chimborazo, with 8,000 beds in 150 buildings on a 125-acre site that treated 76,000 patients during the war. The Union deployed dozens of hospital steamships for the western rivers. It was easier to clean a floating than a ground hospital as medical debris was dumped overboard to float away rather than fester in nearby streets and lots. That saved lives. For instance, of the USS *Red Rover*'s 1,697 patients, only 157 died.[52] The Union also had hospital railroad trains with all the cars painted red and each equipped with fifty-one berths, an operating table, stove, toilet, supply closet, doctor, nurse, and cook.

Farsighted Americans drew ideas from Britain's tragic experience in the Crimean War from 1853 to 1856. Most critical was the finding that disease bred in filth. Philanthropists setup the British Sanitary Commission to alleviate filth in and behind the lines. The American equivalent was the United States Sanitary Commission with Unitarian minister Henry Bellows the president and public park designer Frederick Law Olmstead the executive secretary.[53] Olmstead had called for the Sanitary Commission's creation in his 1861 *Report on the Demoralization of the Volunteers*. Eventually there was an autonomous Western Sanitary Commission headquartered at St Louis. The Sanitary Commission mobilized thousands of volunteers to hold Sanitary Fairs where they raised money, medical supplies, and blankets that its Special Relief Service distributed to the needy. The Sanitary Commission's Bureau of Vital Statistics compiled numbers from army camps and hospitals. The Hospital Directory used the statistics to locate dead or wounded soldiers for inquiring loved ones. Sanitary Commission agents inspected army camps and hospitals then wrote up and submitted to authorities reports that recommended essential improvements. A massive Sanitary Commission report led Congress to pass a law that expanded the Medical Bureau with ten more surgeons and twenty more assistant surgeons on August 3, 1861. Yet, rather than welcome such oversight, most Medical Bureau members resented the Sanitary Commission for exposing their deficiencies.

William Hammond initiated sweeping life-saving reforms of the Medical Department as its chief from April 25, 1862 to August 14, 1864. Working with his assistant Jonathan Letterman, he provided a standard organization for hospitals that split among wards, each with teams of doctors and nurses. They issued medical workers standard equipment depending on their status. They did the same for the ambulance corps, nationalizing what was previously a private auxiliary. They initiated the triage system for sorting wounded among those with minor wounds that received first aid, the grievously wounded who needed immediate surgery, and the dying that were set aside unattended. On May 4, 1863, he banned calomel for its disastrous effects on those who ingested it. That provoked a backlash from suppliers and enemies he made from his imperious leadership. He was court martialed on an array of charges, found guilty, and forced to leave the service.

Two other men contributed significant medical innovations. Silas Weir Mitchell was a surgeon at Philadelphia's Turner Lane Hospital where he developed the rest cure for shell-shocked soldiers, often condemned as "malingerers" for their listlessness and reluctance to return to their regiments. During rainy seasons, malaria and yellow fever plagued civilians and soldiers alike in swampy regions like the lower Mississippi valley with New Orleans an epicenter, and the southeast coast. To his credit, General Benjamin Butler had work crews purge New Orleans' canals and streets of their filth after his army occupied the city in April 1862. That plus widespread use of quinine, caused yellow fever and malaria deaths to plummet from annually thousands during the 1850s to just eleven cases from 1861 to 1865![54] Most New Orleans residents did not appreciate that stunning transformation, instead condemning "Beast Butler" for his strict administration of the city.

Military nurses were men before the Civil War. Walt Whitman was the most famous male nurse. He got involved when he journeyed to Virginia to take care of his brother who was wounded at Fredericksburg in December 1862. He spent several months of 12-hour shifts in an army hospital before the horrors of caring for grotesquely wounded men and incessant deaths finally forced him to leave: "The crushed head I dress … From the stump of the arm, the amputated hand I undo the clotted lint … wash off the matter and blood … a gnawing and putrid gangrene, so sickening."[55]

The overwhelming need for nurses forced the army to employ women. On April 23, 1861, the Union Medical Department established the Women's Nursing Bureau with Dorothea Dix the superintendent. Dix was already famous for her efforts to alleviate the plight of insane people and improve the institutions that held them. She imposed strict standards of appearance and behavior including "the applicant must be over thirty, plain looking, dressed in brown or black ... and no bows, no curls, no jewelry, and no hoop skirts."[56] Over 20,000 women served as army nurses during the Civil War including Louisa May Alcott who related her experiences in *Hospital Sketches* published in 1863.

Clara Barton was inspired by Florence Nightingale, who formed a nursing corps for British troops during the Crimean War. She was forty years old, unmarried, and working in the Patent Office when the war began. She conveyed medical supplies and pressed congressmen to improve medical facilities for soldiers. In 1865, she founded the Office of Correspondence with Friends of Missing Men of the United States Army to help people learn what happened to their loved ones. Over the next three years, she answered 68,182 letters and found remnants of over 20,000 missing men.[57]

Elizabeth Blackwell is among the most influential American women who remains largely unknown today. She became the first female professional doctor after graduating from Geneva Medical College in upstate New York in 1849. She continued her studies and served as a doctor in London and Paris before returning to start a practice in New York City. She spearheaded a rally by over 3,000 women for helping the Union effort at the Cooper Institute on April 29, 1861. From that, she helped form the Women's Central Relief Association for the Sick and Wounded of the Army that worked closely with the Women's Nursing Bureau.

The Confederacy's female nurses were mostly private volunteers organized through local Ladies Aid Societies that eventually acquired state organizations. Southern socialite Mary Chesnut tried to hide the heartbreaking anguish she endured as a part-time nurse: "Horrors upon horrors ... Long rows of them dead, dying. Awful smells, awful sights. A boy from home sent for me. He was lying on a cot, ill of fever. Next to him a man died of convulsions while we stood there." She tried to emulate the stoicism of an older woman who "closes the eyes of the dead, writes letters to the friends of the dying, and ... nurse many a fine fellow shot to pieces back to life." One incident especially disgusted her: "He had been a stalwart creature over six feet and had that day for the first time attempted to walk out. Some brutes on the lawn, wounded soldiers themselves, laughed at him. And he came back, threw himself on his cot, and was weeping hysterically as a woman." That "hospital haunts me all day long – worse night. So much suffering, loathsome wounds, distortions, stumps of limbs exhibited to all and not half cured ... One was shot in the eye, but his whole jaw was paralyzed. Another ... had his tongue cut away by a shot and his teeth with it." Day after day, she "was really upset and came home ill." She literally tried to

scrub away her angst with this daily cleansing ritual: "I came into my room …
stood on the bare floor and made Ellen undress me and take every thread I had
on and throw them all into a washtub out of doors. She had a bath ready for me
and a dressing gown."[58] But that could never scrub the horrors from her mind.

Chapter 12

The 1862 Campaigns

West of the Appalachians, the Confederacy had at least one key wedge over the Union – unified command. With his headquarters at Bowling Green, Kentucky, General Albert Johnston headed the South's Western Military Department that stretched from the Appalachian Mountains to the Great Plains. He faced two Union commands. At St Louis, General Henry Halleck headed the Department of Missouri that included that state and Kentucky west of the Cumberland River. At Louisville, General Don Carlos Buell headed the Department of the Ohio from the Cumberland east to the Appalachians. Halleck and Buell vied for troops, supplies, draft animals, and transports, while ignoring President Lincoln's orders that they launch coordinated offensives against Johnston's forces.

Fortunately for the Union's fate, one general was determined to act.[1] At Cairo, General Ulysses Grant mulled General Leonidas Polk with 12,000 troops at Columbus, Kentucky; General Lloyd Tilghman with 2,500 at Fort Henry on the Tennessee River; General John Floyd with 10,000 troops at Fort Donelson; and Johnston with 25,000 troops at Bowling Green. He was determined to drive a wedge through those rebel forces. By capturing Forts Henry and Donelson, he would be placed to sever the retreats of Polk from Columbus or Johnston from Bowling Green. He asked Halleck's permission to do so. Although Halleck was as cautious as Grant was bold, he reluctantly agreed.

Naval power was essential to Grant's plan. For that, he had two brilliant leaders. One was Captain Andrew Foote who commanded the fleet of transports and ironclads. The ironclads came from the engineering and entrepreneur skills of James Eads who owned a riverboat construction company at Carondelet near St Louis. On August 6, 1861, he won a contract to build eight gunboats with 175ft lengths, 50ft beams, and 6ft drafts, and armed with thirteen cannons within sloped walls covered with 2½in-thick iron sheets. To expedite his order, he began another gunboat construction site at Mound City, Illinois. His 4,000 workers finished the vessels in late January 1862.

Grant packed his 15,000 soldiers in transports and steamed up the Ohio then Tennessee Rivers to Fort Henry. On February 6, he landed his troops while Foote's gunboats bombarded the fort. After sending most of his men to Fort Donelson, Tilghman surrendered. Grant dispatched three gunboats 15 miles upriver to destroy the Memphis and Ohio railroad bridge then beyond to destroy any rebels boats they encountered 150 miles to Muscle Shoals, Alabama, the highest navigable point. Meanwhile Foote steamed downstream, then up the Ohio and Cumberland Rivers to Fort Donelson. Grant garrisoned Fort Henry and led the rest of his troops 11 miles overland to Fort Donelson. As Grant anticipated, Polk and Johnston withdrew southward to avoid being cut off. Johnston sent reinforcements to Fort Donelson, bringing its garrison to 17,000 troops.

Grant deployed his troops in a cordon around Fort Donelson on February 12. The gunboats lost an artillery duel with the rebel batteries and Foote withdrew his battered ironclads from range. Floyd ordered an attack against the Union forces on February 15, but was repelled. He turned over command to General Simon Buckner, Grant's West Point roommate, and escaped with a couple thousand troops, including a cavalry regiment led by Colonel Nathan Bedford Forrest. Had Grant bagged Forrest he would have prevented dozens of subsequent devastating raids against Union supply lines over the next three years. On February 16, Buckner asked for terms. Grant's reply became legendary: "No terms except an unconditional and immediate surrender can be accepted. I propose to move immediately upon your works."[2] Buckner surrendered. Grant had captured his first of three rebel armies during the war. At Fort Donelson, his troops inflicted 16,623 casualties, mostly prisoners, on the enemy while suffering 2,832. An elated President Lincoln promoted Grant to major general.

Nathan Bedford Forrest was arguably the war's most brilliant overall commander for winning all but one of the fifty-four engagements where he led.[3] He excelled as a strategist, tactician, leader, and warrior. He conducted a score of raids with hundreds or thousands of hard-riding horsemen deep behind enemy lines that routed troops, captured garrisons, and burned bridges, supply depots, wagon trains, and rail cars. He was a master of the soft power of bluff that intimidated often more numerous Union forces to surrender rather than fight. His courage was unexcelled. He led most charges, boasted killing thirty-one Union soldiers, and was wounded eight times. Yet, he was conciliatory after the Confederacy's defeat. When his military region surrendered, he issued this last order to his men before disbanding them: "Reason dictates and humanity demands that no more blood be shed ... it is your duty and mine to lay down our arms, submit to the 'powers that be,' and ... aid in restoring peace and establishing law and order through the land."[4]

Forrest naturally excelled as a commander without having received any formal military training before the war. He was born in poverty but through his adult years enriched himself trading land, horses, and slaves. Although he opposed secession, like most southerners his loyalty to his state exceeded that for the United States. On July 10, 1861, he wrangled a captain's commission from Tennessee Governor Isham Harris to form a cavalry company and began recruiting in western Tennessee and Kentucky. By October, he commanded a regiment's worth of troopers, was promoted to lieutenant colonel, and was posted to Fort Donelson. From there he began the devastating raids that soon won him acclaim among southerners, and dread among northerners. One battle made him notorious. On April 12, 1864, after overrunning Fort Pillow, his troops slaughtered a couple hundred black and a hundred white troops as they tried to surrender.[5] Although his culpability is disputed, his racism was not. In 1867, he was elected the Ku Klux Klan's Grand Wizard and served for a year. Yet, afterward, he reconsidered and publicly called for racial harmony if not equality.

Ulysses Grant was not the only victorious Union general west of the Appalachians in early 1862. In eastern Kentucky, General George Thomas with 4,400 troops defeated General George Crittenden with 5,900 troops at Mills Springs on January 19, inflicting 629 casualties while suffering 246. Because of supply shortages and his own natural over-caution, Thomas did not follow up his victory by advancing further south. Emboldened by the victories of Thomas and Grant, General Don Buell finally began a slow advance from Louisville against General Albert Johnston at Bowling Green.

To avoid being cutoff, Johnston withdrew to Nashville and Leonidas Polk from Columbus, Kentucky to Union City, Tennessee. Grant ignored Polk and advanced up the Cumberland River toward Johnston. Johnston withdrew all the way to Decatur, Alabama, then west to Corinth, Mississippi where Polk joined him. Grant captured Clarksville, Tennessee with its iron-works complex. With a small contingent, he steamed on to Nashville but learning of Johnston's whereabouts, returned to the Tennessee River and advanced upstream. By early April, he and 42,682 troops split among 7 divisions were encamped from Pittsburg Landing westward for a couple of miles with Shiloh church near the center and flanked by Owl Creek and Snake Creek northwest and Lick Creek southeast. There Grant waited for Buell to join him.

At Corinth, 23 miles southwest, Johnston had massed 40,335 troops. He sought to defeat Grant before Buell reinforced him. He split and marched his army along two parallel roads to attack the Union army on the morning of April 6.[6] The assault caught Grant's troops by surprise and routed two of his four divisions in the front line. Those of Generals William Sherman and Benjamin Prentiss fought off the rebels. Sherman withdrew to a new position where Grant deployed all his divisions except that of Prentiss who the Confederates forced to surrender. A bullet killed Johnston and General Pierre Beauregard replaced him.

Among Grant's attributes that made him a great general was his unflappability during crises that would rattle most others. When General James McPherson asked Grant whether he planned to retreat, he replied, "Retreat? No, I propose to attack at daylight and whip them."[7] Buell's advanced division reached the river that night and was ferried across to bolster Grant's line. The next morning, Grant ordered an artillery barrage then assault that routed the rebels who retreated to Corinth. Over two days of fighting, the Federals and Confederates suffered 13,047 and 10,609 respective casualties. Shiloh was the war's bloodiest battle so far. That carnage provoked critics to demand that President Lincoln cashier Grant. To that, Lincoln replied: "I can't spare this man, he fights."[8] For Grant, Shiloh transformed his outlook on the war: "I gave up all idea of saving the Union except by complete conquest."[9]

Grant was preparing to quick-march against Corinth when Halleck appeared and ordered him to halt. Halleck sat tight until April 30 then timidly advanced toward Corinth less than a mile a day and each evening had the troops build breastworks even though with reinforcements his 100,000 troops vastly outgunned Beauregard's 51,690 active duty troops and 18,000 on the sick list. On May 25, Halleck finally deployed his army before Corinth but did not attack. Instead, over the next five days, Beauregard launched several attacks while evacuating first his disabled then fit soldiers. He deceived the Union army by having his men cheer each time an empty train arrived to take more of them away while capped scarecrows and black-painted logs filled their empty places along the breastworks. Halleck believed Beauregard was receiving reinforcements rather than steadily transferring ever more of his army to Tupelo, Mississippi, 50 miles south. The last of his men departed on the night of May 30. The Union army occupied Corinth the next day. Halleck had captured a strategic rail junction but let the rebel army escape.

Meanwhile, Union expeditions took over swaths of the Mississippi River from different directions.[10] Heading downstream, General John Pope captured 7,000 Confederate troops on Island Number 10 between Missouri and Kentucky on April 8. The next battle came on May 10, when Commodore Charles Davis with seven gunboats neared eight rebel rams led by Captain James Montgomery at Plum Point Bend, 4 miles above Fort Pillow. The rams sank two gunboats before withdrawing to Memphis. Engineers later raised and repaired the two vessels but not in time to join Davis's next operation. He fought his way past Fort Pillow and Fort Randolph 15 miles below on June 4. That forced the rebels to evacuate those forts. Then, on June 6, he led five gunboats and four rams against Montgomery's eight rams defending Memphis. This time the Federal fleet sank every ram except one that escaped downriver. Union troops disembarked to occupy Memphis on June 6.

Captain David Farragut led a flotilla of 14 gunboats, 19 mortar sloops, 8 steam sloops, and transports packed with 15,000 troops commanded by General Benjamin Butler up the Mississippi River in early April. Two rebel forts and three gunboats guarded the river 75 miles below New Orleans. On April 24, Farragut's flotilla fought its way past, pounding the forts and sinking the gunboats while losing a sloop. The next day, Farragut's flotilla destroyed the batteries guarding the river south of New Orleans. Butler's army disembarked unopposed at New Orleans on April 30. Farragut steamed upstream to receive the surrender of Baton Rouge and Natchez. When he appeared with the same demand before Vicksburg, General Earl Van Dorn, who led its 10,000 defenders, refused. The Confederates literally had the upper hand. Vicksburg's cannons could blast the Union fleet from both river and bluff levels while Farragut's gunboats could only fire at the river level but could not elevate against the bluff-top batteries. Farragut withdrew to Natchez, evacuated its exposed garrison, and returned to Baton Rouge. Now the Confederates effectively commanded the Mississippi River only between Vicksburg and Port Hudson.

Occupying Union troops faced varying degrees of rebel passive and aggressive resistance. Nowhere was that more humiliating than in New Orleans. There, rebel ladies verbally and literally showered abuse on the bluecoats, especially officers. The worst incident was when a woman dumped the contents of her chamber pot on the head of Commodore Farragut walking below. That enraged General Butler, who commanded the occupation. He issued General Order Number 28 that threatened any female who acted unladylike with being treated as a "woman of town plying her profession." That outraged southerners who condemned the general as "Beast Butler." Nonetheless, the proclamation deterred copycat vile acts.

Capturing ports was crucial for the Union blockade. That began in 1861 with expeditions that took Forts Hatteras and Clark guarding North Carolina's Pamlico Sound on August 27 and 28, and Port Royal, South Carolina on November 7. That was the first stage for a massive armada led by General Ambrose Burnside of 15,000 troops packed aboard transports and guarded by warships commanded by Captain Samuel Du Pont that steamed into Pamlico Sound on February 7, 1862. General Henry Wise commanded 3,000 troops defending Roanoke Island. After a bombardment, 10,000 Union troops landed and soon overwhelmed the defenders who surrendered. Burnside and Du Pont won a victory at the cost of 264 casualties while inflicting 2,675. They then steamed on to capture New Bern on March 14, routing the 4,000 defenders and inflicting 578 casualties while suffering 471.

Fort Pulaski overlooked the confluence of the Savannah River with the Atlantic Ocean and so protected Savannah a dozen miles upstream from seaborne invaders. The Union effectively plugged the seaport of Savannah by pummeling and capturing Fort Pulaski on April 11.

After Virginia seceded, the American navy abandoned its naval yard at Norfolk on April 21, 1861. Before leaving sailors burned facilities on shore and several ships including the USS *Merrimack*. The fire only burned the *Merrimack*'s upper structure. Confederate engineers rebuilt the vessel, rechristened the CSS *Virginia*, with an inward-sloping structure 24ft high above the waterline with ten apertures for cannons, and covered it with two layers of 2in thick iron plating; 1in iron plate covered the hull 3ft below the waterline. There were six 9in smoothbore cannons, two 6.4in rifled cannons, and two 7in pivot rifled cannons. A 4ft iron ram extended just below water from the bow. The draft was 22ft. The two 600hp engines propelled it at a top speed of 5 knots. The *Virginia*'s full crew numbered 350 commanded by Commodore Franklin Buchannan. The *Virginia* was ready for action on March 5, 1862.

Meanwhile, at Brooklyn's naval yard, brilliant engineer John Ericsson, who invented the screw propeller, was supervising construction of an ironclad warship he had designed. The USS *Monitor* had a revolving turret with two apertures for 11in smoothbore cannons atop a deck just 3ft above the waterline. The *Monitor*'s 8-knot speed and 11ft draft gave it key advantages over the *Virginia*. The *Monitor* was launched on January 30, 1862, just two months after work began on October 25, 1861. After a month of trial runs and crew training, another ship towed the *Monitor* and its fifty-eight-man crew commanded by Captain John Worden to Hampton Roads. It arrived just in time to save the blocking flotilla from complete destruction

Five American warships blockaded the James River. On March 8, the *Virginia* steamed against them. First, it pummeled the twenty-four gun USS *Cumberland* before sinking it with the ram. Then it turned against the fifty-gun *Congress* that exploded after a shell hit its magazine. The USS *Minnesota* ran aground. The *Virginia* withdrew to replenish its ammunition and rest its crew.

The *Monitor* and *Virginia* squared off on March 9.[11] They pounded each other for several hours with neither capable of penetrating the other's armor. The *Virginia* sailed back to its anchorage. They became the prototypes for ironclad warships. During the war, the United States and Confederate navies built fifty-eight and twenty-one, respectively.[12] Neither the *Virginia* nor the *Monitor* survived the war. With its 22ft draft, the *Virginia* could not ascend the James River to safety at Richmond. To prevent its capture as Union troops advanced up the Peninsula, the crew burned the *Virginia* on May 11, 1862. The *Monitor* continued to conduct operations but sank in a storm off Hatteras Island on January 7, 1863.

General Joe Johnston commanded 45,000 troops at Manassas. In February 1862, General George McClellan conceived a plan to outflank him by packing his 100,000 troops on transports, steaming down the Potomac River into Chesapeake Bay, then up the Rappahannock River to Urbana. President Lincoln initially worried that too few troops would remain to repel an attack by Johnston against Washington. McClellan assured Lincoln that he would move so quickly that he would get between Johnston and Richmond, forcing Johnston to attack him. Lincoln reluctantly approved.

Johnston got wind of McClellan's plan and withdrew his army to Fredericksburg in March. McClellan used that as his latest excuse not to move. On April 9, Lincoln wrote McClellan that "your dispatches complaining that you are not properly sustained … pain me … it is the precise time for you to strike a blow … you must act."[13] After another long delay, McClellan proposed transporting his army to Fort Monroe at the tip of the peninsula between the James and York Rivers, then marching to Richmond. Lincoln raised the same objections. Once again, McClellan promised that he would swiftly capture Richmond then defend it against Johnston. And again, Lincoln grimly assented.

Typically, McClellan failed to keep his promise.[14] On April 4, he began disembarking his army at Fortress Monroe. It was an extraordinary achievement of mobilization, transportation, and supply as "389 vessels delivered … 121,500 men, 14,592 animals, 1,224 wagons and ambulances, 44 artillery batteries."[15] Yet, McClellan refused to move that vast army rapidly against General John Magruder's 13,000 troop at nearby Yorktown as Lincoln repeatedly urged him to do. Instead, he prepared to besiege Yorktown by inching troops and cannons forward. That let Johnston march his army to join Magruder. On May 4, Johnston abandoned Yorktown and withdrew to Williamsburg. McClellan occupied the abandoned trenches at Yorktown then marched to Williamsburg. Johnston withdrew with most of his troops, but left behind General James Longstreet's division. On May 5, McClellan launched a limited attack that Longstreet's men repelled, inflicting 2,239 casualties while suffering 1,703. Longstreet then withdrew to join Johnston's army further west. It had taken McClellan a month to advance a dozen miles and fight one battle.

With 102,236 troops, McClellan slowly followed Johnston's 53,688 troops. The Chickahominy River runs from its source a dozen miles northwest of Richmond east until it angles south to mingle with the James River near Charles City. McClellan's army straddled that river, with two corps south and four corps north. On May 30, a severe storm wrecked the two rickety bridges that engineers had constructed over the river. The next morning, Johnston launched 39,000 troops against those 2 isolated corps with 34,000 troops whose center was at the rail hamlet called Fair Oaks. Fighting desperately, the Union troops drove off the rebels, inflicting 6,134 casualties while suffering 5,031. A bullet ploughed into Johnston's shoulder; he would need six months to recover. The man that replaced him would win fame as the war's greatest Confederate general.

President Davis appointed General Robert Edward Lee the Army of Virginia's commander on June 1. Arguably, Lee was the Civil War's best army strategist and tactician, although, unlike Ulysses Grant, he never directed the South's grand strategy.[16] He graduated from West Point second in his class of 1829, served in an array of posts across the country, was West Point's superintendent from 1852 to 1855, and led the troops that captured John Brown and his gang at Harpers Ferry in 1859. His early career peaked as an officer on General Winfield Scott's staff during the Mexico War. It was Lee's daring scouts that found ways to outflank General Antonio Lopez de Santa Anna's army at Cerro Gordo and Contreras. On April 18, 1861, Scott offered Lee command of the army swelling at Washington. In doing so, he would vault the lieutenant colonel over twenty officers with more seniority. But Lee turned him down and two days later resigned his commission. Both Scott and Lee were Virginians but with different loyalties; for Scott, his nation came first while for Lee it was his state. Lee's first campaign in West Virginia was undistinguished. Nonetheless, President Davis named Lee his chief of staff on March 3, 1862. Soon Lee would collaborate with a general who was nearly as brilliant, although their relationship got off to a disappointing start.

No Civil War general was at once as brilliant and eccentric as Thomas "Stonewall" Jackson.[17] His early resume was standard enough. He was a West Point graduate who fought in the Mexican War, where he won two promotions for bravery and leadership. His quirks became more renowned with time and prompted annoyed or amused students and soldiers to dub him "Tom fool." After the war, he taught at the Virginia Military Institute (VMI) where he memorized his lectures that he would restart if any student disrupted his flow with so much as a question. He sucked lemons to dilute his indigestion and forbad liquor for himself or his men. He was a devout Presbyterian who prayed throughout the day and asserted Biblical eye for an eye rather than loving grace justice. That made him a humorless martinet who severely punished miscreants even for minor infractions. He held his right hand high to balance his blood's circulation; a bullet painfully wounded that hand at First Manassas but did not deter his ritual. He was unflappable under fire. He earned his nickname "Stonewall" at that same battle. Just moments before a Union bullet killed him, General Bernard Bee exclaimed: "Look at Jackson standing there like a damned stonewall." Jackson was a master of strategy and tactics that he explained as "always mystify, mislead, and surprise the enemy."[18] That meant hitting the enemy where they least expected it and were most vulnerable, especially their flank as at Second Manassas and Chancellorsville. On a minor scale, his 1862 Shenandoah Valley campaign was as dazzling as any of Napoleon's greatest.

Virginia's Shenandoah Valley runs 150 miles southwest from the Potomac River. The valley is narrow, squeezed an average dozen or so miles between the Allegheny Mountains westward and Blue Ridge Mountains eastward. Massanutten Mountain is a smaller range 50 miles long, that splits the lower valley between Harrisonburg and Strasburg with Shenandoah River branches flowing on either side. Valley farms produced enormous amounts of crops and livestock. That alone made it vital for feeding Confederate armies in Virginia. Atop that, its configuration strategically boosted the rebel cause. Union armies marching up the valley headed away from campaigns east of the steep Blue Ridge Mountains with its few high passes. Confederate armies marching down the valley headed toward Potomac River fords just a few score miles above Washington City. Two critical transportation lines linked Washington with the Ohio River Valley, the Baltimore and Ohio Railroad that crossed the Potomac River into Virginia at Harpers Ferry and the Chesapeake and Ohio Canal that followed the Potomac River. The most important town was Winchester, a rail and road juncture just 25 miles from the Potomac, which changed hands forty-six times during the war. Union and Confederate troops battled fiercely to control the Shenandoah Valley through all four years of war.

Of those campaigns, Thomas "Stonewall" Jackson fought the most dazzling in spring 1862.[19] President Davis promoted him to major general and assigned him command there in October 1861. On New Year's Day 1862, Jackson launched his first campaign. It was not a success and did not endear him to his men. With 5,000 troops, he sought to capture a 1,400 man Union garrison at Bath but it withdrew across the Potomac. He then turned toward 5,000 Union troops at Romney but they also retreated. He gained both towns with a score of his men killed and wounded in skirmishes but several thousand debilitated by near zero temperatures, snowstorms, and diseases.

In early March, Jackson's army numbered 4,200 troops at Winchester. He faced General Nathaniel Banks with 40,000 troops at Martinsburg, just 21 miles away. Although the Union army outgunned Jackson's by ten to one, he was determined to surprise attack them at dawn. Instead, his officers convinced him to abandon Winchester and withdraw south up the valley when the enemy advanced on March 11. The Union army slowly advanced after them. Jackson attacked Banks and an advanced force of 9,000 troops at Kernstown on March 23.

The Union troops held steady and repelled his attack, inflicting 718 casualties while suffering 590. Jackson withdrew to Staunton.

President Lincoln was determined to crush Jackson and secure the valley. He had 2 other armies converge with Banks against Jackson, Generals John Fremont's 25,000 troops from Moorefield and Irwin McDowell's 35,000 from Centerville. Reinforcements brought Jackson's army to 10,000 troops while 7,000 troops led by General Richard Ewell entered the valley in early May. Jackson then launched his campaign of quick-marching his troops to defeat the scattered Union forces. He trounced General Robert Milroy at McDowell on May 8; General John Kenly at Front Royal on May 23; Banks at Winchester on May 25; Fremont at Cross Keys on June 8; and General James Shields at Port Republic on June 9. All along Colonel Turner Ashby and his several hundred hard-riding cavalry attacked Federal supply depots and wagon trains, slowing and diverting enemy troops; Ashby was killed leading a charge near Harrisonburg on June 6.

Jackson and his footsore men literally left the enemy in the dust on June 18 as they headed over the Blue Ridge Mountains to Charlottesville where they boarded trains bound to join the Confederate army defending Richmond. Lincoln made a crucial mistake when he diverted McDowell against Jackson in the valley instead of joining forces at Richmond with George McClellan advancing west up the Peninsula. Richmond would have fallen had McDowell and McClellan cornered Lee there. Instead, Jackson joined Lee in the Seven Days' campaign that forced McClellan to withdraw.

General Robert E. Lee first displayed his brilliance during the Seven Days' campaign.[20] After the battle of Fairs Oaks, also known as Seven Pines, McClellan transferred most of his army south of the Chickahominy River, but left General Fitz-John Porter's 30,000-man corps on the north side. Lee was determined to destroy that isolated corps but Porter had deployed his troops behind Beaver Dam Creek. A frontal assault would likely fail against such a strong position, but might succeed if combined with a flank attack. On June 12, Lee arched General James E.B. "Jeb" Stuart with 1,200 cavalry to ride around that right flank to see if it was vulnerable. Stuart learned that the Union flank was indeed unanchored to any defensible position like a stream or woods. Rather than head back, he pushed onward all the way around the Union Army, riding 100 miles over 4 days, each day destroying supply wagons and depots, routing pockets of Union troops, and returning with 170 prisoners and 300 horses and mules.

Lee planned to launch a limited attack on Porter's front while Jackson smashed his right flank on June 26. General Ambrose Powell "A.P." Hill attacked at Mechanicsville but Jackson did not appear. The Union troops repelled the rebels, inflicting 1,350 casualties while suffering 361. Nonetheless, that night Porter withdrew several miles to align his corps with the other Union corps south of the Chickahominy. On June 27, Lee ordered his entire army, including Jackson who had finally arrived, to attack. He had wanted Jackson to outflank Porter's flank at Gaines Mill, but Jackson began his attack late and sent his men directly against the Union line. After 6 hours of relentless rebel attacks they finally punched back the Union troops, inflicting 6,837 casualties at the cost of 7,993. On June 29, Lee again attacked, this time against General Edwin Sumner's 26,000-man corps at appropriately named Savage Station, inflicting 1,038 casualties and losing 473. The following day, Lee ordered his latest attack at Glendale, but Jackson failed to send his troops into the battle. The losses were nearly equal, 3,797 to 3,673. McClellan withdrew his army to the James River with his central position at Malvern Hill. On July 1, Lee launched his army against McClellan's but massed Union artillery and rifles devastated the advancing Confederates, inflicting 5,650 casualties to 3,000 Federals. Typically, McClellan failed to counterattack and instead retreated during the night to a defensive arch around Harrison Landing on the James River.

Lee had decisively defeated not the Union army, but McClellan. During a week of fierce fighting, Federal troops repelled almost every Confederate attack, inflicting 20,614 casualties while suffering 16,261. The Federals actually lost more than the Confederates, around 14,000 to 12,500, since they retreated and most of their wounded were captured while most of the rebel wounded were patched up and eventually returned to their regiments. The entire Peninsula campaign cost the Union and Confederacy respectively 25,370 and 30,450 casualties.[21] The crucial Union casualty was McClellan, psychologically devastated by Lee's relentless offensive. Each day McClellan transformed his tactical victory into a defeat by withdrawing rather than hitting the rebels with a massive counterattack where they were most vulnerable.

Historian James McPherson argues that Lee's Peninsula campaign victory was ironic because it made slavery's demise more likely:

If McClellan's campaign had succeeded, the war might have ended. The Union probably would have been restored with minimal destruction in the south. Slavery would have survived in only slightly modified form, at least for a time. But by defeating McClellan, Lee assured a prolongation of the war until it destroyed slavery, the Old South, and nearly everything the Confederacy was fighting for ... After the Seven Days, Union policy took a decisive step toward total war.[22]

Lincoln journeyed to Harrison Landing and met McClellan on July 11. He informed McClellan that he would retain command of the Army of the Potomac but General Henry Halleck would replace him in command of all federal armies. The president then hurried back to Washington. Lee had launched another campaign and this one ignored McClellan and instead appeared to be heading for the United States capital.

Lincoln appointed General John Pope to command the 50,000 troops in northern Virginia called the Army of Virginia.[23] Pope had captured Island Number 10 on the Mississippi River and Lincoln hoped that he could be as decisive in waging war on the eastern front. Pope promised that he would. After arriving, he issued this proclamation to his soldiers that did not exactly endear them to him:

> I come to you out of the West, where we have always seen the backs of our enemies. I am sorry to find so much in vogue amongst you ... certain phrases like ... "lines of retreat." ... Let us look before us and not behind. Success and glory are in the advance, disaster and shame lurk in the rear.[24]

From Culpeper, Pope advanced south with his first objective the rail junction of Gordonsville.

After intimidating McClellan into retreating to Harrison Landing, Lee turned his guns against Pope. He sent Jackson with 25,000 troops to head off Pope's advance. General Nathaniel Banks's division spearheaded the Union army and on August 9 was encamped at Cedar Mountain, 20 miles north of Gordonsville. As Jackson's troops deployed before him, Banks ordered his men to attack. The Confederates repelled the Federals then counterattacked, routing them, inflicting 2,353 casualties while suffering 1,338. Pope massed his army and marched toward Jackson. Outnumbered, Jackson withdrew to Gordonsville.

Lee left 20,000 troops to defend Richmond and joined Jackson with the rest of the army, bringing its total to 55,000 men. He sent Jackson to curl around Pope to cut his supply line.[25] On August 26, Jackson and his footsore troops captured Manassas 25 miles in Pope's rear. That forced Pope to about-face his army and hurry north. Lee followed Jackson's route in a race to get around Pope and reinforce Jackson at Manassas. Jackson withdrew from Manassas a few miles westward to deploy his 22,000 men in a powerful position centered on a sunken railroad line near Groveton. On August 29, Pope and 32,000 troops or half of his army caught up to Jackson. He launched his divisions piecemeal directly against the rebels who slaughtered them. The rest of Pope's army arrived on August 30, giving him 60,000 troops. But Lee also appeared on Pope's left flank, attacked, and routed him. During the Second Battle of Manassas or Bull

Run, the Federal and Confederate armies respectively suffered 16,054 and 9,197 casualties. Pope withdrew his battered army toward Washington. Lee pursued and routed the rear guard of two Union divisions at Chantilly on September 1.

Lincoln merged the Army of Virginia into the Army of the Potomac with McClellan in charge as he and his corps arrived in Washington. With 100,000 troops, McClellan outnumbered Lee's 55,000. Yet, McClellan deployed his men in a defensive arc to guard Washington rather than obey Lincoln's urgings to attack the enemy.

Lee devised his boldest plan yet. He would cross the Potomac River upstream of Washington, threaten to cut off the capital, and force McClellan to march against him. The army waded across at White's Ford then marched to Frederick. There Lee split his army. He sent General Lafayette McLaws and his division to the Potomac just across from the 13,000-man garrison at Harpers Ferry. Jackson would quick-march in a circle that took him upstream of Harpers Ferry that he would then besiege. Lee and most of the rest of the army marched to Boonsboro and Hagerstown, leaving contingents to guard two passes across South Mountain, a long ridge running north and south.

McClellan gingerly advanced his army toward Lee.[26] On September 13, the Union cause received a stunning instance of good luck. Near Frederick, a soldier picked up a sheet of paper wrapped around three cigars left behind by a rebel officer. The paper was a copy of Lee's orders that scattered his army. The soldier showed the order to his officer who sent it up the chain of command until it reached headquarters.

For once, McClellan acted decisively. On September 14, he sent his army forward in three columns to fight their way across South Mountain's passes. Lee concentrated his troops behind Antietam Creek at Sharpsburg. On September 15, Harpers Ferry surrendered after a three-day siege, freeing Jackson to join Lee. That same day, McClellan's advanced corps began deploying along Antietam Creek's east side and the rest of his army arrived the following day.

McClellan had the opportunity to destroy Lee's entire army. He had 87,164 troops, more than twice as many as Lee's 38,000. The Potomac River was just a few miles behind the rebel army. A carefully devised attack could cave in the Confederate line and force Lee to surrender. Tragically, for the American cause, McClellan failed to do that. On September 17, he launched a series of piecemeal attacks along the line that Confederates repelled. The Union and Confederate forces suffered 13,724 and 12,469 casualties, respectively. McClellan did not resume his attack the next day despite his overwhelming numbers including two fresh corps. That night Lee withdrew his army south of the Potomac.

Lincoln repeatedly stated his intention to reunite the nation, not abolish slavery. Yet, the fate of 3,953,762 slaves was inseparable from the war. Some commanders initiated abolition policies long before Lincoln thought it prudent. In August 1861, Generals John Fremont in St Louis and Benjamin Butler at Fortress Monroe issued orders confiscating all property, including slaves, from rebels. Butler argued that if rebel property could legally be taken and slaves were property, then freeing and putting them to work for the Union army was justified. Lincoln feared that would push slaveholding fence-sitters and unionists in the border slave states into the Confederacy: "Kentucky would be turned against us. I think to lose Kentucky is nearly the same as to lose the whole game. Kentucky gone, we cannot hold Missouri, nor I think, Maryland."[27] He revoked both generals' orders for now. Yet on August 6, Congress passed and Lincoln signed the Confiscation Act that empowered federal authorities to confiscate rebel property including slaves, which would be freed.

Lincoln took a series of steps toward abolition in 1862.[28] On March 6, he asked Congress to compensate any states that abolished slavery. On April 16, he signed a law that abolished slavery in the District of Columbia and compensated slaveholders $300 for each of the 3,100 slaves. Yet, he revoked a May 9 abolition proclamation by General David Hunter for his Department of the South that included South Carolina, Georgia, and Florida. He signed a bill on June 19 that abolished slavery in the western territories, although that freed only forty-six people.[29] On July 17, Congress passed the Second Confiscation Act that established a due legal process for trying those accused of committing treason and liberating slaves from those found guilty.

Rather than applaud these measures, abolitionists condemned them for not completing the process. Horace Greeley, the *New York Tribune*'s editor, published an essay on August 19 called "The Prayer of Twenty Million" in which he demanded that Lincoln abolish slavery everywhere immediately. Lincoln explained to Greeley that for now, abolition could only be a means to reunifying the nation, not an end in itself, especially if it thwarted reunification: "If I could save the Union without freeing any slave I would do it; and if I could save it by freeing all the slaves I would do it; and if I could save it by freeing some and leaving others alone, I would also do that."[30]

Lincoln believed that colonizing blacks in some other country would be best for both races. He did not initiate that idea which eighteenth-century philanthropists had originated and the African Colonization Society, founded in 1816, had tried to realize by founding a settlement in Liberia. He never explained just how 4.4 million blacks could be uprooted and sent to Liberia or elsewhere. In August 1862, a delegation of black leaders arrived at the White House to talk him out of his scheme. He replied:

Your race is suffering ... the greatest wrong inflicted on any people. But even when you cease to be slaves, you are yet far removed from ... equality with the white race. You are cut off from many of the advantages which the other race enjoys ... Go where you are treated the best ... It is better for us both to be separated.[31]

A group of abolitionists urged Lincoln to declare emancipation in early September 1862 just as Lee led his army into Maryland. On September 13, he replied: "I view this matter as a practical war matter to be decided on according to the advantages or disadvantages it may offer to the oppression of this rebellion." He then cited practical reasons for not doing so. A proclamation could push the Border States into the Confederacy, appear an act of desperation if not preceded by a decisive victory, and would strain Union resources to feed and arm all the slave refugees.[32]

Antietam was not the decisive battle that Lincoln had envisioned. Yet, on September 22, after forging a consensus in his cabinet, he used it as the excuse to issue his Emancipation Proclamation. From January 1, 1863 "all persons held as slaves within any State or designated part of a State ... in rebellion against the United States, shall be ... forever free."[33] He reassured slaveowners in the Border States that the proclamation did not apply to them and that the United States would compensate them for any loss of their slaves. In other words, Lincoln was liberating slaves beyond Union control while tolerating slavery within Union control. But to critics who called that hypocritical or contradictory, he replied that he was merely upholding the Confiscation Act that empowered the government to confiscate property, including slaves, from rebels while protecting the property of those who remained loyal to the United States.

Lincoln fully recognized how revolutionary the Emancipation Proclamation would be. When he signed the document, he remarked that: "I never, in my life, felt more certain that I was doing right ... If my name ever goes into history it will be for this act, and my whole soul is in it."[34] In his 1863 State of the Union, he explained abolition's most profound meanings: "In giving freedom to the slave, we assure freedom to the free – honorable alike in what we give and what we preserve. We shall nobly save or meanly lose the last best hope on earth ... The way is plain, peaceful, generous, just – a way which, if followed, the world will forever applaud and God must forever bless."[35]

During the Civil War, the threats to the United States nearly spanned the continent, including the Far West.[36] Confederate armies invaded New Mexico in 1861 and 1862. Secessionists raised the rebel flag above Tucson and skirmished with Union troops 50 miles northwest on the trail to California in 1862.

Elsewhere, the thinning or withdrawal of garrisons from forts across the West emboldened neighboring tribes. There were rebellions by the Dakota Sioux in the Minnesota River valley in 1862 that spread to other Sioux bands across the northern plains in 1863 and 1864; by the Cheyenne across the high plains of Colorado and Kansas in 1864; and by the Navaho in northern Arizona and New Mexico in 1864. That forced President Lincoln to divert troops and supplies from key fronts in the east to rescue those far western fronts. Some of those bluecoats were "galvanized Yankees," Confederate prisoners who agreed to turn coat as long as they fought Indians rather than their former comrades.

The Confederacy's western-most campaign began on July 23, 1861, when Colonel John Baylor led 300 troops from El Paso, Texas to Mesilla, New Mexico. Major Isaac Lynde commanded the 380-man garrison at nearby Fort Filmore. On July 25, Lynde led his men to attack Baylor but withdrew after a short skirmish. Fearing that he would be cut off, Lynde abandoned Fort Filmore and withdrew toward Fort Stanton 140 miles away in the Organ Mountains. Baylor pursued and two days later caught up to Lynde and forced him to surrender. On August 1, Baylor proclaimed the Confederate Territory of Arizona that included all land south of the 34th Parallel with Mesilla its capital.

That easy victory inspired Richmond to authorize a campaign led by General Henry Sibley to conquer all of New Mexico. The Federals had abandoned Fort Stanton and withdrawn the garrison to Albuquerque. In the Rio Grande valley, Fort Craig lay halfway between Fort Filmore and Albuquerque. General Edward Canby commanded the 3,810-man garrison, of which only 1,200 were regulars and the rest volunteers led by Lieutenant Colonel Kit Carson. Sibley led 2,515 troops and 15 cannons north on February 7 and they began skirting around Fort Craig on February 21. Craig led his men out to attack Sibley at the riverside hamlet of Valverde. They fought for two days before Canby withdrew back in the fort after suffering 432 casualties to Sibley's 157.

Sibley turned his back on Canby and marched north up the valley as Federal outposts in towns fled before him. The footsore rebel invaders marched unopposed into Albuquerque on March 1 and Santa Fe on March 5. Fort Union on the Santa Fe Trail 95 miles northeast was the only significant Union stronghold left in New Mexico. With his ranks now thinned to 1,100 men, Sibley marched toward Fort Union and its 1,342 men commanded by General John Slough. Learning of Sibley's advance, Slough quick-marched south to block his way at Glorieta Pass where they fought from March 26 to 28. The turning point came when Colonel John Chivington led his Colorado regiment around the rebel rear and destroyed its eighty-five-wagon supply train. That forced Sibley to retreat after losing 147 men to Slough's 222. Sibley withdrew first to Albuquerque then down the valley.

Learning of Glorieta Pass, Canby marched with half of Fort Craig's garrison to cut off Sibley's retreat. Sibley's men repelled him at Albuquerque then hurried down the Rio Grande valley. Reinforced from Fort Union, Canby pursued. Near Fort Craig, Sibley veered southwest into the mountains to avoid being trapped between the Union forces. Sibley finally reached El Paso in May.

Meanwhile, General James Carleton with 2,350 men headed east from Yuma. The advanced guard skirmished with a rebel force at Picacho Peak on April 15 and marched unopposed into Tucson on May 20. After resupplying, Carleton's army resumed their eastward trek and reached abandoned Fort Thorn on the Rio Grande River on July 4. He soon received reinforcements from Fort Craig. Faced with overwhelming odds, Sibley withdrew with his remaining troops all the way to San Antonio, Texas. Although the scale of troops involved in the New Mexico and Arizona campaigns were miniscule compared with those in the east, the distances were epic.

The 6,500 Dakota Sioux lived in 2 adjacent upper and lower reservations 70 miles long and 20 miles wide straddling the middle Minnesota River.[37] For years, they had endured broken treaty promises that the Great Father in Washington would annually give them stipends and plenty to eat. Fort Ridgely stood at the lower reservation's eastern border. The Dakota contrasted their poverty with the well-fed and furnished white homesteaders who farmed land on either side of the river from Fort Ridgely for 20 miles down to the prosperous town of New Ulm. Chief Little Crow vainly protested the corruption of reservation officials who pocketed most of the money they were supposed to give the tribe and sold them shoddy supplies at extortionist prices. They burned with rage when trader Andrew Myrick retorted to their complaints of starvation with: "So far as I am concerned, if they are hungry, let them eat grass."[38] On August 4, several hundred Dakota on the upper reservation emptied the agent's warehouse of all its food and other supplies. On August 17, four warriors murdered a white family and looted their farm. When the Dakota tribal council learned what happened, they decided to drive out all the white troops and settlers. The following day, they began a series of attacks that slaughtered homesteaders down the valley and besieged Fort Ridgely and New Ulm along with Fort Abercrombie on the Red River. Some Winnebago Indians, who also had a reservation in Minnesota, joined the revolt.

Minnesota Governor Alexander Ramsey implored Washington for Federal troops and appointed Henry Sibley colonel of a volunteer regiment to form at Fort Snelling near St Paul and march to the rescue. Sibley led 1,400 troops up the Minnesota River valley to relieve the settlement, then fort, and finally march through the reservation, defeating numerous attacks on his column along the way. Most Dakota surrendered, but many others fled west onto the plains where the Yankton and Yankatonais Sioux sheltered and allied with them. During the war in the Minnesota River valley, around 500 whites and 21 Dakota died; Myrick was among the dead, his mouth stuffed with grass.[39]

President Lincoln appointed General John Pope to command the 1863 campaign to crush the Sioux on the plains. One column led by General Sibley defeated the Sioux at the battles of Big Mound on July 24, Dead Buffalo Lake on July 26, and Stony Lake on July 28, while another column led by General Alfred Sully routed the Sioux at Whitestone Hill on September 3. That broke the back of Sioux resistance. Those bands eventually surrendered at forts along the Missouri River. As for the Dakota and Winnebago, their reservations in Minnesota were eliminated and they were transferred to reservations in Dakota Territory.

Meanwhile, military courts put on trial 392 Dakota warriors on charges of murder, robbery, and rape, and eventually sentenced 303 to death and 20 to prison. Lincoln carefully examined the trial transcripts and spared all from the gallows but 39 with overwhelming evidence of their guilt. On December 26, 1862, 38 were hanged at Mankato, Minnesota, the largest mass execution in American history. Despite that, most Minnesotans condemned Lincoln for pardoning nearly all the accused. Democrats trounced Republicans in the 1864 election, with Governor Alexander Ramsey among the defeated. When Ramsay complained to Lincoln that Republicans could have held the state had he issued fewer pardons, Lincoln sadly replied: "I could not afford to hang men for votes."[40]

During a White House conference with a delegation of western chiefs, Lincoln explained:

It is the object of this government to be on terms of peace with you, and with all our red brethren. We make treaties with you, and try to observe them; and if our children should sometimes behave badly, and violate their treaties, it is against our wish. You know it is not always possible for any father to have his children do precisely as he wishes them to do.[41]

That was rarely more tragically true than on November 29, 1864, when Colonel John Chivington launched an attack by 700 Colorado volunteers against the village led by the one Cheyenne chief who was committed to peace.[42] Black Kettle and his band of several hundred people were camped at Sand Creek on the high plains. An American flag and a white flag flew from a pole near Black Kettle's tepee. The best estimate is that Chivington's troops killed 53 men along with 110 women and children, while suffering 10 killed and 38 wounded.[43]

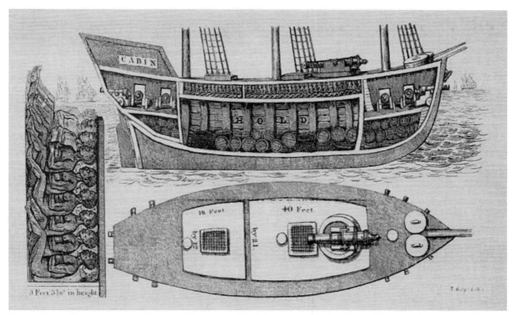

An eighteenth-century woodprint of slaves in a British merchant ship bound for the American colonies. Of the estimated 250,000 of 9.3 million slaves brought from Africa to the western hemisphere from 1450 to 1850, 250,000 reached what became the United States. (*Library of Congress*)

Slaves picking cotton. Cotton accounted for about one-quarter of the South's economy and slaves were the largest source of wealth. (*Currier and Ives, Library of Congress*)

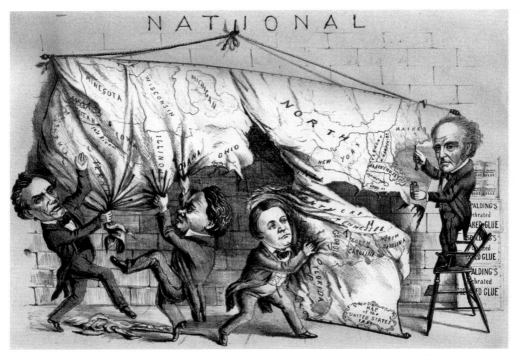

The 1860 Election and America divided, with presidential candidates Abraham Lincoln, Stephen Douglas, John Breckinridge, and John Bell. (*Library of Congress*)

The Confederate bombardment of Federal Fort Sumter in Charleston Bay. (*Currier and Ives, Library of Congress*)

Union troops on parade. (*Library of Congress*)

'Charge of the Gallant 69th New York at First Bull Run, July 21,1861,' *Harper's Weekly*, August 10, 1861. (*Library of Congress*)

Generals Robert Lee and Thomas Jackson conferring before the battle of Chancellorsville, their greatest victory, April 30–May 6, 1863. Jackson was accidently mortally wounded by his men. (*Library of Congress*)

Alexander Gardner, *President Abraham Lincoln, General George McClellan, and his staff*, September 1862. (*National Archives*)

A typical makeshift hospital. (*Library of Congress*)

Dead at Gettysburg. (*Library of Congress*)

Confederate prisoners. (*Library of Congress*)

Union gunboats and transports on the Mississippi River. (*National Archives*)

Abraham Lincoln delivering the Gettysburg Address, November 19, 1863. (*Library of Congress*)

General William Sherman and his army's destructive march to the sea. (*Library of Congress*)

George Healy, *The Peacemakers*, 1868, the White House. From left, General William Sherman, General Ulysses Grant, President Abraham Lincoln, and Admiral David Porter.

President Jefferson Davis ordered anything of military value destroyed in the Confederate capital of Richmond when his government fled that city on April 2 for Danville, Virginia. (*Library of Congress*)

Louis Guillaume, *Surrender of General Lee to General Grant*, April 9, 1865, Appomattox National Park.

The assassination of Abraham Lincoln, April 14, 1865. (*Library of Congress*)

A Ku Klux Klansman, *c.* 1870s. The Ku Klux Klan and other white supremacist groups terrorized blacks to prevent them from enjoying economic, political, and social benefits after their emancipation from slavery. (*Library of Congress*)

The movie *Gone With the Wind* based on Margaret Mitchell's novel epitomized Lost Cause romanticism. (*Library of Congress*)

White supremacists defend a stature of Robert E. Lee statue against protesters who demanded its removal at the University of Virginia at Charlottesville on August 11, 2017. A riot ensued.

Rage and racism vented that massacre. Over the previous two years, mostly Cheyenne but also Arapaho, Comanche, Kiowa, and Kiowa-Apache warriors had attacked towns, wagon trains, and stagecoaches across the high central plains. The only significant army victory came at Adobe Spring just five days before Sand Creek, when Colonel Kit Carson routed several hundred Kiowa-Apache warriors. Otherwise, the bands evaded the few expeditions sent against them.

After an investigation, the Joint Committee on Conduct of the War found that Chivington had:

> Deliberately planned and executed a foul and dastardly massacre ... having full knowledge of their friendly character, having himself been instrumental ... in placing them in their position of fancied security ... Chivington ... surprised and murdered in cold blood, the unsuspecting men, women, and children on Sand creek, who had every reason to believe they were under the protection of the United States authorities.[44]

The government never prosecuted Chivington for his genocide.

General Samuel Curtis led 10,500 troops from Springfield, Missouri into northwestern Arkansas in early March and encamped them south of Pea Ridge near Elkhorn Tavern. General Earl Van Dorn commanded 16,500 troops at Fayetteville. Learning of Curtis's advance, he resolved to cut off and destroy the invaders. During the night of March 6, he sidestepped the federals with Sterling Price's division attacking from the north and Ben McCulloch's division from the west. Although initially surprised, the Union troops held their ground and beat off the attacks on March 7 and 8. Van Dorn finally withdrew after suffering 2,000 casualties to Curtis's 1,391. With reinforcements and supplies, Curtis marched to capture Little Rock then Helena on the Mississippi River.

Late that year, General Thomas Hindman with 11,500 rebel troops advanced north from Fort Smith. On December 7, he tried to get between two converging Federal forces, Generals James Blunt's 7,000 and General Francis Herron's 6,000 bluecoats, and defeat each separately at Prairie Grove. Instead, Herron held the line while Blunt struck Hindman's left flank and rear. Hindman's men drove off Blunt's attack. Each side withdrew on its supply lines with the Federals and Confederates suffering 1,251 and 1,317 casualties, respectively. Union forces held most of central and northwestern Arkansas while the south remained a rebel stronghold.

President Davis replaced Pierre Beauregard with Braxton Bragg as commander of what was then called the Army of Mississippi on June 17. Bragg would become one of the war's most controversial southern generals for his strategies and abrasive personality.[45] He split his army, leaving 32,000 troops with Generals Earl Van Dorn and Sterling Price in northern Mississippi, while he led 34,000 troops east into northern Alabama. He sent cavalry generals Nathan Forrest and John Morgan on long separate raids deep into Tennessee and Kentucky to destroy depots, garrisons, and railroad bridges.

General Henry Halleck in turn split his own army, leaving Ulysses Grant in northern Mississippi and sending Don Buell east to shadow Bragg. On July 11, Lincoln replaced George McClellan with Halleck as general-in-chief. Although Halleck returned to Washington, he ordered Grant and Buell to stay on the defensive and scatter their divisions to occupy key places.

Bragg launched an offensive with his army from Chattanooga and Kirby Smith's 21,000 troops from Knoxville in mid-August. Their objective was to march into Kentucky and unite against Buell, defeat him, and impose a Confederate government over the state. Smith demolished a division of 6,850 federals led by General William Nelson at Richmond, Kentucky on August 29 and 30, inflicting 5,353 casualties while losing only 451 men. He then marched on to occupy Lexington. Meanwhile, Bragg captured 4,148 federals troops at Munfordville on September 17, then sent word to Smith to converge at Bardstown.

Buell was slow to mass his army and pursue. He reached his supply base at Louisville in late September then turned southeast to search for the Confederate army. On October 7, he attacked Bragg at Perrysville and drove him off as his men suffered 4,201 casualties while inflicting 3,296. Bragg withdrew to eastern Tennessee. Buell did not follow up his victory with a rapid advance but instead cautiously crept forward to occupy prominent towns.

George McClellan's limited victory at Antietam further bloated his egomania but did nothing for his courage. He was oblivious to the reality that a skillfully planned and executed attack the second day would have bagged General Lee's entire army with the Potomac at its back. He actually demanded that President Lincoln fire Secretary of War Stanton and General Halleck, and that he take Halleck's place as commander of all the armies. To Lincoln's pleas that he move against Lee, McClellan spewed specious excuses. Lincoln reminded him of "my speaking to you of what I called your over-cautiousness. Are you not over-cautious when you assume that you cannot do what the enemy is constantly doing? Should you not claim to be at least his equal in prowess and act upon the claim?" He urged him to act on "one of the standard maxims of war ... to 'operate upon the enemy's communications as much as possible without exposing your own.'"[46] But that failed to shame or inspire McClellan. On October 24, Lincoln wired McClellan this barbed retort: "I have just read your dispatch about sore tongued and legged horses. Will you pardon me for asking what the horses of your army have done since the battle of Antietam that fatigues anything?"[47]

McClellan finally began moving his 120,000 troops in 6 corps south of the Potomac on October 26, and slowly moved toward Lee's 70,000 troops in 2 corps and 8,000 cavalry led by Jeb Stuart. Lincoln finally removed McClellan from the Army of Potomac's command on November 5, and replaced him with Ambrose Burnside. Burnside did not want the job, protesting that he was unqualified.[48] Lincoln did not take him at his word and instead welcomed his modesty after enduring a year and a half of McClellan's pomposity. Word of the command change prompted Lee to quip: "I hate to see McClellan go. He and I had grown to understand each other so well."[49]

Burnside did accelerate the army's movement and on November 17 reached Falmouth north of the Rappahannock River from Fredericksburg where Lee had deployed his army along the low heights beyond the town, with General James Longstreet's corps on the left and General Thomas Jackson's corps on the right.[50] Burnside packed several regiments in pontoon boats and they rowed across to flush snipers from the town. With those bridgeheads secured, he had three pontoon bridges built at Fredericksburg and three downstream on December 11. On the morning of December 13, he had the corps of Edwin Sumner, Joe Hooker, and William Franklin cross to assault the rebel line. The result was slaughter as the Union troops advanced across open fields against massed rifles and cannons on the heights. The Union suffered 12,653 casualties to the Confederacy's 4,201. The next day, Burnside did not resume the battle despite having two fresh corps. Instead, on December 15, he withdrew his battered army north of the river. That easy yet blood-soaked victory prompted Lee to remark: "It is well that war is so terrible – we should grow too fond of it."[51]

General Ulysses Grant spent month after month at his Memphis headquarters chaffing at being forced to stay on the defensive. Finally, in mid-September, an opportunity arose for a decisive blow against the enemy after General Sterling Price led 15,000 to the rail juncture at Iuka. Grant issued orders that he be cut off and destroyed between Generals Edward Ord marching eastward and General William Rosecrans northward. Price blunted Rosecrans' advance, inflicting 790 casualties and sustaining 515, then sidestepped him and withdrew to join General Earl Van Dorn at Holly Springs. Ord was supposed to attack when he heard Rosecrans' guns open fire, but a stiff wind carried away the roar of battle. After resupplying, Price and Van Dorn marched their 22,000 troops to attack Rosecrans' 21,000 troops at Corinth on October 3 and 4. The Union troops finally drove off the Confederates, inflicting 4,233 casualties and suffering 2,520.

Grant followed up that victory by massing his army and leading it south along the Mississippi Central Railroad with Vicksburg the ultimate objective. He got as far as Oxford when he learned of a disaster. Van Dorn with 3,500 troops captured and destroyed his supply depot at Holly Springs on December 20. Meanwhile, General Nathan Bedford Forrest led 2,100 cavalry on a raid through western Tennessee that eliminated a dozen or so other garrisons, depots, and train trestles, and captured 1,300 Federals, 10,000 rifles, and a million cartridges. That forced Grant to withdraw to restore his supply system. He had sent General William Sherman with his corps from Memphis down the Mississippi to take Vicksburg. Sherman landed his 32,500 men at Chickasaw Bayou a few miles north of Vicksburg and assaulted the 14,000 Confederates entrenched atop Chickasaw Bluffs on December 29. The rebels decimated the attackers, inflicting 1,776 casualties while suffering 207. Sherman withdrew upriver to Milliken Bend on the Mississippi River's west bank a dozen miles upriver from Vicksburg.

Meanwhile, General Rosecrans led his 43,400-man Army of the Cumberland from Nashville against General Bragg's 37,717 troops at Murfreesboro on Stones River. Bragg sent Generals John Morgan and Joe Wheeler on separate cavalry raids to devastate Rosecrans' supply network. Morgan's was the most successful as his 2,140 troops captured or killed 2,069 Union troops while suffering 139 casualties at Hartsville on December 7. Those raids forced Rosecrans to divert another 7,400 troops to bring his total rear echelon troops to 27,657.[52]

That delayed but did not halt Rosecrans whose army appeared before Murfreesboro on December 31, Bragg launched a massive attack against the enemy's right flank. The Confederates drove the Federals back nearly all the way to the river where the bluecoats rallied and held their ground. In two days of fighting each side suffered three of ten men killed, wounded, or captured, making Stones River the war's bloodiest battle as a portion of those who fought, with 13,249 Federal and 11,739 Confederate casualties. With his men and ammunition exhausted, Bragg withdrew his army southeast 35 miles to another strong position. Rosecrans's army was too battered to follow.

Chapter 13

Auxiliaries

A First Lady's venerable public duties include being an adoring wife and a charming hostess; privately, like any spouse, she must offer her husband understanding, support, advice, and affection. Mary Todd Lincoln may be the most controversial First Lady.

She grew up in an affluent slaveholding family in Lexington, Kentucky.[1] She received a good boarding school education. Vivacious and loquacious, she loved being the center of attention at parties and balls. She was moody and could be jealous, petty, petulant, and vindictive. Abraham Lincoln's law partner, William Herndon, described her seesaw nature as "cultured – graceful and dignified" and her as "the belle of the town, leading the young men of the town a merry dance," but also "sarcastic-haughty-aristocratic."[2] She was bright and enjoyed reciting poetry. Politics fascinated her and she lent her mind to any discussions that arose.

What did Lincoln see in Mary? She mesmerized him. A family friend and socialite named Matilda Edwards explained that: "Mary led the conversation – Lincoln would listen and gaze upon her as if drawn by some superior power ... He was charmed with Mary's wit and fascinated with her quick sagacity – her will – her nature – and her culture."[3]

Yet Lincoln had mixed feelings about wedding her. He reveled when she was passionate or tender, but winced at her henpecking. He worried he might be unable to support her financially or emotionally. He got cold feet and did not show up for their first scheduled wedding. Somehow, he overcame his deep reservations and her hurt feelings, and they married on November 4, 1842. She was a loving, if at times nagging, wife and mother. Of their four sons, they deeply mourned the death of one before they entered the White House and another while they lived there.[4]

Being First Lady was a dream come true for Mary. At first, she joyfully played that role as the queen bee at balls, state dinners, and informal teas. But she soon became a political liability rather than asset for her husband. Her vanity and cattiness alienated ever more women and thus their husbands. Seeking to refurbish the White House's tattered furnishings, she embarked on extravagant shopping sprees that she charged to the $20,000 allocated for White House operating expenses. She swiftly exceeded that limit. Lincoln bristled at the mounting bills that somehow he would have to pay from his own pocket. She soon learned that one full brother, three half-brothers, and three brothers-in-law married to her sisters fought for the Confederacy. Critics reviled her as a shrew, spendthrift, and rebel sympathizer.

Then came the death of their son Willie of fever on February 20, 1862. That plunged Mary and Lincoln into deep depression. She sought to reunite with her boy through seances conducted by renowned psychic medium Nettie Colburn. Lincoln was so distraught that several times he had his son's tomb opened so that he could see him again. Witnessing her husband's murder before her eyes pitched Mary into an emotional abyss. She suffered other losses, two brothers during the war and a third son afterward. Her surviving son Robert committed her to an insane asylum in 1875.[5]

Edwin Stanton was among the most controversial war secretaries.[6] With his stern visage, granny glasses, and chest-long thick beard, he resembled some avenging prophet or John Brown-type zealot. He was two-faced and hypocritical, a sycophant to those more powerful and an autocrat to his underlings. Navy Secretary Gideon Welles warned that he was "an intriguer, courts favor, is not faithful in his friendships, is given to secret, underhanded combinations."[7] He was a "control freak." Grant complained that: "Owing to his natural disposition to assume all power and control in all matters ... he boldly took command of the armies, and ... prohibited any order from me going out ... until he had approved it." He was cruel. Grant exposed him as someone who "cared nothing for the feelings of others. In fact it seemed pleasanter to him to disappoint than gratify."[8] Inner demons filled him with deep insecurities and barely concealed rage that he vented at those who crossed him. He was arrogant and condescending. He initially dismissed Lincoln as "a low cunning clown" replete with "idiocy." Over time as they interacted, his views changed to grudging respect.

Stanton had no military experience before Lincoln tapped him to replace Simon Cameron as war secretary on January 20, 1862. Lincoln grimly admired Stanton's killer-instinct as an attack-dog lawyer whether he was prosecuting or defending someone. He knew that Stanton sneered at him but set that aside because he was confident that he would be an effective war secretary.

Stanton did have a first-rate mind. He graduated from Kenyon College in Ohio, studied law, passed the bar, and eventually specialized in expensive business cases first in Pittsburg then in Washington. He originated the insanity defense to win an acquittal for Daniel Sickles, a congressman from Massachusetts who murdered his wife's lover. He proved to be a largely effective if controversial secretary of war for six years. He improved logistics by standardizing track widths and signaling systems, and establishing priority lists for freight car use.

He established a War Board or general staff with Generals Ethan Hitchcock the chief, Montgomery Meigs the quartermaster general, Lorenzo Thomas the adjutant general, Joseph Totten the engineer chief, James Ripley the ordnance chief, and Joseph Taylor the commissary general. Regardless, those who knew him almost universally loathed him.

Secession had one positive effect for America. In Congress, the mass slavocrat departure removed the worst obstacle to action.[9] Republicans dominated both houses for the next two sessions. The 37th Congress from March 4, 1861 to March 4, 1863, held 105 Republicans (57.7 percent), 44 Democrats (24.2 percent), 31 Unionists (17.0 percent), 1 Independent Democrat (0.5 percent), and 1 Constitutional Unionist (0.5 percent) in the House of Representatives, and 30 Republicans (62.5 percent), 11 Democrats (22.9), and 7 Unionists (14.6 percent) in the Senate. The 38th Congress from March 4, 1863 to March 4, 1865, held 84 Republicans (45.9 percent), 72 Democrats (39.3 percent), 16 Unconditional Unionists (8.7 percent), 9 Unionists (4.9 percent), and 2 Independent Republicans (1.1 percent) in the House of Representatives, and 33 Republicans (66.0 percent), 10 Democrats (20 percent), 4 Unconditional Unionists (8 percent), and 3 Unionists (4.0 percent) in the Senate.[10]

The result was a record number of bills that addressed an array of festering national problems. Congress passed 428 laws from December 1861 to December 1863, and 411 from December 1863 to December 1865. Each was more than double the previous peak from 1841 to 1843. There were also a record number of investigative committees with 19 from 1861 to 1863 and 16 from 1863 to 1865 compared with 11 during the 1850s[11] Behind those achievements lurked deep divisions.

The Republican Party was split between radicals who demanded immediate abolition and civil rights for blacks versus conservatives who sought to delay either until there was a national consensus.[12] All along President Lincoln tried to slow the radicals and hurry the conservatives. The leading radicals included Senators Benjamin Wade of Ohio, Charles Sumner of Massachusetts, Zachariah Chandler of Michigan, and James Grimes of Iowa along with Representative Thaddeus Stevens of Pennsylvania. The radicals criticized Lincoln for his caution on abolition and black civil rights. They also insisted that the president should follow Congress rather than lead even in wartime, expressed most zealously by Wade: "It does not belong to the President to devise a policy for the country. His duties are well performed if he has caused the laws to be faithfully executed … It devolves upon Congress to devise a policy."[13] No Republican was more blistering of Lincoln than Wade and he was never more searing than on January 31, 1862: "Mr. President, you are murdering your country by inches in consequence of the inactivity of the military and the want of a distinct policy in regard to slavery."[14]

Wade chaired the Joint Committee for the Conduct of the War established after the Bull Run debacle in July 1861.[15] The seven members included four senators, three representatives, five Republicans and a Democrat from each House. The committee's role was to investigate any allegations of wrongdoing by generals and contractors. Lincoln met frequently with the Committee to address their concerns and wielded threat of Committee investigations to spur cautious generals who feared the wrath of the politicians. Other important committees included the Senate's Military Affairs chaired by Henry Wilson of Massachusetts, Territories by Wade, Commerce by Chandler, District of Columbia by Grimes, and the House's Ways and Means by Stevens and Government Contracts by Charles Van Wyck of New York.

The Democratic Party was split between War and Peace factions; the former wanted to crush the Confederacy, the latter wanted peace at any price including the South's independence if need be. Although Democrats were a minority, they still held considerable power.[16] Lincoln faced a Faustian dilemma with the War Democrats. He could placate them only by appointing some among them generals like Benjamin Butler of Massachusetts, Daniel Sickles of New York, John McClernand and John Logan of Illinois, and Lew Wallace of Indiana. All were inept commanders.

Corruption is the illegal or unethical exploitation of public resources for private gain. Corrupt American politics did not begin with the Civil War, but the unprecedented vast amounts and types of government spending gave unscrupulous politicians, bureaucrats, and businessmen vast opportunities to enrich themselves.[17] That grossly violated the original intent of America's revolutionary leaders who sought to create a republic led by virtuous public servants. Of course, they understood that virtue was an ideal and some men were easily led astray. So they designed a system of institutions with overlapping powers that minimized opportunities for corruption.

That system worked well until the late 1820s. Three forces combined to increase corruption: the emergence of political machines in cities; the rise of powerful banking, manufacturing, railroad, and shipping companies; and the election of Andrew Jackson to the White House in 1828. The result was an unabashed "spoils system" whereby those in power sold offices, contracts, and privileges to those who could afford them. The payback could also be political. Company presidents forced their employees to vote for a party or politician. Election officials stuffed ballot boxes.

Democrats tended to be far more rapacious than Whigs. Indeed, the Democratic Party machines that monopolized votes and offices in cities were a major reason for the Whig Party's demise in 1852. Two years later, the Republican Party arose dedicated to combating corruption. That did not prevent some Republicans from blatantly selling out like Simon Cameron of Pennsylvania.

The most egregious corruption involved Civil War contracts won by manufacturers who put profits above patriotism. They banked vast sums for guns that exploded in the firers' faces, shoes that fell apart after a day's march, and rancid barrels of flour, pork, and beef. In that, they were abetted by many politicians and bureaucrats, who palmed kickbacks to approve the contracts or ignore the defects.

President Lincoln abhorred corruption yet ended up with Cameron as his Secretary of War.[18] That came from a deal his campaign manager David Davis struck with Cameron during the 1860 Republican Party convention to head the War Department in return for backing Lincoln's nomination. Cameron shamelessly enriched himself in his latest office. An egregious example of Cameron's greed involved obsolete Hall Rifles. He authorized the sale of 5,000 of them for $3.50 each to crony Arthur Eastman who slightly modified them with costs from $0.75 to $1.25 each, then resold them to crony Simon Stevens for $12.50 each and he resold them back to the War Department for $22 each. How much kickback Cameron palmed from each transaction was unrecorded.[19] Lincoln got Cameron to resign on January 14, 1862, in return for naming him ambassador to Russia, at once a prestigious post and exile from American politics and temptations. He also spared Cameron a congressional investigation with a letter disingenuously claiming that he and other cabinet secretaries "were at least equally responsible … for whatever error, wrong, or fault was committed."[20] That political cloak gained Cameron's gratitude.

Lincoln did intervene to rescue one class of profiteers that he felt had been unfairly singled out. On December 17, 1862, General Grant ordered "the Jews, as a class" to have their goods confiscated and themselves expelled from his region because their speculations in the cotton trade and other commodities had driven up prices that hurt his army's supplies. A delegation of Jewish merchants sought and received an audience with the president. Lincoln received them with words that mingled humor and sympathy: "And so the children of Israel were driven from the happy land of Canaan." The leader replied: "Yes, and that is why we have come unto Father Abraham's bosom, asking protection." Smiling, Lincoln said: "And this protection they shall have at once."[21] He rescinded the order.

The White House and Congress imposed regulations to combat corruption. Bids for contracts were supposed to be open, competitive, and won by the lowest offer. Each department had strict standards for contract compliance and penalties for violations. Although Quartermaster General Montgomery Meigs was personally honest, he did ensure that contracts were distributed to reward Republican and War Democrat districts. Over four years, the War Department administered $3.2 billion worth of contracts with tens of thousands of businesses. Given that vast scale of deals and temptations, the "killings" of profiteers shadowed those on battlefields.

The Civil War began with nearly identical home fronts, North and South.[22] Each experienced that initial heady rush to war, especially young men who believed their side would swiftly crush the other and wanted to share that glory before it was over. In city squares and village commons politicians made stirring speeches, brass bands played, and women, children, and old men cheered the brave local recruits as they marched away.

The battle of Bull Run killed that romantic fantasy in late July 1861. Thereafter, Washington and Richmond sought hundreds of thousands of more volunteers for a war that increasingly appeared endless. As recruits dwindled, each side eventually established conscription. Daily with pounding hearts northerners and southerners scanned newspapers for the latest battles and list of dead or they opened letters from officers informing them that their loved one had bravely died in combat or succumbed from disease. Ever more men and teenage boys reappeared with amputated limbs, empty eye sockets, and haunted faces. Ever more men shirked recruiting officers and dodged the draft. Women especially but many men as well-found solace by dedicating more of their life to their religious beliefs and practices.[23]

Women experienced their own varying transformations in outlook, duties, and, for some, livelihoods. They tried to ease some of their anguish with their friends by knitting socks for soldiers. They filled jobs vacated by men whether at farms, offices, or factories. Many became more outspoken on political issues.[24] Countless echoed this lament by plantation mistress Caroline Davis who contrasted their homebound supportive role with the extraordinary events that men witnessed and shaped: "we poor women have no name or existence of our own, we pass silently down the stream of time without leaving a single trace behind – we die unknown."[25] In her journal, Louisa May Alcott confessed: "I long to be a man; but I can't fight, will content myself with working for those who can."[26] She was a nurse most of the war.

Gradually daily life on the home fronts diverged. Only a few northern states experienced any fighting, notably Pennsylvania and Maryland with brief invasions and little destruction, Kentucky that suffered more widespread fighting and raids, and Missouri where rebel invasions and guerrillas devastated swaths of countryside and towns. Elsewhere across the North, the war was mostly a faraway abstraction except for those who mourned dead or crippled loved ones. Nonetheless, that common war effort for unification and eventually abolition forged greater American nationalism among northerners.[27]

Meanwhile, the tightening blockade and rampaging or occupying Union forces devastated the Confederacy's economy. Southerners suffered worsening shortages of essential goods including food, and paid ever more in paper money for what little was available. Malnutrition spread. In spring 1863, hundreds of desperate women looted stores and warehouses in Richmond and Petersburg, Virginia, Salisbury and High Point, North Carolina, Mobile, Alabama, and Atlanta, Savannah, Milledgeville, and Columbus, Georgia. Morale among soldiers and civilians was inseparable. Letters from home lamenting worsening hardships and dangers induced countless soldiers to desert.

The worst worry concerned slavery. Slaves worked less, defied more, or escaped after southern men departed for distant fronts, often never to return. No slaveholder was immune from slave disruptions. The slaves at President Davis's Brierfield and neighboring brother's plantation revolted after learning of General Grant's approaching army. They looted the houses and other buildings, refused to work, and many ran off to the Union forces. That revolt belied the assertion by Davis then and apologists since that his slaves were obedient and loving to him and his family.[28] Mississippi Governor John Pettus lamented the potential double-blow against the Confederacy when slaves, especially males, fled to the Union lines: "Every able bodied negro man that falls into the hands of the enemy is not only a laborer lost to the country, he is also, under the current policy of the U.S. government, a soldier gained to his army."[29]

Wives and especially widows of soldiers pleaded for help with their unruly slaves, food shortages, and other problems from Richmond and their state governments. Congress did grant draft exemptions for any men with twenty or more slaves. Naturally, that provoked resentment by slaveowners with fewer slaves who had to leave them in their wives' care while they were off fighting. Countless people grumbled at the unfairness of a "rich man's war, poor man's fight."

Mary Boyd Chesnut was a rich southern belle with a Charleston townhouse, plantation near Camden, South Carolina, and a husband who had been an American senator and now was a Confederate official and general. They spent much of the war in Richmond where Mary befriended First Lady Varina Davis. Her wartime diary is the best account of the home front, albeit from the elite's lofty perch where they suffered far less than most southerners.[30]

Learning of the Confederacy's formation, she committed herself to support it with "calm determination and cool brains. We have risked all, and we must play our best, for the stake is life or death." Her glimpses of the war's horrors during her stints as a nurse, the deaths of loved ones, and the sight of ever more maimed veterans eroded that sanguine view. She had an especially poignant experience one evening seeing a string of flatbed railcars packed with sleeping soldiers "like swathed mummies" bound for the front: "A feeling of awful depression laid hold of me. All these fine fellows going to kill or be killed. Why?" She tried to bury such feelings by reveling in the Old South's balls, dinners, strolls, concerts, flirtations, and carriage rides that persisted among the elite nearly to the war's end. A typical ladies luncheon hosted by Varina Davis in January 1864 included: "Gumbo, ducks and olives, supreme de volaille, chickens in jelly, oysters, lettuce salad, chocolate jelly cake, claret soup, champagne." Yet she deplored vicious social politics, especially those closest to home: "Wrangling, rows, heartburnings, envy, hatred and malice, unbrotherly love, family snarls, neighborhood strife, and ill blood ... Everybody knows where to put in a knife." The hyperinflation eventually ruined virtually everyone. In November 1864, she was to "spend five hundred dollars today for sugar, candles, and a lamp."[31]

Like countless other slaveowners, Mary at once benefited from yet hated the institution, and felt both compassion and repulsion for black people. She took pride in how well she treated her slaves and taught them "such good manners" and they were "so well behaved and affection – a little bit lazy but that is not crime." Yet she condemned them for being so "dirty, slatternly, idle, ill-smelling by nature." She worried how much she could trust them, especially after Lincoln declared their emancipation: "Not by one word can we detect any change in the demeanor of these negro servants ... Are they solidly stupid or wiser than we are." She was confident her own people "will not rise and cut our throats ... yet I believe they are all spies for the other side." The murder of an elderly female cousin by her slaves provoked more soul searching: "Hitherto I have never thought of being afraid of negroes. I have never injured any of them. Why should they want to hurt me? Two-thirds of my religion consists in trying to do good to negroes because they are so in my power ... Somehow today I feel that the ground is cut away from under my feet." Ultimately, she concluded that slavery "has to go ... All that has been gained by it goes to the North and to negroes. The slaveowners, when they are good men and women, are the martyrs."[32] Eventually the war caught up the Chesnut family when General Sherman's troops burned their plantation's mill, gin, and barn packed with a hundred cotton bales, although they spared the mansion and slave cabins.

Amidst the war, President Lincoln rendered annual what had previously been sporadic and rare – a national day of Thanksgiving. He first called for a thanksgiving day in 1863 and made it permanent in 1864.[33] In his proclamation, he cited all the things that Americans should be grateful for despite all the horrendous deaths, maimings, and destruction they were suffering. Most importantly, the nation's population, enterprises, and prosperity continued to expand. Ever since, most Americans cherish Thanksgiving as cozy time to count their blessings and feast together with family and friends.

Of the 4,000 or so newspapers and other periodicals across the United States in 1860, around 80 percent backed a political party.[34] The leading Republican newspapers included New York's *Evening Post, Times,* and *Tribune,* Chicago's *Tribune,* St Louis's *Missouri Democrat,* and Washington's *National Republican.* German Americans and their newspapers were mostly Republican like the *Pittsburger Volksblatt,* Pittsburgh *Freiheits Freund und Courier,* St Louis *Westliche Post,* and *Illinois Staats-Zeitung.* The nation's four most bestselling and influential newspapermen were Horace Greeley and his *Tribune,* William Cullen Bryant and his *Evening Post,* Henry Raymond and his *New York Times,* and James Bennett and his Democrat-leaning *New York Herald.* Their newspapers were within shouting distance of each other near New York's City Hall.

The Civil War was the first war that artists illustrated as it happened. Fletcher Harper founded *Harper's Weekly* in 1857 modeled after the *Illustrated London News.* Woodblock prints of people and scenes supplemented the stories. Politically *Harper's* initially championed the Democratic Party and conservative policies but by 1863 fully backed the Lincoln administration. A new chief editor, George Curtis, and cartoonist Thomas Nast led that transformation. Artists Alfred Wald and Theodore Davis sent back vivid battle sketches from various fronts. Circulation averaged 120,000 throughout the war. *Harper's* chief rival was *Frank Leslie's Illustrated News* with the same mix of stories and pictures, and nearly as many readers. From 1835 to 1907, Currier and Ives produced over 7,500 lithographs "suitable for framing," including hundreds of Civil War scenes.

Winslow Homer created the war's most beautiful and haunting paintings including *Rainy Day in Camp, Prisoners from the Front, Sharpshooter on Picket Duty, Home Sweet Home, The Bright Side,* and *Veteran in a New Field* from 1862 to 1866. Many were inspired by his scores of war drawings as a *Harper's Weekly* correspondent and which he published as *Campaign Sketches* in 1863. Conrad Chapman was the South's greatest wartime painter whose *59th Virginia, Battery Laurens Street,* and *Flag of Sumter* were especially striking. However, Chapman painted in Charleston and did not visit other fronts.

The Civil War was the first photographed war. Photographers recorded thousands of poignant images of living and dead soldiers along with their equipment, wagons, trains, camps, towns, countryside, and civilians. Most famous and prolific was Mathew Brady and his New York studio that included Alexander Gardner, Timothy O'Sullivan, George Barnard, and James Gibson.[35]

Journalism increasingly professionalized during the mid-nineteenth century. In 1846, a group of editors established the Associated Press to pool their stories with standards for objective reporting. Despite their Republican Party affiliation, New York's *Tribune, Evening Post,* and *Times,* and Chicago's *Tribune* initiated investigative reporting of complex problems. The Civil War expanded professional journalism. The most vital skill was reporting accurately and dispassionately the war itself, an experience new to all journalists. An average 350 reporters from dozens of newspapers deployed on various fronts throughout the war. The largest contingent came from the *New York Herald* with 30 reporters in 1862 and 63 in 1865. Reporter Edmund Stedman admitted that the "early correspondents, of whom I was one, knew nothing of military life, tactics, modern warfare."[36] Fortunately, they had a model in *London Times* correspondent William Russell who had reported on numerous wars before, most notably the Crimean War. The shared hardships and at times dangers of being a war reporter inspired those journalists to call themselves the "bohemian brigade."

Greeley and his editors devised a doctrine for wartime reporting that they published on June 8, 1863:

> While we … emphatically disclaim and deny any right … in journalists or others, to incite, advocate, abet, uphold or justify treason or rebellion, we respectfully but firmly assert … the right of the Press to criticize freely and fearlessly the acts of those charged with the administration of the Government, also those of all their civil and military subordinates … to secure greater energy, efficiency, and fidelity in the public service.[37]

Censorship actually spurred professional journalism's development. On January 31, 1862, Lincoln signed a bill that empowered the president to nationalize the telegraph system and two days later, he authorized War Secretary Stanton to do so. Stanton issued orders to newspaper editors that stories had to be approved before they were sent and that journalists who tried to send or editors who tried to publish sensitive military information would be prosecuted and their newspapers shut down. Eventually the War Department issued a list of 154 newspapers whose stories it deemed seditious. Generals issued or revoked passes to journalists based on their reporting. That forced journalists and editors to be very prudent about the accuracy of their sources and subsequent stories as well as when they sent or published them. General Grant was liberal with reporters, reassuring them that: "You yourself must determine what is proper to send. I trust your discretion and your honor to give no information of value to the enemy."[38]

President Lincoln was adept at currying the favor of journalists and editors by amusing them with homespun stories, and playing them off against each other for dollops of inside information. He used them not just to spin favorable or stifle unfavorable news about himself, his administration, and the war effort, but to extract information unknown to his advisors and secretaries. His favorite paper was the *National Republican* for its usually favorable editorials and accurate reports. Lincoln's attempts to woo the press failed with most Democratic newspapers.

The Democratic press included the *New York World*, *Chicago Times*, St Louis *Republican*, *Cincinnati Enquirer*, and *Dayton Empire*. Prominent "Copperhead"-leaning newspapers included the *New York Daily Post*, *The Crisis*, the *Detroit Free Press*, and the *Indiana State Sentinel*. Some editorials certainly appeared to advocate sedition. For instance, the *New York Daily Post* actually insisted that, "the call of Mr. Lincoln for soldiers is not binding in Law upon the people of New York."[39]

Union commanders often bristled at war coverage and editorials by local newspapers. General Ambrose Burnside got so upset with what he called seditious reporting and editorials by the *Chicago Times* that he ordered it suspended on June 1, 1863. Lincoln lifted the suspension three days later. After capturing Savannah, General Sherman issued this order:

> Not more than two newspapers will be published ... their editors and proprietors will be held to the strictest accountability, and will be punished severely, in person and property, for any libelous publication, mischievous matter, premature news, exaggerated statements, or any comments whatever upon the acts of the constituted authorities; they will be held accountable for such articles even if copied from other papers.[40]

The South's cities had their own daily newspapers and the region boasted publications like the *Southern Literary Messenger*, *Debow's Review*, *Magnolia Weekly*, and *Southern Field and Fireside* that had presented short stories, poems, and essays since the 1830s.[41] Before the war, most newspapers shrilly promoted fire-eater slavocrat and secessionist views.[42] During the war, they increasingly criticized government incompetence and corruption. President Davis had an antagonistic relationship with the press. As the blockade tightened, southern publishers suffered worsening shortages of paper, parts for presses, and ink that crimped circulation. Nonetheless, in September 1862, a group of Richmond publishers founded the *Southern Illustrated News*, although the quality of its war reporting and pictures fell far short of its northern inspirations, *Harper's* and *Leslie's*.

Memoirs by the Civil War's participants provide historians with invaluable if at times questionable primary sources. "Memories," of course, can be tailored to settle scores, scapegoat others, absolve oneself, and obscure damning facts. Among the scores published, the best overall were those of Ulysses Grant and William Sherman for their clear, accurate accounts of their campaigns, battles, key decisions, conflicts with fellow generals and politicians, and own mistakes that haunted them. Other leading memoirs by generals included Phil Sheridan, Joshua Chamberlain, James Longstreet, Braxton Bragg, Jubal Early, Richard Taylor, and Edward Alexander. Jefferson Davis's memoirs were as stilted and biased as his character. From common soldiers, those of Sam Watkins and Robert Rhodes provide the best respective Confederate and Union memoirs. John Ransom chronicled the horrors he survived as a prisoner at Andersonville. The three best accounts by nurses were Louisa May Alcott's *Hospital Sketches* (1863), Phoebe Pember's *A Southern Woman's Story* (1879), and African American Susie King Taylor's *Reminisces* (1902). Mary Boyd Chesnut's wartime journals, published posthumously as *A Diary from Dixie* in 1905, brilliantly reveals what life was like on the southern home front.

The war inspired novels, short stories, and poems from soldiers, doctors, nurses, and civilians engulfed by its horrors and by other gifted writers who imagined it through the tales of those who survived it.[43] The greatest was Ambrose Bierce who joined the Union army at age 18 and endured four years of war, including the killing fields of Chickamauga.[44] After the war, he became a free-lance journalist. No combat veteran was more prolific or brilliant in writing about his experiences through essays and short stories. His "An Occurrence at Owl Creek Bridge" from his *Tales of Soldiers and Civilians* (1892) is a classic. He is probably most famous for his *Devil's Dictionary* of cynical, insightful definitions like this of "History": "an account mostly false, of events mostly unimportant which are brought about by rulers mostly knaves, and soldiers mostly fools." John De Forest also fought in numerous battles for the Union. Critics consider his *Miss Ravenel's Conversion from Secession to Loyalty* (1867) the best novel about the Civil War penned by a veteran, although most of the story is a behind-the-lines love triangle. Albion Tourgee was a Union veteran who participated in South Carolina's Reconstruction until the Ku Klux Klan forced him to flee. His novel *A Fool's Errand* (1879) is based on some of his experiences. Disillusioned Confederate veteran George Cable conveyed some of that in his *The Cavalier* (1901) and *Kincaid's Battery* (1908). Walt Whitman served in several posts in Washington from 1863 to 1865, including several months nursing mangled and diseased soldiers. Although nearly every poem in his collection *Drum Taps* (1865) addressed the war lyrically rather than brutally, "The Wound Dresser" depicted crushed faces, amputations, and gangrenous gaping wounds. Silas Mitchell was chief surgeon at Philadelphia's Turner Lane Hospital that treated wounded soldiers. He devised the "rest cure" for shell-shocked soldiers. He was also a novelist whose *In War Time* (1884) most clearly reflected his own experiences.

Then there were the writers who never experienced the war directly. Herman Melville spent most of the war years at his home Arrowhead near Pittsfield, Massachusetts. Yet newspaper and veteran accounts inspired a collection of poems called *Battle-Pieces and Aspects of the War* (1866) that explored the meaning of life and death, religious belief and disbelief, and afterlife and extinction. Stephen Crane's *Red Badge of Courage* (1895) is considered the best Civil War novel by a late nineteenth-century writer who never experienced combat. Like countless young men, protagonist Henry Fleming enlisted in romantic hopes of being a hero only to discover combat's horrors and terrors. He fled from battle, was clubbed by another fleeing Union soldier, bandaged his wound, was treated like a hero rather than coward, and returned to battle determined to realize his "red badge of courage." African American writer Paul Dunbar explored relations between whites and blacks during the war in his *The Fanatics* (1901). Rebecca Harding Davis is known only by experts today but was a prolific writer of hundreds of novels of which *Waiting for Verdict* (1867) involved the war and relations between whites and blacks. Emily Dickinson was even more cloistered in neighboring Amherst but like Melville and using the same sources was inspired to write her own war-related poems with the same themes.

Mark Twain was forever haunted by his two weeks with the "Marian Rangers," a Confederate militia company. They spent most of their time hiding from Union forces hunting them. Their only "action" happened one night when they shot to death someone approaching their camp:

The man was not in uniform and was not armed. He was a stranger in the country; that was all we found out about him. The thought of him got to preying on me every night. I could not get rid of it … the taking of that unoffending life seemed such a wanton act. And it seemed the epitome of war; … the killing of strangers against whom you feel no personal animosity; strangers whom in other circumstances, you would help if you found them in trouble, and who would help you if you needed it. My campaign was spoiled … I resolved to retire from this … sham soldiership while I could save something of my self-respect.[45]

Some of the most moving depictions of the war were carved in stone or cast in iron. Augustus Saint Gaudens created the stone relief sculpture of Colonel Robert Shaw leading the 54th Colored Massachusetts Regiment, displayed on Boston's Common. Daniel Chester French created two brilliant, moving Lincoln tributes. That in Washington is at the Mall's west end in a massive Greek-style temple with a majestic, seated Lincoln gazing east toward the Capitol a mile and a half away and flanked by his Gettysburg Address chiseled on one wall and the key excerpt from his Second Inaugural Address on the other. That in Nebraska has a standing Lincoln with his head bowed before a wall engraved with the Gettysburg Address.

Chapter 14

The 1863 Campaigns

West of the Mississippi, the year began with a Confederate victory. On New Year's Day, General John Magruder with 500 troops and 2 gunboats attacked Galveston defended by 600 Union troops and 6 gunboats anchored nearby. The rebel gunboats took or sank four Union gunboats while Magruder's men captured 420 Federals as General Isaac Burrell evacuated the port with the rest of his troops. The Confederates held Galveston for the rest of the war, although the Union blockade persisted.

That same day, General John Marmaduke led 2,300 cavalry from Lewisburg, Arkansas toward the Federal supply depot at Springfield, Missouri, 187 miles north. On January 8, the rebels overwhelmed Springfield's defenders and destroyed the supplies, then rode east to Hartville, 45 miles away, to rout a garrison and burn the depot on January 11. That forced General Samuel Curtis to withdraw his army from Fayetteville back to Springfield to secure his rear and replenish his supplies.

Meanwhile, Federal troops elsewhere scored a significant victory. After Sherman's defeat at Chickasaw Bluffs, General Henry Halleck had General John McClernand supersede him in command. McClernand led the army 50 miles up the Arkansas River to attack Fort Hindman on January 10, 1863. The Union troops bagged the entire 5,000-man garrison while suffering 1,061 casualties. The army then withdrew to Milliken's Bend on the Mississippi River a dozen miles north of Vicksburg.

Richard Taylor was among the most enterprising Confederate generals who is little known today. He operated mostly in Louisiana and Arkansas. On June 7, he launched simultaneous assaults on Federal depots at Milliken's Bend and Young's Point on the Mississippi River's western shore, hoping to divert Grant from his Vicksburg campaign. The garrisons drove off the attackers. He then led 5,000 troops down Bayou Teche to capture a Federal depot at Brashear City with 1,700 prisoners, a dozen cannons, 5,000 rifles, and other critical supplies on June 22. Union troops repulsed his attack against Fort Butler on the Mississippi River. He advanced as far as Kenner, a dozen miles from New Orleans, but withdrew after learning that Vicksburg and Port Hudson had fallen.

Much further north up the Mississippi River, Union General Benjamin Prentiss and 4,129 troops occupied Helena, Arkansas. General Theophilus

Holmes sought to eliminate that toehold when he launched his 7,646 troops against it on July 4. The defenders repulsed the rebels, inflicting 1,614 casualties while sustaining only 239.

The Union soon racked up another victory westward. General James Blunt with 3,000 troops with 12 cannons headed south from Fort Gibson 35 miles and routed 5,000 rebels with four howitzers led by General Douglas Cooper at Honey Springs on July 17. Honey Springs was the largest battle in Indian Territory and was fought mostly by Indians on either side. After receiving reinforcements, Blunt marched down the Arkansas River valley to occupy abandoned Fort Smith on September 1.

The Union followed up those victories with an effort to conquer central Arkansas with its capital. After replacing Prentiss, General Frederick Steele marched with 6,000 troops west, while General John Davidson led 6,000 cavalry south from Bloomfield, Missouri. They joined forces at Clarendon, Arkansas on August 15, then advanced toward Little Rock. General Sterling Price had 7,700 troops at Bayou Metou on their route, but Steele arced Davidson toward his rear, forcing him to retreat to Little Rock. On September 11, Steele again threatened to cut off Price who, outgunned and outmaneuvered, withdrew toward Arkadelphia 65 miles south. The Union troops marched into Little Rock late that day.

Among that year's Union targets was Charleston, with an armada jointly led by Admiral Samuel Du Pont and General David Hunter given the mission. On April 15, seven ironclads churned into Charleston bay to bombard Forts Sumter and Moultrie. The forts' cannons opened fire and eventually disabled five of the gunboats, forcing them all to withdraw; one sank that night. Hunter would not begin an army offensive for more than two months. Then, on July 10, six ironclads bombarded Fort Wagner on Morris Island while 6,000 troops landed for an assault.

Among the regiments was the 54th Massachusetts with black soldiers and white officers led by Colonel Robert Shaw. Determined to show his "colored" troops were just as valiant as white troops, Shaw received permission for the 54th to spearhead the assault. The Confederates repelled the attack, inflicting 1,515 casualties while suffering 174; 270 of the 54th's 600 men were killed, wounded, or captured, with Shaw among the dead. The survivors reembarked in their longboats and rowed back to the armada. Over the next six months, the warships bombarded the forts, reducing them to rubble but not surrender.

President Abraham Lincoln did not immediately relieve General Ambrose Burnside of command after his Fredericksburg debacle, but instead gave him a second chance. Burnside sought to outflank Lee by leaving a corps before Fredericksburg and marching with five corps up the Rappahannock and crossing over at fords above the town. The advance began on January 20 but soon bogged down into a "mud march" as heavy rains inundated the roads and swelled the rivers. Burnside canceled his offensive two days later. On January 25, Lincoln replaced Burnside with Joseph Hooker, the 5th Corps commander.

Hooker's men adored him because he led from the front, earning him the nickname "Fighting Joe," and tried to alleviate their miseries.[1] He revitalized the army's dismal morale with furloughs, better food, cleaner camps, amnesty for deserters, back pay, and insignias for each corps to promote pride and friendly rivalry. Emulating the rebel army, he united the cavalry regiments into one corps. Yet he had his detractors. Apparently, he enjoyed the charms of ladies innocent of traditional virtue. Charles Francis Adams described his headquarters as "a place where no self-respecting man liked to go, and no decent women could go. It was a combination of barroom and brothel."[2] The general's proclivities inspired the word hooker for prostitute.

Far worse, Hooker talked about overthrowing the government and becoming dictator. Just how serious he was cannot be determined, but Lincoln took him at his word and confronted it in a curious letter:

> I have heard, in such a way to believe it, of your recently saying that both the army and the government needed a dictator. Of course, it was not for this, but in spite of it, that I have given you the command. Only those generals who gain successes can set up dictators. What I now ask of you is military success, and I will risk the dictatorship.[3]

Hooker knew his only sensible offensive plan was to repeat what Burnside had tried in January and hope he had better weather.[4] On April 26, he left 23,600 troops under General John Sedgwick to distract Lee at Fredericksburg while he led 65,000 infantry preceded by 11,500 cavalry east up the Rappahannock River then crossed over at several fords to outflank the rebel army. Spring rains slowed the march by inundating the roads and swelling the rivers. He established his headquarters near a crossroads called Chancellorsville, 12 miles west of Fredericksburg and there hesitated for several crucial days.

Faced with being crushed between two overwhelming enemy forces, most commanders would have hastily retreated. Typically, Lee attacked. On May 2, he split his army in three parts, left 10,000 men under General Jubal Early in Fredericksburg, marched 15,000 troops directly toward Hooker, and arced Jackson's 30,000-man corps preceded by General Jeb Stuart's cavalry toward the Union rear. On May 3, as Lee's men assaulted Hooker's front, Jackson hit his rear. They punched back but did not break the Union army. That same day, Sedgwick attacked and routed Early at Fredericksburg then advanced a couple of miles west of town and then stalled. On May 4, Lee marched eastward with two divisions to link with Early and drive back Sedgwick. Hooker did not order an assault to break through the rebels before him and join forces with Sedgwick. At his headquarters, a cannon ball struck a pillar that Hooker was leaning against, stunning him. His aides revived him and led him to the rear beyond range. On May 6, Hooker and Sedgwick withdrew their forces across the Rappahannock, despite the fact that four corps had experienced little fighting and in a massive attack likely would have overwhelmed the exhausted rebels.

Lee had won a stunning campaign, routing two enemy armies and inflicting 17,287 casualties while suffering 12,821. His worst loss was Thomas Jackson who rebel pickets mistakenly shot in the dark when he was riding back from a reconnaissance. Surgeons amputated his shattered left arm. Learning of that tragedy, Lee sadly remarked, "he has lost his left arm, but I have lost my right."[5] That loss was permanent when pneumonia killed Jackson on May 10.

Although Hooker's army still outnumbered Lee's by 90,000 to 60,000 troops, his defeat at Chancellorsville demoralized him. Lee got President Davis's permission to follow up his victory by marching into the North. Like his invasion the previous year, he hoped that a decisive victory on northern soil could force President Lincoln into peace talks and encourage Britain, France, and other European powers to ally with the Confederacy. And if not that, invading the North would ruin any pending Union offensive plans, force Hooker to abandon most of northern Virginia as he pursued, and let the Confederate army sustain itself from captured enemy supplies or civilian requisitions. While Lee's campaign did achieve the second if not the first set of goals, it ended in defeat at Gettysburg.[6]

Reinforced, Lee's army numbered 75,000 troops split among 3 corps commanded by Generals James Longstreet, Richard Ewell, and Ambrose Hill. With General Jeb Stuart and his 9,500-man cavalry corps screening his rear, Lee led his army toward the Shenandoah Valley in early June. Learning of Lee's movement, Hooker sent General Alfred Pleasanton's 11,000-man cavalry corps westward to determine where Lee was heading. On June 9, Pleasanton attacked Stuart at Brandy Station in what became the war's largest cavalry battle. In desperate fighting, the Confederate horsemen finally drove off the Federals, inflicting 936 casualties while suffering 523.

As Lee marched north, Hooker asked Lincoln's permission to head toward Richmond. Lincoln rejected that notion, arguing that: "I think Lee's army, not Richmond, is your true objective point. If he comes toward the upper Potomac, follow on his flank and on his inside track, shortening your lines while he lengthens his. Fight him, too, when opportunity offers. If he stays where he is, fret him and fret him."[7]

Meanwhile, Lee's army captured 4,000 Union troops, 23 cannons, and 300 supply wagons at Winchester and Martinsburg on June 15, at a cost of 269 casualties. Lee and his men crossed the Potomac River on June 22. Three days later, Stuart led his corps in a raid that eventually circled the Union army but deprived Lee of his best source of intelligence for nearly ten days. Hooker tried to keep pace with Lee as he marched north.

Exasperated with Hooker's inability or unwillingness to catch up to Lee, Lincoln replaced him with General George Meade, the 5th Corps' commander, on June 28. As Lee's army marched through Maryland and into Pennsylvania toward Harrisburg, Meade advanced cautiously, determined to keep his army between the enemy and Washington. Indeed, caution and, at times timidity, were Meade's dominant traits as a general. He was at heart an engineer who instinctively sought methodically to entrench his men rather than decisively outmaneuver and outfight the enemy.[8]

The epic three-day battle of Gettysburg began on July 1, when a Confederate division dispatched to capture a supply of shoes said to be warehoused there ran into a Union cavalry brigade defending the town. Learning of the fighting, Lee and Meade hurried other units there. By the first day's end, Confederate troops drove Union troops south and east of the town. Meade stabilized a line in a fishhook with his east flank on Culp Hill, his arced center on Cemetery Hill a few hundred yards south of town, and the shaft along Cemetery Ridge. Lee deployed his troops in his own fishhook north and west of the Union line.

Lee's plan for the second day was for Longstreet directly to attack the Union left while Ewell and Hill launched limited attacks along the line to distract the enemy. He rejected Longstreet's advice to arc around the Union flank and strike the rear. Longstreet got a late start and by the time he attacked in late afternoon, Union forces already manned two strategic hills, Little Round Top and Round Top to anchor the left flank. In fierce fighting the bluecoats repelled greycoat assaults all along the line. Stuart and his saddle-sore horsemen finally rejoined Lee late that day.

Lee believed that an all-out assault on July 3 would rout the Union army. He sent Stuart to assail the Union rear, massed 150 cannons and bombarded the Union line for 2 hours, then had 14,000 troops of 3 divisions led by General George Pickett, James Pettigrew, and Isaac Trimble charge the Union center while Ewell assaulted Culp Hill. Union troops repelled all 3 attacks. In 3 days of fighting, the 65,000 Confederates and 85,000 Federals suffered 28,063 and 23,049 casualties, respectively.

The following day, Lee prepared for a Union attack that never came. That night, he reluctantly ordered a withdrawal in heavy rain that persisted for days. Although with reinforcements Meade outnumbered Lee by 95,000 to 40,000 troops and two of his corps had not fired a shot, he did not immediately follow let alone attack. A Union cavalry raid destroyed the Confederate pontoon bridge across the Potomac at Williamsport on July 6. Word of that did not spur Meade to assault Lee trapped north of the river. Engineers hastily constructed a rickety bridge and Lee was able to withdraw his battered army across to safety on July 13.

Lincoln was devastated when he learned that Meade had let Lee escape. He expressed his sorrow in a letter to Meade that he never sent:

> I have been oppressed nearly ever since the battle of Gettysburg ... that you ... were not seeking collision with the enemy, but were trying to get him across the river without another battle ... You fought and beat the enemy at Gettysburg ... He retreated, and you did not ... pressingly pursue him; but a flood in the river detained him ... and yet you stood and let the flood run down, bridges be built, and the enemy move away at his leisure without attacking him ... I do not believe you appreciate the magnitude of the misfortune involved in Lee's escape. He was within your easy grasp, and to have closed upon him would, in connection with our other late successes, have ended the war. As it is, the war will be prolonged indefinitely.[9]

He did write General Oliver Howard, the 11th Corps commander, that:

> I was deeply mortified by the escape of Lee across the Potomac, because the substantial destruction of his army would have ended the war, and because I believed such destruction was perfectly easy – believed that General Meade and his noble army had expended all the skill and toil and blood up to the ripe harvest, and then let the crop go to waste.[10]

A proclamation from Meade congratulating his troops for driving "from our soil every vestige of the presence of the invader" further riled Lincoln. "Will our generals never get that idea out of their heads," the president lamented. "The whole country is our soil." He feared he had saddled the nation with another McClellan.[11]

Throughout August and September, Meade advanced slowly as far as the Rapidan River and then encamped his army north of it. Lee was so confident that he faced another McClellan that he dispatched Longstreet's corps to reinforce Bragg in Tennessee. When Meade still refused to move against him despite his diminished numbers, Lee planned his own attack. On October 14, he sent

Ambrose Hill and his 17,218 men against Gouverneur Warren's 8,383-man corps guarding the Union right at Bristoe Station. Warren's troops stood firm and blasted the attackers, inflicting 1,380 casualties while suffering 540. On November 27, Meade launched his army on a wide arc east and then south to cut the enemy off from Richmond. Lee quick-marched his troops to get into Meade's rear at Mine Run. Learning of danger, Meade hastily withdrew his troops on December 2. Each army then went into winter quarters.

Ulysses Grant was determined to take Vicksburg.[12] The devastating raids by Confederate cavalry commanders against his supply network convinced him that a river-bound campaign offered the best chance of success. With naval superiority, he would worry little about his supplies as long as they were aboard steamboats. The jump off for his campaign was Milliken's Bend a dozen miles north of Vicksburg on the west bank where General John McClernand had withdrawn after capturing Fort Hindman. By February, Grant massed 45,000 troops there. His initial plan was to dig a canal so that his flotilla could safely bypass the cannons massed along Vicksburg's bluffs and shore. He deployed his men on four different possible canal routes from February through April 1863. Low water defeated each attempt.

Grant conceived a brilliant plan that solved that strategic Gordian knot. He arced two of his corps west of the river until they reached the Mississippi 50 miles south of Vicksburg, while Admiral David Porter led his flotilla downstream to meet them. To mislead General John Pemberton, the regional commander headquartered at Vicksburg, he launched two forces in the opposite direction. He retained General William Sherman's corps at Milliken's Bend and had him deploy a division east of the Mississippi River to threaten Chickasaw Bluffs. He dispatched General Benjamin Grierson with 1,700 cavalry from La Grange, Tennessee south through Mississippi on what became a 17-day raid destroying train trestles and supply depots all the way to join General Nathaniel Banks' army at Baton Rouge.

Eight gunboats and three transports steamed past Vicksburg's batteries on the night of April 16. Sentinels ignited bonfires on the opposite shore to silhouette the gunboats and transports. The rebel batteries fired 525 rounds of which 68 struck vessels but only sank one transport. A few nights later, six transports began that daunting gauntlet and five survived to join the flotilla downstream. On April 30, the vessels ferried Grant and the corps of Generals McClernand and James McPherson across the river at Bruinsburg as Sherman marched his corps south to join them. Grant later recalled his quiet elation at this triumphant moment:

I was now in the enemy's country, with a vast river and the stronghold of Vicksburg between me and my base of supplies. But I was on dry ground on the same side of the river with the enemy. All the campaigns, labors, hardships, and exposures from the month of December previous to this time that had been made and endured were for the accomplishment of this one object.[13]

Rather than march directly north against General John Pemberton at Vicksburg, Grant led his army northeast toward Jackson where General Joe Johnston massed an army. His troops routed a rebel force at Port Gibson on May 1, another at Raymond on May 12, and finally Johnston at Jackson on May 14. Grant kept Sherman in Jackson to guard his rear while he headed west with his other two corps to Vicksburg. He defeated Pemberton at Champion Hill on May 16, Big Black River on May 17, and arrived before Vicksburg on May 19. He immediately ordered an attack that the defenders in their elaborate entrenchments easily repulsed, and a larger attack the next day with worse losses.

Despite those repulses, Grant had fought a brilliant campaign. Over 17 days, he marched his army 180 miles, trounced the rebels in 5 battles, inflicted 7,200 casualties while suffering 4,379, captured Jackson, and trapped Pemberton with 31,600 men and 172 cannons in Vicksburg. He deployed his troops to construct their own entrenchments as siege guns were emplaced along the line and began firing, killing soldiers and civilians alike. Mary Chesnut recorded this horrific incident experienced by friends:

They had been at Vicksburg during the siege and during the bombardment sought refuge in a cave. The roar of the cannon ceasing, they came out gladly for a breath of fresh air. At the moment they emerged, a bomb burst … among them … struck the son already wounded and smashed off the arm of a beautiful little grandchild not yet three years old. There was this poor little girl with her touchingly lovely face – and her arm gone.[14]

Meanwhile, Sherman burned Jackson and marched to Vicksburg. When Johnston approached with 31,000 men, Grant had Sherman deploy his corps west of the Big Black River. Johnston dared not attack and eventually withdrew to Jackson's ruins. Grant had Sherman pursue Johnston but Johnston retreated into eastern Mississippi.

Pemberton surrendered his army on July 4. The Union and Confederate armies had suffered 4,910 and 2,872 respective casualties during the siege. Grant paroled 2,166 officers, 27,230 troops, and 114 officials, and sent to prison camps an officer and 708 men who rejected parole. The Union also captured 172 cannons, 60,000 firearms, and huge stores of munitions.

The last Confederate stronghold on the Mississippi at Port Hudson with 6,340 defenders surrendered to General Banks' 20,000 troops 5 days later; the Union army suffered 4,362 casualties during the 4-week siege. That exhilarating news prompted Lincoln to reflect, "The father of waters again goes unvexed to the sea."[15]

Volunteers dwindled as the war persisted and the lists of dead buried in distant grounds and the sight of crippled veterans soared. The Federal government had no choice but to fill the depleted ranks of regiments with conscripts. The first draft round was scheduled for July 11, 1863. The only serious violent resistance to the draft came in New York City.[16] Rich men who were drafted could avoid service by paying a $300 fee. That price was far too high for tens of thousands of unskilled laborers, of whom many were Irish immigrants. The Irish competed for menial jobs with blacks. Employers played off blacks and Irish eager for jobs against each other to keep wages as low as possible. The result were worsening class and racial tensions. Wages fell further behind inflation, exacerbating the poverty plaguing blacks and Irish. Strikes and riots increasingly erupted.

Atop this came the draft that began on Saturday, July 11. There was no resistance that day but on Sunday, Irish workers congregated at saloons, vented their rage, and swore to resist on Monday when the lottery resumed. On July 13, mobs attacked draft officials and surged into black neighborhoods to beat black men and burn numerous businesses along with the *New York Tribune* office and a black orphanage although the children escaped. The riots lasted 4 days and resulted in 104 deaths before the government was able to blanket the city with troops. Of the dead, 83 or nearly all were rioters, 11 were blacks, 8 were soldiers, and 2 were policemen. When officials resumed the draft on August 19, 20,000 troops ensured that they were peaceful.

In central Tennessee, General William Rosecrans ignored repeated entreaties by President Lincoln and General Halleck to march with his 87,800 troops against General Braxton Bragg and his 46,250 troops deployed along the Duck River with his headquarters at Tullahoma. Having lost a third of his army at Stones River, Rosecrans feared suffering another devastating battle with Bragg. Then, in March, General Nathan Bedford Forrest led a raid that destroyed key links in Rosecrans' supply network that had to be repaired. Rosecrans sought to retaliate by sending General Abel Streight with 1,500 cavalry to raid behind Bragg's army in April 1863. Forrest led 600 cavalry in pursuit, cornered Streight on May 3, and intimidated him into surrendering.

Rosecrans finally launched his offensive in late June and eventually outmaneuvered Bragg from Tennessee with no more than a few skirmishes along the way.[17] First, from Murfreesboro, he split his army into four columns with the two outer ones curling around Bragg's rear from June 24 to 30. That forced Bragg to withdraw to Chattanooga on July 4. After pausing for six weeks, Rosecrans repeated his maneuver and Bragg retreated into northern Georgia on September 8. The next day Union troops marched into Chattanooga. The entire campaign cost the Army of the Cumberland just 570 casualties. Meanwhile, General Ambrose Burnside's 24,000-man Army of the Ohio drove General Simon Buckner's 10,000 troops from Knoxville on September 3. Of course, any war's key object is destroying enemy armies, and Rosecrans and Burnside failed to do that. Buckner joined Bragg in northern Georgia.

Throughout 1863, cavalry raids by Nathan Forrest and John Morgan sharply stunted those Union operations in scale and prolonged them in time by destroying their supplies and diverting their troops. On June 27, Morgan led 2,460 cavalry across the upper Cumberland River on an epic 700-mile raid through parts of Tennessee, Kentucky, Indiana, and Ohio. Along the way, they captured numerous small garrisons, destroyed supply depots, tore up railroads, burned bridges, and fired on steamboats. Thousands of bluecoat cavalry split among different columns pursued them. Morgan lost ever more of his men from skirmishes and exhaustion. Union forces finally cornered Morgan and his remaining 364 troopers at Salineville in eastern Ohio on July 26. They were confined in the state penitentiary at Columbus.

President Davis sent General James Longstreet with his 20,000-man corps to reinforce Bragg.[18] That brought Bragg's army to 65,000 troops, superior to Rosecrans's 60,000 troops. When Rosecrans tried to outmaneuver Bragg from his latest position, this time the rebel leader stood his ground. He blunted the advance of three separate Union columns from September 10 to 13. Both commanders massed their armies on either side of Chickamauga Creek a dozen miles south of Chattanooga. Bragg launched his army against Rosecrans's on September 19. The Union troops fought off the Confederates that day. Bragg renewed his attack the next morning and this time the rebels punched through, routing most of the Union army. Only General George Thomas's corps held its position and so let most of the army evade capture and retreat to Chattanooga. The battle of Chickamauga was the bloodiest west of the Appalachians, with 16,170 Union and 18,454 Confederate casualties.[19]

Bragg pursued and captured 400ft Missionary Ridge and 1,500ft Lookout Mountain on the city's southeast and western outskirts.[20] Confident that his command of the high ground was impregnable, he dispatched Longstreet's corps to retake Knoxville and Joe Wheeler with 4,000 cavalry to devastate the Union supply lines stretching back to Nashville. He hoped to starve and bombard Rosecrans into surrender.

Rosecrans soon received reinforcements. Sherman's corps was already on its way before Chickamauga, and Lincoln had Hooker's corps transferred from Meade's army to Chattanooga. On October 16, Lincoln replaced Rosecrans with Thomas, created the Division of the Mississippi that included the territory between the Mississippi River and Appalachian Mountains, and named Ulysses Grant its commander.

Ulysses Grant hurried to Chattanooga, arriving on October 21.[21] His first step was to secure the city's supply line. By late November, he had done that and massed 72,500 troops against Bragg's 49,000 troops. His plan was for Sherman to attack Braxton Bragg's right flank while Hooker took Lookout Mountain, and Thomas feinted toward Missionary Ridge. The battle opened on November 23, when Thomas's men captured Orchard Knob and Bushy Knob a mile and a half from Missionary Ridge. The next day, Patrick Cleburne's troops repelled Sherman's attack but Lookout Mountain's defenders fled. On November 25, Grant ordered an all-out assault against Missionary Ridge with Hooker against the rebel left, Thomas the center, and Sherman the right. The Confederates blunted the attacks by Hooker and Sherman, but Thomas's troops fought their way up the ridge and routed the defenders. In three days of combat, the Union suffered 5,824 casualties while inflicting 8,681 on the Confederates. Bragg withdrew his army 30 miles south to Dalton, Georgia.

Meanwhile, Longstreet launched three separate attacks on Burnside's army deployed in forts and entrenchments around Knoxville. Union troops repelled the Confederates at Campbell's Station on November 16 and Fort Sanders on November 24. The Confederates captured Bean's Station on December 14, but the bluecoats withdrew into an inner line of fortifications. President Davis ordered Longstreet to return to Lee's army in Virginia.

Abraham Lincoln delivered what became known as America's greatest public address at Gettysburg on November 19, 1863.[22] He was there to help commemorate the first National Cemetery. The cemetery was laid out in a half circle with symmetrical curling lines of graves extending from a central park with now withered winter grass. The graves were organized by states with one section reserved for the unknown. The cemetery was reserved solely for the five thousand or so Union soldiers who had died in the battle four-and-a-half months earlier; the rebel dead were buried in scattered plots near where they fell.

Only about half the Union dead had been transferred there from their shallow temporary graves dispersed across the surrounding countryside. Each day the burial squads could only dig up, cart, drop, and shovel over around a hundred cadavers in the neat rows of freshly dug graves. Many corpses had either not been buried or had been extracted and gnawed by hungry hogs and dogs. And then there were still hundreds of the once thousands of mangled horses that had not yet been laboriously buried. No matter what way the breeze blew, it carried the lingering stench from countless rotting corpses.

The speakers, other dignitaries, and 5,000 or so spectators packed that central half-moon park. The keynote speaker was actually America's most acclaimed orator, Edward Everett, whose previous career included being a representative and senator from and governor of Massachusetts as well as Harvard University's president. In his 2-hour lecture replete with allusions to ancient Greek and Roman writers, wars, and warriors, Everett expounded the theme that the battle of Gettysburg surpassed in scale, stakes, leadership, and heroism any preceding historical or mythical combats.

Then it was Lincoln's turn. He delivered his 272-word address in a few minutes. Here is what he said:

Four score and seven years ago our fathers brought forth on this continent a new nation, conceived in liberty and dedicated to the proposition that all men are created equal.

Now we are engaged in a great civil war, testing whether that nation, or any nation so conceived and so dedicated, can long endure. We are met on a great battlefield of that war. We have come to dedicate a portion of that field as a final resting place for those who here gave their lives that that nation might live. It is altogether fitting and proper that we should do this.

But, in a larger sense, we cannot dedicate – we cannot consecrate – we cannot hallow – this ground. The brave men, living and dead, who struggled here, have consecrated it far above our poor power to add or detract. The world will little note nor long remember what we say here, but it can never forget what they did here. It is for us, the living, rather, to be dedicated here to the unfinished work which they who fought here have thus far so nobly advanced. It is rather for us to be here dedicated to the great task remaining before us – that from these honored dead, we take increased devotion to that cause for which they gave the last full measure of their devotion, that we here highly resolve that these dead shall not have died in vain, that this nation, under God, shall have a new birth of freedom; and the government of the people, by the people, and for the people, shall not perish from the earth.'[23]

The immediate response was favorable. Several times the crowd interrupted his address with applause. Later newspapers printed his speech and most editors lauded the eloquence and profundity of his words. To his credit, Everett recognized its brilliance. The next day, he wrote the president that: "I should be glad if I could flatter myself that I came as near to the central idea of the occasion in two hours as you did in two minutes."[24]

Lincoln had composed the address in three stages, the evening before he took the train to Gettysburg, on the train, and the evening before his delivery. He structured his address like a classical Greek funeral oration, first extolling the dead and then uplifting the mourners by explaining the larger meaning of that death. What Lincoln sought was to dedicate the Union war effort to fulfilling the Declaration of Independence's natural rights principles of equality, life, liberty, and the pursuit of happiness for all men, and thus complete America's revolution.

Chapter 15

The 1864 Campaigns

President Abraham Lincoln got Congress to pass a bill establishing the rank of lieutenant general, last held by George Washington, and awarding it to Ulysses Grant for his brilliant series of victorious campaigns. Majorities approved in the House of Representatives on February 1, the Senate on February 24, and Lincoln signed it into law on February 29. On March 3, General Henry Halleck ordered Grant to report to Washington.

Grant and his son Fred arrived on March 8. No one met him at the station nor recognized him when he checked into the Willard Hotel. He was relieved when the clerk informed him they could have the last available room despite it being among the worst. Only when he signed the register did the clerk, to his embarrassment, recognize the visitor. Grant received the Willard's best suite. That evening, Lincoln held a reception for Grant at the White House. It was the first time they had met, although they had corresponded many times. The following day, Lincoln formally promoted Grant to lieutenant general and replaced Halleck with him as commanding general; he retained Halleck as his chief military advisor with the title chief of staff.

Among Grant's talents was promoting men as ruthless and skilled as he was at war. He named William Sherman his successor to command the Mississippi Division between the Appalachian Mountains and Mississippi River. He summoned Philip Sheridan east to head the Army of the Potomac's 12,000 cavalrymen. Although he retained Gordon Meade as the Army of the Potomac's commanding general, Grant would actually be in charge and use him as a chief of staff to implement his plans. He wanted to replace inept leaders like Benjamin Butler, Franz Sigel, and Nathaniel Banks but for now, Lincoln prevented him from doing so. Although Lincoln shared that desire, he felt compelled to keep them because of their latent political power.

Grant understood how to win the war: "From an early period of the rebellion, I had been impressed with the idea that active and continuous action of all the troops that could be brought into the field, regardless of seasons and weather, were necessary to a speedy termination of the war." To that end, his orders to the regional commanders was simple – march against the nearest rebel army and destroy it. Those armies included Sherman's in northern Georgia; Butler's at Fortress Monroe on the Peninsula; Sigel's at Winchester in the Shenandoah; and Banks's at Baton Rouge.

Grant began the campaign on May 2 at Culpepper Court House with 115,000 troops, nearly twice as many as Lee's 64,000 at Orange 20 miles south.[1] His plan was to arc east of Lee's army and get between it and Richmond. Typically, Lee attacked rather than withdrew. On May 5, he launched his army against Grant's as it marched through the Wilderness, a mostly forested region west of where the previous battle of Chancellorsville was fought. Despite being outnumbered, Lee's army fought Grant's army to a standstill in 2 days of fierce fighting that cost them 11,033 and 17,666 casualties, respectively.

Rather than withdraw, Grant again tried to sidestep Lee but Lee got to Spotsylvania, a critical crossroads, before him. They battled there from May 6 to 21, as Grant launched a series of attacks that the Confederates repelled with heavy losses; the Union and Confederate armies suffered 18,399 and 12,687 casualties, respectively.

Meanwhile, Grant dispatched Sheridan with his 12,000-man cavalry corps to raid all the way to Richmond. General Jeb Stuart with 4,500 horsemen headed off Sheridan at Yellow Tavern 6 miles north of Richmond on May 10. The Federal troopers routed the rebels, with Stuart among the dead, and freed 400 Union prisoners. With his ammunition short and horses jaded, Sheridan withdrew.

Grant tried his latest flanking move on the night of May 21, and Lee stopped him at Hanover on the North Anna River. Grant's latest lunge came on June 3, when he advanced as far as Cold Harbor just a dozen miles northeast of Richmond. Lee again got there first and entrenched his army. Grant ordered a massive attack on the rebel lines that day and the next. The result was slaughter, with 12,738 Union and 5,287 Confederate casualties.

Grant tried to break the stalemate by sending Sheridan and his 9,286 horsemen on their latest raid deep in Lee's rear. The 6,762-man rebel cavalry corps, now led by Wade Hampton, headed Sheridan off at Trevilian Station, 60 miles northwest of Richmond on June 11. The troopers fought that day and into the next before Sheridan finally withdrew, losing 1,512 men to Wade's 803.

In little more than a month from May 5 to June 12, the Union and Confederate armies suffered 39,259 and 25,000 casualties.[2] Critics blasted Grant as a "'butcher" deadset on destroying Lee through sheer attrition. Actually, the opposite was true, at least strategically. Grant sought to outmaneuver Lee while Lee sought to grind down Grant by exploiting interior lines to get to and fortify strategic crossroads just in time. Time after time, Lee won that race. As for tactics, Grant did try to steamroll Lee at each battle. Of those, he regretted only one – Cold Harbor.

Grant's next maneuver was his most sweeping yet.[3] He had a 2,100ft-long pontoon bridge built across the James River and began marching his army across on June 12. The objective was Petersburg, a strategic rail and road junction just 20 miles south of Richmond. If he took Petersburg, Lee would have to abandon Richmond and race westward toward Lynchburg then angle south into North Carolina. Grant would enjoy the inside tract in that race.

The spearhead Union corps led by General William Smith approached Petersburg's defenses on June 15. General Pierre Beauregard's 2,500 troops thinly lined the entrenchments. Smith launched a limited attack that captured an outer stretch of rebel line. Had Smith pushed through to the town and defended the bridge across the Appomattox River, he would have brilliantly achieved Grant's plan. Instead, he believed prisoners who falsely claimed that Lee and his army would soon arrive. He ordered his men to prepare to defend against an attack that never came.

Lee eventually did arrive with his army as did Grant with the rest of his. Grant deployed his corps in an arc with the right anchored on the Appomattox River but with his left open. Whenever he stretched his line further west, Lee mimicked him. That creeping deadlock would last another ten months. Lee countered Grant's attempts to sever the railroad running south at Globe Tavern on August 18, Reams Station on August 25, Peebles Farm from September 30 to October 2, and Hatcher's Run on October 27 and from February 5 to 7, 1865.[4]

The Army of the Potomac's right flank was just half a dozen miles from the Army of the James that had arrived a month earlier. Butler was among the war's worst generals. In early May, he advanced with 30,000 troops up the James River. Beauregard repelled both ironclads on the river, and Union troops on land at Drewry's Bluff 8 miles from Richmond on May 15. In their latest lopsided victory, the Confederates inflicted 5,546 casualties while suffering 2,506. Butler retreated to Bermuda Hundred where the James and Appomattox Rivers mingled. Beauregard advanced and had his 5,000 troops construct entrenchments that penned in Butler. There, Butler and his men sat virtually useless month after month.

Lincoln sympathized with Grant's advice to cashier Butler and replace him with a skilled general. Tragically, political rather than military necessity trumped that decision. Before the war, Butler was a very influential Massachusetts Democratic politician who supported slavery and states' rights. After Fort Sumter, he wrangled a general's commission from Lincoln in return for a promise of loyalty and support for the Republican Party. With an eye to the approaching November election, Lincoln hesitated to cashier such an outspoken, volatile, mercenary politician from a key state.

General Grant approved a plan in mid-June that might have led to a breakthrough at Petersburg.[5] The colonel of a Pennsylvania regiment with many former coal miners suggested digging a tunnel to culminate beneath a rebel fort, packing the end chamber with gunpowder, igniting a massive explosion that destroyed the fort, then charging through that gap. The tunnel eventually extended 511ft with an 80ft cross-shaft. Politics and bad tactics caused the latest debacle.

Burnside commanded the sector where the scheme was developed. Initially, he designated a brigade of black troops to spearhead the attack and had them trained for the mission. A few days before the assault, colonels of white regiments protested letting black troops conduct such a vital attack, doubly fearing either that they would fail for lack of courage and skill or would succeed to prove themselves equal to white troops. Hours before the mission, Meade objected on related political and humanitarian grounds: "if we put the colored troops in front ... and it should prove a failure, it would then be said ... that we were shoving those people ahead to get killed because we did not care anything about them." Grant succumbed to his argument.[6]

The plan initially worked. At dawn on July 30, the mine exploded, destroying a fort manned by 278 troops and erupting a crater 170ft long, 60ft wide, and 30ft deep. The black troops had been instructed to avoid the crater with some troops rolling up each exposed and dazed rebel flank, while others pushed forward along either rim. The white regiments poured into the crater and struggled to climb the far wall. Lee ordered reserves to converge and attack the bluecoats packing the crater. The result was slaughter, with the Union suffering 3,798 casualties and inflicting 1,491 before they retreated. Grant confessed to Halleck that the defeat "was the saddest affair I have witnessed in the war. Such an opportunity for carrying fortifications I have never seen and do not expect again to have."[7]

Admiral David Farragut led the fleet of four ironclad and fourteen wooden warships that battled its way into Mobile Bay past three forts on August 5, 1864.[8] A mine, then called a torpedo, sank the lead ironclad USS *Tecumseh*. When his officers talked about turning back, Farragut shouted: "Damn the torpedoes! Full speed ahead!"

Defending Mobile was the ironclad CSS *Tennessee* and three smaller warships. Farragut's fleet bombarded and sank them. Over the next three weeks, the warships shelled and the troops landed to capture each fort. Although the Union fleet had effectively plugged Mobile, the city's defenders would hold out until April 12, 1865. Nonetheless, Farragut's battle cry ranks with Captain James Lawrence's "Don't give up the ship!" and Captain Oliver Perry's "We have met the enemy fleet and they are ours!" as stirring symbols of the American navy's fighting spirit.

Americans led the world in submarine warfare. During America's War of Independence, David Bushnell designed and built a one-man wooden egg-shaped vessel dubbed the USS *Turtle*, propelled by peddling, submerged or surfaced by flooding or expelling water from a chamber, and armed with a gunpowder cask that could be screwed into a vessel's hull. In 1776, he tried and failed to sink a British warship in New York harbor. In 1862, Horace Hunley designed and built a much larger submarine – 30ft long, 4ft wide, and 5ft high – with eight men hand-cranking the propeller and tanks that could be filled or emptied with water to surface or submerge, and a ninth man at the rudder. Initially, it was armed with a mine pulled by a 200ft rope. The tactic was to dive beneath an enemy warship and pull the mine against the vessel's far side.[9]

Launched in Charleston harbor, the CSS *Hunley* became an unintended suicide bomb. It sank twice, drowning its crews. One sinking happened when the chain dragging the mine entangled the propeller. To avoid that, the *Hunley* was armed with a mine capping a 22ft spar protruding from the bow. The tactic now was simply to ram that spar into an enemy vessel. On the night of February 17, 1864, the *Hunley* fulfilled its mission by sinking the USS *Housatonic*. The crew's elation was short-lived. The *Hunley* sank on the way back to port. The *Hunley* inspired the great powers, including the United States, eventually to develop their own submarines, which revolutionized naval warfare.

Sherman received command of the western department that stretched between the Mississippi River and Appalachian Mountains on March 18. He had earned the job, although it was a steep learning curve to get there.[10] He was a West Point graduate, sixth in his class of forty-three in 1840. He served in both the Seminole and Mexican Wars, but never came under fire in either. His most persistent duty was quartermaster. He resigned his commission in 1850 after he married Ellen Ewing, the interior secretary's daughter. To support his steadily growing family, he deployed his quartermaster skills as a banker and real estate developer first in San Francisco then in New York. In 1859, he accepted an appointment as the president of a military academy at Pineville, Louisiana which much later would evolve into Louisiana State University. After Fort Sumter, he resigned and headed north.

Sherman was tall and lean, with receding reddish hair. He spoke rapidly and usually confidently. He was a manic-depressive who seesawed between bouts of elation and despair. Despite his fierce continence and mood swings, he was a loving husband, father, and friend. He knew his limits but tried to stretch them as far as possible. In May 1861, he actually turned down War Secretary Simon Cameron's offer to be a brigadier general. He doubted his ability to command such large numbers of troops and regiments. Instead, he preferred to earn his way to the top by methodically mastering each rank along the way. So he readily accepted promotion from lieutenant to colonel and a regiment's command.

Sherman fought at the first battle of Bull Run then was transferred to the western theater. There he received twenty days medical leave after declaring to visiting War Secretary Cameron that a couple hundred thousand troops were needed to prevail on that front. Newspaper editors called him "insane." Thereafter he kept his views to himself and through diligence and luck received promotions to command first a brigade then a division. His resolute defense against the rebel onslaught at Shiloh won him Grant's undying gratitude and support. His first independent campaign died when Confederates repelled his corps' assault at Chickasaw Bluffs in January 1863. He overcame that stigma during the Vicksburg campaign when he defeated Joe Johnston's army at Jackson while most of Grant's army advanced west, defeating Pemberton along the way then besieging him in Vicksburg. At Chattanooga, General Patrick Cleburne repulsed his attack on the rebel right flank and it was General Thomas who routed the Confederates by capturing Missionary Ridge.

Sherman advocated total war as the most moral way to destroy the Confederacy and reunite the nation: "We are not only fighting hostile armies but a hostile people, and must make old and young, rich and poor, feel the hard hand of war, as well as their organized armies."[11] Devastating the enemy's transportation infrastructure, especially railroads, was critical. He explained the process:

> The track was heaved up in sections the length of a regiment, then separated rail by rail; bonfires were made of the ties ... on which the rails were heated, carried to trees or telegraph poles, wrapped around and left to cool. Such rails could not be used again; and to be more certain, we willed up many deep cuts with trees, brush, and earth, and commingled with them loaded shells, so arranged that they would explode on the attempt to haul out the bushes.[12]

In January 1864, Grant authorized Sherman to march from Vicksburg with 21,000 troops 134 miles all the way to Meridian and destroy that rail and supply center. They set forth on February 4, faced no opposition along the way, entered the city on February 14, for the next five days systematically looted, burned, or destroyed anything of military value, then returned to Vicksburg. As for railroads, they wrecked 115 miles of track, sixty-one trestles, twenty locomotives, and hundreds of cars.[13] He would later see the raid as a dress rehearsal for his "march to the sea" later that year.

Grant's marching orders to Sherman arrived on April 4: "You I propose to move against Johnston's army, to break it up, and to get into the interior of the enemy's country as far as you can, inflicting all the damage you can against their war resources."[14] To that end, Sherman commanded 3 armies in northern Georgia, John McPherson's 50,000-man Army of the Tennessee, George Thomas's 35,000-man Army of the Cumberland, and John Schofield's 15,000-man Army of the Ohio. Facing them at Rocky Face Ridge was Joe Johnston's 65,000-man Army of Tennessee.[15]

Sherman's campaign depended on the unimpeded round-the-clock chugging of supply trains along the single track linking Chattanooga and Atlanta. Each day his 100,000 troops and 35,000 horses consumed supplies conveyed by 160 railroad cars. He recalled that it "would have required thirty-six thousand eight hundred wagons of six mules each, allowing each wagon to have hauled two tons twenty miles each day, a simple impossibility in roads such as then existed in the region of the country."[16]

Sherman opened his campaign on May 7 with the first of a series of attempts to pin down Johnston with Thomas and Schofield while outflanking him with McPherson. Like Lee against Grant in Virginia, Johnston always deftly withdrew just in time as his troops staved off Union attacks. They battled at Rocky Face from May 7 to 13, Resaca from May 13 to 15, Adairsville on May 17, New Hope Church on May 25 and 26, Dallas from May 26 to June 1, Kolb's Farm on June 22, Kennesaw Mountain on June 27, Paces Ferry on July 5, and culminated with Peachtree Creek on July 9. Johnston withdrew with his army into Atlanta's well-prepared defenses.

Sherman and his men had marched and fought their way to Atlanta's outskirts in 7 weeks while suffering 17,000 casualties to Johnston's 14,000. The carnage in Georgia was a quarter that in Virginia because Sherman was far more cautious than Grant. Only at Kennesaw Mountain did he launch a massive attack against Johnston's entrenched men, suffering 3,000 to 1,000 casualties. Meanwhile, Sherman's steadily stretching supply line, with its core the single-track railroad linking Chattanooga and Atlanta, endured repeated destructive raids by rebel cavalry led by Joe Wheeler.

Johnston fought a masterly campaign, repeatedly evading and stinging Sherman's maneuvers and attacks despite being outnumbered two to one. Yet, on July 17, President Davis replaced him with John Hood. His excuse was Johnston's withdrawal to Atlanta, although that was inevitable given Sherman's overwhelming power. Actually, Davis and Johnston loathed each other, an animosity that began long before the war and may have involved their rivalry over a southern belle. Regardless, Davis's choice would prove to be disastrous. Hood was not just brave but reckless. He was a Texan with a prickly sense of honor that drove him to lead every charge. That cost him a crippled arm at Gettysburg and an amputated leg at Chickamauga. An aide had to strap him in the saddle.[17]

Hood launched a series of attacks against the Union line expanding around Atlanta with each repulsed at Peachtree Creek on July 20, Atlanta on July 22, and Ezra Church on July 22. The Confederates suffered 15,000 casualties to the Union's 6,000. Sherman's worst loss was McPherson, killed on July 22. Sherman replaced him General Oliver Howard, a one-armed general who after the war founded Howard College for black students.

Five weeks then ensued as Sherman settled into a siege. In extending his line, he cut all the roads and rails radiating from Atlanta except those heading south through Jonesborough 20 miles away. Hood tried to distract Sherman by dispatching Wheeler with 4,500 troopers against the Union supply line in northern Georgia. They destroyed 30 miles of railroad, skirmished with the Federal garrison at Dalton for two days, then rode north to threaten the garrison at Loudon, Tennessee. On September 10, the saddle-sore troopers finally reached safety at Tuscumbia, Alabama. That raid disrupted but did not sever Sherman's supply line.

Sherman was actually more concerned about raids by General Nathan Forrest several hundred miles away in western Tennessee and northern Mississippi. Forrest fought there rather than with first Johnston and then Hood in Georgia because of his own acrimonious relationship with Braxton Bragg that had smoldered for years. Before the battle of Missionary Ridge, Forrest finally erupted in rage at Bragg: "I have stood your meanness as long as I intend to. You have played the part of a damned scoundrel, and are a coward."[18] He got President Davis's permission to form an independent command for northern Mississippi and western Tennessee. That feud actually aided the Confederacy. He would have bedeviled Sherman had he been on the Georgia front, but at best would have merely delayed Atlanta's inevitable fall. Instead, he decisively saved his new command from being overrun.

Forrest's first raid in 1864 was his most controversial. Starting on March 16, he led 2,500 horsemen on a month-long series of attacks on garrisons, supply depots, railroad tracks, and bridges across western Kentucky and Tennessee. Fort Pillow sat on a bluff above the Mississippi River 40 miles north of Memphis. Its 600 defenders were split between companies of white and black Union troops. On April 12, Forrest launched an assault that overran the garrison, initially killing 231 soldiers, some after they surrendered, and capturing the rest at the cost of 14 killed and 86 wounded; only 58 of 262 black soldiers survived. That "Fort Pillow massacre" darkened Forrest's reputation.[19]

Sherman understood the strategic threat that Forrest posed to his own operations. He ordered General Andrew Smith, that region's commander:

> To pursue Forrest on foot, devastating the land over which he passed or may pass, and make him and the people of Tennessee and Mississippi realize that although [he is] a bold, daring, and successful leader, he will bring ruin and misery on any country where he may ... tarry. If we do not punish Forrest and the people now, the whole effect of our conquests will be lost.[20]

Smith tapped General Samuel Sturgis to lead 4,800 infantry, 3,300 cavalry, and twenty-two cannons from Memphis into northern Mississippi in June. With just 3,500 cavalry, Forrest double-enveloped and routed the invaders at Brice's Crossroads on June 10, inflicting 2,249 casualties while losing 492.

Smith led the next campaign to hunt Forrest. In early July, he marched with 13,000 infantry, 3,000 cavalry, and 24 guns from Memphis toward Tupelo. Defending Tupelo was General Stephen Lee's command, which included 2,100 infantry, 7,000 cavalry, and 20 guns; Forrest led the cavalry. After the Union army arrived on July 14, Lee ordered a series of attacks that day and the next. The bluecoats repelled each assault, inflicting twice as many casualties, 1,340 to the 674 they suffered; Forrest was among the wounded. Yet rather than follow up his victory, Smith withdrew to Memphis. Thus, did Smith win tactically but yield strategically. Forrest was soon back in the saddle again. Sherman sent Smith another order to hound Forrest relentlessly.

Smith marched with 18,000 infantry and cavalry south from Memphis along the Mississippi Central railroad. They reached Oxford on August 9. Forrest led 1,500 troopers against Memphis, trotting into the city on August 21. The raiders destroyed Federal supplies then withdrew. That raid prompted Smith to withdraw to Memphis.

Sherman implemented a plan on August 25 designed eventually to capture Hood and Atlanta. He stretched one corps to occupy the entire semicircle of entrenchments and marched with six corps to Jonesborough. That forced Hood to abandon Atlanta and assault Sherman at Jonesborough on August 31 and September 1. Sherman's troops repelled the attacks and counterattacked. Hood managed to escape with most of his army, having suffered 2,700 casualties to the Union's 1,149. Sherman's victorious army entered Atlanta the next day. In all, the Atlanta campaign culminating with its capture cost the Union and Confederate 31,687 and 34,979 respective casualties. Sherman had fought a brilliant campaign in which he achieved one of his two strategic goals with fewer losses than the enemy.

Sherman soon realized that holding Atlanta was as much a curse as an asset. First Forrest and then Hood threatened to cut him off from his supply base at Chattanooga. Forrest launched his latest raid from Tuscumbia on September 20, not long after Wheeler and his tattered but triumphant men rode into town. Forrest led 2,000 troopers through middle Tennessee wrecking railroads, capturing garrisons, and burning supplies. Sherman tried to coordinate a convergence of available forces against the raiders, but Forrest evaded them and returned to his lair in northern Alabama.

After the battle of Jonesborough, Hood withdrew to Palmetto, Georgia, on the railroad that linked Atlanta and Pensacola, and there replenished his ranks and supplies. On October 1, Hood led his army north toward Allatoona to sever that crucial link in Sherman's supply line. Sherman left a corps at Atlanta and marched north with his other five corps. On October 5, there was a fierce fight between a detached division from each army at Allatoona. Hood withdrew west then headed north to capture Resaca on October 17, then hurried west into Alabama as Sherman nearly caught up to him.

Frustrated, Sherman conceived a plan that decisively changed the war. He asked Grant's permission to assign Thomas's Army of the Cumberland to defend Tennessee while he returned with the Army of the Tennessee to Atlanta, which he would destroy and then march to Savannah, cutting a swath of destruction all the way: "I can make this march and make Georgia howl!" Grant replied that: "If you see a chance of destroying Hood's army, attend to that first, and make your other move secondary." Sherman replied that: "No single army can catch Hood and I am convinced that the best results will follow from defeating Jeff Davis's cherished plan of making me leave Georgia by maneuvering ... If I turn back, the whole effect of my campaign will be lost ... I am clearly of the opinion that the best results will follow my contemplated movement through Georgia."[21] Grant grimly approved.

Grant initially wanted Nathaniel Banks to march east to capture Mobile, Alabama, one of the South's major ports. Instead, Lincoln and Halleck talked Grant into diverting Banks up the Red River valley against General Richard Taylor and take Shreveport in northwestern Louisiana. The objective was more political than military. Seizing Shreveport would extend Louisiana's reconstructed government over most of the state and gain revenues from the rich cotton plantations along the way. Lincoln was also concerned about Napoleon III's imposition of a regime in Mexico headed by Maximilian, an Austrian archduke made emperor. He hoped that Shreveport could be a staging area for a backdoor invasion of Texas that secured its border with Mexico. He explained to Grant that: "I see ... that you incline strongly toward an expedition against Mobile.

This would be tempting to me also, were it not that, in view of recent events in Mexico, I am greatly impressed with the importance of re-establishing the national authority in Western Texas as soon as possible."[22] Of course, if Maximilian posed a genuine threat to Texas, the logical place to deter it was not Shreveport high on the Red River but Brownsville at the Rio Grande mouth.

After setting forth from New Orleans on March 12, Banks and his 28,000 troops got no further than 35 miles from Shreveport. On April 8, Taylor hurled his 14,000 troops against the advanced Union force of 12,000 troops at Sabine Crossroads near Mansfield, and routed them, inflicting 2,245 casualties while suffering 1,000. The next day he hit Banks at Pleasant Hill, but was repelled, losing 1,626 killed, wounded, and captured to the Union's 1,369 losses. Banks did not follow up his victory but instead withdrew down the Red River to the Mississippi and then to New Orleans. His excuse was that low river waters impeded his supplies.

Banks partly redeemed himself on November 6, when he led 6,000 troops into Brownsville, Texas, at the Rio Grande's mouth, which a small rebel force hastily evacuated. Banks returned with most troops to New Orleans after garrisoning Brownsville with 1,000 soldiers led by General Francis Herron. On July 30, 1864, Herron abandoned Brownsville as 1,300 rebel troops led by Colonel John "Rip" Ford, a famed Texas Ranger, approached. The Confederacy held Brownsville for the rest of the war.

Meanwhile, General Sterling Price led 12,000 troops north from Camden in south central Arkansas on August 28, in what would be an epic march. General Thomas Ewing commanded the 1,456-man garrison of Fort Davidson at Pilot Knob. On September 27, the Union troops repelled attacks by the invaders, inflicting over 1,000 casualties while enduring 213, then escaped as they blew up the fort behind them. Price angled northeast aiming at St Louis, but veered westward after learning that Generals Alfred Pleasonton and Andrew Smith were advancing against him with overwhelming forces. His new objective was Kansas City where General Samuel Curtis massed troops. Along the way, Price's troops won skirmishes at Glasgow, Sedalia, Lexington, Little Blue River, Independence, and Bryam's Ford. As Price approached, Curtis deployed his 22,000 troops at Westport a dozen miles southeast of Kansas City. On October 23, Price attacked, but was repelled then routed when Curtis counterattacked, with each side losing around 1,500 men. For several weeks, Curtis pursued Price to the Arkansas border. Price finally escaped with 6,000 remaining troops to Laynesport, Arkansas on the Red River on December 2. Price and his men had fought an astonishing campaign during which they marched over 1,400 miles and fought forty-three engagements. But that was the Confederacy's last hurrah for Missouri.

General Franz Sigel advanced with 6,500 troops up the Shenandoah Valley in early May. On May 15, General John Breckinridge with 5,150 troops, including 241 Virginia Military Institute (VMI) cadets, attacked and routed him at New Market, inflicting 841 casualties while suffering 531, including 10 cadets dead and 47 wounded.

Grant replaced Sigel with David Hunter and diverted reinforcements and supplies to his army. With 15,000 troops, Hunter began his offensive on June 1. His objective was to destroy any rebel army in the valley then march over the divide, capture Lynchburg, then head east along the railroad to Richmond. That was a tall order. Hunter nearly pulled it off. His army scattered a rebel force at Piedmont on June 5. Behind Hunter's army, Colonel John Mosby and his guerilla fighters on fast horses attacked isolated garrisons and supply trains, destroying many.

Lee sent Jubal Early and his division to Lynchburg just days before Hunter arrived on June 17. Early's troops repelled Hunter's probing attacks that day and the next. Hunter withdrew with the excuse that his munition and food supplies were dwindling. Early followed hard on Hunter's heels, skirmishing with his rear guard and nabbing hundreds of stragglers. As Hunter veered toward Washington, Early headed north for Maryland, crossed the Potomac on July 6, and routed General Lew Wallace and 5,800 troops at a Monocacy River ford on July 7, inflicting 1,294 casualties and suffering around 800. He advanced toward Washington, halting before Fort Stevens, one of the capital's key fortifications, on July 11.

Early had skirmishers probe the fort's defenses. General Horatio Wright commanded Washington's defenses that included 37 miles of entrenchments studded by 68 forts, 93 batteries, and 800 cannons manned by 10,000 troops.[23] On July 12, Wright and a tall, gangly, bearded civilian wearing a stovepipe hat appeared and peered at the rebel lines as bullets whizzed past. Captain Oliver Wendall Holmes, later a Supreme Court justice, was nearby and shouted, "Get down you damned fool before you get shot!" The man obeyed the captain's order. Holmes soon learned that the civilian was President Lincoln who was determined to see the war firsthand.[24]

Early recognized that Washington's defenses were too powerful to penetrate and withdrew into Virginia. General George Crook with 10,000 troops pursued and attacked Early's 14,000 troops at Kernstown on July 24. The Confederates routed the Federals, inflicting 1,200 casualties while suffering 600. Early followed up that victory by recrossing the Potomac into Maryland, determined to inflict as much destruction or extract as much ransom from northern towns as was possible. He spared Frederick and Hagerstown, Maryland in return for $200,000 and $20,000 in greenbacks, respectively. He sent his cavalry north to demand $500,000 from Chambersburg, Pennsylvania. On July 20, after the government refused to pay, the rebels looted and burned the town. Early and his footsore men along with scores of wagons packed with supplies finally crossed the Potomac into Virginia on August 3.

Grant dispatched Sheridan to rebuild the Army of the Shenandoah and "put himself south of the enemy and follow him to the death. Wherever the enemy goes, let our troops go also." Atop that he was to "do all the damage to railroads and crops you can. Carry off stock of all description and negroes so as to prevent further planting. If the War is to last another year we want the Shenandoah Valley to remain a barren waste."[25]

Sheridan proved to be an outstanding choice.[26] Although he spent most of his career as an infantryman, he was just as adept commanding horsemen. He was short and stocky, with stubby-legs, a thick neck, and short-cropped hair. He was a hothead; a fistfight with a fellow cadet got him suspended for a year from West Point. In 1853, he finally graduated thirty-fourth of fifty-two classmates. He spent most of the next seven years fighting Indians in the northwest. Captain George Sanford explained the effects of Sheridan's courage and charisma:

> He was the only commander I have ever met whose personal appearance in the field was an immediate ... stimulus to battle – a stimulus strong enough to turn beaten and disorganized troops into a victorious army ... They simply believed he was going to win, and every man ... was determined to be on hand and see him do it.[27]

With 37,000 troops, Sheridan attacked Early's 15,000 at Winchester on September 19; the rebels fought fiercely, inflicting 5,020 casualties while suffering 3,610 before retreating in good order. Sheridan pursued and attacked Early at Fisher's Hill on September 22, inflicting 1,234 casualties and incurring 528. Early withdrew 60 miles. Rather than try to catch him, Sheridan unleashed his men to devastate the valley. He later reported that: 'I have destroyed over 2,000 barns filled with wheat, hay, and farming implements; over 70 mills filled with flour and wheat, and have driven in front of the army over 4,000 head of stock, and have killed and issued to the troops not less than 3,000 sheep ... The people here are getting sick of the war.'[28]

Astonishingly, Early scraped together reinforcements and supplies then headed north for another fight. At dawn on October 19, his 14,000 troops hit the 31,000 Federals by surprise and routed them at Cedar Hill. Sheridan was in Winchester a dozen miles away when he heard the distant rumble. He mounted his horse and galloped toward the battle. He rallied his men and counterattacked, driving off the rebels. Although, once again Early inflicted more casualties than he lost, 5,665 to 2,910, that was his last hurrah in the Shenandoah. The Union would dominate the lower valley for the war's remainder.

Abraham Lincoln faced the challenge of winning a second term in 1864.[29] The first step to that end was easy enough. The Republican Party held its convention at Baltimore on June 7. Delegations gathered from all the northern states along with Arkansas, Louisiana, and Tennessee. They voted to call themselves the National Union Party to entice moderate Democrats. Lincoln won on the first ballot with 506 of 528 votes. For vice president, Lincoln replaced Hannibal Hamlin of Maine with Andrew Johnson who he had appointed Tennessee's provisional governor on March 12, 1862. Johnson was a slaveowner who now supported abolition. Lincoln faced two inept, angry, and resentment generals who aspired to win the presidency.

The newly formed Radical Democracy Party held a convention at Cleveland from May 29 to 31. Most delegates were Radical Republicans disgruntled with Lincoln for not championing immediate abolition of slavery and racial equality. They nominated John Fremont as their presidential candidate and John Cochrane, a former congressman and current general, as vice president. Fremont accepted on June 4.

George McClellan received the Democratic Party's nomination for president at the convention in Chicago on the first ballot on August 29, with Ohio Congressman and Copperhead George Pendleton for vice president. McClellan did not hide how he intended to end the war: "If I am elected, I will recommend an immediate armistice and a call for a convention of all the states and insist upon exhausting all and every means to secure peace without further bloodshed."[30]

Lincoln was so certain he would lose that on August 23, he composed a letter, sealed it, and required his cabinet secretaries to promise to uphold it without telling them what it said. The letter read: "This morning, as for some days past, it seems exceedingly probable that this Administration will not be reelected. Then it will be my duty to so cooperate with the President-elect as to save the Union between the election and the inauguration, as he will have secured his election on such ground that he cannot possibly save it afterwards."[31]

Lincoln and his campaign supporters tried to assure voters that the North was winning the war and complete victory was inevitable with the current strategy. That appeared to be true. By fall 1864, Union forces had conquered vast swaths of the South, including the Mississippi River valley, Tennessee, and coastal pockets. The blockade was increasingly effective. The Union army numbered 860,733 troops, nearly twice the Confederate army's 463,181.[32] Nonetheless, the North's attrition strategy was enormously costly in death and destruction with no immediate decisive results. For instance, from June to December 1863, Confederate muster rolls diminished merely from 473,058 to 464,646 or 8,412 men although the decline was sharper for those actually with their regiments, from 307,464 to 277,970 or 29,494.[33]

Lincoln's reelection campaign got a major boost with news that Sherman had captured Atlanta on September 2. After Richmond, no rebel city held more symbolic importance. He enjoyed another vital victory on September 22, when his emissaries talked Fremont into abandoning his third party campaign in return for the resignation of his archenemy Montgomery Blair, the postmaster general. However, Fremont not only did not endorse Lincoln, he persisted in publicly criticizing him.

Lincoln won a landslide with 2,218,358 votes or 55.0 percent of those cast to McClellan's 1,812,807 or 45.0 percent, and 212 to 21 in the Electoral College with every state except New Jersey, Delaware, and Kentucky. The soldier vote was critical to the election. Nineteen states provided ballots for their troops in the field. The soldiers voted overwhelmingly for Lincoln, 119,754 or 79 percent compared with 34,291 or 22 percent for McClellan. Lincoln had long coattails. Republicans captured the governorships and legislatures of all states except New Jersey, Delaware, and Kentucky. In the House of Representatives, Republicans won 150 seats to the Democrats' 33, Conservative Party's 5, Radical Party's 4, and 1 independent. In the Senate, the Republicans won 33 seats to the Democrat's 10, the Unconditional Unionists' 4, and the Unionists' 2.

With his election mandate, Lincoln wielded his State of the Union address to boost the nation's morale by celebrating its power, and depress that of the rebels:

> The important fact remains demonstrated that we have more men now than when the war began; that we are not exhausted, nor in process of exhaustion, that we are gaining strength, and may, if need be, maintain the contest indefinitely. This as to men. Material resources are now more complete and abundant than ever ... They can at any moment have peace simply by laying down their arms and submitting to the national authority under the Constitution ... The war will cease ... whenever it shall have ceased on the part of those who began it.[34]

General George Thomas established the Army of the Cumberland's headquarters at Nashville. He split his army, keeping 30,000 troops there and deploying General John Schofield with 30,000 at Pulaski 75 miles south. That was enormously risky. Hood's 40,000 troops were at Decatur, Alabama, 50 miles due south of Pulaski. If Thomas wanted to wield Schofield as bait, Hood might quick-march and defeat him before Thomas reinforced him, or Schofield could withdraw to join Thomas.

Thanks to spies and scouts, Hood was well aware of Schofield's vulnerability and was determined to crush him by cutting him off from Nashville. On October 26, he marched west to Tuscumbia then north toward Columbia, 30 miles beyond Pulaski. Schofield learned of Hood's advance and withdrew his army to Columbia where he deployed them for battle on November 26. Hood again sidestepped Schofield, this time around his left flank. Schofield evaded the encirclement by withdrawing. On November 29, he deployed his army at Franklin, just 15 miles southwest of Nashville and implored Thomas to join him.

Hood hurled his army directly at Schofield's on November 30. The Union line held, pouring volleys of Minnie balls and canister into the rebel ranks. After dark fell, Schofield withdrew his army to Nashville. Hood won a pyrrhic victory, having driven off the enemy but suffering 6,252 casualties to Schofield's 2,326; among the dead was Patrick Cleburne, among the greatest southern division commanders.

Hood marched on to deploy his army before Nashville. With around 25,000 troops, he tried to besiege Thomas with 55,000 troops in the entrenchments and forts ringing Nashville. Thomas had failed to march to Schofield's support at Franklin. Had he done so, the Union army would have steamrolled Hood. Now he waited passively within his defenses as Hood's men erected their own breastworks and Grant repeatedly implored him to attack.

Thomas methodically devised an attack plan. On the morning of December 15, two weeks after Hood appeared before him, Thomas finally launched his army against Hood's with feints on the enemy right and center and a massive assault on the left. Despite being outgunned more than two to one, the rebels repelled the attacks. Thomas resumed the assault the next day, and this time the Union troops finally routed the rebels inflicting 6,000 casualties while suffering 3,061. Grant urged Thomas ruthlessly to pursue Hood but he advanced no further than the Duck River before ending the chase on December 29. Hood withdrew to Decatur, arriving with 20,000 or half the number he started with 6 weeks earlier. He resigned on January 13, 1865. President Davis replaced him with General Richard Taylor.

Atlanta's destruction began during the siege with the Union bombardment. Part of the city was destroyed on the night of September 2 when retreating rebels detonated 81 train cars packed with munitions to prevent their capture. On September 7, Sherman expelled all 20,000 of the city's inhabitants. After more than two months of Union occupation, Sherman ordered burned any buildings that might aid the Confederate war effort including the train station, city hall, warehouses, cotton mills, machine shops, and gristmills; the fires spread to destroy hundreds of private homes and businesses.

With black smoke darkening the sky behind them, Sherman and his army began their march to the sea on November 12.[35] He recalled their jubilant first day:

> We turned our horses' heads to the east; Atlanta was soon lost behind the screen of trees, and became a thing of the past. Around it clings many a thought of desperate battle, of hope and fear, that now seems like the memory of a dream ... The day was extremely beautiful, clear sunlight, with bracing air, and an unusual feeling of exhilaration seemed to pervade all minds – a feeling of something to come, vague and undefined, still full of venture and intense interest.

He knew that the campaign he and his men had embarked on was perhaps unique in history, with:

> Two hostile armies marching in opposite directions, each in the full belief that it was achieving a final and conclusive result in a great war, and I was strongly inspired with the feeling that the movement on our part was a direct attack upon the rebel army and the rebel capital at Richmond, though a full thousand miles of hostile territory intervened, and that, for better or worse, it would end the war.[36]

His army numbered 62,000 troops split among 4 corps. He divided them into two wings commanded by Generals Oliver Howard and John Slocum that marched on parallel roads toward Savannah 250 miles southeast. Each corps had around 800 ammunition, supply, and ambulance wagons packed with 10 days of provisions and 40 rounds for each of the 68 cannons. He ordered his men to carry forty rounds each, live off the land, and destroy anything that supported the rebel cause except private homes. His soldiers, soon called "bummers," gleefully followed orders. They looted and burned their way day after day across a swath of Georgia that ranged from 30 to 60 miles wide. Eventually around 25,000 blacks escaped their masters to follow Sherman's army and pillage anything that evaded the soldiers. By one estimate, Sherman's men "confiscated 6,871 mules and horses, 13,294 head of cattle, 10.4 million pounds of grain, and 10.7 million pounds of fodder as Georgia farmers unwillingly contributed about 6 million rations of beef, bread, coffee, and sugar."[37]

The only enemy troops between the Army of the Tennessee and Savannah were 3,500 cavalrymen led by Joe Wheeler and local militia companies. Skirmishes occasionally flared but mostly the rebels fled before the Federal juggernaut. Savannah was defended by 10,000 troops led by General William Hardee. Sherman reached Savannah's outskirts on December 10. His troops captured Fort McAllister that guarded the Ogeechee River below the city on December 13. With the blockade fleet now free to steam directly upstream, Hardee and his men fled north into South Carolina on December 20. The Army of the Tennessee marched into Savannah the next day. Sherman's victorious campaign had cost him merely 103 killed, 428 wounded, and 278 prisoners. Yet, as with Hood at Atlanta, he captured a city not Hardee's army.

Sherman sent Lincoln this celebratory message: "I beg to present you, as a Christmas gift, the city of Savannah, with 150 heavy guns and … about 25,000 bales of cotton." To Halleck, he explained the logic behind his total war campaign that destroyed Atlanta and anything of military value from there to the sea:

We are not only fighting hostile armies, but a hostile people, and must make old and young, rich and poor, feel the hard hand of war, as well as their organized armies. I know this recent movement of mine through Georgia has had a wonderful effect in this respect. Thousands who had been deceived by their lying papers into the belief that we were being whipped all the time, realized the truth.[38]

Chapter 16

Traitors

Espionage is said to rival prostitution as the world's oldest profession. Regardless, certainly one's interests are better defended or enhanced the better informed one is about the intentions and power of one's foes and friends. That applies to individuals and their respective groups whether they are devoted to family, tribe, business, revolution, terrorism, or nation, to name the more prominent. National intelligence involves collecting, analyzing, and using information critical to defending or enhancing one's national interests. Military intelligence vitally concerns learning the deployments, numbers, and intentions of enemy forces, and secondarily their supplies and morale. Covert actions are secret attempts to influence an adversary's political, economic, or military power that can include sabotage and subversion. Deception is crucial to shield one's operations and mislead the enemy. That includes making secret codes for oneself and breaking the enemy's secret codes, and successfully running spies in enemy territory and catching the enemy's spies in one's own territory. During the Civil War, the North and South conducted the full array of espionage and covert operations.[1]

When the war began, the United States had no organization that conducted intelligence or covert actions. The State, War, and Navy Departments each had a bureau of several men who collected and analyzed information but almost exclusively from open sources. None of them trained and deployed intelligence officers covertly to steal foreign documents, recruit prominent foreigners to betray their countries by revealing secrets vital to American interests, and conduct covert actions. Nor did any have departments devoted to catching foreign spies. Each army and smaller forces were responsible for collecting, analyzing, and wielding their own intelligence.

For all that, Allan Pinkerton, who headed a detective agency in Chicago, filled the void for what became the Army of the Potomac. The Central Illinois Railroad commissioned Pinkerton to provide security for Abraham Lincoln during his whistle-stop journey from Springfield on February 11 to Washington on February 23. Learning of an assassination plot in Baltimore, Pinkerton had Lincoln wear a disguise and take an earlier train that got him there midnight the day before he was expected to appear. A coach conveyed him across Baltimore from the north to the south station where he boarded a train for the capital.

Pinkerton also discovered a plot for a mob to disrupt the Electoral College vote on February 13; General Winfield Scott deployed enough troops around the Capitol to deter any attack.

In Washington, Pinkerton established a twenty-four man organization with five spies in Richmond gathering intelligence. Only one of his agents, Timothy Webster, was caught, tried, found guilty, and executed for espionage. Yet ultimately, Pinkerton's agency failed at espionage. He grossly exaggerated rebel troop numbers by at least 50 percent more than their actual numbers. General McClellan then further bloated those numbers to give himself an excuse for inaction, claiming he faced twice more foes than his own troops.

General Joseph Hooker established a Bureau of Military Information on February 4, 1863. To lead it, he tapped Colonel George Sharpe, a prewar New York lawyer who had traveled overseas and spoke several foreign languages.[2] Sharpe worked closely with cavalry commanders and civilian informants to gather intelligence. He evaluated and integrated intelligence from an array of sources including spies, deserters, prisoners, refugees, escaped slaves, cavalry scouts, enemy newspapers, tapped telegraph lines, and observers in hot air balloons. He assigned a Signal Corps team to observe and learn the Confederate flag alphabet and thus its messages. He also ran agents behind enemy lines, many with covers as smugglers to gain them welcome and underwrite their expenses. One of his most informative was Elizabeth Van Lew, a wealthy Richmond spinster who knew President Davis and other leading officials. Sharpe's estimates of rebel troop strength were far more accurate than Pinkerton's. When Ulysses Grant took command, he placed the Military Intelligence Bureau under the Provost Marshal and made Sharpe the deputy.

One technical advantage the Army of the Potomac enjoyed was aerial reconnaissance. In good weather on a stalled front, hot-air balloons rose above the Union lines to roughly 500ft with a rope tethering them to the ground. Inside the basket, two men with a telescope noted the disposition of enemy troops and estimated their numbers. Although the South also deployed hot-air balloons, theirs were not as reliable or numerous.

The Confederacy exploited the same array of intelligence sources as the United States. They were superior in two methods. Confederate cavalry ranged further and usually outrode and outshot any Union cavalry they encountered, and so could gather more information. Another advantage was that spies infested Union troops wherever they marched, camped, or occupied across the South. General William Sherman explained the conundrum: "Our enemies have a great advantage in the fact that in our midst, in our camps, and along our avenues of travel, they have active partisans, farmers, and businessmen who seemingly pursue their usual calling, but are in fact spies. They report all our movements and strength, while we can procure information only by circuitous and unreliable means."[3] A study of Federal and Confederate operations found thirteen and twelve successes and nine and six failures, respectively.[4]

The most famous if not successful rebel spy was Rose O'Neal Greenhow, a widow and Washington socialite who charmed ranking officers, officials, and politicians into revealing secrets that she then had couriers carry to General Pierre Beauregard. Her most important message was General Irwin McDowell's pending march against Manassas in July 1861. Pinkerton got wind of her espionage, had her watched, and then arrested on August 23. A search of her home uncovered eight intelligence reports and a cypher code. Her gender saved her from being tried, found guilty, and executed. Instead, she was placed under house arrest. Despite that restriction, she kept collecting information and having it carried South. Caught again she was sent to Old Capitol Prison in January 1862. Lincoln had her expelled to the rebel lines in May 1862. That effectively ended her time as a spy. She became a southern celebrity.

President Lincoln had to fight the war Janus-faced, at once overseeing the war against the Confederacy and the possibility of subversion, sabotage, and outright rebellion on the home front.[5] Although Republicans dominated Congress, they battled Democrats for control over state governorships and assemblies.[6] Democrats split between majority War and minority Peace factions, with the latter openly sympathetic to the Confederacy, slavery, and peace at any price.

American patriots contemptuously likened Peace Democrats to poisonous "copperhead" snakes that hid in the undergrowth and sank their fangs into passersby.[7] Many Peace Democrats not only proudly called themselves Copperheads but defiantly wore copper badges bearing the Goddess of Liberty cut from a copper penny. Copperhead groups included the underground pro-Confederate Sons of Liberty, Knights of the Golden Circle, and Order of American Knights. To counter Copperheads, American patriots formed the Union League and the Loyal Publication Society.

During the 1862 midterm election, Democrats won the governorships of New York, New Jersey, Pennsylvania, Ohio, Indiana, and Illinois, and the New York and New Jersey assemblies. Nonetheless, Republicans controlled the other governorships and sixteen legislatures among the free states. Peace Democrats captured the lower houses of Illinois and Indiana, and issued resolutions calling for a truce and peace talks with the Confederacy, and demanding that Lincoln retract the Emancipation Proclamation. Indiana Governor Oliver Morton was a War Democrat loyal to the United States but many of his state's legislators were not. The Indiana legislature's resolution actually called for "acknowledging the Southern Confederacy and urging the states of the Northwest to dissolve all constitutional relations with the New England states."

Union troops hated Copperheads who sought to cancel all their sacrifices by embracing the Confederacy. After Peace Democrats took over Illinois's legislature, 55 of the state's infantry regiments, 4 of the cavalry regiments, and 4 artillery batteries representing 50,000 troops issued petitions that condemned any word of armistice and compromise with the rebels, while 22 units offered to march to Springfield and arrest the Copperhead politicians.[8]

Clement Vallandigham was the most outspoken Peace Democrat.[9] He had served three terms as an Ohio congressman when he lost his reelection campaign in 1862. In 1863, he campaigned to be Ohio's governor on a platform of armistice, peace negotiations, and condemnation of Lincoln and his administration. After he made a fiery speech on May 1, General Ambrose Burnside, the Department of the Ohio's commander, had him arrested at his home in Dayton but could not find a violated law with which to charge him. That provoked his followers to burn the local Republican newspaper office, while Vallandigham filed for a writ of habeas corpus.

Lincoln recognized that Vallandigham's detention without charges by the military was unconstitutional since civilian courts were operating and Ohio was free of martial law. He thought of a way to get rid of Vallandigham without either releasing him in Ohio or imposing trumped up treason charges against him. On May 26, he had Vallandigham escorted to the rebel lines and freed to join the Confederacy. That too was constitutionally dubious. Lincoln justified his decision by arguing: "Must I shoot a simple-minded soldier boy who deserts, while I must not touch a hair of a wily agitator who induces him to desert? ... I think that in such a case to silence the agitator and save the boy is not only constitutional, but withal a great mercy."[10]

Vallandigham made his way to Canada then back to Ohio in time to attend the state's Democratic convention that issued resolutions demanding an immediate cease-fire and peace talks with the Confederacy. The Sons of Liberty named Vallandigham its president. Lincoln learned of his return but wisely chose to leave him alone to avoid making him a martyr. Actually, a conspiracy existed in which Vallandigham's expected arrest was supposed to trigger a Copperhead uprising. Astonishingly, Vallandigham won the Democratic Party's nomination for governor in 1863, although he lost the election with 187,492 votes to War Democrat John Brough's 288,374. Yet, that revealed the depth of anti-war and pro-rebel sentiment in Ohio.

The Confederacy suffered an array of Unionist enclaves, mostly in mountainous regions with few slaves like western Virginia, eastern Tennessee, northern

Alabama, northern Georgia, and western North Carolina. Jones County in southern Mississippi was mostly marshland, but was still Unionist. Unionist strongholds strengthened as deserters fled there.[11]

Yet, of Unionist regions, only Virginia's broke away to become a new state.[12] On June 20, 1861, a convention at Wheeling denounced the secessionist vote in Richmond, declared itself the rightful government, and elected Francis Pierpont governor and symbolically two senators to Congress. The convention declared the state of West Virginia with its capital at Wheeling on August 6, 1861, subject to popular approval. On August 24, the referendum passed by 18,404 to 781 votes. The next step was to draft a constitution that began on November 26, was finished on February 18, and approved by 18,162 to 514 votes on April 11, 1862. West Virginia applied for statehood to Congress on May 13. Congress passed a law approving statehood if West Virginia amended its constitution to outlaw slavery. West Virginia did so on March 26, 1863 and Lincoln proclaimed its statehood on June 20, 1863. West Virginia elected two senators and three representatives who took their seats in Congress on July 13, 1863.

Lincoln replied to criticisms of hypocrisy for allowing West Virginia's secession from Virginia:

> The division of a state is dreaded as a precedent. But a measure made expedient by a war is no precedent for times of peace. It is said that the admission of West Virginia is secession, and tolerated only because it is our secession. Well, if we call it by that name, there is still difference enough between secession against the Constitution and secession in favor of the Constitution.[13]

East Tennessee nearly seceded from the rest of the state. Secession bitterly divided the state.

During the referendum on June 8, 1861, more than twice as many across the state voted in favor – 104,913 to 47,238 – but more than twice as many in the eastern region, voted to remain American – 32,923 to 14,780. East Tennessee's Unionist leaders called for a convention at Greeneville to consider seceding from the state on June 17. Greeneville was the hometown of loyalist Senator Andrew Johnson. The 292 delegates issued a declaration of loyalty to the United States:

> The Constitution of the United States has done us no wrong. The Congress of the United States has made no threat against the law-abiding people of Tennessee. Under the Constitution of the United States, we have enjoyed as a nation more of civil and religious freedom than any other people under the whole Heaven … The cause of secession has no charm for us, and its

progress has been marked by the most alarming and dangerous attacks upon the public liberty. In other states, as well as our own, its whole course threatens to annihilate the last vestige of freedom.

They then voted to petition Nashville for permission to secede but meekly stayed put when the state government rejected their petition. The region's 297,596 people included 27,539 slaves. Whether they wanted to remain American or join the rebellion, nearly all whites initially opposed abolition, fearing it would lead to anarchy and economic collapse.[14]

After Union forces overran and occupied a state, Lincoln appointed a military governor to administer it and organize its unionists for self-rule once they surpassed 10 percent of those who voted in the 1860 election. The first came on March 3, 1862, when he issued Andrew Johnson the rank of brigadier general and made him Tennessee's governor with the power to appoint civilian officials who took a loyalty oath to the United States, organize a constitutional convention, and suspend habeas corpus under America's Constitution.

The trouble with Tennessee and other states that received military governors like Louisiana, North Carolina, Louisiana, Arkansas, Virginia, and Texas was that they remained battlegrounds throughout the war. As rump states, their provisional governments lacked legitimacy in the eyes of most people living there. Atop that were widespread complaints of corruption, incompetence, and brutality for each occupation government. All that crimped their progress toward rejoining the United States. Meanwhile, two territories transformed themselves into states, Kansas on January 29, 1861 and Nevada on October 10, 1864.

Guerilla warfare involves small groups of usually ununiformed men behind the lines attacking both enemy soldiers and civilians, and looting or destroying both public and private property. Between attacks, guerillas usually disperse among the population. Enemy forces rarely catch guerrillas. Most people where guerillas hide are either sympathetic or terrorized so they refuse to reveal their whereabouts.

During America's Civil War, guerillas were almost exclusively a rebel phenomenon.[15] Nowhere was the guerrilla fighting more destructive and murderous than in western Missouri. The war for neighboring Kansas in the 1850s never ended but instead spread into Missouri where it swelled in scale and viciousness. A common rebel tactic was wearing Union uniforms, riding in among a group of Union troops camped or marching, and slaughtering them. William Quantrill, his associate "Bloody Bill" Anderson, and their gang that included Jesse and Frank James committed the most atrocities. Quantrill's usual order was "to kill every man big enough to carry a gun." Their worst came at Lawrence, Kansas on August 21, 1863, when Quantrill and 500 guerrillas murdered 182 men and burned 185 buildings. Their second worst was at Centralia, Missouri on September 27, 1864, when Anderson and 80 bushwhackers captured and murdered 24 soldiers then ambushed and killed 124 of 147 militiamen who pursued them.

Guerilla warfare's anarchic and rapacious nature provokes mass paranoia, rage, hatred, and desire for vengeance. Union General Clinton Fisk, who commanded a Union garrison at St Joseph, Missouri, expressed that pathology: "There is scarcely a citizen in the county but wants to kill someone of his neighbors for fear that said neighbor may kill him."[16] To deter and punish guerrillas, Federal commanders in Missouri asserted ever-harsher measures against them. General Henry Halleck issued on March 13, 1862 this order: "All persons are hereby warned that if they join any guerrilla band they will not, if captured, be treated as ordinary prisoners of war, but will be hung as robbers and murders."[17] On June 23, 1862, General John Schofield imposed a statewide Board of Assessment to extract taxes from all rebel supporters who refused to sign a loyalty oath to the United States. The Lawrence massacre prompted General Thomas Ewing, the regional commander, to issue on August 25, 1864, an order that forced all civilians to evacuate four Missouri counties bordering Kansas; more than 20,000 people became refugees.

Richmond's policy toward guerrillas changed as high officials debated whether morality or necessity should prevail. On June 18, 1861, Adjutant General Robert Chilton ordered all guerrilla units to join the nearest regular unit. On March 19, 1862, War Secretary Judah Benjamin declared that: "Guerilla companies are not recognized as part of the military organization of the Confederate States, and cannot be authorized by this Department."[18] Then, on April 28, 1862, Richmond issued the Partisan Ranger Act that offered commissions for leaders who raised companies to operate behind enemy lines.

Of the partisan forces raised, the most effective was led by Colonel John Mosby, known as "the Grey Ghost," who for several years launched hit and run attacks against Union forces in northern Virginia.[19] He and his men wore uniforms, took prisoners, and respected civilians. Among his greatest coups was leading twenty-nine men to capture General Edwin Stoughton, thirty-two other soldiers, and fifty-eight horses at Fairfax County Courthouse on March 15, 1863.

Mosby was an exception among "partisan rangers." Confederate General Thomas Rosser complained that guerrillas "were a nuisance and an evil" lacking "discipline, order, or organization; they roam ... over the country, a band of thieves, stealing ... and doing every manner of ... crime. They are a terror to the citizens and an injury to the cause."[20] The Confederate government abolished all ranger units except Mosby's and another led by Captain John McNeill on April 21, 1864. That did not prevent the gangs from continuing their depredations.

President Davis and the Confederate Congress authorized and funded several guerilla operations in the North.[21] On February 15, 1864, they authorized $5 million for an operation led by Captain Thomas Hines to organize saboteurs, Confederate prisoner escapes, peace groups, and sympathizers across the North. He and his men managed to torch half a dozen steamboats at St Louis, an army warehouse at Mathoon, Illinois, and on November 25, 1864, start nineteen fires in buildings across New York City. Hines's most ambitious operation was gathering seventy armed men to overwhelm the guards and liberate the prisoners at Camp Douglas near Chicago. He had to cancel the attack when police arrested some of his men and learned of the plot. For the same reasons Thompson called off an attack on a prison camp near Indianapolis. On October 18, 1864, Lieutenant Bennett Young led nineteen men from Canada to nearby St Albans, Vermont, forced the townspeople to hand over $200,000, burned several buildings, killed a man who resisted, then fled back across the border.

The only significant guerilla operation the Union launched became known as Andrew's Raid or the Great Locomotive Race.[22] James Andrew was a Union spy who repeatedly penetrated rebel lines as a quinine salesman, gathered information, then returned to Union lines. He conceived a plan to sabotage the railroad running between Atlanta and Chattanooga that supplied General Braxton Bragg's army. He and twenty-one volunteers separately made their way to Marietta, Georgia by April 12, 1862, boarded a northbound train, hijacked it at Big Shanty, and chugged away. They had intended to wreck trestles and cut telegraph wires behind them but a group of railroad workers and soldiers pursued them on another train. The raiders abandoned their train just short of the Tennessee border and scattered in the woods. Soldiers soon captured them. Eventually eight, including Andrews, were hanged as spies, eight escaped, and six were exchanged. President Lincoln issued all twenty-one raiders the Congressional Medal of Honor.

Guerilla warfare was extremely effective in draining Union troops and supplies. Just a few score guerillas that periodically attacked isolated supply depots, garrisons, and troop trains forced the Union to divert hundreds or even thousands of troops to search for them. General Sherman explained the dilemma of having to fight both front and rear where guerillas operate: "Though our armies pass across and through the land, the war closes in behind and leaves the same enemy behind. We attempt to occupy places, and the people rise up and make the detachments prisoners."[23]

Lincoln understood that victory ultimately depended on winning the hearts and minds of most rebels. His instructions to General John Schofield revealed the balance he sought between military and political goals: "Let your military measures be strong enough to repel the invader and keep the peace, and not so strong as to unnecessarily harass and persecute the people. It is a difficult role, and so much great will be the honor if you perform it well."[24]

President Lincoln's most controversial acts involved his suspensions of habeas corpus or the right for criminal suspects to be freed from arrest if authorities make no formal charges against them.[25] The Constitution's Article I, Section 9 permits suspension only when "in cases of Rebellion or Invasion the public safety may require it." He first did so on April 27, 1861 for arrests of suspected saboteurs of the railroad and telegraph between Philadelphia and Washington. That literally proved too narrow as sabotage and agitation by Confederate sympathizers spread over the border and northern states. On September 24, 1862, he extended the suspension across the entire country for "all persons discouraging volunteer enlistments, resisting militia drafts, or guilty of any disloyal practice affording aid and comfort to the rebels." Eventually the provost marshals arrested and imprisoned without trial of "several hundred draft resisters and antiwar activists, including five newspaper editors, three judges, and several minor political leaders."[26]

Supreme Court Justice Roger Taney, notorious for his 1857 Dred Scott decision, condemned Lincoln for suspending habeas corpus.[27] He argued that Lincoln violated the Constitution because the authority to suspend appears in the First Article about Congressional powers rather than the Second Article about presidential powers. Lincoln justified his act by arguing that Congress was not in session when the rebellion erupted so as commander-in-chief he suspended habeas corpus then received Congress's approval after it reconvened. In doing so, he helped save rather than violate the Constitution and republic. He rhetorically asked:

> Was it possible to lose the nation and yet preserve the constitution? By general law, life and limb must be protected; yet often a limb must be amputated to save a life; but a life is never wisely given to save a limb. I felt that the measures, otherwise unconstitutional, might become lawful, by becoming indispensable to the preservation of the nation.[28]

Congress passed the Habeas Corpus Act on March 3, 1863, that permitted the suspension of habeas corpus but required civilians to be tried in civilian not military courts. War Secretary Stanton defied that law and ordered military authorities to arrest any dissenters and hold them indefinitely without trial. In doing so, biographer William Marvel explained that Stanton essentially "abolished the First Amendment, overrode the Fourth, ignored the Fifth, and eviscerated the Sixth. He essentially criminalized every American's right to

Traitors   175

criticize the government."²⁹ In the 1866 Milligan case, the Supreme Court ruled unconstitutional the trial of civilians in military courts if civilian courts are functioning.

After that round of mass arrests appeared to quell the threat, Lincoln lifted the suspension. Dissent steadily spread and grew more subversive. Lincoln again suspended habeas corpus on September 15, 1863. Overall, the Lincoln administration arrested and held without charges 13,535 civilians during the war. Of 4,271 trials, 1,940 or 45.4 percent were in Border States, 1,339 or 31.4 percent in occupied regions of rebel states, and 212 or 5.0 percent in northern states. They also censored or suspended over 300 newspapers accused of printing seditious editorials or secret information that gave aid and comfort to the enemy.³⁰

Lincoln asked General-in-Chief Halleck to draft a law of war code to guide Federal officers and soldiers alike.³¹ On August 6, 1863, Halleck transferred that task to Francis Lieber, a distinguished legal scholar, who gathered and chaired a six-man committee of other experts. On April 24, 1863, the War Department issued *Instructions for the Governance of Armies of the United States in the Field*, soon popularly known as Lieber's Code, as General Orders Number 100. The 157 articles listed crimes like robbery, rape, maiming, arson, murder, and espionage; defined procedures for requisitioning private property with compensation; required prisoners to be well housed and fed; forbad torture, poisoning, assassination, gratuitous cruelty, slavery, confiscations for private gain, and the destruction of schools, hospitals, museums, and libraries; formed commissions to try all offenses including enemy spies and guerillas; and permitted takeovers and use of enemy property. Otherwise, any acts were justified by "military necessity" or "those measures which are indispensable for securing the ends of the war." Five thousand copies of Lieber's Code were distributed to officers. The Lieber Code became the foundation for international law of war developed through the Hague Conventions of 1899 and 1907, and Geneva Conventions of 1948 and 1977, Convention against Torture of 1985, and International Criminal Court Treaty of 1998.

Among Lincoln's most onerous duties was determining whether soldiers condemned to death for various crimes might be pardoned. He carefully examined the trial transcripts and pardoned hundreds. Eventually 252 soldiers were executed for capital crimes during the war, including 141 chronic deserters.³² On March 11, 1865, he issued a Proclamation Offering Pardon to Deserters if they reported to duty within sixty days until May 10; otherwise they would forfeit their citizenship rights. It is unlikely many men took advantage of that amnesty as the war ended before the deadline.

Chapter 17

The 1865 Campaigns

D uring his 1864 reelection campaign, President Abraham Lincoln tried to counter the peace movement by announcing his willingness to grant rebels amnesty but only after the Confederate states abolished slavery and rejoined the United States. That, of course, diametrically opposed President Jefferson Davis's insistence that the United States recognize Confederate independence and slavery. Nonetheless, for propaganda, Davis dispatched Clement Clay and James Holcombe to Niagara Falls, Canada for peace talks. Lincoln sent his secretary John Hay and Horace Greeley, the *New York Tribune*'s editor, to meet them. The delegations merely expressed their respective irreconcilable positions. That let Lincoln and Davis accuse each other of intransigence. Lincoln explained that standoff to Congress: "He cannot voluntarily reaccept the Union; we cannot voluntarily yield it. Between him and us the issue is … inflexible. It is an issue which can only be tried by war, and decided by victory."[1]

In early February 1865, Davis sent word that he wanted to negotiate the war's end. Lincoln hurried Secretary of State William Seward to General Ulysses Grant's headquarters at City Point where the talks would occur. Davis selected a high-level delegation that included Vice President Alexander Stephens, President *pro tem* of the Senate Robert Hunter, and Secretary of War John Campbell. But he dispatched them with these words: "Say to Mr. Lincoln … that I shall at any time be pleased to receive proposals for peace on the basis of our Independence. It will be useless to approach me with any other."[2]

The envoys crossed the lines at Petersburg and were escorted to Grant's headquarters at City Point on February 2. Hoping to sway Stephens, an old friend from their time as congressmen, Lincoln sent word that he would join Seward in the talks to be held aboard the steamboat *River Queen* on February 3. Although their meeting began amiably enough, they soon talked past each other. The envoys demanded recognition of the Confederacy's independence while the president insisted on capitulation, abolition, and reunification. Lincoln promised $400,000,000 in compensation to slaveowners for liberating their chattel, but the envoys rejected that notion. Lincoln reluctantly ended the talks and had the envoys escorted back to the Confederate lines. Davis used the failed diplomacy to boost the rebel will to fight on, informing Congress that: "The enemy refused to enter into negotiations with the Confederate states or with any of them separately, or to give to our people any other terms or guaranties than those which the conqueror may grant, or to permit us to have [peace] on any other basis than our unconditional submission to their rule."[3]

Wilmington lay on the Cape Fear River's north bank 28 miles upstream of its mouth on the Atlantic. By late 1864, Wilmington was the last major port for blockade-runners. From Wilmington extended a slender peninsula like an arm that ended in a fist. Atop that fist sat Fort Fisher bristling with 47 cannons and 2,000 troops. Defending Wilmington were 6,400 troops led by General Robert Hoke. He deployed them on Sugar Loaf Hill 4 miles north of Fort Fisher.

An armada of 60 warships and transports packed with 6,500 troops anchored just beyond range of Fort Fisher's cannons in late December 1864. Admiral David Porter commanded the vessels and General Benjamin Butler the soldiers. Butler was just as inept in his latest command as he was in previous ones. His plan was to pack 215 tons of gunpowder in a ship and detonate it near the fort. On December 24, the explosion damaged nothing more than countless eardrums. The warships bombarded Fort Fisher but the sand walls absorbed most of the shells. Butler landed his troops on the peninsula wrist's north beach just beyond the fort's cannon range then reembarked them when the fort appeared only lightly damaged. Lincoln relieved Butler of command and replaced him with General Alfred Terry on January 8.

The warships pounded Fort Fisher as Terry disembarked a mixed force of 8,000 soldier, sailors, and marines on the wrist's north beach on January 13. He split his men with half to assault the fort and the other half to face any attack by Hoke and his men. Over three days, the warships bombarded the fort and knocked out all but four of its guns. Terry ordered an assault on January 15. The defenders inflicted casualties of 684 on the soldiers and 393 on the marines and sailors, but suffered 583 before the survivors surrendered.

Grant had trains convey General John Schofield's 20,000-man Army of the Ohio from Nashville to Washington where they embarked on transports bound for the armada in the Cape Fear River. Schofield's orders were to take Wilmington then march to join General William Sherman at Goldsboro, a strategic rail juncture. Hoke withdrew before Schofield's overwhelming army and abandoned Wilmington. The Union troops marched into Wilmington on February 22.

Elsewhere, Mobile remained in rebel hands even though Admiral David Farragut's fleet was anchored in Mobile Bay and Union troops occupied the three forts. Grant had three forces converge on Mobile, General Edward Canby with 20,000 troops from New Orleans, 8,000 cavalry from Vicksburg, and 13,480 cavalry led by General James Wilson from Eastport Mississippi. Outnumbered two to one, Mobile's defenders withdrew from the city on April 8. By mid-April, Union forces controlled Mobile and most other Alabama cities.

After resting in Savannah for 6 weeks, Sherman and his 60,000 troops resumed their march on February 1. The plan was to devastate South Carolina as thoroughly as they had a swath of Georgia then head to Goldsboro, North Carolina, where they would rendezvous with Schofield's army marching from Wilmington. By one count as they marched north, Sherman's "foragers stripped the countryside of at least 7 million pounds of foodstuffs, 11.6 million pounds of corn, 83 million pounds of fodder, and 11,825 horses and mules."[4]

The first major objective was Columbia, South Carolina's capital. On February 17, as Sherman's army approached, the rebel defenders ignited cotton bales to prevent their capture. The fires spread, burning down much of the downtown. Sherman had his men try to suppress the fire. Terrified that Charleston would suffer the same fate as Atlanta and Columbia, the defenders surrendered to the blockade fleet on February 18.

Sherman rested his troops in Columbia several weeks before heading north again in early March. Grant ordered General George Stoneman with 5,000 cavalry at Knoxville to join forces with Sherman in North Carolina. General Pierre Beauregard commanded the remaining Confederate troops in North Carolina until February 23, when President Davis replaced him with Joe Johnston. At most, Johnston could muster about 20,000 troops. Outnumbered three to one, Johnston could merely fight delaying battles at Averasborough on March 16 and Bentonville on March 19 and 21, while cavalry led by Wade Hampton and Joe Wheeler harassed the Union advance. Sherman did not press his attacks but instead sought to maneuver Johnston into a position where he had to surrender.

President Lincoln met with Generals Grant and Sherman on March 27 at City Point, where they discussed how to end the war as swiftly and decisively as possible. Sherman recalled that:

> Grant and myself supposed that one or the other of us would have to fight one more bloody battle, and that it would be the last. Mr. Lincoln exclaimed, more than once, that there had been blood enough shed, and asked us if another battle could not be avoided. I remember well to have said that we could not control that event; that this necessarily rested with our enemy.[5]

Indeed, General Robert Lee initiated the climatic final campaign replete with battles.[6] He recognized that his ability to hold Petersburg was increasingly imperiled. It was only a matter of time before Grant sent Phil Sheridan's cavalry corps and an infantry corps westward to outflank and sever the Confederate retreat. Meanwhile, Sherman's army was steadily driving General Johnston's army further north. Lee sought to divert Grant with a spoiling attack on Fort Stedman on the eastern part of the defense lines. Early on the morning of March 25, General John Gordan's division attacked and overran the fort. General John Parke, the local Union commander, massed his reserves and counterattacked, routing the rebels. In all the Confederates suffered 4,000 casualties and the Federals only 1,044.

Grant ordered Sheridan's cavalry corps and Gouverneur Warren's 5th corps to dash westward on March 29.[7] Lee dispatched General George Pickett to head them off at Five Forks. Sheridan routed Pickett and overran the rail line on April 1, inflicting 2,950 casualties while suffering 830. With Lee's army stretched to the physical and emotional breaking point, Grant ordered the entire army to assault all along the line on April 2. The Union troops broke through and scattered the Confederates. Davis granted Lee's request to abandon the Petersburg and Richmond defenses and quick-march his army westward toward Danville. After ordering anything in the capital of military value burned or blown up, Davis and the rest of his government and their families fled with the army.

Lincoln and Grant triumphantly toured Petersburg on April 3. Lincoln elatedly told Admiral Porter: "Thank God I have lived to see this. It seems to me that I have been dreaming a horrid dream for four years, and now the nightmare is gone."[8] On April 4, he had troops escort him to Richmond where exuberant and awed blacks followed him as their Moses amidst the city's desolation.

Sheridan's corps relentlessly advanced and overran the Danville–Richmond railroad track on April 5. Lee was with his 35,000 remaining troops at Amelia Courthouse when he learned that route was severed. His last chance of escape was toward Lynchburg. On April 6, Andrew Humphrey's 2nd Corps attacked Lee's rear guard at Sayler's Creek, and captured 7,700 rebels and much of the supply train while suffering 1,148 casualties. The following day Grant sent Lee a request to surrender to avoid "any further effusion of blood." Lee replied, asking what terms Grant intended. Grant wrote that he would offer Lee the same terms that he granted Pemberton at Vicksburg, parole.

Sheridan cut off Lee's retreat at Appomattox Court House on April 8. Lee and his remaining 28,356 troops were almost entirely surrounded and were down to their last rations and cartridges. Since March 29, he had lost 19,132 troops and 689 cannons.[9] Heartbroken, Lee sent word to Grant that he was ready to meet on the morning of April 9.

The surrender took place in the parlor of Wilbur McLean's house at Appomattox. Immaculate in his dress uniform, Lee arrived with just one staff officer. Grant soon appeared with a dozen staff and leading generals; he was mud splattered and disheveled. As the two generals shook hands and sat down, Grant wondered:

> What General Lee's feelings were, I do not know. As he was a man of much dignity, with an impassible face, it was impossible to say whether he felt inwardly glad that the end had finally come, or felt sad over the result and was too manly to show it … but my own feelings, which had been quite jubilant on the receipt of his letter, were sad and depressed. I felt like anything rather than rejoicing at the downfall of a foe who had fought so long and valiantly, and had suffered so much for a cause, though that cause was … one of the worst for which a people ever fought.

Grant tried to put Lee at ease by recalling their earlier careers including their Mexican War experiences: "Our conversation grew so pleasant that I almost forgot the object of our meeting" until Lee reminded him.[10] Grant called over his secretary Captain Ely Parker, a Seneca, and introduced him to Lee, who remarked, "I am glad to see a real American here." Parker sagely replied, "We are all Americans here."[11]

Grant was generous. He paroled Lee's entire army, let officers keep pistols and swords, and all men with horses their mounts. He had his quartermaster distribute three days of rations to the starving soldiers and issued train passes so that they had free passage home. This moved Lee to say, "This will have the best possible effect upon the men and will do much toward conciliating our people."[12]

President Lincoln related a disturbing dream to his bodyguard Ward Lamon in early April. He heard the sound of weeping and followed it into the White House's East Room where mourners and soldiers crowded around a casket: "'Who is dead in the White House?' I demanded of one of the soldiers. The president,' was his answer: 'he was killed by an assassin!' Then came a loud burst of grief from the crowd, which awoke me from my dream. I slept no more that night."[13] Nearly two weeks later he related another dream, this time to his cabinet on April 14. They were awaiting news that General Sherman had received General Johnston's surrender. Lincoln reassured them that they would soon get word because of a recurring dream he had the previous night that he often had after a great event. He always stood on the deck of a vessel sailing toward a dark unknown shore.

That evening Lincoln and Mary planned to attend a performance of the comedy, *Our American Cousin*, playing at Ford's Theater. Lincoln had asked General Grant and Julia to join them but they already had plans to go to their home in Burlington, New Jersey. Lincoln then invited family friends Major Henry Rathbone and his fiancé Clara Harris. They arrived late at the presidential box seat overlooking the stage. The actors and audience applauded the president then the performance resumed.

John Wilkes Booth was a renowned actor and rabid rebel sympathizer.[14] In early 1865, he formed a cabal of half a dozen or so members to kidnap Lincoln and convey him to the Confederacy. Then on April 11, Booth attended Lincoln's speech in which he spoke about reconstructing the rebel states with slavery abolished and civil rights for blacks. Enraged, he was now deadset on decapitating the American government's leadership with Booth murdering the president, George Atzerodt the vice president, and Lewis Paine the secretary of state at 10 o'clock on the night of April 14.

That evening, the assassins only partly achieved their goal. Outside Andrew Johnson's home, Atzerodt lost his nerve and hurried away. Powell got into Seward's house by claiming he had medicine for the secretary of state who was bedridden. He stabbed but did not kill Seward and stabbed or bludgeoned four other male family members before escaping. Booth entered the presidential box seat, aimed a single-shot derringer at the back of Lincoln's head, and pulled the trigger. The bullet penetrated Lincoln's skull, cut through his brain and exited his jaw. Booth then stabbed Rathbone and jumped to the stage. He broke his leg in the drop, rose, and cried "*Sic semper tyranus*" or "Thus always to tyrants!" He managed to hobble out, mount a horse, and ride off. Lincoln was carried across the street to a boarding house where doctors attended him. He died the next morning.

War Secretary Edwin Stanton took charge of the investigation. Booth evaded capture for twelve days until Union cavalry caught up to him hiding in a barn and shot him on April 26. Eventually eight other conspirators were captured and tried at the Old Arsenal Penitentiary in Washington from May 9 to June 30. The jurors found all eight guilty of conspiracy to assassinate Lincoln and Seward. Four were hanged – Lewis Powell, David Atzerodt, David Herold, and Mary Surratt – on July 7. Three received life prison terms – Michael O'Laughlin, Samuel Arnold, and Samuel Mudd – and Edmund Spangler received a six-year term.

Lincoln's coffined body lay in state in the White House's East Room while 25,000 people filed past. His body then was conveyed to the Capitol where it lay it state under the dome. Finally, his body was taken by train in a 1,700-mile journey with stops for mourners at Baltimore, Harrisburg, Philadelphia,

New York, Albany, Buffalo, Cleveland, Columbus, Indianapolis, Chicago, and, finally, to Springfield where it was interned in Oak Ridge Cemetery on May 4. Staunton was present when Lincoln died and may have expressed Lincoln's most profound elegy: "Now he belongs to the ages."[15]

After Appomattox, the Confederacy's last frail props swiftly collapsed. President Davis was with General Johnston when word arrived of Lee's surrender. Even then, he refused to admit defeat. While "our late disasters are terrible," he insisted that, "we should not regard them as fatal. I think we can whip the enemy yet if our people turn out." He asked Johnston's view. The general replied that "our people are tired of the war, feel themselves whipped, and will not fight."[16]

Angered, Davis left Johnston and with his entourage continued their flight south with no clear destination. At Bennett Place near Durham, North Carolina, Johnston and Sherman negotiated an initial agreement on April 17, whereby all rebel troops in the Carolinas, Georgia, and Florida surrendered and were paroled. Unfortunately, Sherman exceeded instructions and pledged the restoration of civil rights to rebel soldiers and civilians. Grant had him renegotiate the agreement to simply parole and dismiss to their distant homes the 36,817 soldiers solely under Johnston's command. Sherman and Johnston signed that document on April 26. At Citronelle, Alabama, General Richard Taylor surrendered to General Edward Canby all remaining 52,453 rebel troops east of the Mississippi on May 3. Union cavalry captured Jefferson Davis at Irwinville, Georgia on May 10. Acting on behalf of General Kirby Smith, General Simon Buckner surrendered to Canby all rebel troops west of the Mississippi at New Orleans on May 26, 1865.[17]

Two victorious American armies marched in parades amidst cheering crowds down Pennsylvania Avenue, that of the Potomac led by General Meade on May 23 and that of the Tennessee led by General Sherman the next day. Sherman recalled that event with great pride: "It was in my judgement the most magnificent army in existence – sixty-five thousand men, in splendid physique, who had just completed a march of nearly two thousand miles in a hostile country." Now he reveled in: "The steadiness and firmness of the tread … the uniform intervals between the companies, all eyes directly to the front, and the tattered and bullet-riven flags, festooned with flowers."[18]

Chapter 18

Death and Destruction

More Americans died in the Civil War than all of America's other wars combined. At least 360,222 Union and 258,000 Confederates died or one in six and four, respectively of those who served. Atop that carnage, the war killed directly or indirectly at least 50,000 civilians.[1] Casualty rates varied among the armies. In the first dozen battles in which casualties exceeded 6,000, the Federals deployed 809,456 troops and suffered 113,160 losses or 13.9 percent of the total while the Confederate figures were 622,265, 152,841, and 24.6 percent.[2] Battles were much deadlier on the Virginia front than westward. As for the fifty regiments with the highest battle casualties, forty-one of the Union's and forty of the Confederate's fought in Virginia. Union troops in Virginia suffered 23 percent higher combat casualties than their counterparts on western fronts, although death from disease was 43 percent higher for the latter. In battles, Lee actually lost a higher portion of his army than Grant, 20 percent to 16 percent. That was mostly because Lee was usually outgunned. But Lee also launched some disastrous attacks with no chance of success, most notoriously at Malvern Hill, Cemetery Ridge, and Fort Stedman.[3] The South lost a far larger share of its military age men than the North, 31 percent to 16 percent.[4] Officers led from the front, with those killed in action 15 percent and generals 50 percent more likely to be killed than a private. A far worse share of Confederate than Federal generals died in or from battle, 18 percent to 8 percent. A slightly higher portion of Federal than Confederate generals resigned before the war ended, 36 percent to 30 percent.[5] Disease killed twice as many soldiers as combat. The deadliest diseases were dysentery, typhoid, and pneumonia. Although less fatal, malaria and syphilis also plagued troops in certain regions or with certain temptations. Slightly more Confederates than Federals died from their wounds, 18 percent to 14 percent, with gangrene the usual cause.[6]

War	Years	Deaths	Population	Death Portion of Population
Civil War	1861–5	625,000	31,443,000 (1860)	1.988%
World War II	1941–5	405,399	133,402,000 (1940)	0.307%
World War I	1917–18	116,516	103,268,000 (1910)	0.110%
Vietnam War	1961–71	58,209	179,323,175 (1970)	0.030%
Korean War	1950–3	36,516	151,325,000 (1950)	0.020%
American War for Independence	1775–83	25,000	2,500,000 (1780)	0.899%
1812 War	1812–15	15,000	8,000,000 (1810)	0.297%
Mexican War	1846–8	13,283	21,406,000 (1850)	0.002%
Wars against Iraq and Al Qaeda	2001–10	6,717	294,043,000 (2000)	0.002%
Philippine War	1899–1902	4,196	72,129,001 (1900)	0.006%

Figure 18.1: Top Ten American Wars Ranked by Total Number of American Military Deaths[7]

Most combat dead were hastily buried in mass graves near where they fell. On July 16, 1862, Congress passed a law that authorized the Federal government to purchase land for national cemeteries where the war dead were reburied with each grave marked by a simple white stone chiseled with the soldier's name and regiment if known. The reinterment program ended in 1871 after 303,536 soldiers were buried among 74 cemeteries at a cost of $4,000,306.[8] With time, those cemeteries became places of haunting beauty and melancholy. Some families that could afford it were able to get their loved ones disinterred, transported, and buried in their local cemeteries. If the chemicals and time were available, many who died of wounds or disease were embalmed for shipment home. Arlington National Cemetery is the most revered. That land and its mansion was General Robert Lee's when the war began. The Federal government confiscated it and began burying soldiers there in May 1864. Today there are over 400,000 honored dead at Arlington.

Mourning had social rules during the nineteenth century.[9] Widows and widowers mourned for two-and-a-half years and three months, respectively. Women wore all black clothing while men only had to wear a black ribbon around an arm or as a hatband. Mothers mourned a year for her child. Children mourned a year for their parents and six months for their siblings. The tragic deaths of hundreds of thousands of men, mostly young, provoked countless people to question God and others to worship more fervently.[10]

The national holiday of Memorial Day to commemorate the war dead developed from the Decoration Days of cities and states following the Civil War, with Charleston initiating the practice on May 1, 1865. National organizations emerged to lead ceremonies, tend graves, and build monuments, chiefly the North's Grand Army of the Republic and Northern Women's Relief Corps, and the South's the Confederated Southern Memorial Association, United Confederate Veterans, and Daughters of the Confederacy.

Part III

Conflict and Violence, 1865–Present

Chapter 19

Reconstruction and Resistance

Looking back two decades, Ulysses Grant reflected that: "It is probably well that we had the war when we did. We are better off than we would have been without it, and have made more progress than we otherwise should have made ... The war has made us a nation of great power and intelligence."[1] That was certainly true for the free states and the country as a whole.[2]

The defection of slavocrats from Congress to the Confederacy was critical to the passage of an array of bills that enabled the United States not just to crush the rebellion but develop the economy.[3] From 1861 to 1865, Lincoln and Congress crafted a series of bills that established a modern financial system and currency. In 1862 alone, they passed laws that enhanced western settlement, transportation, and education. With the Homestead Act of May 20, a settler would receive 160 acres of public land after living on and improving it for five years and paying a small license fee; before the war ended, Washington transferred title to 5 million acres of public land to homesteaders. With the Morrill Act of July 2, the government created a Department of Agriculture and gave each state 30,000 acres of public land for each congressman and senator for sale solely to finance education. With the Pacific Railroad Act of July 1, Washington would give a corporation 6,400 acres of public land per mile and loans of $16,000 per mile on flat land and $48,000 on mountainous land to build a railroad from Omaha to Sacramento; two companies, the Union Pacific and the Central Pacific, received charters to build railroads toward each other from east and west, respectively. Vermont representative Justin Morrill spearheaded or jointly led the drafting of all these laws.

The North's manpower and production steadily expanded during the war. In his 1864 address to Congress, Lincoln confidently reported that: "We have more men now than we had when the war began; that we ... may, if need be, maintain the contest indefinitely. This as to men. Material resources are now more complete and abundant than ever. The national resources ... are ... inexhaustible."[4] In just four years, the North's economy expanded by 50 percent and the railroad network from 31,000 to 35,000 miles. The Springfield arsenal produced 14,000 rifles in 1861, 102,000 in 1862, 218,000 in 1863, and 276,000 in 1864. The Colt factory made 27,000 pistols in 1861 and 137,000 in 1863. Farm labor shortages encouraged mechanization with mowers, reapers, grain drills, corn planters, and threshers swelling productivity. The number of sheep and wool production more than doubled with 60,000,000lb of wool in 1860 and 140,000,0001b in 1865. Government demand for goods and services comprised around half of the economy. Overall, Washington spent $3.2 billion over four years with the national debt at $2.8 billion in 1865. Although the North's production soared, the average northerner was worse off than before the war as wages and prices rose respectively 43 percent and 117 percent from 1861 to 1865.[5]

The war devastated the South. Historian James McPherson succinctly and vividly conveyed what the defeated rebellion inflicted on the rebels:

> The South was not only invaded and conquered, it was utterly destroyed. By 1865, the Union forces had ... destroyed two-thirds of the assessed value of Southern wealth, two-fifths of the South's livestock, and one-quarter of her white men between the ages of 20 and 40. More than half the farm machinery was ruined, and the damages to railroads and industries were incalculable ... Southern wealth decreased by 60 percent.[6]

The South accounted for 30 percent of the nation's economy in 1860 and 12 percent in 1870. The per capita income of southerners was two-thirds that of northerners in 1860 and two-fifths in 1870. The eleven southern states had $4,363,030,367 worth of wealth in 1860 and $1,603,402,429 in 1865; that loss included $1,634,105,341 worth of nearly 4 million liberated slaves and $1,125,522,577 of other property. The war devastated the South's economy with factories, livestock, crops, and railroads worst hit; in all, the South's agricultural and manufacturing production plummeted 46 percent from 1860 to 1870. The South would not fully recover its 1860 economic level until 1900; by rebelling, slavocrats squandered two generations of their region's wealth.[7]

The American victory immediately brought legal if not national unity. McPherson observed: "Before 1861, the two words 'United States' were generally rendered as a plural noun: 'the United States' are a republic. The war marked a transition of the United States to a singular noun. The 'Union' also became a nation, and Americans now rarely speak of their Union except in an historical sense."[8] As for the notion of being American, for southerners bitter at their loss the embrace of that identity took years for most, decades for others, generations for many, and never occurred for some.

Reconstruction was the process whereby the rebel states were shorn of slavery and reunited with the United States.[9] How to do that was fiercely debated. President Lincoln's views evolved on the South's reconstruction after reunification as they did for all controversial issues as he listened, read, experimented, reflected, and learned. All along, he tried to slow radicals who demanded immediate abolition and civil rights for black men, and hurry conservatives who backed abolition but not immediately civil rights.[10] For most of the war, he was split over what civil rights, if any, blacks should enjoy. He leaned toward granting well-to-do, educated, and veteran black men the right to vote and run for office, while delaying those rights for all others until they reached similar levels of income and schooling in a generation or so. Toward the war's end, he mulled a swifter pace of years rather than generations although he would leave the timetable to each state.

A far more pressing question was what civil rights to restore to former rebels now under Union occupation.[11] For that, he devised a plan to split the South's population and turn the factions against each other, thus weakening the Confederacy while enticing states back into the Union. On December 8, 1862, he offered amnesty, pardon, and restoration of full civil rights except the ownership of slaves for anyone other than ranking rebel politicians and generals who swore a loyalty oath to the United States. After 10 percent of the voting population in 1860 did so, they could form a state government and be readmitted to the United States.

Radical Republicans denounced Lincoln's policy as too lenient. Firebrand Thaddeus Stevens, who chaired the House Ways and Means Committee, insisted that Reconstruction must "revolutionize Southern institutions, habits, and manners. The foundation of their institutions … must be broken up and relaid, or all our blood and treasure have been spent in vain."[12] Senator Benjamin Wade and Representative Henry Davis respectively chaired the Committees on Territories and Reconstruction. They devised the Wade-Davis Bill for "reconstructing" rebel states only after the war ended. States would be readmitted with full equal rights if they abolished slavery and half the male population signed loyalty oaths. Those who attended a state constitutional convention would be limited to those who took an "iron-clad oath" that they never supported the rebellion. Congress passed the Wade-Davis Bill on July 2, 1864. Lincoln pocket-vetoed the bill, explaining that it would undermine the integrity of Arkansas and Louisiana that had already accepted his terms for readmission and discourage other states from doing so. That 10 percent was much more likely than 50 percent to grant black men the right to vote and run for office. For governors to guide the transformation of occupied rebel states, he appointed Andrew Johnson to Tennessee, Edward Stanley to North Carolina, George Shepley to Louisiana, John Phelps to Arkansas, and Andrew Hamilton to Texas; all were former unionist representatives or senators from those states.

Lincoln voiced his last words on reconstruction in a speech on April 11, 1865, three days before his assassination. Typically, he began by explaining the related political, economic, social, and psychological challenges to transforming the South's slavocracy into democracy. He cited Louisiana as a successful example where occupation authorities had worked with unionists to draft a constitution that outlawed slavery and instituted a government. He acknowledged conflicts and mistakes along that path, but lauded Louisiana's unionist leaders for their accomplishments. Louisiana reached Lincoln's 10 percent threshold in 1864, held a convention from April to June, and approved a constitution that abolished slavery, opened the judicial system to equality for blacks with whites, required schooling for black children, let blacks join the militia, and empowered legislators to grant blacks the franchise. He anticipated benefits for both races if all men enjoy full civil rights, and vaguely warned of chronic problems if that did not happen.[13]

He grounded reconstruction on the moral principle that he articulated during his inaugural address a month earlier. In words designed to inspire, sooth, and reconcile all Americans, he declared:

> With malice toward none; with charity toward all; with firmness in the right, as God gives us to see the right, let us strive on to finish the work we are in; to bind up the nation's wounds; to care for him who shall have borne the battle, and for his widow and the orphan – to do all which may achieve and cherish a just and lasting peace among ourselves and with all nations.[14]

Lincoln's greatest contribution to reconstruction was abolition that he achieved in two stages.[15] His first came by proclamation as commander-in-chief, justified as military necessity to weaken the enemy by freeing their slaves from January 1, 1863. That freedom did not extend to the 450,000 slaves in Missouri, Kentucky, Maryland, and Delaware loyal to the United States or the 275,000 slaves in regions of rebel states then under Union control. Nonetheless, it did legally liberate 3 million slaves, although only a portion of them would free themselves or be freed by Union troops before the war's end.

The next was a constitutional amendment that abolished slavery everywhere across the United States. The Constitution can be amended with favorable votes for a proposal by at least two-thirds of both houses of Congress and ratifications by at least three-fourths of the states. Lincoln found sponsors in both houses for the proposed Thirteenth Amendment that abolished slavery and empowered Congress to ensure that happened. When several congressional leaders expressed doubt over whether they could get two key votes and asked his advice, he replied:

I am President of the United States, clothed with great power. The abolition of slavery by constitutional provision settles the fate for all coming time, not only the millions now in bondage, but of unborn millions to come – a measure of such importance that those two votes must be procured. I leave it to you to determine how it shall be done, but … I expect you to procure those votes.[16]

The Senate voted 38 to 6 in favor on April 8, 1864 but the House fell short of the two-thirds threshold. The 1864 election gave Republicans more than two-thirds of the House of Representatives. On January 31, 1865, the House approved the proposal by 119 to 56. For ratification, 27 of the 36 states had to approve. Tragically, Lincoln was murdered before he could savor that triumph. The Thirteenth Amendment surpassed the ratification threshold on December 6 and President Andrew Johnson formally declared it part of the Constitution on December 18, 1865.

Had Lincoln finished his second term, he would undoubtedly have guided the South's reconstruction as skillfully as he did its military defeat. The resistance and violence would have been much less and black civil rights deeper imbedded. Instead, Lincoln's death inaugurated a political tug-of-war between Congressional Radicals who demanded immediate and full black civil rights and President Johnson who would only end slavery.[17]

Johnson was born into poverty then worked his way to wealth as a tailor, businessman, and landowner.[18] He had a distinguished political career as a Tennessee alderman, assemblyman, Congressional representative, two-term governor, and United States senator. Lincoln tapped him first to govern occupied Tennessee then to be his vice president in 1864. Johnson was an unabashed racist who would gradually abolish slavery but deny blacks equal economic, political, and educational opportunities with whites. He explained: "This country is for white men and by God, as long as I am President, it shall be governed by white men."[19] To that end, he vetoed a series of civil rights laws.

Most northerners fell somewhere between those extremes. General William Sherman represented that pragmatic middle ground. He saw the immediate need for liberated blacks was not abstract political rights but land with which to sustain themselves. On January 16, 1865, he issued Special Field Order Number 15 that designated a swath of land from Savannah, Georgia to Jacksonville, Florida from the ocean 30 miles inland to be confiscated from its rebel plantation owners and given to blacks, with each family receiving 40 acres and a mule. He then appointed General Rufus Saxton to implement the order. Over the next year, Saxton distributed land among 40,000 former slaves on 400,000 acres.[20]

General Nathaniel Banks conceived a different plan in occupied Louisiana in January 1863. He negotiated a deal with plantation owners to sign contracts with blacks that guaranteed them $3 a month along with food, shelter, clothing, and medical care in return for full days of work six days a week and not leaving the land without permission. At its peak, the system included 50,000 blacks on 1,500 plantations in Louisiana and 700,000 blacks up the Mississippi River valley. Monthly wages rose to $7 for men and $5 for women. Radicals criticized this system for transforming slaves into serfs and demanded that the land be confiscated and distributed among black families.[21]

After the war, Sherman expressed the nuanced views of countless Americans over how far to liberate blacks from their subjection as slaves or second-class citizens. He genuinely sympathized with black people and sought to improve their lives:

> I will do as much to ameliorate his political and social condition as Mr. Gerrit Smith, Wendell Philips, and Greeley, and others who seem to me mere theorists and not practical workers ... we find plenty of people contending to make negroes voters, and even ... to comingle their blood with ours. On these points I think men may honestly differ very widely and I ... would be slow in going to such extremes. The negro should of course be protected in his industry and encouraged to acquire property, knowledge, trade, and every means possible to better his condition, but I think we should all be rather too slow than too fast in extending political rights. These in turn will adjust themselves according to the laws of Nature and experience ... I believe you and I have done more acts of kindness to the negros of America than all the philanthropists put together; but our acts are quiet and unknown, whereas theirs have been noisy and demonstrative.[22]

Congress passed a bill establishing the Bureau of Refugees, Freedmen, and Abandoned Lands to assist newly emancipated slaves on March 3, 1865. One-armed General Oliver Howard successfully headed the Freedmen's Bureau from May 1865 to July 1874. Most of the Bureau's initial work involved providing food, clothing, and shelter for blacks who had fled their masters. During its first 15 months, the Bureau distributed 13 million rations with each a week's worth of corn meal, flour, and sugar for each person, with two-thirds going to blacks and a third to whites. The Bureau's Freeman's Savings Bank encouraged thrift and enterprise. The 1862 Confiscation Act let the Federal government eventually take title to 850,000 acres either abandoned or forfeited by white owners. The Bureau distributed it in 40-acre sections to black families. The 1866 Southern Homestead Act gave land to unmarried black women. Despite those policies, blacks only got about a third of that land while pardoned owners won back most or all of what they had lost. Most landless blacks became sharecroppers on white plantations and kept one-third of the crop in return for seed, fertilizer, tools, plows, and mules from the owner who extracted two-thirds of production.[23]

Howard recognized that education was critical to the ability of blacks to improve their lives.[24] Before the war, every southern state except Tennessee outlawed teaching slaves to read and write. That left 90 percent of the South's black population illiterate. The Freedmen's Bureau organized 3,000 schools with 150,000 students by 1869. In November 1866, Howard gathered ten philanthropists to found Howard University in Washington with himself as its first president. Other black colleges established during Reconstruction included Atlanta, Fisk, Hampton, and Tugaloo.[25] Private philanthropic groups like the National Freedmen's Relief Association, the New England Freedman's Aid Society, the Western Freedmen's Aid Commission, and the American Missionary Association supplemented the Freedmen's Bureau.

Radical Republicans expanded their domination of Congress in the 1866 election as their House seats rose from 150 to 173 and their Senate seats from 37 to 39. The Democrats also picked up House seats, with their share rising from 33 to 47 while they retained 10 Senate seats. That greater electoral support for Republicans, including Radicals among them, reflected the Union victory that appeared to vindicate abolitionism. Radical Republicans believed that they had won a mandate to impose full civil rights for blacks. They formed the Joint Committee on Reconstruction to oversee this latest crusade as strictly as they had tried to do so for the previous one through the Joint Committee on the War.

President Johnson vehemently opposed that and instead intended to pardon and restore civil rights to all the South's white men whether they took an iron-clad oath or not. He pardoned over 7,000 southerners with prewar wealth over $20,000 that were excluded from the original pardons. Gradually nearly everyone got amnesty. Vice President Alexander Stephens received a pardon after a couple months' incarceration. One exception was President Jefferson Davis who was held without charges in Fort Monroe for two years; on May 11, 1867, he won release when eighteen sympathizers pooled $100,000 for bail money.[26] Only one rebel leader was indicted for any crime. A court found Henry Wirz, Andersonville prison camp's commandant, guilty of war crimes and had him executed on November 10, 1865.

Johnson zealously blocked two Reconstruction bills that Congress passed in 1866. The first was the Freedman Bureau Act that bolstered the original law; Johnston vetoed it on February 19. Although Congress failed to override the veto, it passed another version that Johnson vetoed on June 26 but Congress overrode it on July 16. On March 13, Congress passed the Civil Rights Act that defined citizenship and granted equal protection to all citizens. Johnson vetoed it on March 27 and Congress overrode it on April 9.

The Republicans' most far-reaching law was the Reconstruction Act that became law on March 2, 1867 after Congress overrode Johnson's veto. The Act split the eleven former rebel states among five regions, each with a military governor and troops, and a process whereby each state could be reinstated after the drafting and approval by referendum of a constitution that outlawed slavery and granted equal rights to all citizens including the right to vote and run for office. Congress retaliated against Johnson's obstructionism on February 18, 1867 by passing the Tenure of Office Act that required Senate approval for the president's firing of any officeholder that the Senate previously approved. On March 2, Johnson vetoed that bill and Congress promptly overrode the veto. Most importantly, Republicans thwarted the attempts of Johnson and the Democrats to kill the Fourteenth Amendment whose key tenets defined citizenship and the rights of due process and equal protection. The Fourteenth Amendment was ratified on July 9, 1868.[27]

At first, Johnson grudgingly complied with the Tenure of Office Act. On August 12, he fired War Secretary Edwin Stanton but sent his justification to the Senate. On January 13, 1868, the Senate voted to reinstate Stanton. On February 21, Johnson fired Stanton again but without sharing his reason with the Senate. That was the excuse for the House's Republican majority to vote by 128 to 47 for eleven articles of impeachment against Johnson on February 24. The Senate tried him but failed to convict him by one vote, 35 to 19, on May 16.[28]

Nonetheless, Johnson's political career was effectively over. New York Governor Horatio Seymour won the Democratic Party's presidential nomination. Meanwhile, the Republicans nominated Ulysses Grant. In the election held on November 3, 1868, Grant won 3,013,650 popular votes to Seymour's 2,708,740, and 214 to 80 electoral votes. On March 4, 1869, Grant took the presidential oath determined to fulfill Reconstruction.

White southern racists bitterly mourned their defeat then occupation by the Union army and Freedmen's Bureau, and the liberation of their slaves and attempt to grant blacks equal rights with themselves. They condemned the influx of "Yankee" businessmen who hoped to profit from Reconstruction as "carpetbaggers" and those among themselves who collaborated as "scallywags." A North Carolina veteran expressed the pervasive fear and rage against newly freed blacks: "To see the slaves ... go with arms in hand and threaten the lives of our fair ladies ... and ... insulting ... take their rings and furniture from their houses ... and left to the mercy of those brutal black negroes, is this not enough to rouse the hearts of all true southern men."[29]

A portion of white southerners organized themselves in a variety of terrorist groups with the Ku Klux Klan the most powerful alongside the White Brotherhood, White League, Redshirts, and Knights of the White Camellia.[30] These groups terrorized blacks by beating or murdering their leaders and burning their homes, businesses, churches, and schools. For instance, in Louisiana alone, 2,141 blacks were killed and 2,115 were wounded during Reconstruction.[31] Several times mobs rampaged through black neighborhoods, murdering and burning. In Memphis on May 1, 1866, a cart accident between a white driver and a black driver led to three days of violence that left forty-six blacks and two whites dead and hundreds of black homes and businesses torched. In New Orleans on July 30, 1866, a white mob attacked a black civil rights meeting, and killed thirty-four black and three white Radical Republicans, and wounded over a hundred others. In Camilla, Georgia on September 19, 1868, a mob attacked a black election parade, murdered as many as fifteen people and beat scores more then and over the following weeks. The deadliest fighting came at Opelousas, Louisiana, on September 28, 1868, when as many as 250 blacks and 50 whites died.

One by one, the states met the home rule requirements, Tennessee in 1869, Virginia and North Carolina in 1870, Georgia in 1871, Arkansas, Alabama, and Texas in 1874, Georgia in 1871, and Mississippi in 1875. White southern politicians instituted an array of non-violent means to subject blacks called the Black Codes or Jim Crow that forced them to sign year-long contracts for subsistence wages; forbad "vagrancy"; prevented them from leaving their masters' plantations, filing lawsuits, owning land, testifying in court, and voting; imposed onerous taxes on livelihoods other than farmer or servant; outlawed sex and marriage between the races; and forbad blacks from using the same public transportation, hotels, restaurants, and restrooms as whites.[32] Although the 1866 Civil Rights Act outlawed Black Codes, enforcement proved nearly impossible.

Nonetheless, blacks won some fleeting political victories during Reconstruction. Black state legislators included Alabama's 17, Arkansas's 8, Florida's 19, Georgia's 36, Louisiana's 50, Mississippi's 16, North Carolina's 14, South Carolina's 71, Texas's 10, and Virginia's 24. In Mississippi's state legislature, 9 of 37 senators and 55 of 115 assemblymen were black in 1874. There was one black governor, Pinkney Pinchback of Louisiana. Sixteen blacks won seats in the House of Representatives and two won Senate seats, Hiram Revels and Blanche Bruce of Mississippi.[33]

The Union League was an association dedicated to promoting equal rights whose chapters mushroomed across the nation with black and white members. The Union League worked with the National Equal Rights League that 145 black leaders formed at a convention at Syracuse, New York in October 1864.

Frederick Douglass chaired the committee that drafted its charter. The League soon had branches in all northern states.

Ulysses Grant naturally sympathized with underdogs and wanted all people to enjoy equal civil rights: "It is too late in this age of enlightenment to persecute any one on account of race, color, or religion."[34] As the army's commanding general, he acted to ensure that blacks enjoyed equal legal protection with whites in the South. On January 12, 1866, he issued General Order Number 3 that required occupation authorities to protect "colored persons from prosecutions" where they are "charged with offenses for which white persons" were immune.[35] He suspended the *Richmond Examiner* for its seditious editorials. As president, he worked with Congress to strengthen civil rights and fight terrorism. The most important measures were the Fifteenth Amendment, ratified on March 30, 1870, the Enforcement Act of May 31, 1870, and the Enforcement Act of April 20, 1871; those laws were also called the Ku Klux Klan acts.

The Fifteenth Amendment's wording was clear enough: "The right of citizens of the United States to vote shall not be denied or abridged by the United States or by any State on account of race, color, or previous condition of servitude. The Congress of the United States shall have power to enforce his article by appropriate legislation." Abolitionist William Lloyd Garrison celebrated "this wonderful, quiet, sudden transformation of four million human beings from ... the auction block to the ballot box."[36] Yet, as with all other civil rights amendments and laws, the challenge was enforcing it.

Grant faced the same widespread violence against blacks and white Republicans across the South as his predecessor, but was determined to crush rather than appease it. On October 12, 1871, he wielded the Enforcement Acts to condemn the "combinations and conspiracies" in nine South Carolina counties and gave them five days to disperse peacefully to their homes. When the deadline passed, he suspended habeas corpus in those counties, ordered troops to arrest any insurgents, and had Attorney General Amos Akerman spearhead the prosecutions. Within six weeks, authorities arrested several thousand suspects. Federal courts eventually issued 3,384 indictments and won 1,143 convictions against Ku Klux Klan members. Akerman reasoned that: "If you cannot convict, you, at least, can expose, and ultimately such exposure will make the community ashamed of shielding the crime."[37] The 1875 Civil Rights Act outlawed the Jim Crow laws that systematically discriminated against blacks.

Despite Grant's crackdown on the Klan and other white terrorist groups, violence persisted. The worst massacre was at Colfax, Louisiana on April 13, 1873, when white militia murdered as many as 153 blacks while suffering 3 dead. Appalled, Grant ordered American troops to restore order and round up suspects. Eventually Federal courts indicted 72 whites on various charges including murder, tried 9, and convicted 3. The White League murdered 6 white Republican officials and 20 blacks at Coushatta, Louisiana in August 1874. Although officials arrested 25 suspects, none were charged. A battle erupted between 2,500 White League militia and black militia and police in New Orleans on September 14, 1874. The White League suffered 21 dead and 19 wounded while killing 11 and wounding 60 law-enforcement officers. Grant dispatched 5,000 troops to New Orleans to quell that insurrection. At Hamburg South Carolina on July 8, 1876, a hundred Redshirts attacked 25 black militia, killing 6 while suffering 1 dead. Although officials indicted 94 men, none were prosecuted.

The Supreme Court's conservative majority aided and abetted white racism and violence with its devastating rulings in *Slaughterhouse Cases* (1873) against the Fourteenth Amendment, *United States v. Cruikshank* (1876) against the Enforcement Act, and *United States v. Reese* (1876) against the Fifteenth Amendment. *Slaughterhouse* limited the Fourteenth Amendment's citizenship rights to Federal jurisdictions, upholding state discrimination. *Cruikshank* overturned the convictions of three men in the Colfax massacre with claims that the court had violated their civil rights. *Reese* permitted officials to prevent blacks from registering to vote.

In the 1876 presidential election, Democrat Samuel Tilden won the popular vote with 4,286,546 to Republican Rutherford Hayes's 4,034,311, and was ahead 184 to 165 in the Electoral College, one short of victory. The trouble was that four states with twenty electoral votes – Louisiana, Florida, South Carolina, and Oregon – had disputed counts. Secret negotiations between the candidates' managers resolved the issue. Although the details remain murky, Tilden appears to have conceded those states and the election in return for Hayes' pledge to end Reconstruction. Regardless, Hayes did withdraw the remaining troops from the South shortly after entering the White House.[38]

Looking back at Reconstruction, Grant recognized that "the wisest thing would have been to have continued for some time the military rule. That would have enabled the Southern people to pull themselves together and repair material losses. Military rule would have been just to all: the negro who wanted freedom, the white man who wanted protection, the Northern man who wanted Union." He condemned the delusions and ignorance of most former rebels, especially the demagogues who still led them: "If the Southerners could only put aside the madness of their leaders, they would see that they are richer now than before the war. Money is not held in as few hands as before the war, and the people per capita are richer. And that, after all, is what we want to see in a republic." Looking ahead, he asserted that for blacks: "Suffrage once given can never be taken away and all that remains now is to make good that gift by protecting those that received it."[39] Looking ahead, Grant predicted this: "If we are to have another contest in this country in the near future of our natural existence ... the dividing line will not be Mason and Dixon, but between patriotism and intelligence on the one side, and superstition, ambition, and ignorance on the other."[40] Actually, those two camps have split Americans for over four centuries with only the respective strengths, issues, and zeal changing through time.

The Confederacy may have lost the actual war and been forced to give up slavery, but ever since sympathizers have fought to supplant that history with a mythology called "the Lost Cause," inaugurated by John Pollard in his 1866 book with that title.[41] The myth was that the southern states seceded to uphold states' rights, that slavery had nothing to do with the war, and that nearly all slaves were happy and treated like family by their masters. Abraham Lincoln had a succinct reply to the mythologizers: "Without slavery the rebellion could never have existed; without slavery it could not continue."[42]

That simple truth is anathema to believers. The Lost Cause is quasi-religious with its saints like Robert Lee, Stonewall Jackson, and Jefferson Davis. That trinity is literally carved in granite at Stone Mountain, 20 miles east of Atlanta; the 150ft-tall profiles are the world's largest bas relief. The place where Jackson died is actually called the "Stonewall Jackson Shrine." Lee is the most revered as a near Christ-like figure.[43] Like most religions, the Lost Cause has a villain. Neo-Confederates scapegoat General James Longstreet for the defeat at Gettysburg, claiming that not just the battle but the war could have been won had he attacked earlier on the second day.[44]

Three organizations spearheaded the Lost Cause campaign, the Confederated Southern Memorial Association, United Confederate Veterans, and United Daughters of the Confederacy, respectively founded in 1872, 1889, and 1894. Women actually led most fund-raising campaigns to erect statues of Confederate generals and soldiers.[45] Lost Cause leaders like former generals Jubal Early, John Gordon, and Porter Alexander sought to ground their beliefs on evidence. They formed the Southern Historical Society at New Orleans in 1869 and began publishing documents and reports as the Southern Historical Society Papers in 1876. Jefferson Davis's 2-volume 1,279-page *Rise and Fall of the Confederate Government* (1881) epitomized that mythical Lost Cause substitution for history.

Believers also promoted the Lost Cause through novels and eventually films. Leading late nineteenth-century fiction writers included Joel Harris and his *Uncle Remus: His Songs and Sayings* (1880) and Thomas Page and his novel *Marse Chan: A Tale of Old Virginia* (1887). Thomas Dixon romanticized the Ku Klux Klan in his 1905 novel *The Clansman* that director D.W. Griffith made into the 1915 brilliant if racist film *Birth of a Nation*. Margaret Mitchell's novel

Gone With The Wind (1936), and the 1939 movie it inspired, epitomized the "moonlight and magnolia" vision of the antebellum south with Scarlett O'Hara the quintessential "steel magnolia" of southern womanhood.

The reasons for the Lost Cause are obvious enough. People hate to lose anything, especially a devastating war that could have been avoided had reason rather than fanaticism prevailed. The former slaveholders who championed secession and war against the United States especially sought to evade history's condemnation. Clement Evans, who headed the United Confederate Veterans, at once explained and sugar-coated that burden: "If we cannot justify the South in the act of Secession, we will go down in History solely as a brave, impulsive but rash people who attempted in an illegal manner to overthrow the Union of our country."[46] So ever since the war, neo-Confederates have tried to subvert history with their Lost Cause mythology. It is so much easier to accept a soothing delusion that celebrates one's cause rather than admit the truth – that Southerners seceded from and warred against the United States to protect slavery.

Then there was the "victorious cause," although adherents never used that term. In 1866, veterans founded the Grand Army of the Republic (GAR) appropriately in Springfield, Illinois. The GAR dedicated itself to quiet memory, not myth. They sponsored veterans' gatherings at encampments and lobbied government for pensions, health care, battlefield parks, and monuments to their valor.

History is the Lost Cause's antidote, at least for the relative few who bother to study it. Scholars have written tens of thousands of books on the Civil War. There are also scores of historical novels that unsentimentally depict the horrors, complexities, dilemmas, and paradoxes of slavery and the war.[47] Among the best are Michael Shaara's *The Killer Angels* (1974); Jeff Shaara's *Gods and Generals* (1996) and *The Last Full Measure* (1998); Richard Slokin's *The Crater* (1980); and John Frazier's *Cold Mountain* (1997). William Styron's *The Confessions of Nat Turner* explored the mind of the man who led the most murderous slave revolt. Two novels explored John Brown, Russell Banks' *Cloudsplitter: A Novel* (1998) and James McBride's tragic-comic *The Good Lord Bird* (2013). William Faulkner depicted the struggles among southerners with the war's legacy in his novels *Satoris* (1927), *Light in August* (1932), and *The Unvanquished* (1938). Film directors have produced their own powerful works, most notably Ken Burns' haunting nine-part documentary *The Civil War* that appeared in 1990.

Chapter 20

Civil Rights and Fulfillments

Confederates are said to have lost the war but won Reconstruction. The Black Codes and Jim Crow laws effectively subjected blacks as laborers; stripped them of their political rights including voting, serving on juries, and running for office; and forbad them from sharing public schools, restaurants, hotels, parks, theaters, and restrooms with whites. The white establishment enforced these measures both through the courts and violence, including murder by vigilantes and mobs. The Tuskegee Institute calculated that across the United States from 1882 to 1968 4,743 people were lynched, including 3,446 blacks and 1,247 whites.[1]

The Supreme Court upheld Jim Crow with three late nineteenth-century rulings. In the 1883 *Civil Rights* cases, the justices struck down the 1875 Civil Rights Act as unconstitutional. In the 1896 *Plessy versus Ferguson* case, they ruled segregation was legal as long as it was separate but equal. In the 1898 *William versus Mississippi* case, they deemed voter restrictions like poll taxes and literacy tests constitutional.

Conditions for most blacks changed little from slavery. The political gains that blacks made during Reconstruction disappeared after it ended. Most black farmers were sharecroppers who gave as much as half their production to white landowners. Most blacks remained illiterate as children were denied public schools.

In the early twentieth century, two men asserted opposite views of how blacks could improve their lives. Booker T. Washington was the president of the Tuskegee Institute for black students. He encouraged blacks to excel at ethics, education, and enterprise; full political rights could be won only after blacks impressed whites with their economic, intellectual, and moral feats. He used his own life as an example in his book *Up from Slavery* (1901). William (W.E.B.) Dubois was the first black Harvard University graduate and his most acclaimed book was *Souls of Black Folks* (1903). He called on blacks to demand segregation's immediate end and full equality with whites.

It was Dubois's vision rather than Washington's that inspired white and black liberals to form two civil rights organizations in 1910.[2] The National Association for the Advancement of Colored People (NAAC) spearheaded black civil rights by launching lawsuits that challenged racist laws on constitutional grounds.

That inevitably patient, incremental legal strategy took more than four decades before it began winning decisive victories. The National Urban League formed to lobby city and state governments to end discrimination.

President Theodore Roosevelt tried to improve conditions for blacks symbolically by inviting Booker T. Washington to dine with him at the White House and by opening the federal civil service to qualified black applicants. President Woodrow Wilson ended that progress by forbidding blacks from federal jobs. During World War I, hundreds of thousands of black men served in segregated divisions while hundreds of thousands of other southern blacks moved north to take factory jobs vacated by whites who joined the army. When the war was over, a couple million decommissioned soldiers struggled to find jobs and housing. The result was race riots in numerous cities with the worst in East St Louis, Chicago, and Tulsa from 1919 to 1921. During the 1920s, the Ku Klux Klan revived and committed violence against blacks.

During World War II, over a million black men served in segregated units alongside 11 million whites while a million or so southern blacks moved to fill factory jobs. Philip Randolph headed the Sleeping Car Porters Union. In 1941, he organized a mass protest at the Lincoln Memorial in Washington against federal civil service discrimination. President Franklin Roosevelt issued an executive order that opened the federal administration to qualified blacks.

The greatest civil rights victories came during the two decades following World War II. In 1948, President Harry Truman ordered the armed forces integrated. The NAACP won a decisive victory in 1954 when the Supreme Court upheld its client's case in its *Brown versus Topeka Board of Education*; the justices declared unconstitutional the "separate but equal" concept because segregation was inherently unequal. In 1955, police arrested a black woman named Rosa Parks when she refused to move from the white section of a bus in Montgomery, Alabama. That inspired local Reverends Martin Luther King and Ralph Abernathy to organize a black boycott of the city buses. Eventually, the city government desegregated the bus system but not before King and hundreds of other protesters were arrested for civil disobedience. In 1957, President Dwight Eisenhower sent the 101st Airborne Division to Little Rock, Arkansas to enforce school integration when Governor Orval Faubus refused to implement it.

The civil rights movement became nationwide during the 1960s as many local groups and initiatives merged. In 1960, black students occupied Woolworth lunch counters to protest the banning of black patrons, and eventually forced that company to end discrimination. "Freedom Riders" violated segregation rules on interstate Greyhound and Trailways buses, eventually forcing them to end discrimination. The Southern Christian Leadership Conference (SCLC), the

Student Nonviolent Coordinating Committee (SNCC), and Congress of Racial Equality (CORE) emerged to spearhead mass demonstrations across the nation. Symbolically, the most powerful protest occurred before the Lincoln Memorial in Washington on August 28, 1963, when a quarter million people massed to hear a series of civil rights speeches keynoted by King's "I have a dream."

President John Kennedy and Attorney General Robert Kennedy worked with King and other civil rights leaders to overcome discrimination at the city and state levels, while they tried to advance a sweeping Civil Rights Bill through Congress. After Kennedy's assassination, President Lyndon Johnson led that effort and eventually rallied enough congressional votes to enact three laws whose implementation systematically ended Jim Crow: the Civil Rights Act signed on July 2, 1964, the Voting Rights Act of August 6, 1965, and the Fair Housing Act of April 11, 1968. More controversially, he initiated "affirmative action" that gave blacks an advantage in job hiring and school admission. He justified that as a corrective for centuries of discrimination suffered by blacks. Opponents decried that as reverse discrimination. Regardless, those victories cost civil rights leaders terrible losses with thousands arrested, hundreds beaten, and dozens murdered including the Kennedy brothers and King.

Over the next four decades, African Americans made enormous economic, political, and social progress. By 2020, eight of ten blacks were middle or upper class, and countless male and female blacks had through merit – intellect and character – risen to the highest levels of every profession. As vitally, most other Americans progressed with black Americans, in attitudes as well as incomes. During the 2008 and 2012 elections, a majority of voters embraced for president someone who, in his own words "as a black man with a Muslim name," would never have had a chance just a decade or so earlier. An African American man was inaugurated president 200 years after Abraham Lincoln's birth and 152 years after his death and slavery's abolition.

Barack Hussein Obama won the 2008 election against Republican candidate John McCain with 69,496,516 votes or 52.9 percent and 365 electors to 59,948,323 or 45.7 percent and 173 electors. He nearly as decisively defeated Republican challenger Mitt Romney in the 2012 election, with 65,915,795 votes or 51.1 percent and 332 electors to 60,933,504 votes or 47.2 percent and 206 electors. That certainly revealed that most Americans no longer embraced racism, or in Martin Luther King's vision, now judged people by the content of their character rather than the color of their skin. And most of those who voted against Obama did so not because of what he looked like, but because of what he proposed to do as president.

Among Obama's heroes was Abraham Lincoln whose character and career he tried to emulate. He was born in Honolulu, Hawaii to a white American mother and a Kenyan Muslim father. He went to Columbia University as an undergraduate and then Harvard Law School where he edited its *Law Review*. He was an Illinois state senator from 1997 to 2004, and a United States senator from 2005 to 2008. He is an eloquent orator and fine writer with each of his four books a bestseller, *Dreams of My Father* (1995), *The Audacity of Hope* (2007), *Of Thee I Sing* (2010), *A Promised Land* (2020). He is a loving husband to Michelle and loving father to their daughters Sasha and Malia.

America had achieved a post-racial society in 2008 brilliantly symbolized by that "black man with a Muslim name," Barack Hussein Obama's election to the White House. Then tragic deaths and radical movements destroyed that progress by a generation or more.

Chapter 21

New Battles in Old Wars

The Black Lives Matter (BLM) movement arose in 2014 after controversial killings of black criminal suspects by police officers in Ferguson, Missouri and New York City. The movement was inspired by Critical Race Theory that claims all white Americans are racist and have constructed "systemic racism" that suppresses and exploits everyone else who are called "people of color." Critics blast the theory as itself racist and ahistorical, arguing that myths contrived from blackwashed history are as odious as whitewashed versions. For instance, how did alleged "systemic racism" prevent Asian Americans from far surpassing Caucasians in income, education degrees, test scores, and longevity especially given the grievous discrimination that Chinese and Japanese Americans once genuinely suffered. In reality, each person's life is determined by a unique dynamic among intellect, character, ambition, skill, and luck. Regardless, in cities across America, BLM leaders organized mass protests that demanded ending "systemic racism," defunding police and replacing them with social workers, amnestying convicts then in prison, freeing arrested criminal suspects without bail, and paying slavery reparations to blacks.[1]

The movement surged in the months following the apparent suffocation of criminal suspect George Floyd by Officer Derek Owen who sat on his head after he resisted arrest in Minneapolis on May 25, 2020. As many as 25 million people joined protests in over 2,000 cities and towns that peaked on June 6 with ½ million people in 550 sites. Although most rallies were peaceful, protestors in dozens of cities fought police and looted and burned businesses and public buildings, causing nineteen deaths, hundreds of injuries, and from $1 billion to $2 billion in damages. The most destructive riots were in New York, Minneapolis, and especially Seattle and Portland where BLM, Antifa, and other radical groups captured districts then battled police for months.[2]

How true are Black Lives claims that police killings of black men represent systematic racism? Extensive studies by the National Academy of Sciences, Education Fund to Stop Violence, and Coalition to Stop Gun Violence provide vital statistics to answer that question.[3] In 2019, blacks numbered 46,800,000 or about 13 percent of America's 328,000,000 people. That year police killed 1,089 criminal suspects including 406 whites, 259 blacks, 212 unknowns, 182 Hispanics, 17 Asians, and 13 American Indians. Of the 259 blacks killed, 246 were armed and 13 were unarmed. That same year, of 14,414 homicides, 7,639 were blacks, with around 95 percent murdered by other blacks. Statistically the overwhelming evidence is that police kill criminal suspects of all races that appear to pose an imminent threat to themselves and other innocent people. The number of black criminal suspects killed by police is a fraction of the number of blacks killed by other blacks and a virtual nullity among 46,800,000 blacks. Official investigations, grand juries, and juries exonerate virtually all police killings of any armed or unarmed criminal suspects of any ethnicity because public safety not racism was the reason. Nonetheless, the Black Lives Movement spotlights the few controversial killings by police then characterizes all police killings of black criminal suspects as systemic racism while ignoring killings by police of non-black criminal suspects and the killings of blacks by other blacks. Meanwhile, in 2019, 151 police officers died in the line of duty with 49 murdered by gunfire, 8 by vehicular assault, and 3 beaten to death.[4]

Tragically, the Black Lives Movement to defund the police and empty prisons ruined countless black lives. Police officers wield deadly force against criminal suspects that appear to pose a danger to themselves or innocent other people. Official investigations nearly always find that police shootings of criminal suspects are justified. Two scholarly studies reached similar conclusions. The Black Lives Movement intimidated thousands of police to retire and demoralized tens of thousands of police from vigorously enforcing the law. Police killings of criminal suspects dropped by around 200 while around 3,000 more murders occurred, mostly by blacks against other blacks. Another study found that every dollar invested in police results in an average $1.65 savings in crime costs, and that American cities are actually underpoliced given chronic crime rates. Yet another study found that police – black and white – display "bias" or mingled cynicism, suspicion, and fear against blacks in high-crime districts that makes them more inclined to use force rather than talk for arrests.[5]

Confederate memorials became a BLM target. Confederate heritage groups, often spearheaded by the Daughters of the Confederacy, erected around 1,700 memorials in the century following the war, with most statues of leaders and anonymous soldiers, and obelisks with names of local or regimental dead. Most are located at county court houses, battlefield parks, or cemeteries.[6] During demonstrations, protesters defaced and even toppled Confederate memorials and statues of other Americans they considered racists like George Washington, Thomas Jefferson, Abraham Lincoln, Ulysses Grant, and Theodore Roosevelt. A riot ensued at the University of Virginia on August 11 and 12, 2017, when an array of white supremacist groups held a Unite the Right protest against BLM and other groups that sought to remove a Robert E. Lee statue. One Unite the Right protester drove his car into a crowd of anti-monument protesters, and killed one of them, while 33 other people were injured in fights between the movements.

The choices for what to do about Confederate and other controversial historical monuments are clear: Leave them alone, tear them down, or teach them up. Those who want to tear them down succeeded in forcing state and city governments to raze 168 monuments in 2020 alone, atop scores of others over preceding years. The most visible change was removing Confederate battle flags imbedded in the state flags of Georgia and Mississippi in 2003 and 2020, respectively.[7]

The radical right also surged in power, enflamed by the election of the first black president in 2008. Governor Rick Perry declared his hope that Texas would secede a second time from the United States. So-called "patriot" groups skyrocketed in number from 149 in 2008 to 512 in 2009 and 1,274 in 2011. Of those groups, 127 were explicitly militia groups. Whatever the category, many groups openly called for vandalism, beatings, and outright murder of liberal politicians.[8] Not just leaders of self-styled "patriot" groups but even some Republican politicians openly advocated violence to advance their agenda. Former Minnesota governor Tim Pawlenty told a cheering group that they should "take a nine-iron and smash the window out of big government in this country." Dick Morris, a Republican political advisor, stated on Fox News that, "Those crazies in Montana who say ... kill AFT agents because the U.N.'s going to take over – well, they're beginning to have a case."[9]

Obama endured years of false accusations that he was a secret Muslim who was born outside the United States and was thus ineligible to be president. Ironically, the leader of that "birther" movement would replace him as president.

Donald Trump was elected president on November 8, 2016, after he won the Electoral College vote by 306 to 227, although he lost the popular vote with 62,984,828 or 46.1 percent to Democratic candidate Hillary Clinton's 65,853,514 or 48.2 percent. Over the next four years, he presided over, exacerbated, and often instigated racial conflicts. He openly appealed to the array of white supremacist groups in the Unite the Right movement and frequently advocated violence by them against his political foes. Daily he uttered or tweeted inflammatory lies and conspiracy theories that reached a stunning 30,574 "false or misleading statements" by the time he left office.[10] In doing so, Trump accelerated the Republican Party's transformation from the reform party of Abraham Lincoln, Theodore Roosevelt, and Richard Nixon into a vehicle for his own authoritarian, venal, and hateful ambitions. How was that possible?

What happened was that the political parties had essentially traded ideological places over the preceding century and a half. The Democratic Party was conservative – Jeffersonian and increasingly Jacksonian – from its founding in the early 1790s until Franklin Roosevelt became president in 1933 and remade it into an increasingly progressive party. Like its predecessors the Federalist and Whig parties, the Republican Party was initially progressive and Hamiltonian, then diluted by a strengthening conservative wing until Ronald Reagan completed that transformation after becoming president in 1981. Thereafter the Republicans became the party of massive tax cuts for the wealthy and attempts to repress voting by minorities, especially blacks, among other conservative measures. Under Trump, far right-wing media like Fox, Breitbart, and Infowars and groups like QAnon, Oath Keepers, and Proud Boys warped how most Republicans interpreted and acted in the political world.

Trump openly violated American democracy's laws, institutions, and mores. There were attempts to investigate and prosecute Trump on an array of charges. The Justice Department investigated allegations that he and his campaign had conspired with the Russians to undermine America's 2016 election.[11] Robert Mueller, the chief investigator, issued a report that did not find convictable evidence of conspiracy but did find ten examples of Trump's obstruction of justice. In 2019, the House of Representatives voted to impeach Trump for obstructing Congress and abuse of power, but the Senate Republican majority acquitted him.

During the 2020 election, Democratic Party challenger Joe Biden decisively defeated Trump with 306 to 232 electors and 81,283,501 or 51.3 percent to 74,223,975 or 46.8 percent popular votes. Yet, Trump refused to concede and instead falsely claimed that he was the victim of massive voter fraud that robbed him of reelection. He called on his followers to mass in Washington on January 6, 2021, the day Congress was scheduled to certify the election result. That noon in a speech before around 20,000 supporters, some waving Confederate flags, he urged them to march on the Capitol to prevent the certification. At the Capitol, 2,000 Trumpians overran the thin blue line of police and broke in to ransack the building and hunt down representatives and senators, calling for killing their leaders including Vice President Mike Pence and House Speaker Nancy Pelosi. Thus did Trump's followers achieve what Jefferson Davis's could only dream of doing – triumphantly waving Confederate flags inside the captured American Capitol.

Minutes before the mob surged into the House and Senate chambers, police escorted the members to safety. Then, with reinforcements, the police eventually expelled the rioters. In the fighting, 143 police were injured, 1 was murdered, and 2 later committed suicide, while 1 rioter was killed, heart attacks killed 3, and scores were injured. Late that night, Congress certified the election result, although far from the standard routine unanimous vote. Although all Democrats voted in favor, among Republicans 140 representatives and 7 senators voted against certifying Biden's victory, thus supporting the lie that Trump had won the election. The Trumpian mobs' ransack of the Capitol enraged Americans for whom the Capitol is a semi-sacred symbol of their democracy and nation. By January 2023, Justice Department had indicted over 999 January 6 insurgents for various misdemeanors and felonies, of which 465 pleaded guilty, 185 of 335 sentenced were in prison, and 2, Oath Keeper President Stuart Rhodes and Florida chapter chief Kelly Meigs, received convictions for seditious conspiracy.[12]

During his inaugural address on January 20, 2021, Joe Biden emphasized themes of national unity, compromise, reason, and justice. As for those themes, Biden's running mate Kamala Harris symbolized three extraordinary political firsts in American history as a woman racially half black and half Asian. Yet, the Black Lives Matter movement dismissed the meaning of Harris's achievement as they had Obama's presidential electoral victories to persist in claiming that systemic racism existed.

As for justice, House Speaker Nancy Pelosi had articles of impeachment drafted against Trump for instigating an insurrection. The House of Representatives voted 323 to 197 in favor on January 26. The Senate trial lasted from February 10 to 14 and resulted in a vote of fifty-seven senators, including seven Republicans, to convict, and forty-three Republicans to acquit. Thus did Trump escape conviction because fewer than two-thirds of senators voted in favor.

America remains split over the 2020 election and a myriad of other issues. An American Enterprise Institute poll found that only 32 percent or one-third of Republicans accepted the election results as accurate, while two-thirds or 66 percent believed it was fraudulent; four of five or 79 percent favored Trump; three of four or 74 percent denied that he instigated the January 6 insurrection; and 55 percent or more than half believed that violence was sometimes necessary in a democracy.[13] Within two months of Biden's inauguration, Republicans introduced over 250 bills in 47 state assemblies to suppress voting by various methods with they claim that they were trying to prevent voter fraud. In fact, the 2020 election resulted in only 16 charged cases of voter fraud of 156,006,056 votes cast. Biden denounced that systematic assault on American democracy as "Jim Crow on steroids in the 21st century." He worked with House of Representative Speaker Nancy Pelosi and Senate Majority Leader Chuck Schumer to draft a voters' rights bill that would eliminate gerrymandering, allow automatic voter registration, expand early voting, and cut the power of corporate money to corrupt politics. Republicans prevented that from becoming law.[14]

The House of Representatives voted 222 to 190 on June 20, 2021, to form the "Select House Committee on the January 6 Attack." The committee's nine members included seven Democrats and two Republicans, with Democrat Bennie Thompson the chair and Republican Liz Cheney the vice chair. By December 2022, the Committee interviewed over 1,000 witnesses, amassed over 1 million pages of documents for evidence, and submitted an 864-page report to the Justice Department and the American people. The referred charges included obstructing an official procedure, conspiring to defraud the United States, and conspiring to commit insurrection against the United States.[15]

During his six decades as a businessman, Trump fended off scores of civil lawsuits for fraud, tax evasion, breach of contract, campaign finance violations, racial discrimination, and sexual assault. His mastery of crime boss and legal defense tactics enabled him to evade any criminal indictments until 2023, when he received four separate packages of criminal felony indictments.

Two came from Special Counsel Jack Smith, who Attorney General Merrick Garland appointed on November 18, 2022, nearly twenty-two months after Trump incited the January 6, 2020 insurrection. Smith proved to be as decisive and bold a prosecutor as Garland was timid and hesitant. His two decades of experience as a prosecutor included serving as chief prosecutor against Kosovo war criminals at the International Criminal Court at The Hague, in the Netherlands. He launched 2 investigations, 1 on Trump's attempts to overturn the 2020 election and the other for stealing over 13,000 federal documents, of which 304 were top secret, and trying to prevent officials from recovering them.

The document theft case was straightforward. A president must return all documents to the National Archives and Records Administration (NARA) when he leaves office; no secret document can be revealed to anyone without a security clearance. Trump not only took over 13,000 documents and stored them in public places at his Mar-a-Largo Florida resort where he lived and repeatedly refused official requests to return them, but revealed top-secret documents to people without security clearances. Smith announced on June 8, that a Miami grand jury had indicted Trump on thirty-seven counts, with thirty-two under the Espionage Act and the others for willful retention of national defense information, false statements and obstruction of justice; two co-conspirators were also charged. On July 27, Smith filed a superseding indictment of new felony charges against Trump and his co-conspirators that included altering, mutilating, destroying, and concealing official documents.

Trump's attempts to overthrow the American government and install himself as dictator was a far more complex case to investigate. For months preceding and during the two months following the presidential election, Trump repeatedly claimed that the election was rigged against him and called on his followers to overturn the results. The core of that effort involved mobilizing alternative sets of electors in seven states – Arizona, Georgia, Michigan, Nevada, New Mexico, Pennsylvania, and Wisconsin – who would falsely claim to be legitimate on January 6, the day that Congress certified the state election results. That would coincide with Trump provoking a mob to storm and overrun the Capitol to prevent certification. On August 1, a grand jury in Washington indicted Trump on four felony counts that included conspiracy to defraud the United States, conspiracy to obstruct an official proceeding, obstruction of an official proceeding, and conspiracy to violate rights; the indictment referred to Trump's six unindicted and unnamed co-conspirators who may be charged later. Noticeably missing was the charge that Trump incited an insurrection. Smith anticipated the defense arguing that Trump merely expressed his First Amendment right of free speech when he did so.

District Attorney Fani Willis of Fulton County, Georgia, issued on August 14, a 41- count indictment of Trump and 18 co-conspirators for violating the Corrupt Organization and Racketing Organizing (RICO) Act with a "criminal enterprise" that asserted 161 separate attempts to overturn the 2020 election in Georgia.

The least serious criminal indictment against Trump was the first filed. On March 30, Manhattan District Attorney Alvin Brag issued thirty-four felony charges against Trump for falsifying business records. Trump had $130,000 paid to buy the silence of porn star Stormy Daniels with whom he had an affair and could have revealed the story during his 2016 election campaign. Trump concealed the payment through a series of illicit channels. Although falsifying business records is a misdemeanor it becomes a felony if used for another crime. His aide Michael Cohen, who made the payment, pleaded guilty to eight felonies on August 21, 2018, and received a three-year sentence and $50,000 fine.

Whether any of these trials results in convictions and prison for Trump and his co-conspirators remains to be seen. What is clear is that America's legal system at the federal, states, and local levels is still committed to prosecuting crimes and championing justice. Anyone who commits a legal or moral crime repeatedly without remorse is pathological. By that measure, the overwhelming evidence is that Trump is a pathological bully, liar, and criminal. Yet, it is also clear that all the congressional and legal investigations against Trump bolstered rather than diminished the adoration of his supporters. Polls reveal that about 45 percent of people zealously believe in Trump and everything he tells them, and reject all contrary evidence. Trump is the latest "Lost Cause" in America's unending civil war.

Appropriately, Abraham Lincoln will have the last words:

> At what point shall we expect the approach of danger? ... Shall we expect some transatlantic military giant to ... crush us at a blow? Never! All the armies of Europe, Asia, and Africa combined, with all the treasure of the earth (our own excepted), with a Bonaparte for a commander, could not by force take a drink from the Ohio ... in a trial of a thousand years.... At what point, then, is the approach of danger[?] ... If ever it reach us it must spring up amongst us ... If destruction be our lot we must ourselves be its author ... As a nation of free men we must live through all time, or die by suicide.[16]

Notes

Introduction

1. For the traditional lower carefully calculated figure, see: Thomas Livermore, *Numbers and Losses in the Civil War, 1861–65* (New York: Houghton, Mifflin, 1900). For the higher recent estimate, see: David Hacker, "A Census Based Count of the Civil War Dead," *Civil War History*, vol. 54, no. 4 (December 2011), 307–48.
2. For a brilliant and hilarious exploration of the reenacting world, see: Tony Horwitz, *Confederates in the Attic: Dispatches from the Unfinished Civil War* (New York: Pantheon, 1998).
3. For leading books, see: William Taylor, *Cavalier and Yankee: The Old South and American National Character* (New York: Braziller, 1957); Brian Reid, *The Origins of the American Civil War* (London: Longman, 1996); Michael Morrison, *Slavery and the American West: The Eclipse of Manifest Destiny and the Coming of the Civil War* (Chapel Hill: University of North Carolina Press, 1997); Lorman Ratner and Dwight Teeter, *Fanatics and Fire-eaters: Newspapers and the Coming of the Civil War* (Champlain: University of Illinois Press, 2002); Stephen Berry, *All That Makes a Man: Love and Ambition in the Civil War South* (New York: Oxford University Press, 2003); Edward Ayers, *What Caused the Civil War: Reflections on the South and Southern History* (New York: W.W. Norton, 2005); Bruce Levine, *Half Slave and Half Free: The Roots of the Civil War* (New York: Hill and Wang, 2005): Chandra Manning, *What This Cruel War Was Over* (New York: Vintage, 2008); Elizabeth Veron, *Disunion!: The Coming of the Civil War, 1789–1857* (Chapel Hill: University of North Carolina Press, 2008); Marc Egnal, *Clash of Extremes: The Economic Origins of the Civil War* (New York: Hill and Wang, 2009).
4. Jefferson Davis, *The Rise and Fall of the Confederate Government* (New York: D. Appleton and Company, 1881), 518.
5. C. Vann Woodward, ed., *Mary Chesnut's War* (New Haven: Yale University Press, 1981), 25.

Chapter 1

1. William Nester, *The Struggle for Power in Colonial America, 1607–1776: The Art of American Power during the Early Republic* (New York: Lexington Books, 2017).
2. Milton Meltzer, *Slavery: A World History* (New York: Da Capo Press, 1993).
3. John Reader, *Africa: A Biography of the Continent* (New York: Vintage, 1999), 291.
4. Philip Curtin, *The Atlantic Slave Trade: A Census* (Madison: University of Wisconsin Press, 1969), 268, 287; Paul Lovejoy, "The Impact of the African Slave Trade on Africa: A Review of the Literature," *Journal of African History*, vol. 30, 368, 365–94; Hugh Thomas, *The Slave Trade: The Story of the Atlantic Slave Trade, 1440–1870* (New York: Touchstone Books, 1997), 432–3, 631–2, 804.
5. Ira Berlin, *Many Thousands Gone: The First Two Centuries of Slavery in North America* (Cambridge Mass.: Harvard University Press, 1998); James Horton and Lois Horton, *Slavery and the Making of America* (New York: Oxford University Press, 2005); Betty Wood, *Slavery in Colonial America, 1619 to 1776* (New York: Rowman and Littlefield, 2005); John Spear, *The American Slave Trade: An Account of Its Origin, Growth, and Suppression* (New York: Read and Company, 2020).
6. "Trans-Atlantic Slave Trade Estimate," Emory University, website.

7. William Lerner, ed., *Historical Statistics of the United States, Colonial Times to 1970,* 2 vols (Washington DC: US Department, Bureau of the Census, 1975), 2:1168.

Chapter 2
1. William Nester, *The Revolutionary Years, 1775–1789* (Washington DC: Potomac Books, 2011); William Nester, *The Hamiltonian Vision, 1789–1800: The Art of American Power during the Early Republic* (Washington DC: Potomac Books, 2012).
2. Sean Wilentz, *No Property in Man: Slavery and Antislavery at the Nation's Founding* (Cambridge, Mass.: Harvard University Press, 2019).
3. Lerner, ed., *Historical Statistics of the United States,* 1:22.
4. Nester, *Hamiltonian Vision*; William Nester, *The Jeffersonian Vision, 1801–1815: The Art of American Power during the Early Republic* (Washington DC: Potomac Books, 2013).
5. David Howe, *The Political Culture of the American Whigs* (Chicago: University of Chicago Press, 1984); Michael Holt, *The Rise and Fall of the American Whig Party: Jacksonian Politics and the Onset of Civil War* (New York: Oxford University Press, 2003).

Chapter 3
1. Douglas North, *The Economic Growth of the United States, 1790–1860* (Englewood Cliffs: Prentice Hall, 1961); David Jeremy, *Transatlantic Industrial Revolution: The Diffusion of Textile Technology between Britain and America, 1790–1830s* (Cambridge, Mass.: MIT Press, 1981); Otto Mayr and Robert Post, eds, *Yankee Enterprise: The Rise of the American System of Manufactures* (Washington DC: Smithsonian, 1982); Thomas Cochran, *Frontiers of Change: Early American Industrialization* (New York: Oxford University Press, 1983); John Houndshell, *From the American System to Mass Production, 1800–1932* (Baltimore: Johns Hopkins university Press, 1984); Donald Hoke, *Ingenious Yankees: The Rise of the American System of Manufacturing in the Private Sector* (New York: Oxford University Press, 1990); Walter Licht, *Industrializing America: The Nineteenth Century* (Baltimore: Johns Hopkins University Press, 1995); David Meyer, *The Roots of America's Industrialization* (Baltimore: Johns Hopkins University Press, 2003); David Meyer, *Networked Machinists: High Technologies Industries in Antebellum America* (Baltimore: Johns Hopkins University Press, 2006); Barbara Tucker and Kenneth Tucker, *Industrializing Antebellum America: The Rise of Manufacturing Entrepreneurs in the Early Republic* (New York: Palgrave Macmillan, 2008); Charles Morris, *The Dawn of Innovation: The First American Industrial Revolution* (New York: Public Affairs, 2012).
2. Carol Sheriff, *The Artificial River: The Erie Canal and the Paradox of Progress, 1817 to 1862* (New York: Oxford University Press, 1997); Evan Cornog, *The Birth of Empire: Dewitt Clinton and the American Experience* (New York: Oxford University Press, 2000); Peter Bernstein, *Wedding of the Waters: The Erie Canal and the Making of a Great Nation* (New York: W.W. Norton, 2006).
3. George Taylor, *The Transportation Revolution, 1815–1860* (New York: Routledge, 1977); James Flexner, *Steamboats Come True: America Inventors in Action* (Boston: Little Brown, 1978).
4. Lerner, ed., *Historical Statistics of the United States,* 2:731.
5. Bray Hammond, *Banks and Politics in America: From the Revolution to the Civil War* (Princeton: Princeton University Press, 1991); Howard Bodenhorn, *The History of Banking in Antebellum America* (Cambridge, Mass.: Harvard University Press, 2000).
6. Robert Gallman and John Wallis, eds, *American Economic Growth and Standards of Living Before the Civil War* (Chicago: University of Chicago Press, 1992).
7. James McPherson, *Battle Cry of Freedom: The Civil War Era* (New York: Oxford University Press, 1988), 19, 40.
8. Ibid., 25.

Chapter 4

1. David Davis, *The Problem of Slavery in the Age of Revolution* (Ithaca: Cornell University Press, 1975); Donald Robinson, *Slavery in the Structure of American Politic, 1765–1820s* (New York: W.W. Norton, 1979); Kenneth Stampp, *The Peculiar Institute: Slavery in the Antebellum South* (New York: Vintage, 1989); Michael Tadman, *Speculators and Slaves: Masters, Traders, and Slaves in the Old South* (Madison: University of Wisconsin Press, 1998); Roger Ransom, *Conflict and Compromise: The Political Economy of Slavery* (New York: Cambridge University Press, 1989); Berlin, *Many Thousands Gone*; Ted Owsley, ed., *Black and White: Cultural Interaction in the Ante-Bellum South* (Oxford: University of Mississippi Press, 2008); Manning, *What This Cruel War Was Over*; Eugene Genovese, *Fatal Self Deception: Slaveholding Paternalism in the Old South* (New York: Cambridge University Press, 2012); Robert Fogel and Stanley Engerman, *Time on the Cross: The Economics of American Negro Slavery* (New York: W.W. Norton, 2013).

2. Eric Foner, *Free Soil, Free Labor, Free Men: The Ideology of the Republican Party before the Civil War* (New York: Oxford University Press 1995), 41, 47.

3. Levine, *Half Slave and Half Free*, 37, 41.

4. Ibid., 23.

5. William Freehling, *The Road to Disunion: Secessionists at Bay, 1776–1854* (New York: Oxford University Press, 1990), 43.

6. Fogel and Engerman, *Time on the Cross*, 132.

7. Gavin Wright, *The Political Economy of the Cotton South: Households, Markets, and Wealth in the Nineteenth Century* (New York: W.W. Norton, 1978); John Moore, *The Emergence of the Cotton Kingdom in the Old Southwest* (Baton Rouge: University of Louisiana Press, 1988); Harold Woodman, *King Cotton and His Retainers: Financing and Marketing the Cotton Crop of the South, 1800–1926* (New York: Beard Books, 2000).

8. Freehling, *Road to Disunion: Secessionists at Bay*, 24.

9. Taylor, *Cavalier and Yankee*; W.J. Cash, *Mind of the South* (New York: Vintage, 1991); Elizabeth Fox-Genovese and Eugene Genovese, *The Mind of the Master Class: History and Faith in the Southern Slaveholders' World View* (New York: Cambridge University Press, 2005); Susan Delfino, Michele Gillespie, and Louis Kyriakoukis, eds, *Southern Society and Its Transformation, 1790–1860* (Columbia: University of Missouri Press, 2011).

10. Keri Leigh Merritt, *Masterless Men: Poor Whites and Slavery in the Antebellum South* (New York: Cambridge University Press, 2017).

11. Dickson Bruce, *Violence and Culture in the Antebellum South* (Austin: University of Texas Press, 1979); Bertram Wyatt-Brown, *Southern Honor: Ethics and Behavior in the Old South* (New York: Oxford University Press, 1982); Jack Williams, *Dueling in the Old South: Vignettes of Social History* (College Station: Texas A & M University Press, 2000); Joanne Freeman, *Affairs of Honor: National Politics in the New Republic* (New Haven: Yale University Press, 2001); Berry, *All That Makes a Man*.

12. William Tecumseh Sherman, *Memoirs of General W.T. Sherman* (New York: Library of America, 1990), 363.

13. Vann Woodward, ed., *Mary Chesnut's Civil War*; Catherine Clinton, *The Plantation Mistress: Woman's World in the Old South* (New York: Pantheon books, 1982); Elizabeth Fox-Genovese, *Within the Plantation Household: Black and White Women of the Old South* (Chapel Hill: University of North Carolina Press, 1988); Victoria Bynum, *Unruly Women: The Politics of Social and Sexual Control in the Old South* (Chapel Hill: University of North Carolina Press, 1992).

14. Vann Woodward, ed., *Mary Chesnut's Civil War*, 46.

15. Fox-Genovese, *Within the Plantation Household*, 23.

16. Clinton, *Plantation Mistress*, 103.

17. Vann Woodward, ed., *Mary Chesnut's Civil War*, 29.

18. Drew Gilpin Faust, *The Ideology of Slavery: Pro-Slavery Thought in the Ante-Bellum South* (Baton Rouge: Louisiana State University Press, 1981); Drew Gilpin Faust, *A Sacred Circle: The Dilemma of the Intellectual in the Old South, 1840–1860* (Baton Rouge: Louisiana State University Press, 1982); Larry Tise, *Proslavery: A History of the Defense of Slavery in America, 1701–1840* (Athens: University of Georgia Press, 1987); Drew Gilpin Faust, *The Creation of Southern Nationalism: Ideology and Identity in the Civil War South* (Baton Rouge: Louisiana State University Press, 1989); Eugene Genovese, *The Slaveholders' Dilemma: Freedom and Progress in Southern Conservative Thought, 1820–1860* (Columbia: University of South Carolina Press, 1992); Michael Snay, *Gospel of Disunion: Religion and Separatism in the Antebellum South* (New York: Cambridge University Press, 1993); David Ericson, *The Debate Over Slavery: Antislavery and Proslavery Literature in Antebellum America* (New York: New York University Press, 2000); Mason Lowance, ed., *A House Divided: The Antebellum Slavery Debates in America, 1776–1865* (Princeton: Princeton University Press, 2003); Paul Finkelman, *Defending Slavery: Proslavery Thought in the Old South* (Boston: Bedford-St Martin's Press, 2003); Michael O'Brien, *Conjectures of Order: Intellectual Life and the American South*, 2 vols (Chapel Hill: University of North Carolina Press, 2004); Adam Tate, *Conservatism and Southern Intellectuals, 1789–1861: Liberty, Tradition, and the Good Society* (Columbia: University of Missouri Press, 2005).

19. H.W. Brands, *Heirs of the Founders: The Epic Rivalry of Henry Clay, John Calhoun, and Daniel Websters, the Second Generation of American Giants* (New York: Doubleday, 2018), 250.

20. Levine, *Half Slave and Half Free*, 140.

21. Jefferson to John Holmes, April 22, 1820, Adrienne Koch and William Peden, eds, *The Life and Selected Writings of Thomas Jefferson* (New York: Modern Library, 1998), 637.

22. Freehling, *Road to Disunion: Secessionists at Bay*, 108.

23. Ibid., 147.

24. William Cooper, *Liberty and Slavery: Southern Politics to 1860* (New York: Knopf, 1982); Leonard Richards, *The Slave Power: The Free North and Southern Domination, 1780–1860* (Baton Rouge: Louisiana State University Press, 2000).

25. Freehling, *Road to Disunion: Secessionists at Bay*, 323.

26. Veron, *Disunion!*, 113.

27. Stanley Campbell, *The Slave Catchers: Enforcement of the Fugitive Slave Act, 1860–1860* (Chapel Hill: University of North Carolina Press, 1970), 207.

28. Robert May, *Manifest Destiny's Underworld: Filibustering in Antebellum America* (Chapel Hill: University of North Carolina Press, 2002).

Chapter 5

1. Timothy McCarthy and John Stauffer, eds, *Prophets of Protest: Reconsidering the History of American Abolitionism* (New York: New Press, 2006); Manisha Sinha, *The Slave's Cause: A History of Abolition* (New Haven: Yale University Press, 2017); Stanley Herrold, *American Abolition: Its Direct Political Impact from Colonial Times to Reconstruction* (Charlottesville: University of Virginia Press, 2019).

2. Eric Burin, *Slavery and the Peculiar Solution: A History of the American Colonization Society* (Gainesville: University of Florida Press, 2005).

3. Lewis Perry, *Radical Abolitionists: Anarchy and Government of God in Antislavery Thought* (Ithaca: Cornell University Press, 1973); Ronald Walters, *The Antislavery Appeal: American Abolitionism after 1830* (Baltimore: Johns Hopkins University Press, 1976); James Stewart, *Holy Warriors: The Abolitionists and American Slavery* (New York: Hill and Wang, 1976); Richard Sewall, *Ballots for Freedom: Antislavery Politics in the United States, 1837–1860* (New York: Oxford University Press, 1976); Lawrence Friedman, *Gregarious Saints: Self and Community in American Abolitionism, 1830–1870* (New York: Cambridge University Press, 1982); Edward Magdol, *The Antislavery Rank and File: A Social Profile of the Abolitionist*

Constituency (Westport: Greenwood Press, 1986); Stanley Harrold, *The Abolitionists and the South, 1831–1861* (Lexington: University Press of Kentucky, 1995); Richard Newman, *The Transformation of American Abolitionism: Fighting Slavery in the Early Republic* (Chapel Hill: University of North Carolina Press, 2002); Louis Filler, *The Crusade Against Slavery: Friends, Foes, and Reforms, 1820–1860* (New York: Routledge, 2017).

4. Foner, *Free Soil, Free Labor, Free Men*, 46.

5. Aileen Kraditor, *Means and Ends in American Abolitionism: Garrison and His Critics on Strategy and Tactics, 1834–1850* (New York: Pantheon Books, 1969); Henry Mayer, *All On Fire: William Lloyd Garrison and the Abolition of Slavery* (New York: W.W. Norton, 2008).

6. Filler, *Crusade Against Slavery*, 67.

7. Jean Fagan Yellin and John Van Horne, eds, *The Abolitionist Sisterhood: Women's Political Culture in Antebellum America* (Ithaca: Cornell University Press, 1994); Julie Roy Jeffrey, *The Great Silent Army of Abolitionism: Ordinary Women in the Antislavery Movement* (Chapel Hill: University of North Carolina Press, 1998); Michael Pierson, *Free Hearts, Free Homes: Gender and American Abolitionist Politics*, Chapel Hill: University of North Carolina Press, 2003).

8. Foner, *Free Soil, Free Labor, Free Men*, 52, 53.

9. Freehling, *Road to Disunion: Secessionists at Bay*, 321.

10. Ann Hagedon, *Beyond the River: The Untold Story of the Heroes of the Underground Railroad* (New York: Simon & Schuster, 2004); Eric Foner, *Gateway to Freedom: The Hidden History of the Underground Railroad* (New York: W.W. Norton, 2016).

11. Catherine Clinton, *Harriet Tubman: The Road to Freedom* (New York: Back Bay Books, 2005); Earl Conrad, *Harriet Tubman* (New York: Associated Publishers, 1943), 214.

12. Corey Brooks, *Liberty Power: Antislavery Third Parties and the Transformation of American Politics* (Chicago: University of Chicago Press, 2016); Reinhard Johnson, *The Liberty Party, 1840–1848: Antislavery Third Party Politics in the United States* (Baton Rouge: Louisiana State University Press, 2021).

13. David Grimsted, *American Mobbing, 1828–1861: Toward Civil War* (New York: Oxford University Press, 1998); John McKivigan and Stanley Herrold, eds, *Antislavery Violence: Sectional, Racial, and Cultural Conflict in Antebellum America* (Knoxville: University of Tennessee Press, 1999).

14. David Bright, *Frederick Douglass' Civil War* (Baton Rouge: Louisiana State University Press, 1989); Philip Foner, ed., *Frederick Douglas on Slavery and the Civil War: Selections from His Writings* (Mineola: Dover, 2003); Timothy Sandefur, *Frederick Douglass: Self-Made Man* (Washington DC: Cato Institute, 2018); Damon Root, *A Glorious Liberty: Frederick Douglass and the Fight for an Anti-Slavery Constitution* (Lincoln: Potomac Books, 2020).

15. Kwame Appiah, ed., *Narrative of the Life of Frederick Douglass, an American Slave & Incidents in the Life of a Slave Girl* (New York: Modern Library, 2000).

16. Ibid., 18, 19, 34, 38, 24, 26–7, 32, 75, 93.

17. Ibid., 45, 48, 50, 68.

18. Ibid., 69, 104.

19. Frederick Douglass, *The Life and Times of Frederick Douglass* (New York: Dover Books, 2003), 302.

Chapter 6

1. Reginald Horsman, *Race and Manifest Destiny: The Origins of the American Racial Anglo-Saxonism* (Cambridge, Mass.: Harvard University Press, 1981); Thomas Hietala, *Manifest Design: American Exceptionalism and Empire* (Ithaca: Cornell University Press, 1985); Amy Greenberg, *Manifest Manhood and the Antebellum American Empire* (New York: Cambridge University Press, 2005).

2. For books on the early republic and antebellum decades that explore the themes of manifest destiny, territorial, and slavery expansion, see: Sean Wilentz, *The Rise of American Democracy:*

Jefferson to Lincoln (New York: W.W. Norton, 2005); Daniel Howe, *What Hath God Wrought: The Transformation of America, 1815–1848* (New York: Oxford University Press, 2007); Nester, *Hamiltonian Vision*; Nester, *Jeffersonian Vision*; William Nester, *The Age of Jackson and the Art of America Power, 1815–1848* (Washington DC: Potomac Books, 2013); William Nester, *The Age of Lincoln and the Art of American Power* (Washington DC: Potomac Books, 2013).

3. Robert Forbes, *The Missouri Compromise and Its Aftermath: Slavery and the Meaning of America* (Chapel Hill: university of North Carolina Press, 2009).

4. Congressional Globe, 29 Congress, 1st Session, 1217.

5. Mark Steigmaier, *Texas, New Mexico, and the 1850 Compromise: Boundary Dispute and Sectional Crisis* (Kent: Kent State University Press, 1996); John Waugh, *On the Brink of Civil War: The Compromise of 1850 and How It Changed the Course of American History* (Wilmington: Scholarly Resources, 2003).

6. David Sachsman, Kittrell Rushing, and Roy Morris, *Memory and Myth: The Civil War in Fiction and Film from Uncle Tom's Cabin to Cold Mountain* (Richmond: Purdue University Press, 2007), 8.

7. Joan Hedrick, *Harriet Beecher Stowe: A Life* (New York: Oxford University Press, 1994).

8. Harriet Beecher Stowe, *Uncle Tom's Cabin* (New York: Barnes and Noble, 2012), vii.

9. Elizabeth Moss, *Domestic Novelists in the Old South: Defenders of Southern Culture* (Baton Rouge: Louisiana State University Press, 1992).

10. Van Woodward, ed., *Mary Chesnut's War*, 245.

11. James Rawley, *Race and Politics: "Bleeding Kansas" and the Coming of the Civil War* (Lincoln: University of Nebraska Press, 1979); Nicole Etcheson, *Bleeding Kansas: Contested Liberty in the Civil War Era* (Lawrence: University Press of Kansas, 2004).

12. Congressional Globe, 33 Congress., 1st Session, Appendix 769.

13. McPherson, *Battle Cry of Freedom*, 146.

14. Michael Fellman, *Inside War: The Guerilla Conflict in Missouri during the American Civil War* (New York: Oxford University Press, 1989), 14.

15. William Gienapp, *The Origins of the Republican Party* (New York: Oxford University Press, 1988); Foner, *Free Soil, Free Labor, Free Men*; Robert Engs and Randall Miller, eds, *The Birth of the Grand Old Party: The Republicans' First Generation* (Philadelphia: University of Pennsylvania Press, 2002).

16. John Bicknell, *Lincoln's Pathfinder: John C. Fremont and the Violent Election of 1856* (Chicago: Chicago Review Press, 2017); William Nester, *The Old West's First Power Couples: The Fremonts, the Custers, and Their Epic Quest for Manifest Destiny* (Tucson: Rio Nuevo Publishers, 2020).

17. Paul Finkelman, *Dred Scott v. Sandford: A Brief History with Documents* (Boston: Bedford-St Martin's Press, 1997); Don Fehrenbacher, *The Dred Scott Case: Its Significance in American Law and Politics* (New York: Oxford University Press, 2001).

18. James Simon, *Lincoln and Chief Justice Taney: Slavery, Secession, and the President's War Powers* (New York: Simon & Schuster, 2006), 16.

19. For overviews of the opposing legal arguments over slavery, see: Earl Maltz, *Slavery and the Supreme Court, 1825–1861* (Lawrence: University of Kansas Press, 2009); Paul Finkelman, *Supreme Injustice: Slavery in the Nation's Highest Court* (Cambridge, Mass.: Harvard University Press, 2018); Martha Jones, *Birthright Citizenship: A History of Race and Rights in Antebellum America* (New York: Cambridge University Press, 2018).

20. Foner, *Free Soil, Free Labor, Free Men*, 76.

21. Benjamin Quarles, *Allies for Freedom: Blacks and John Brown* (New York: Da Capo, 2001); John Stauffer and Zoe Trodd, eds, *Meteor of War: The John Brown Story* (Maplecrest: Brandywine Press, 2004); David Reynolds, *John Brown, Abolitionist: The Man Who Killed Slavery, Sparked the Civil War, and Seeded Civil Rights* (New York: Vintage, 2006); Tony Horowitz, *Midnight Rising: John Brown and the Raid that Sparked the Civil War* (New York: Picador, 2012).

22. Paul Finkelman, ed., *His Soul Goes Marching On: Responses to John Brown and the Harpers Ferry Raid* (Charlottesville: University of Virginia Press, 1995); Reynolds, *John Brown, Abolitionist*; Peggy Russo and Paul Finkelman, eds, *Terrible Swift Sword: The Legacy of John Brown* (Athens: Ohio University Press, 2005).

23. H.W. Brands, *The Zealot and the Emancipator: John Brown, Abraham Lincoln, and the Struggle for America's Freedom* (New York: Doubleday, 2020).

Chapter 7

1. For Lincoln in the context of his time, see: Nester, *Age of Lincoln*. For the most evocative if not scholarly biography, see Carl Sandburg, *Abraham Lincoln: The Prairie Years and the War Years* (New York: Mariner Books, 2002). For other excellent biographies, see: Michael Burlingame, *Abraham Lincoln: A Life*, 2 vols (Baltimore: Johns Hopkins University Press, 2013); Sidney Blumenthal, *A Self-Made Man: The Political Life of Abraham Lincoln, 1809–1849* (New York: Simon & Schuster, 2017); Sidney Blumenthal, *Wrestling with his Angel: The Political Life of Abraham Lincoln, 1849–1856* (New York: Simon & Schuster, 2018); Sidney Blumenthal, *All the Powers of the Earth: The Political Life of Abraham Lincoln, 1856–1860* (New York: Simon & Schuster, 2020). For other good political biographies see: Philip Paludan, *The Presidency of Abraham Lincoln* (Lawrence: University Press of Kansas, 1994); James McPherson, *"We Cannot Escape History": Lincoln and the Last Best Hope of Earth* (Urbana: University of Illinois Press, 1995); David Donald, *Lincoln* (New York: Simon & Schuster, 1995); Richard Carwardine, *Lincoln: A Life of Purpose and Power* (New York: Vintage, 2007); Miller, *President Lincoln*.

2. Lincoln to A.G. Hodges, April 4, 1864, Philip Van Doren, ed., *The Life and Writings of Abraham Lincoln* (New York: Modern Library, 1940), 807.

3. Speech at Peoria, October 16, 1854, Van Doren, ed., *The Life and Writings of Abraham Lincoln*, 362.

4. William Herndon, *The Herndon's Lincoln: The True Story of a Great Life* (Springfield: The Herndon's Lincoln Publishing Company, 1921), 405–6.

5. Lincoln to A.G. Hodges, April 4, 1864, Van Doren, ed., *The Life and Writings of Abraham Lincoln*, 809.

6. John Briggs, *Lincoln's Speeches Reconsidered* (Baltimore: Johns Hopkins Press, 2005).

7. Annual Message to Congress, January 1, 1863, Van Doren, ed., *The Life and Writings of Abraham Lincoln*, 738.

8. Lincoln's First Public Address, March 9, 1832, Van Doren, ed., *The Life and Writings of Abraham Lincoln*, 224.

9. Reply in Debate at Ottawa, August 21, 1858, Van Doren, ed., *The Life and Writings of Abraham Lincoln*, 472–3.

10. Speech at Peoria, October 16, 1854, Van Doren, ed., *The Life and Writings of Abraham Lincoln*, 376.

11. Message to Congress, July 4, 1861, Van Doren, ed., *The Life and Writings of Abraham Lincoln*, 667–8.

12. Lyceum, January 23, 1838, Van Doren, ed., *The Life and Writings of Abraham Lincoln*, 233, 236.

13. Message to Congress, July 4, 1861, Van Doren, ed., *The Life and Writings of Abraham Lincoln*, 667–8.

14. Harold Holzer, *Lincoln at Cooper Union: The Speech That Made Him President*, (New York: Simon & Schuster, 2004).

15. Cooper Union Speech, February 27, 1860, Van Doren, ed., *The Life and Writings of Abraham Lincoln*, 591.

16. Meditation on the Divine Will, September 30, 1862, Van Doren, ed., *The Life and Writings of Abraham Lincoln*, 728.

17. Springfield Speech, June 16, 1858, Van Doren, ed., *The Life and Writings of Abraham Lincoln*, 429.

18. Harold Holzer, ed., *The Lincoln-Douglas Debates: The First Complete, Unexpurgated Text* (New York: HarperCollins, 1993); Alan Guelzo, *Lincoln and Douglas: The Debates That Defined America* (New York: Simon & Schuster, 2008).

19. Blumenthal, *All the Powers of the Earth*, 364.

20. Douglas, Egerton, *Year of Meteors: Stephen Douglas, Abraham Lincoln, and the Election that brought on the Civil War* (New York: Bloomsbury Press, 2010); Michael Holt, *The Election of 1860: A Campaign Fraught with Consequences* (Topeka: University Press of Kansas, 2017).

21. Foner, *Free Soil, Free Labor, Free Men*, 315.

22. Ibid., 72.

Chapter 8

1. Ralph Wooster, *The Secession Conventions of the South* (Princeton: Princeton University Press, 1962); Maury Klein, *Days of Defiance: Sumter, Secession, and the Coming of the Civil War* (New York: Vintage, 1999); Charles Dew, *Apostles of Disunion: Southern Secession Commissions and the Causes of the Civil War* (Charlottesville: University of Virginia Press, 2002); Freehling, *The Road to Disunion: Secessionists Triumphant, 1854–1861* (New York: Oxford University Press, 2009); Adam Goodheart, *1861: The Civil War Awakening* (New York: Vintage, 2012).

2. Drew Gilpin Faust, *The Creation of Confederate Nationalism: Ideology and Identity in the Civil War South* (Baton Rouge: Louisiana State University Press, 1989), 55.

3. Miller, *President Lincoln*, 15.

4. William Freehling, *Prelude to Civil War: The Nullification Controversy in South Carolina, 1816–1836* (New York: Oxford University Press, 1965); Richard Ellis, *The Union at Risk: Jacksonian Democracy, States' Rights, and the Nullification Crisis* (New York: Oxford University Press, 1987).

5. Jean Baker, *James Buchannan: The 15th President, 1857–1861* (New York: Times Books, 2004).

6. John McCardell, *The Idea of a Southern Nation: Southern Nationalists and Southern Nationalism, 1830–1860* (New York: W.W. Norton, 1981); Faust, *Creation of Southern Nationalism*; Emory Thomas, *The Confederacy as a Revolutionary Experience* (Columbia: University of South Carolina University Press, 1992); Paul Escott, *After Secession: Jefferson Davis and the Failure of Confederate Nationalism* (Baton Rouge: Louisiana State University Press, 1992); Wiley Sword, *Southern Invincibility: A History of the Confederate Heart* (New York: St. Martin's Griffin, 2000); Anne Sarah Rubin, *A Shattered Nation: The Rise and Fall of the Confederacy* (Chapel Hill: University of North Carolina Press, 2005); George Rable, *The Confederate Republic: A Revolution against Politics* (Chapel Hill: University of North Carolina Press, 2007); Stephanie McCurry, *Confederate Reckoning: Power and Politics in the Civil War South* (Cambridge, Mass.: Harvard University Press, 2010).

7. John Coski, *The Confederate Battle Flag: America's Most Embattled Emblem* (Cambridge, Mass.: Harvard University Press, 2005).

8. William Cooper, *Jefferson Davis, American* (New York: Vintage, 2001); James McPherson, *Embattled Rebel: Jefferson Davis as Commander in Chief* (New York: Penguin, 2014); William Davis, *Jefferson Davis: The Man and His Hour* (New York: Lume Books, 2016).

9. Klein, *Days of Defiance*, 248.

10. Steven Woodworth, *Jefferson Davis and His Generals: The Failure of Confederate Command in the West* (Lawrence: University Press of Kansas, 1990); Steven Woodworth, *Davis and Lee at War* (Lawrence: University Press of Kansas, 1995); Joseph Harsh, *Confederate Tide Rising: Robert E. Lee and the Making of Southern Strategy, 1861–1862* (Kent: Kent State University Press, 1998).

11. Herman Hattaway and Archer Jones, *How the North Won: A Military History of the Civil War* (Urbana: University of Illinois Press, 1991), 286–77.

12. Richard Beringer et al., *The Elements of Confederate Defeat: Nationalism, War Aims, and Religion* (Athens: University of Georgia Press, 1989); Gary Gallagher, *The Confederate War:*

How Popular Will, Nationalism, and Military Strategy Could Not Stave Off Defeat (Cambridge, Mass.: Harvard University Press, 1997); Armstead Robinson, *Bitter Fruits of Bondage: The Demise of Slavery and Collapse of the Confederacy* (Charlottesville: University of Virginia Press, 2005); Rubin, *A Shattered Nation.*

13. Vann Woodward, ed., *Mary Chesnut's Civil War*, 83.
14. Address at Cleveland, February 15, 1861, Van Doren, ed., *The Life and Writings of Abraham Lincoln*, 639.
15. Farewell Address at Springfield, February 11, 1861, Van Doren, ed., *The Life and Writings of Abraham Lincoln*, 635–6.
16. Doris Kearns Goodwin, *Team of Rivals: The Political Genius of Abraham Lincoln* (New York: Simon & Schuster, 2006).
17. Inaugural Address, March 4, 1861, Van Doren, ed., *The Life and Writings of Abraham Lincoln*, 649–50, 654.
18. William Marvel, *Mr. Lincoln Goes to War* (Boston: Houghton Mifflin, 2006); Russell McClintock, *Lincoln and the Decision for War: The Northern Response to Secession* (Chapel Hill: University of North Carolina Press, 2008).
19. Vann Woodward, ed., *Mary Chesnut's Civil War*, 46.

Chapter 9
1. George Turner, *Victory Rode the Rails: The Strategic Place of Railroads in the Civil War* (New York: Bobbs-Merrill, 1953); Paul Koistenen, *Beating Plowshares into Swords: The Political Economy of American Warfare, 1606–1865* (Lawrence: University Press of Kansas, 1996); John Clark, *Railroads in the Civil War: The Impact of Management on Victory and Defeat* (Baton Rouge: Louisiana State University Press, 2004); Peter Onuf, *Nations, Markets, and War: Modern History and the American Civil War* (Charlottesville: University of Virginia Press, 2006); Mark Wilson, *The Business of Civil War: Military Mobilization and the State, 1861–1865* (Baltimore: Johns Hopkins University Press, 2006); Baron Hacker, *Astride Two Worlds: Technology and the American Civil War* (Washington DC: Smithsonian Institute Scholarly Press, 2016); Earl Hess, *Civil War Logistics: A Study of Military Transportation* (Baton Rouge: Louisiana State University Press, 2017).
2. For overviews, see: David Donald, ed., *Why the North Won the Civil War* (New York: Collier Books, 1960); Roman Heleniak and Lawrence Hewitt, eds, *The Confederate High Command* (Shippensburg: White Mane Publishing, 1990); Hattaway and Jones, *How the North Won*; Archer Jones, *Civil War Command and Strategy: The Process of Victory and Defeat* (New York: Free Press, 1992); Donald Stoker, *The Grand Design: Strategy and the U.S. Civil War* (New York: Oxford University Press, 2010). For the Southern failure, see: Beringer et al., *Elements of Confederate Defeat*; Woodworth, *Jefferson Davis and His Generals*; Archer Jones, *The Politics of Command: Factions and Ideas in Confederate Strategy* (Baton Rouge: Louisiana State University Press, 1998); Gallagher, *The Confederate War*; Robinson, *Bitter Fruits of Bondage*; Rubin, *A Shattered Nation.*
3. McPherson, *Battle Cry of Freedom*, 318.
4. Lerner, ed., *Historical Statistics of the United States*, 1:8, 14; 2:666, 731; Hattaway and Jones, *How the North Won*, 17–18.
5. Richard Beringer, Herman Hattaway, Archer Jones, and William Still, *Why the South Lost the Civil War* (Athens: University of Georgia Press, 1986), 10.
6. Beringer et al., *Why the South Lost*, 9.
7. McPherson, *Battle Cry of Freedom*, 325.
8. Mark Grimsley, *The Hard Hand of War: Union Military Policy toward Civilians, 1861–1865* (New York: Cambridge University Press, 1995); Robert Daughty, Ira Gruber, et al., *The American Civil War: The Emergence of Total Warfare* (Lexington, Mass.: D.C. Heath, 1996);

Daniel Sutherland, *The Emergence of Total Warfare: Civil War Campaigns and Commanders* (Abilene: McWhiney Foundation Press, 1998).

9. Beringer et al., *Why the South Lost*, 247.

10. Sherman, *Memoirs*, 585.

11. Hattaway and Jones, *How the North Won*, 721.

12. Grady McWhiney and Perry Jamieson, *Attack and Die: Civil War Military Tactics and the Southern Heritage* (Tuscaloosa: University of Alabama Press 1984); Earl Hess, *Civil War Infantry Tactics: Training, Combat, and Small Unit Effectiveness* (Baton Rouge: Louisiana State University Press, 2015); Stephen Hysop, *Atlas of the Civil War: A Complete Guide to the Tactics and Terrain of Battle* (Washington DC: National Geographic, 2009); Paddy Griffith, *Battle Tactics and the Civil War* (London: Crowood Press, 2014).

13. McPherson, *Battle Cry of Freedom*, 513.

14. Hattaway and Jones, *How the North Won*, 29–30, 501–5.

15. Ibid., 324.

16. Ibid., 357.

17. Richard West, *Mr. Lincoln's Navy* (New York: Longmans, Green, 1957); James Merrill, *Rebel Shore: The Story of Union Sea Power in the Civil War* (New York: Little, Brown, 1958); Howard Nash, *A Naval History of the Civil War* (New York: A.S. Barnes, 1972); Rowena Reed, *Combined Operations in the Civil War* (Annapolis: Naval Institute Press, 1978); Craig Symonds, ed., *Union Combined Operations in the Civil War* (New York: Fordham University Press, 2010); Paul Calore, *Naval Campaigns of the Civil War* (Jefferson: McFarland and Company, 2001); Craig Symonds, *The Civil War at Sea* (New York: Oxford University Press, 2012); Spencer Tucker, *Blue and Grey Navies: The Civil War Afloat* (Annapolis: Naval Institute Press, 2013).

18. Hattaway and Jones, *How the North Won*, 33–4, 88.

19. Reed, *Combined Operations in the Civil War*; Symonds, ed., *Union Combined Operations in the Civil War*.

20. Charles Hearn, *Grey Raiders of the Sea: How Eight Confederate Warships Destroyed the Union's High Seas Commerce* (Baton Rouge: Louisiana State University Press, 1996).

21. McPherson, *Battle Cry of Freedom*, 380–2; Hattaway and Jones, *How the North Won*, 427.

22. James Soley, *The Blockade and the Cruisers* (New York: Charles Scribner's Sons, 1885); Virgil Jones, *The Civil War at Sea: The Blockaders* (New York: Holt, Rinehart, 1960); Stephen Wise, *Lifeline of the Confederacy: Blockade Running during the Civil War* (Charleston: University of South Carolina Press, 1991).

23. Soley, *Blockade and the Cruisers*, 44–5.

24. McPherson, *Battle Cry of Freedom*, 378–82.

25. Richard Current, "God and the Strongest Battalions," in *Why the North Won the Civil War*, ed. David Donald (New York: Collier Books, 1960), 23.

26. Bodenhorn, *History of Banking*; Irwin Unger, *The Greenback Era: A Social and Political History of American Finance* (Princeton: Princeton University Press, 1964); Bray Hammond, *Sovereignty and an Empty Purse: Banks and Politics in the Civil War* (Princeton: Princeton University Press, 1970); Hammond, *Banks and Politics*; Paul Studenski and Herman Krooss, *The Financial History of the United States* (New York: Beard Books, 2003).

27. Stephen Daggett, *Costs of Major U.S. Wars* (Washington DC: Congressional Research Service, 2010); Robert Hormats, *The Price of Liberty: Paying for America's Wars* (New York: Henry Holt, 2007).

28. Ralph Andreano, ed., *The Economic Impact of the American Civil War* (Cambridge, Mass.: Schenkman Publishing Company, 1962), 174.

29. Douglas Ball, *Financial Failure and Confederate Defeat* (Urbana: University of Illinois Press, 1991).

30. McPherson, *Battle Cry of Freedom*, 447; Andreano, ed., *Economic Impact of the American Civil War*, 15.

31. McCurry, *Confederate Reckoning*, 155, 392.
32. For an overview, see: D.P. Crook, *The North, the South, and the Powers, 1861–1865* (New York: John Wiley, 1974); Dean Mahin, *One War at a Time: The International Dimensions of the American Civil War* (Washington DC: Potomac Books, 1999); Howard Jones, *Blue and Grey Diplomacy: A History of Union and Confederate Foreign Relations* (Chapel Hill: University of North Carolina Press, 2009). For the Confederacy, see: Frank Owsley, *King Cotton Diplomacy: Foreign Relations of the Confederate States of America* (Tuscaloosa: University of Alabama Press, 2008). For the Union, see: Norman Ferris, *Desperate Diplomacy: William H. Seward's Foreign Policy* (Nashville: University of Tennessee Press, 1976). For diplomacy with Britain and France, see: Brian Jenkins, *Britain and the War for the Union*, 2 vols (Montreal: McGill-Queens University Press, 1974, 1980); Amanda Foreman, *A World on Fire: Britain's Crucial Role in the American Civil War* (New York: Random House, 2012); Steve Saulaude, *France and the Civil War: A Diplomatic History* (Chapel Hill: University of North Carolina Press, 2019).
33. Owsley, *King Cotton Diplomacy*, 351.
34. McPherson, *Battle Cry of Freedom*, 548; Andreano, ed., *Economic Impact of the American Civil War*, 51.
35. Shelby Foote, *The Civil War, A Narrative, From Fredericksburg to Meridian* (New York: Vintage, 1986), 150.
36. Gabor Boritt, ed., *Lincoln, The War President: The Gettysburg Lectures* (New York: Oxford University Press, 1992); Gabor Boritt, ed., *Lincoln's Generals* (Lincoln: University of Nebraska Press, 1994); Thomas Goss, *The War within the Union High Command: Politics and Generalship during the Civil War* (Lawrence: University Press of Kansas, 2003); Geoffrey Perret, *Lincoln's War: The Untold Story of America's Greatest President as Commander in Chief* (New York: Random House, 2004); James McPherson, *Tried by War: Abraham Lincoln as Commander in Chief* (New York: Penguin, 2009); Chester Hearn, *Lincoln, the Cabinet, and the Generals* (Baton Rouge: Louisiana State University Press, 2010); Stephen Sears, *Lincoln's Lieutenants: The High Command of the Army of the Potomac* (Boston: Houghton Mifflin, 2017).
37. Burlingame, *Abraham Lincoln*, 2:248.
38. Lincoln to Hooker, June 5, 1863, Van Doren, ed., *The Life and Writings of Abraham Lincoln*, 754.
39. John Eisenhower, *Agent of Destiny: The Life and Times of General Winfield Scott* (New York: Free Press, 1997).
40. Hattaway and Jones, *How the North Won*, 287.
41. Lincoln to Henry Halleck, September 19, 1863, Van Doren, ed., *The Life and Writings of Abraham Lincoln*, 783.

Chapter 10
1. William Freehling, *The South vs. the South: How Anti-Confederate Southerners Shaped the Course of the Civil War* (New York: Oxford University Press, 2001), 57.
2. Message to Congress, July 4, 1861, Van Doren, ed., *The Life and Writings of Abraham Lincoln*, 667–8.
3. Burlingame, *Abraham Lincoln*, 2:181.
4. Sherman, *Memoirs*, 199.
5. Stephen Sears, *George B. McClellan: The Young Napoleon* (New York: Da Capo Press, 1999); Ethan Rafuse, *McClellan's War: The Failure of Moderation in the Struggle for the Union* (Bloomington: University of Indiana Press, 2011).
6. John Waugh, *Lincoln and McClellan: The Troubled Partnership between a President and His General* (New York: St Martin's Griffin, 2011).
7. Jeffrey Wert, *The Sword of Lincoln: The Army of the Potomac* (New York: Simon & Schuster, 2005), 44.

8. Burlingame, *Abraham Lincoln*, 2:197.
9. For the best book on Missouri politics and fighting during the Civil War, see: Fellman, *Inside War*. For the best books on the campaigns in Missouri and elsewhere west of the Mississippi River, see Jay Monaghan, *Civil War on the Western Border, 1854–1865* (Lincoln: University of Nebraska Press, 1955); Alvin Josephy, *The Civil War in the American West* (New York: Alfred Knopf, 1992).
10. Christopher Phillips, *Damned Yankee: The Life of General Nathaniel Lyon* (Baton Rouge: Louisiana State University Press, 1996).
11. Ulysses Grant, *Memoirs* (Princeton: Collectors Reprints, 1998); Jean Smith, *Grant* (New York: Touchstone, 2001); Ron Chernow, *Grant* (New York: Penguin, 2017).
12. Grant, *Memoirs*, 11.
13. Chernow, *Grant*, xix.
14. Harry Williams, *McClellan, Sherman, and Grant* (New Brunswick: Rutgers University Press, 1962), 105.
15. Smith, *Grant*, 15.
16. Ibid., 233.
17. Grant, *Memoirs*, 17.
18. Ibid., 107.

Chapter 11

1. Hattaway and Jones, *How the North Won*, 9–10.
2. McPherson, *Battle Cry of Freedom*, 328.
3. Ibid., 313.
4. Edward Hagerman, *The American Civil War and the Origins of Modern Warfare: Ideas, Organization, and Field Command* (Bloomington: Indiana University Press, 1988); Hess, *Civil War Logistics*.
5. Hattaway and Jones, *How the North Won*, 274–5.
6. Sherman, *Memoirs*, 879.
7. Douglas Freeman, *Lee's Lieutenants: A Study in Command*, 3 vols. (New York: Charles Scribners' Sons, 1942–4); Goss, *War Within the Union High Command*; Wilmer Jones, *Generals in Blue and Gray: Lincoln's Generals* (Mechanicsville: Stackpole Books, 2006); Wilmer Jones, *Generals in Blue and Gray: Davis's Generals* (Mechanicsville: Stackpole Books, 2006).
8. Henry Williams, "The Military Leadership of North and South," in *Why the North Won the Civil War*, ed. David Donald (New York: Collier, 1960), 36.
9. McPherson, *Tried by War*, 42.
10. Taylor, *Cavalier and Yankee*; David Pugh, *Sons of Liberty: The Masculine Mind in Nineteenth Century America* (Westport: Greenwood Press, 1983); Reid Mitchell, *Civil War Soldiers* (New York: Viking, 1988); Mark Carnes and Clyde Griffin, eds, *Meanings for Manhood* (Chicago: University of Chicago Press, 1990); James McPherson, *What They Fought For, 1861–1865* (Baton Rouge: Louisiana State University Press, 1994); Michael Kimmel, *Manhood in America: A Cultural History* (New York: Free Press, 1995); James McPherson, *For Cause and Comrades: Why Men Fought in the Civil War* (New York: Oxford University Press, 1997); Berry, *All That Makes a Man*.
11. Hattaway and Jones, *How the North Won*, 9.
12. McPherson, *Battle Cry of Freedom*, 492.
13. Ibid., 608.
14. Eugene Murdock, *Patriotism Limited 1862–1865: The Civil War Draft and the Bounty System* (Kent: Kent State University Press, 1967); Eugene Murdock, *One Million Men: The Civil War Draft in the North* (Madison: University of Wisconsin Press, 1971); James Geary, *We Need Men: The Union Draft in the Civil War* (Chapel Hill: University of North Carolina Press,

1990); Colleen Glenney Boggs, *Patriotism by Proxy: The Civil War Draft and the Cultural Formation of Citizen Soldiers, 1863–1865* (New York: Oxford University Press, 2020).

15. McPherson, *Battle Cry of Freedom*, 605.
16. Earl Hess, *Liberty, Virtue, and Progress: Northerners and Their War for the Union* (New York: Fordham University Press, 1997); Susan-Mary Grant, *North Over South: Northern Nationalism and American Identity in the Antebellum Era* (Lawrence: University Press of Kansas, 2000).
17. Lincoln Opinion of the Draft, August 15, 1863, *Lincoln Life and Times*, 771.
18. McPherson, *Battle Cry of Freedom*, 432.
19. Ibid., 614.
20. Hattaway and Jones, *How the North Won*, 114–16.
21. Foote, *Civil War: A Narrative, From Fredericksburg to Meridian*, 65.
22. Dudley Cornish, *The Sable Arm: Negro Troops in the Union Army, 1861–1865* (New York: Longmans, Green, 1956); Joseph Glatthaar, *Forged in Battle: The Civil War Alliance of Black Soldiers and White Officers* (Baton Rouge: Louisiana State University Press 1990); James McPherson, *The Negro's Civil War: How America's Blacks Felt and Acted during the War for Union* (New York: Vintage, 2003); Ira Berlin, Joseph Reidy, and Leslie Rowland, eds, *Freedom's Soldiers: The Black Military Experience in the Civil War* (New York: Cambridge University Press, 1998); William Dobak, *Freedom by the Sword: The Official Army History of the U.S. Colored Troops in the Civil War, 1862 to 1867* (New York: Red and Black Publishers, 2020).
23. Cornish, *Sable Arm*, 214–28, 254–8.
24. Ira Berlin, Joseph Reidy, and Leslie Rowland, eds, *Freedom: A Documentary History of Emancipation, 1861–1867: The Black Military Experience* (New York: Cambridge University Press, 1982), 483–516, 633–7.
25. Lincoln to James Conkling, August 26, 1863, Van Doren, ed., *The Life and Writings of Abraham Lincoln*, 779–80.
26. Goodwin, *Team of Rivals*, 550.
27. Berlin et al., *Freedom's Soldiers*, 588–9.
28. Donald, *Lincoln*, 489.
29. McCurry, *Confederate Reckoning*, 326.
30. Sword, *Southern Invincibility*, 319.
31. Robert Durden, *The Gray and the Black: The Confederate Debate on Emancipation* (Baton Rouge: Louisiana State University Press, 1972), 206.
32. McCurry, *Confederate Reckoning*, 351.
33. Genovese, *Fatal Self Deception*, 145.
34. James Robertson, *Soldiers Blue and Gray* (Charleston: University of South Carolina Press, 1998); Peter Carmichael, *The War for the Common Soldiers: How Men Thought, Fought, and Survived in Civil War Armies* (Chapel Hill: University of North Carolina Press, 2018).
35. David Blight, "No Desperate Hero: Manhood and Freedom in a Union Soldier's Experience," Catherine Clinton and Nina Silber, eds, *Divided Houses: Gender and the Civil War* (New York: Oxford University Press, 1992), 59.
36. Ella Lonn, *Desertion during the Civil War* (Lincoln: University of Nebraska Press, 1998); Foote, *Civil War, A Narrative: Fredericksburg to Meridian*, 635; Hattaway and Jones, *How the North Won*, 444.
37. Gerald Linderman, *Embattled Courage: The Experience of Combat in the American Civil War* (New York: Free Press, 1989); Earl Hess, *The Union Soldier in Battle: Enduring the Ordeal of Combat* (Lawrence: University Press of Kansas, 1997); Brent Nosworthy, *The Bloody Crucible of Courage: Fighting Methods and Combat Experience of the Civil War* (New York: Carrol and Graf, 2003).
38. Dave Grossman, *On Killing: The Psychological Cost of Learning to Kill* (Boston: Little, Brown, 1995), ix.

39. Drew Gilpin Faust, *This Republic of Suffering: Death and the American Civil War* (New York: Vintage, 2008), 34, 35, 37–8.
40. George Adams, *Doctors in Blue: The Medical History of the Union Army during the Civil War* (New York: Henry Schuman, 1952), 113.
41. Sherman, *Memoirs*, 885–6.
42. Ibid., 265.
43. Colonel L.M. Dayton report, in Sherman, *Memoirs*, 436–7.
44. Randall Jimerson, *The Private Civil War: Popular Thought during the Sectional Conflict* (Baton Rouge: Louisiana State University Press, 1988), 228.
45. Daniel Aaron, *The Unwritten War: American Writers and the Civil War* (New York: Alfred Knopf, 1973), 185–6.
46. McPherson, *Battle Cry of Freedom*, 802. William Hesseltine, ed., *Civil War Prisons* (Kent: Kent State University Press, 1972); William Hesseltine, *Civil War Prisons: A Study in War Psychology* (Columbus: Ohio State University Press, 1998); Lonnie Speer, *Portals to Hell: Military Prisons of the Civil War* (Lincoln: University of Nebraska Press, 2005).
47. William Marvel, *Andersonville: The Last Depot* (Chapel Hill: University of North Carolina Press, 1994); Ovid Cutch, *The History of Andersonville Prison* (Tallahassee: University Press of Florida, 2011).
48. Derek Maxfield, *Hellmira: The Union's Most Infamous Civil War Prison Camp* (New York: Savas Beattie, 2020).
49. McPherson, *Battle Cry of Freedom*, 793.
50. Alan Nolan, *Lee Reconsidered: General Robert E. Lee and Civil War History* (Chapel Hill: University of North Carolina Press, 2000), 19.
51. Adams, *Doctors in Blue*; Paul Steiner, *Disease in the Civil War: Natural Biological Warfare in 1861–1865* (Springfield: C.C. Thomas, 1968); Frank Freemon, *Gangrene and Glory: Medical Care during the Civil War* (Urbana: University of Illinois Press, 1998).
52. Freemon, *Gangrene and Glory*, 63.
53. William Maxwell, *Lincoln's Fifth Wheel: The Political History of the United States Sanitary Commission* (New York: Longmans, Green, and Company, 1956); Judith Ann Giesberg, *Civil War Sisterhood: The U.S. Sanitary Commission and Women's Politics in Transition* (Boston: Northeastern University Press, 2000).
54. Freemon, *Gangrene and Glory*, 218.
55. Mark Van Doren, ed., *The Portable Walt Whitman* (New York: Penguin, 1977), 228.
56. Sylvia Dannett, ed., *Noble Women of the North* (New York: Thomas Yoseloff, 1959), 60.
57. Elizabeth Pryor, *Clara Barton: Professional Angel* (Philadelphia: University of Pennsylvania Press, 1987), 154.
58. Vann Woodward, ed., *Mary Chesnut's Civil War*, 158, 474, 641, 668, 637.

Chapter 12
1. Kenneth Gott, *When the South Lost the Civil War: An Analysis of the Fort Henry-Fort Donelson Campaign, February 1862* (Mechanicsburg: Stackpole Books, 2003); Timothy Smith, *Grant Invades Tennessee: The 1862 Battles for Forts Henry and Donelson* (Lawrence: University Press of Kansas, 2016).
2. Grant, *Memoirs*, 150.
3. John Wyeth, *That Devil Forrest: A Life of General Nathan Bedford Forrest* (Baton Rouge: Louisiana State University Press, 1989); Samuel Mitcham, *Bust Hell Wide Open: The Life of Nathan Bedford Forrest* (New York: Regnery, 2019); John Scales, *Nathan Bedford Forrest, 1861–1865: The Battles and Campaigns of Confederate General* (New York: Savas Beattie, 2019).
4. Scales, *Nathan Bedford Forrest*, 443.
5. Ward, *River Ran Red*.

6. Winston Groom, *Shiloh, 1862* (Washington DC: National Geographic Society, 2013); Timothy Smith, *Shiloh: Conquer or Perish* (Lawrence: University Press of Kansas, 2016).
7. Smith, *Grant*, 200.
8. Chernow, *Grant*, 211.
9. Grant, *Memoirs*, 168.
10. Barbara Brooks Tomblin, *The Civil War on the Mississippi: Union Sailors, Gunboat Captains, and the Campaign to Control the River* (Lexington: University Press of Kentucky, 2020).
11. James Nelson, *Reign of Iron: The Story of the First Battling Ironclads: The Monitor and the Merrimack* (New York: William Morrow, 2004); Richard Snow, *Iron Dawn: The Monitor, the Merrimack, and the Civil War Sea Battle that Changed History* (New York: Scribner, 2016).
12. McPherson, *Battle Cry of Freedom*, 377.
13. Letter to McClellan, April 9, 1862, Van Doren, ed., *The Life and Writings of Abraham Lincoln*, 698–700.
14. Stephen Sears, *To the Gates of Richmond: The Peninsula Campaign* (New York: Ticknor and Shields, 1992); Gary Gallagher, *The Richmond Campaign of 1862: The Peninsula and the Seven Days* (Chapel Hill: University of North Carolina Press, 2008).
15. Sears, *To the Gates of Richmond*, 24.
16. Douglas Freeman, *R.E. Lee: A Biography*, 4 vols (New York: Charles Scribners' Sons, 1933–5); Emory Thomas, *Robert E. Lee: A Biography* (New York: W.W. Norton, 1997); Nolan, *Lee Reconsidered*; Michael Korda, *Clouds of Glory: The Life and Legend of Robert E. Lee* (New York: Harper Perennial, 2015). For critical accounts, see: Thomas Connelly, *The Marble Man: Robert E. Lee and His Image in American Society* (New York: Knopf, 1977); Nolan, *Lee Reconsidered*; John McKenzie, *Uncertain Glory: Lee's Generalship Reexamined* (New York: Hippocrene Books, 1997). For comparisons, see: J.F.C. Fuller, *Grant and Lee: A Study in Personality and Generalship* (Bloomington: University of Indiana Press, 1957); Gene Smith, *Lee and Grant: A Dual Biography* (New York: McGraw-Hill, 1984).
17. Byron Farwell, *Stonewall: A Biography of General Thomas J. Jackson* (New York: W.W. Norton, 1993); James Robertson, *Stonewall Jackson: The Man, the Soldier, the Legend* (New York: Macmillan, 1997); Donald Davis, *Stonewall Jackson: Lessons in Leadership* (New York: St Martin's Press, 2007); S.C. Gwynne, *Rebel Yell: The Violence, Passion, and Redemption of Stonewall Jackson* (New York: Charles Scribner's Sons, 2015).
18. McPherson, *Battle Cry of Freedom*, 455.
19. Robert Tanner, *Stonewall in the Valley: Thomas J. "Stonewall" Jackson's Shenandoah Valley Campaign, Spring 1862* (Mechanicsburg: Stackpole Books, 1996); Peter Cozzens, *Shenandoah 1862: Stonewall Jackson's Valley Campaign* (Chapel Hill: University of North Carolina Press, 2008).
20. Sears, *To the Gates of Richmond*; Clifford Dowdey, *The Seven Days: The Emergence of Lee* (Lincoln: University of Nebraska Press, 1993); Gallagher, *Richmond Campaign of 1862*.
21. Sears, *To the Gates of Richmond*, 243, 255; Foote, *Civil War: A Narrative, From Fredericksburg to Meridian*, 516.
22. McPherson, *Battle Cry of Freedom*, 490.
23. Wallace Schutz and Walter Trenerry, *Abandoned by Lincoln: A Military Biography of General John Pope* (Urbana: University of Illinois Press, 1990); Peter Cozzens, *General John Pope: A Life for the Nation* (Urbana: University of Illinois Press, 2000).
24. McPherson, *Battle Cry of Freedom*, 524.
25. John Hennessey, *Return to Bull Run: The Campaign and Battle of Second Manassas* (New York: Simon & Schuster, 1993).
26. James McPherson, *Crossroads of Freedom: Antietam* (New York: Oxford University Press, 2002); Stephen Sears, *The Landscape Turned Red: The Battle of Antietam* (New York: Mariner Books, 2003).

27. Lincoln to O.H. Browning, September 22, 1861, Van Doren, ed., *The Life and Writings of Abraham Lincoln*, 682.
28. Ira Berlin et al., eds, *Free At Last: A Documentary History of Slavery, Freedom, and the Civil War* (New York: New Press, 1992); William Blair and Karen Younger, eds, *Lincoln's Proclamation: Emancipation Reconsidered* (Chapel Hill: University of North Carolina Press, 2009); Robinson, *Bitter Fruits of Bondage*.
29. Paludan, *Presidency of Abraham Lincoln*, 135.
30. Lincoln to Horace Greeley, August 22, 1862, Van Doren, ed., *The Life and Writings of Abraham Lincoln*, 719.
31. Lincoln to black delegation, August 15, 1862, Van Doren, ed., *The Life and Writings of Abraham Lincoln*, 715–16.
32. Reply to a Committee of Denominations Asking the President to Issue a Proclamation of Emancipation, September 13, 1862, Van Doren, ed., *The Life and Writings of Abraham Lincoln*, 720–3.
33. Preliminary Emancipation Proclamation, September 22, 1862, Van Doren, ed., *The Life and Writings of Abraham Lincoln*, 723–6.
34. Goodwin, *Team of Rivals*, 499.
35. Annual Message to Congress, January 1, 1863, Van Doren, ed., *The Life and Writings of Abraham Lincoln*, 738.
36. Unless otherwise noted, this chapter's statistics came from Josephy, *Civil War in the American West*.
37. Kenneth Carley, *The Dakota War of 1862: Minnesota's Other Civil War* (St Paul: Minnesota Historical Society Press, 1976).
38. Josephy, *Civil War in the American West*, 109.
39. Carley, *Dakota War*, 1.
40. Donald, *Lincoln*, 394–5.
41. Miller, *President Lincoln*, 322.
42. Duane Schultz, *Month of the Freezing Moon: The Sand Creek Massacre, November 1864* (New York: St Martin's Press, 1990); Thom Hatch, *Black Kettle: The Cheyenne Chief Who Sought Peace But Found War* (New York: John Wiley, 2004).
43. Hatch, *Black Kettle*, 164.
44. Schultz, *Month of the Freezing Moon*, 166.
45. Earl Hess, *Braxton Bragg: The Most Hatted Man of the Confederacy* (Chapel Hill: University of North Carolina Press, 2016).
46. Lincoln to McClellan, October 13, 1862, Van Doren, ed., *The Life and Writings of Abraham Lincoln*, 729–30.
47. Lincoln to McClellan, October 24, 1862, Van Doren, ed., *The Life and Writings of Abraham Lincoln*, 731.
48. William Marvel, *Burnside* (Chapel Hill: University of North Carolina Press, 1991).
49. Hattaway and Jones, *How the North Won*, 266.
50. Gary Gallagher, *The Fredericksburg Campaign* (Chapel Hill: University of North Carolina Press, 1995).
51. Gary Gallagher, *Lee and His Army in Confederate History* (Chapel Hill: University of North Carolina Press, 2006), 80.
52. James Ramage, *Rebel Raider: The Life of General John Hunt Morgan* (Lexington: University Press of Kentucky, 1986), 131, 145.

Chapter 13
1. Jean Harvey Baker, *Mary Todd Lincoln: A Biography* (New York: W.W. Norton, 2008).
2. Donald, *Lincoln*, 84.

3. Ibid., 85.
4. Michael Burlingame, *An American Marriage: The Untold Story of Abraham Lincoln and Mary Todd* (New York: Pegasus, 2021).
5. Jason Emerson, *The Madness of Mary Lincoln* (Carbondale: University of Southern Illinois Press, 2012).
6. William Marvel, *Lincoln's Autocrat: The Life of Edwin Stanton* (Chapel Hill: University of North Carolina Press, 2015).
7. Gideon Welles, *The Diary of Gideon Welles, Secretary of the Navy* (Boston: Houghton Mifflin, 1911), 203.
8. Grant, *Memoirs*, 333, 572.
9. Allan Bogue, *The Congressman's Civil War* (New York: Cambridge University Press, 1989).
10. Kenneth Martis, *Historical Atlas of Political Parties in the United States Congress, 1789–1989* (Englewood Cliffs: Prentice Hall, 1989).
11. Paludan, *Presidency of Abraham Lincoln*, 108–9.
12. Hans Trefousse, *The Radical Republicans: Lincoln's Vanguard for Racial Justice* (New York: Alfred Knopf, 1969); Michael Green, *Freedom, Union, and Power: Lincoln and His Party during the Civil War* (New York: Fordham University Press, 2004).
13. Perret, *Lincoln's War*.
14. Trefousse, *Radical Republicans*, 184.
15. Bruce Tap, *Over Lincoln's Shoulder: The Committee on the Conduct of the War* (Lawrence: University Press of Kansas, 1998).
16. Joel Silbey, *A Respectable Minority: The Democratic Party in the Civil War Era, 1860–1868* (New York: W.W. Norton, 1977); Jean Baker, *Affairs of Party: The Political Culture of Northern Democrat in Mid-Nineteenth Century* (Ithaca: Cornell University Press, 1983).
17. Mark Summers, *The Plundering Generation: Corruption and the Crisis of the Union, 1849–1861* (New York: Oxford University Press, 1987); Wilson, *Business of Civil War*; Kenneth Winkle, *Lincoln's Citadel: The Civil War in Washington DC* (New York: W.W. Norton, 2013); Jeffrey Wert, *Civil War Barons: The Tycoons, Entrepreneurs, Inventors, and Visionaries Who Forged Victory and Shape a Nation* (New York: Da Capo Press, 2018).
18. Paul Kahan, *Amiable Scoundrel: Simon Cameron, Lincoln's Scandalous Secretary of War* (Lincoln: Potomac Books, 2020).
19. Kahan, *Amiable Scoundrel*, 174.
20. Goodwin, *Team of Rivals*, 413.
21. Ibid., 519.
22. Maris Vinovskis, ed., *Toward a Social History of the American Civil War* (New York: Cambridge University Press, 1990); Clinton and Silber, eds, *Divided Houses*; Joan Cashin, ed., *The War Was You and Me: Civilians in the American Civil War* (Princeton: Princeton University Press, 2002); Scott Nelson and Carol Sheriff, *A People at War: Civilians and Soldiers in America's Civil War, 1854–1877* (New York: Oxford University Press, 2007).
23. Randall Miller, Harry Stout, and Charles Wilson, eds, *Religion and the American Civil War* (New York: Oxford University Press, 1998); Mark Noll, *The Civil War as a Theological Crisis* (Chapel Hill: University of North Carolina Press, 2006).
24. For an overview, see: Barbara Cutter, *Domestic Devils, Battlefield Angels: The Radicalization of American Womanhood, 1830–1865* (Dekalb: Northern Illinois University Press, 2003). For northern women, see: Elizabeth Leonard, *Yankee Women: Gender Battles in the Civil War* (New York: W.W. Norton, 1997); Jeannie Attie, *Patriotic Toil: Northern Women and the American Civil War* (Ithaca: Cornell University Press, 1998); Nina Silber, *Daughters of the Union: Northern Women Fight the Civil War* (Cambridge, Mass.: Harvard University Press, 2005); Judith Ann Giesberg, *Army at Home: Women and the Civil War on the Northern Front* (Chapel Hill: University of North Carolina Press, 2009). For southern women, see: Drew

Gilpin Faust, *Mothers of Invention: Women of the Slaveholding South* (Chapel Hill: University of North Carolina Press, 1996); Edward Campbell and Kym Rice, eds, *A Woman's War: Southern Women, Civil War, and the Confederate Legacy* (Charlottesville: University of Virginia Press, 1996); Bell Irvin Wiley, *Confederate Women* (Westport: Praeger, 1975); George Rable, *Civil Wars: Women and the Crisis of Southern Nationalism* (Urbana: University of Illinois Press, 1989).

25. Leeann Whites, "The Civil War as a Crisis in Gender," Catherine Clinton and Nina Silber, eds, *Divided Houses: Gender and the Civil War* (New York: Oxford University Press, 1992), 8.

26. Joel Myerson and Daniel Shealy, eds, *The Journal of Louisa May Alcott* (Athens: University of Georgia Press, 1997), 105.

27. Hess, *Liberty, Virtue, and Progress*; Grant, *North Over South*; Melinda Lawson, *Patriot Fires: Forging a New American Nationalism in the Civil War North* (Lawrence: University Press of Kansas, 2002); Matthew Gallman, *Northerners at War: Reflection on the Civil War Home Front* (Kent: Kent University Press, 2010).

28. McCurry, *Confederate Reckoning*, 254–9.

29. Ibid., 298.

30. Vann Woodward, ed., *Mary Chesnut's Civil War*.

31. Ibid., 3, 470, 551, 176, 668.

32. Ibid., 235, 245, 48, 153, 199, 246.

33. "Proclamation of Thanksgiving," October 3, 1863, Van Doren, ed., *The Life and Writings of Abraham Lincoln*, 783–4.

34. For overviews, see: David Sachsman, Kittrell Rushing, and Debra Reddin van Tryll, eds, *The Civil War and the Press* (New York: Routledge, 1999); David Sachsman, Kittrell Rushing, et al., *Words at War: The Civil War and American Journalism* (West Lafayette: Purdue University Press, 2008); Ford Risley, *Civil War Journalism* (New York: Praeger, 2012); David Sachsman, *A Press Divided: Newspaper Coverage of the Civil War* (New York: Transaction Books, 2014); Harold Holzer, *Lincoln and the Power of the Press* (New York: Simon & Schuster, 2014). For northern journalists, see: Cutler Andrews, *The North Reports the Civil War* (Pittsburgh: University of Pittsburgh Press, 1955); Brayton Harris, *Blue & Grey in Black and White: Newspapers in the Civil War* (Washington DC: Brassey's, 1999); James Perry, *The Bohemian Brigade: The Civil War Correspondents – Mostly Rough, Sometimes Ready* (New York: John Wiley, 2000).

35. Mary Panzer, *Mathew Brady and the Image of History* (Washington DC: Smithsonian Books, 2004).

36. Perry, *Bohemian Brigade*, x.

37. Mark Neely, *The Union Divided: Party Conflict in the Civil War North* (Cambridge, Mass.: Harvard University Press, 2002), 100.

38. Perry, *Bohemian Brigade*, 276.

39. Neely, *Union Divided*, 103.

40. Sherman, *Memoirs*, 714.

41. Cutler Andrews, *The South Reports the Civil War* (Pittsburgh: University of Pittsburgh Press, 1985).

42. Ratner and Teeter, *Fanatics and Fire-eaters*; David Sachsman and George Borchard, *The Antebellum Press: Setting the Stage for the Civil War* (New York: Routledge, 2019).

43. Robert Lively, *Fiction Fights the Civil War: An Unfinished Chapter in the Literary History of the American People* (Chapel Hill: University of North Carolina Press, 1957); Aaron, *Unwritten War*; Edmund Wilson, *Patriotic Gore: Studies in the Literature of the American Civil War* (New York: W.W. Norton, 1994); Alice Fabs, *The Imagined Civil War: Popular Literature of the North and South, 1861–1865* (Chapel Hill: University of North Carolina Press, 2001).

44. Roy Morris, *Ambrose Bierce: Alone in Bad Company* (New York: Oxford University Press, 1995).

45. Aaron, *Unwritten War*, 137–8.

Chapter 14

1. Walter Hebert, *Fighting Joe Hooker* (Lincoln: University of Nebraska Press, 1999).
2. Foote, *Civil War: A Narrative, From Fredericksburg to Meridian*, 233–4.
3. Lincoln to Hooker, January 26, 1863, Van Doren, ed., *The Life and Writings of Abraham Lincoln*, 750.
4. Ernest Furgurson, *Chancellorsville 1863: The Souls of the Brave* (New York: Alfred Knopf, 1992); Stephen Sears, *Chancellorsville* (New York: Mariner Books, 1998).
5. Davis, *Stonewall Jackson*.
6. Edwin Coddington, *The Gettysburg Campaign: A Study in Command* (New York: Charles Scribners' Sons, 1968); Noah Trudeau, *Gettysburg: A Testing of Courage* (New York: Perennial, 2002); Stephen Sears, *Gettysburg* (New York: Mariner Books, 2004); Allen Guelzo, *Gettysburg: The Last Invasion* (New York: Vintage, 2014).
7. James McPherson, *Tried By War: Abraham Lincoln as Commander In Chief* (New York: Penguin, 2008), 180.
8. Tom Huntington, *Searching for George Gordon Meade: The Forgotten Hero of Gettysburg* (Mechanicsville: Stackpole Books, 2013); John Selby, *Meade: The Price of Command* (Kent: Kent State University Press, 2018); Kent Brown, *Meade at Gettysburg: A Study in Command* (Chapel Hill: University of North Carolina Press, 2021).
9. Lincoln to George Meade, July 14, 1863, Van Doren, ed., *The Life and Writings of Abraham Lincoln*, 766.
10. Lincoln to Oliver Howard, July 21, 1863, Van Doren, ed., *The Life and Writings of Abraham Lincoln*, 767.
11. Boritt, ed., *Lincoln's Generals*, 89.
12. Michael Ballard, *Vicksburg: The Campaign that Opened the Mississippi* (Chapel Hill: University of North Carolina Press, 2010); Donald Miller, *Vicksburg: Grant's Campaign that Broke the Confederacy* (New York: Simon & Schuster, 2020).
13. Grant, *Memoirs*, 224.
14. Vann Woodward, ed., *Mary Chesnut's Civil War*, 581.
15. Lincoln to James Conkling, August 26, 1863, Van Doren, ed., *The Life and Writings of Abraham Lincoln*, 779–80.
16. Adrian Cook, *Armies of the Streets: The New York City Draft Riots of 1863* (Lexington: University Press of Kentucky, 1974); Iver Bernstein, *The New York Draft Riots: Their Significance for American Society and Politics in the Age of the Civil War* (New York: Oxford University Press, 1990); Barnet Schecter, *The Devil's Own Work: The Civil War Draft Riots and the Fight to Reconstruct America* (New York: Walker Books, 2007).
17. David Powell and Eric Wittenberg, *Tullahoma: The Forgotten Campaign that Changed the Course of the War* (New York: Savas Beattie, 2010).
18. David Powell, *The Chattanooga Campaign – A Mad Irregular Battle: From the Crossing of the Tennessee River through the Second Day, August 22 to September 19, 1863* (New York: Savas Beattie, 2016).
19. David Powell, *The Chattanooga Campaign – Glory or the Grave: The Breakthrough, the Union Collapse, and the Defense of Horseshoe Ridge, September 9, 1863* (New York: Savas Beattie, 2016).
20. David Powell, *The Chattanooga Campaign – Barren Victory: The Retreat to Chattanooga, the Confederate Pursuit, and the Aftermath of Battle, September 21–October 20, 1864* (New York: Sava Beattie, 2016).
21. Peter Cozzens, *The Shipwreck of Their Hopes: The Battle for Chattanooga* (Champlain: University of Illinois Press, 1996); David Powell, *The Spoils of Victory: Ulysses S. Grant at Chattanooga* (Carbondale: Southern Illinois Press, 2020).
22. Gary Wills, *Lincoln at Gettysburg: The Words That Remade America* (New York: Simon & Schuster, 1992); Gabor Boritt, *The Gettysburg Gospel: The Lincoln Speech That Nobody Knows* (New York: Simon & Schuster, 2006).

23. Gettysburg Address, November 19, 1863, Van Doren, ed., *The Life and Writings of Abraham Lincoln*, 788.

24. Burlingame, *Abraham Lincoln*, 2:576.

Chapter 15

1. Clifford Dowdey, *Lee's Last Campaign: The Story of Lee and His Men against Grant, 1864* (Lincoln: University of Nebraska Press, 1993); Earl Hess, *Trench Warfare Under Grant and Lee: Field Fortifications in the Overland Campaign* (Chapel Hill: University of North Carolina Press, 2007); Alfred Young, *Lee's Army during the Overland Campaign: A Numerical Study* (Baton Rouge: Louisiana States University Press, 2013); Joseph Wheeler, *Bloody Spring: Forty Days That Sealed the Confederacy's Fate* (New York: Da Capo, 2014); Steven Sodergren, *The Army of the Potomac in the Overland and Petersburg Campaigns: Union Soldiers and Trench Warfare* (Baton Rouge: Louisiana State University Press, 2017).

2. Smith, *Grant*, 365.

3. Gordon Rhea, *On to Petersburg: Grant and Lee, June 4–15, 1864* (Baton Rouge: Louisiana State University Press, 2017); Wilson Greene, *A Campaign of Giants: The Battle for Petersburg: From the Crossing of the James to the Crater* (Chapel Hill: University of North Carolina Press, 2018); Edwin, Bearss, *The Petersburg Campaign: The Eastern Front, June–August 1964* (New York: Savas Beattie, 2021).

4. Edwin Bearss, *The Petersburg Campaign: The Western Front Battles, September 1864–April 1865* (New York: Savas Beattie, 2021).

5. Earl Hess, *Into the Crater: The Mine Attack at Petersburg* (Columbia: University of South Carolina Press, 2010).

6. Chernow, *Grant*, 428.

7. Smith, *Grant*, 381.

8. James Duffy, *Lincoln's Admiral: The Civil War Campaigns of David Farragut* (New York: Castle Books, 2008).

9. Richard Bak, *The CSS Hunley: The Greatest Unwater Adventure of the Civil War* (New York: Taylor Trade Publishing, 1999).

10. Lindell Hart, *Sherman: Soldier, Realist, American* (New York: Da Capo Press, 1993); James McDonough, *William Tecumseh Sherman: In the Service of My Country, A Life* (New York: W.W. Norton, 2017): Brian Reid, *The Scourge of War: The Life of William Tecumseh Sherman* (New York: Oxford University Press, 2020).

11. Shelby Foote, *Civil War: A Narrative: Red River to Appomattox* (New York: Vintage, 1986), 714.

12. Sherman, *Memoirs*, 579.

13. Hattaway and Jones, *How the North Won*, 309.

14. Sherman, *Memoirs*, 490.

15. Albert Castel, *Decision in the West: The Atlanta Campaign of 1864* (Lawrence: University of Kansas Press, 1992); Stephen Davis, *A Long and Bloody Task: The Atlanta Campaign from Dalton through Kennesaw Mountain to the Chattahoochee, May 5–July 18, 1864* (New York: Savas Beattie, 2016); Stephen Davis, *All the Fighting They Want: The Atlanta Campaign from Peachtree Creek to the City's Surrender, July 18–September 2, 1864* (New York: Savas Beattie, 2017); Lawrence Peterson, *Decisions of the Atlanta Campaign: The Twenty-one Central Decisions that Defined the Operation* (Chattanooga: University of Tennessee Press, 2019).

16. Sherman, *Memoirs*, 890.

17. Craig Symonds, *Joseph E. Johnston: A Civil War Biography* (New York: W.W. Norton, 1993); Stephen Hood, *John Bell Hood: The Rise, Fall, and Resurrection of a Confederate General* (New York: Savas Beattie, 2013).

18. Foote, *Civil War, A Narrative, Fredericksburg to Meridian*, 813.

19. Ward, *River Ran Red*.

20. Foote, *Civil War, A Narrative: Red River to Appomattox*, 510.

21. Sherman, *Memoirs*, 627, 639, 640.
22. Smith, *Grant*, 162.
23. Winkle, *Lincoln's Citadel*.
24. Gabor Boritt, ed., *Lincoln, The War President*, 34.
25. Grant, *Memoirs*, 454; Smith, *Grant*, 384.
26. Roy Morris, *Sheridan: The Life and Wars of General Phil Sheridan* (New York: Vintage, 1993); Joseph Wheelan, *Terrible Swift Sword: The Life of Philip H. Sheridan* (New York: Da Capo, 2012).
27. Jeffry Wert, *From Winchester to Cedar Creek: The Shenandoah Campaign of 1864* (Carlisle: South Mountain Press, 1987), 93–4.
28. Hattaway and Jones, *How the North Won*, 618.
29. John Waugh, *Reelecting Lincoln: The Battle for the 1864 Presidency* (New York: Da Capo Press, 2001); Jonathan White, *Emancipation, the Union Army, and the Reelection of Abraham Lincoln* (Baton Rouge: Louisiana State University Press, 2014); David Johnson, *Decided on the Battlefield: Grant, Sherman, Lincoln, and the Election of 1864* (New York: Prometheus, 2020).
30. McPherson, *Battle Cry of Freedom*, 771.
31. Memorandum to His Cabinet, August 23, 1864, Van Doren, ed., *The Life and Writings of Abraham Lincoln*, 823.
32. Foote, *Civil War: Fredericksburg to Meridian*, 953.
33. Beringer et al., *Why the South Lost*, 266.
34. Lincoln Annual Message to Congress, December 6, 1864, Van Doren, ed., *The Life and Writings of Abraham Lincoln*, 832–4.
35. Burke Davis, *Sherman's March* (New York: Random House, 1980); Joseph Glatthaar, *March to the Sea and Beyond: Sherman's Troops in the Savannah and Carolina Campaigns* (Baton Rouge: Louisiana State University Press, 1995); Noah Trudeau, *Southern Storm: Sherman's March to the Sea and Beyond* (New York: Harper Perennial, 2009).
36. Sherman, *Memoirs*, 656, 644–5.
37. Glatthaar, *March to the Sea and Beyond*, 130.
38. Sherman, *Memoirs*, 71, 705.

Chapter 16
1. Harnett Kane, *Spies for the Blue and Gray* (New York: Doubleday, 1954); Edwin Fishel, *The Secret War for the Union: The Untold Story of Military Intelligence in the Civil War* (New York: Houghton Mifflin, 1996); Donald Markle, *Spies and Spymasters of the Civil War* (New York: Hippocrene, 2004).
2. Peter Tsouras, *Major George H. Sharpe and the Creation of American Military Intelligence in the Civil War* (New York: Casemate, 2018).
3. Sherman, *Memoirs*, 227.
4. Fishel, *Secret War for the Union*, 563–8.
5. William Blair, *With Malice Toward Some: Treason and Loyalty in the Civil War* (Chapel Hill: University of North Carolina Press, 2014).
6. William Hesseltine, *Lincoln and the War Governors* (New York: Alfred Knopf, 1955).
7. Frank Klement, *Dark Lanterns: Secret Political Societies, Conspiracy, and Treason Trials in the Civil War* (Baton Rouge: Louisiana State University Press, 1984); Jennifer Weber, *Copperheads: The Rise and Fall of Lincoln's Opponents in the North* (New York: Oxford University Press, 2008); Nathan Kalmoe, *With Ballots and Bullets: Partisanship and Violence in the Civil War* (New York: Cambridge University Press, 2020).
8. Neely, *Union Divided*, 44.
9. Frank Klement, *The Limits of Dissent: Clement L. Vallandigham and the Civil War* (New York: Fordham University Press, 1999); Thomas Mackay, *Opposing Lincoln: Clement L. Vallandigham,*

Presidential Powe, and the Legal Battle over Dissent in Wartime (Lawrence: University Press of Kansas, 2020).

10. Lincoln to Erastus Corning, June 12, 1863, Van Doren, ed., *The Life and Writings of Abraham Lincoln*, 761–2.
11. Freehling, *South vs. the South*.
12. Eric Wittenberg, Edmund Sargus, and Penny Barrick, *Seceding from Secession: The Civil War, Secession, and the Creation of West Virginia* (New York: Savas Beattie, 2020).
13. Wittenberg, Sargus, and Barrick, *Seceding from Secession*, 109.
14. William Harris, *With Charity for All: Lincoln and the Restoration of the Union* (Lexington: University Press of Kentucky, 1997), 24–9.
15. Fellman, *Inside War*; Daniel Sutherland, ed., *Guerillas, Unionists, and Violence on the Confederate Homefront* (Fayetteville: University of Arkansas Press, 1999); Daniel Sutherland, *A Savage Conflict: The Decisive Role of Guerrillas in the Civil War* (Chapel Hill: University of North Carolina Press, 2013); Joseph Beilein and Matthew Hulbert, *The Civil War Guerrilla: Unfolding the Black Flag of History, Memory, and Myth* (Lexington: University Press of Kentucky, 2015).
16. Fellman, *Inside War*, 62.
17. Ibid., 88.
18. Ramage, *Rebel Raider*, 89.
19. James Ramage, *Gray Ghost: The Life of Col. John Singleton Mosby* (Lexington: University of Kentucky Press, 1999).
20. Fellman, *Inside War*, 99.
21. Oscar Kinchen, *Confederate Operations in Canada and the North* (North Quincy: Christopher Publishing House, 1970).
22. William Pittenger and James Bogle, *Daring and Suffering: A History of the Andrews Raid* (Nashville: Cumberland House, 1999).
23. Hattaway and Jones, *How the North Won*, 289.
24. Fellman, *Inside War*, 84.
25. Mark Neely, *The Fate of Liberty: Abraham Lincoln and Civil Liberties* (New York: Oxford University Press, 1991).
26. McPherson, *Battle Cry of Freedom*, 493.
27. Simon, *Lincoln and Chief Justice Taney*.
28. Letter to A.G. Hodges, April 4, 1864, Van Doren, ed., *The Life and Writings of Abraham Lincoln*, 807–8.
29. Marvel, *Lincoln's Autocrat*, 220.
30. Neely, *Fate of Liberty*, 130, 168–9, 173.
31. John Witt, *Lincoln's Code: The Laws of War in American History* (New York: Free Press, 2012).
32. Robert Alotta, *Civil War Justice: Union Army Executions under Lincoln* (Shippensburg: White Mane Press, 1989), 30.

Chapter 17

1. Lincoln Annual Message to Congress, December 6, 1864, Van Doren, ed., *The Life and Writings of Abraham Lincoln*, 833.
2. Foote, *Civil War, A Narrative: Red River to Appomattox*, 468.
3. Ibid., 778.
4. Glatthaar, *March to the Sea and Beyond*, 130.
5. Sherman, *Memoirs*, 811–12.
6. Wilson Greene, *The Final Battles of the Petersburg Campaign: Breaking the Backbone of the Rebellion* (Knoxville: University of Tennessee Press, 2012); Edward Alexander, *Dawn of Victory: Breakthrough at Petersburg, March 25–April 2, 1865* (New York: Savas Beattie, 2015).
7. Burke Davis, *To Appomattox: Nine April Days, 1865* (New York: Rinehart, 1959); Elizabeth Veron, *Appomattox: Victory, Defeat, and Freedom at the Civil War's End* (New York: Oxford

University Press, 2013); Joseph Wheelan, *Their Last Full Measure: The Final Days of the Civil War* (New York: Da Capo, 2016); Caroline Janney, ed., *Petersburg to Appomattox: The End of the War in Virginia* (Chapel Hill: University of North Carolina Press, 2018).

8. Jones, *Generals in Blue and Gray: Lincoln's Generals*, 32.
9. Grant, *Memoirs*, 554.
10. Ibid., 545–6.
11. Wheelan, *Their Last Full Measure*, 257.
12. Harry Hansen, *The Civil War: A History* (New York: Signet, 2010), 636.
13. Lincoln to Ward Lamon, April 11, 1865, Van Doren, ed., *The Life and Writings of Abraham Lincoln*, 185.
14. George Forgie, *Patricide in the House Divided: A Psychological Interpretation of Lincoln and His Age* (New York: W.W. Norton, 1973); Brad Meltzer and John Mensch, *The Lincoln Conspiracy: The Secret Plot to Kill America's 16th President and Why It Failed* (New York: Flatiron Books, 2020).
15. Marvel, *Lincoln's Autocrat*, 370.
16. Foote, *Civil War: A Narrative: Red River to Appomattox*, 968.
17. Sherman, *Memoirs*, 835–59.
18. Ibid., 866.

Chapter 18
1. Faust, *This Republic of Suffering*, 255, 257.
2. McWhiney and Jamieson, *Attack and Die*, 8.
3. McPherson, *Battle Cry of Freedom*, 472.
4. James McPherson quoted in Faust, *Republic of Suffering*, 274.
5. McPherson, *Battle Cry of Freedom*, 330; Hattaway and Jones, *How the North Won*, 504.
6. McPherson, *Battle Cry of Freedom*, 485; Freemon, *Gangrene and Glory*.
7. United States military casualties of wars, Wikipedia.com.
8. Faust, *Republic of Suffering*, 236. Monro MacCloskey, *Hallowed Ground: Our National Cemeteries* (New York: Richard Rosens Press, 1968).
9. Mary Louise Kete, *Sentimental Collaborations: Mourning and Middle-Class Identity in Nineteenth Century America* (Durham: Duke University Press, 2000).
10. Noll, *Civil War*.

Chapter 19
1. Grant, *Memoirs*, 576, 579.
2. Lee Soltow, *Men and Wealth in the United States, 1850–1870* (New Haven: Yale University Press, 1975).
3. Heather Cox Richardson, *The Greatest Nation of the Earth: Republican Economic Policies during the Civil War* (Cambridge, Mass.: Harvard University Press, 1997).
4. Annual Message to Congress, December 6, 1864, Van Doren, ed., *The Life and Writings of Abraham Lincoln*, 832–3.
5. Morris, *Dawn of Innovation*, 157; Foote, *Civil War: A Narrative: Red River to Appomattox*, 1041; RalphAndreano, ed., *Economic Impact of the American Civil War*, 53.
6. James McPherson, *Ordeal by Fire: The Civil War and Reconstruction* (New York: Alfred Knopf, 1982), 476.
7. Donald Dodd and Wynelle Dodd, *Historical Statistics of the South, 1790–1970* (Tuscaloosa: University of Alabama Press, 1973); Claudia Goldin and Frank Lewis, "The Economic Cost of the American Civil War: Estimates and Implications," *Journal of Economic History*, vol. 35, no. 2 (June 1975), 299–326; Andreano, ed., *Economic Impact of the American Civil War*, 81.
8. McPherson, *Battle Cry of Freedom*, 859. See also: David Goldfield, *America Aflame: How the Civil War Created a Nation* (New York: Bloomsbury Press, 2011).

9. Dan Carter, *When the War Was Over: The Failure of Self-Reconstruction in the South, 1865–1867* (Baton Rouge: Louisiana State University Press, 1985); Eric Foner, *Reconstruction: America's Unfinished Revolution, 1863–1877* (New York: Harper and Row, 1988); Eric Foner, *A Short History of Reconstruction* (New York: Harper and Row, 1990).
10. Harold Hyman, *The Radical Republicans and Reconstruction, 1861–1870* (Indianapolis: Bobbs-Merrill, 1967).
11. Stephen Ash, *When the Yankees Came: Conflict and Chaos in the Occupied South, 1861–1865* (Chapel Hill: University of North Carolina Press, 1995); Grimsley, *Hard Hand of War*; Thomas Lowry, *Confederate Heroines: 120 Southern Women Convicted by Union Military Justice* (Baton Rouge: Louisiana State University Press, 2006).
12. Fawn Brodie, *Thaddeus Stevens: Scourge of the South* (New York: W.W. Norton, 1966), 231–2.
13. Last Public Address, April 11, 1865, Van Doren, ed., *The Life and Writings of Abraham Lincoln*, 846–51.
14. Second Inaugural Address, March 4, 1865, Van Doren, ed., *The Life and Writings of Abraham Lincoln*, 842.
15. Berlin et al., eds., *Free At Last*; Robinson, *Bitter Fruits of Bondage*.
16. Goodwin, *Team of Rivals*, 687.
17. Eric McKitrick, *Andrew Johnson and Reconstruction* (Chicago: University of Chicago Press, 1960); Annette Gordon-Reed, *Andrew Johnson: The 17th President, 1865–1869* (New York: Time Life Books, 2011).
18. Hans Trefousse, *Andrew Johnson* (New York: W.W. Norton, 1997).
19. McKitrick, *Andrew Johnson and Reconstruction*, 184.
20. Foner, *Reconstruction*, 70–1.
21. Ibid., 55–7.
22. Sherman, *Memoirs*, 1051–2.
23. Foner, *Reconstruction*, 152, 158, 161.
24. Ronald Butchart, *Northern Schools, Southern Blacks, and Reconstruction: Freedmen's Education, 1862–1875* (Westport: Praeger, 1980).
25. Foner, *Reconstruction*, 96, 144.
26. Cynthia Nicoletti, *Secession on Trial: The Treason Prosecution of Jefferson Davis* (New York: Cambridge University Press, 2017).
27. Eric Foner, *The Second Founding: How the Civil War and Reconstruction Remade the Constitution* (New York: W.W. Norton, 2020).
28. David Stewart, *Impeached!: The Trial of President Andrew Johnson and the Fight for Lincoln's Legacy* (New York: Simon & Schuster, 2009); Brenda Wineapple, *The Impeachers: The Trial of Andrew Johnson and the Dream of a Just Nation* (New York: Random House, 2020).
29. Jimerson, *Private War*, 112.
30. Allen Trelease, *White Terror: The Ku Klux Klan Conspiracy and Southern Reconstruction* (New York: Harper and Row, 1971); George Rable, *But There Was No Peace: The Role of Violence in the Politics of Reconstruction* (Athens: University of Georgia Press, 1984); Elaine Frantz Parsons, *Ku Klux: The Birth of the Klan during Reconstruction* (Chapel Hill: University of North Carolina Press, 2019).
31. Chernow, *Grant*, 763.
32. C. Van Woodward, *The Strange Career of Jim Crow* (New York: Oxford University Press, 1974); Jerrold Packard, *American Nightmare: The History of Jim Crow* (New York: St Martin's Press, 2002).
33. Foner, *Reconstruction*, 318, 352–3.
34. Chernow, *Grant*, 643.
35. Ibid., 568.
36. Foner, *A Short History of Reconstruction*, 193.
37. Chernow, *Grant*, 708.

38. C. Van Woodward, *Reunion and Reaction: The Compromise of 1877 and the End of Reconstruction* (New York: Oxford University Press, 1991); Roy Morris, *Fraud of the Century: Rutherford B. Hayes, Samuel Tilden, and the Stolen Election of 1876* (New York: Simon & Schuster, 2004); Michael Holt, *By One Vote: The Disputed Presidential Election of 1876* (Lawrence: University Press of Kansas, 2017).

39. Smith, *Grant*, 571.

40. Ibid., 569.

41. Paul Gaston, The New South Creed: A Study in Southern Mythmaking (New York: Alfred Knopf, 1970); Rollin Osterweis, *The Myth of the Lost Cause, 1865–1900* (Hamden: Archon Books, 1973); Gaines Foster, *Ghosts of the Confederacy: Defeat, the Lost Cause, and the Emergence of the New South* (New York: Oxford University Press, 1987); Charles Wilson, *Baptized in Blood: The Religion of the Lost Cause, 1865–1920* (Athens: University of Georgia Press, 1980); Ralph Widener, *Confederate Monuments: Enduring Symbols of the South and the War between the States* (Washington DC: Andromeda Associates, 1982); Mark Neely, Harold Holzer, and Gabor Boritt, *The Confederate Image: Prints of the Lost Cause* (Chapel Hill: University of North Carolina Press, 1987); Jim Cullen, *The Civil War in Popular Culture: A Reusable Past* (Washington DC: Smithsonian, 1995); Kirk Savage, *Standing Soldiers, Kneeling Slaves: Race, War, and Monument in Nineteenth Century America* (Princeton: Princeton University Press, 1997); Horwitz, *Confederates in the Attic*; Sword, *Southern Invincibility*; Gary Gallagher and Alan Nolan, eds, *The Myth of the Lost Cause in Civil War History* (Bloomington: Indiana University Press, 2010); David Blight, *Race and Reunion: The Civil War in American Memory* (Cambridge, Mass.: Belknap Press, 2012); Edward Bonekemper, *The Myth of the Lost Cause: Why the South Fought the Civil War and Why the North Won* (New York: Regnery History, 2015); Nicole Maurantonio, *Confederate Exceptionalism: Civil War Myth and Memory in the Twenty-First Century* (Topeka: University Press of Kansas, 2019); Ty Seidule, *Robert E. Lee and Me: A Southerner's Reckoning with Lost Cause* (New York: St Martin's Press, 2021).

42. Annual Message to Congress, January 1, 1863, Van Doren, ed., *The Life and Writings of Abraham Lincoln*, 738.

43. Connelly, *Marble Man*; Nolan, *Lee Reconsidered*.

44. Thomas Connelly and Barbara Bellows, *God and General Longstreet: The Lost Cause and the Southern Mind* (Baton Rouge: Louisiana State University Press, 1982); William Piston, *Lee's Tarnish General: James Longstreet and His Place in Southern History* (Athens: University of Georgia Press, 1990); Jeffry Wert, *General James Longstreet: The Confederacy's Most Controversial Soldier* (New York: Simon & Schuster, 1994); Gory Pfarr, *Longstreet at Gettysburg: A Critical Assessment* (Jefferson: McFarland Publishing, 2019).

45. Campbell and Rice, eds, *A Woman's War*.

46. Foster, *Ghosts of the Confederacy*, 4.

47. Sachsman, Rushing, and Morris, *Memory and Myth*.

Chapter 20

1. "Lynchings of Whites and Negroes, 1882–1968," Tuskegee University website.

2. Jeanne Theoharris, *A More Beautiful and Terrible History: The Uses and Misuses of Civil Rights History* (New York: Beacon Press, 2019); Christopher Schmidt, *Civil Rights in America: A History* (New York: Cambridge University Press, 2020).

Chapter 21

1. For the most powerful criticisms of black radicalism by an African American scholar, see: John McWhorter, *Losing the Race: Self-Sabotage in Black America* (New York: Harper Perennial, 2001): John McWhorter, *Woke Racism: How a New Religion Has Betrayed Black America* (New York: Portfolio, 2021).

2. Jennifer Kingson, "Exclusive: $1 Billion-Plus Riot Damage Is Most Expensive in Insurance History," *Axios*, September 16, 2020.

3. John Hagen, "Risk of Being Killed by Police Use of Force in the United States by Age, Race, Ethnicity, and Sex," *Proceedings of the National Academy of Sciences*, August 20, 2019; "A Public Health Crisis Decades in the Making," The Education Fund to Stop Violence and the Coalition to Stop Gun Violence, February 2021, website; Molly Stellino, "Factcheck," *USA Today*, January 23, 2020, website. For scholarly analyses of the relationship between crime and race in America, see: Barry Latzer, *The Myth of Overpunishment: A Defense of the America Justice System and a Proposal to Reduce Incarceration while Protecting the Public* (New York: Republic Books, 2022); Rafael Mangual, *Criminal (In)Justice: What the Rise for Decarceration and Depolicing Gets Wrong and Who It Hurts Most* (New York: Center Street Books, 2022).

4. "FBI Releases 2019 Statistics on Law Enforcement Officers Killed in the Line of Duty," FBI National Press Office, May 4, 2020.

5. Aaron Chalfin and Justin McCray, "Are U.S. Cities Underpoliced? Theory and Evidence," *Review of Economics and Statistics*, vol. 100, no. 1 (2018), 167–86; Tyler Lane, "Police Involved Deaths and the Impact on Homicide Rates in the Post-Ferguson Era," *Sage*, vol. 37, Issue 19–20, July 1, 2021; Thomas Edsall, "America Has Become Both More and Less Dangerous Since Black Lives Matter," *New York Times*, May 17, 2023; Travis Campbell, "Black Lives Matter's Effects on Police Lethal Use of Force," *SSRN*, July 2, 2023.

6. Karen Cox, *Dixie's Daughters: The United Daughters of the Confederacy and the Preservation of Confederate Culture* (Gainesville: University of Florida Press, 2019); Karen Cox, *No Common Ground: Confederate Monuments and the Ongoing Fight for Racial Justice* (Chapel Hill: University of North Carolina Press, 2021); Ryan Newson, *Cut in Stone: Confederate Monuments and Theological Disruption* (Waco: Baylor University Press, 2020); Roger Hartley, *Monumental Harm: Reckoning with Jim Crow Era Confederate Monuments* (Columbia: University of South Carolina Press, 2021).

7. Neil Vigdor and Daniel Victor, "168 Rebel Symbols Removed Last Year," *New York Times*, March 1, 2021.

8. Kim Severson, "Number of U.S. Hate Groups Is Rising," *New York Times*, March 8, 2012.

9. David Barstow, "The Tea Party Movement Lights Fuse for Rebellion by the Right," *New York Times*, February 15, 2010; "The Second Wave: The Return of the Militias," Southern Poverty Law Center, August 1, 2009.

10. Factcheckers, "In Four Years President Trump Made 30,574 False or Misleading Statements," *Washington Post*, January 20, 2021.

11. William Nester, *Putin's Virtual War: Russia's Subversion and Conversion of America, Europe, and the World Beyond* (London: Frontline Books, 2019).

12. Arianna Johnson, "Jan. 6 Insurrection 2 Years After," *Forbes*, January 7, 2023.

13. Daniel Cox, "After the Ballots Are Counted: Conspiracies, Political Violence, and American Exceptionalism," *Survey of American Life*, February 2, 2021.

14. Nicholas Fandos, "Democrats Begin Push for Biggest Expansion of Voting Since the 1960s: Republicans Distort Facts on Hearing," *New York Times*, March 25, 2021; Nick Corasaniti and Reid Epstein, "In Georgia, G.O.P. Fires First Shots of Voting Battle," *New York Times*, March 27, 2021; Philip Bump, "Despite the GPO Rhetoric, there have been fewer than two dozen Charged Case of Voter Fraud," *Washington Post*, May 4, 2021.

15. Adam Schiff, ed., *The January 6 Report: Findings of the Selective Committee to Investigate the January 6 Attack on the United States Capitol* (New York: Random House, 2023).

16. Lyceum Address, January 27, 1838, Van Doren, ed., *The Life and Writings of Abraham Lincoln*, 232.

Select Bibliography

Aaron, Daniel, *The Unwritten War: American Writers and the Civil War*, New York: Alfred Knopf, 1973.

Adams, George, *Doctors in Blue: The Medical History of the Union Army during the Civil War*, New York: Henry Schuman, 1952.

Adler, Joyce Sparer, *War in Melville's Imagination*, New York: New York University Press, 1981.

Alexander, Edward, *Dawn of Victory: Breakthrough at Petersburg, March 25–April 2, 1865*, New York: Savas Beattie, 2015.

Andreano, Ralph, ed., *The Economic Impact of the American Civil War*, Cambridge, Mass.: Schenkman Publishing Company, 1962.

Andrews, Cutler, *The North Reports the Civil War*, Pittsburgh: University of Pittsburgh Press, 1955.

Andrews, Cutler, *The South Reports the Civil War*, Pittsburgh: University of Pittsburgh Press, 1985.

Appiah, Kwame, ed., *Narrative of the Life of Frederick Douglass, an American Slave & Incidents in the Life of a Slave Girl*, New York: Modern Library, 2000.

Ash, Stephen, *When the Yankees Came: Conflict and Chaos in the Occupied South, 1861–1865*, Chapel Hill: University of North Carolina Press, 1995.

Attie, Jeannie, *Patriotic Toil: Northern Women and the American Civil War*, Ithaca: Cornell University Press, 1998.

Ayers, Edward, *What Caused the Civil War: Reflections on the South and Southern History*, New York: W.W. Norton, 2005.

Bak, Richard, *The CSS Hunley: The Greatest Unwater Adventure of the Civil War*, New York: Taylor Trade Publishing, 1999.

Baker, Jean Harvey, *Affairs of Party: The Political Culture of Northern Democrat in Mid-Nineteenth Century*, Ithaca: Cornell University Press, 1983.

Baker, Jean Harvey, *Mary Todd Lincoln: A Biography*, New York: W.W. Norton, 2008.

Ball, Douglas, *Financial Failure and Confederate Defeat*, Urbana: University of Illinois Press, 1991.

Ballard, Michael, *Vicksburg: The Campaign that Opened the Mississippi*, Chapel Hill: University of North Carolina Press, 2010.

Bearss, Edwin, *The Petersburg Campaign: The Eastern Front, June–August 1964*, New York: Savas Beattie, 2021.

Bearss, Edwin, *The Petersburg Campaign: The Western Front Battles, September 1864–April 1865*, New York: Savas Beattie, 2021.

Beilein, Joseph, and Matthew Hulbert, *The Civil War Guerrilla: Unfolding the Black Flag of History, Memory, and Myth*, Lexington: University Press of Kentucky, 2015.

Beringer, Richard, Herman Hattaway, Archer Jones, and William Still, *Why the South Lost the Civil War*, Athens: University of Georgia Press, 1986.

Beringer, Richard, et al., *The Elements of Confederate Defeat: Nationalism, War Aims, and Religion*, Athens: University of Georgia Press, 1989.

Berlin, Ira, *Many Thousands Gone: The First Two Centuries of Slavery in North America*, Cambridge, Mass.: Harvard University Press, 1998.

Berlin, Ira, et al., eds, *Free At Last: A Documentary History of Slavery, Freedom, and the Civil War*, New York: New Press, 1992.

Ira Berlin, Joseph Reidy, and Leslie Rowland, eds, *Freedom: A Documentary History of Emancipation, 1861–1867: The Black Military Experience*, New York: Cambridge University Press, 1998.

Berlin, Ira, Joseph Reidy, and Leslie Rowland, eds, *Freedom's Soldiers: The Black Military Experience in the Civil War*, New York: Cambridge University Press, 1998.

Bernstein, Iver, *The New York Draft Riots: Their Significance for American Society and Politics in the Age of the Civil War*, New York: Oxford University Press, 1990.

Bernstein, Peter, *Wedding of the Waters: The Erie Canal and the Making of a Great Nation*, New York: W.W. Norton, 2006.

Berry, Stephen, *All That Makes a Man: Love and Ambition in the Civil War South*, New York: Oxford University Press, 2003.

Bicknell, John, *Lincoln's Pathfinder: John C. Fremont and the Violent Election of 1856*, Chicago: Chicago Review Press, 2017.

Blair, William, *With Malice Toward Some: Treason and Loyalty in the Civil War*, Chapel Hill: University of North Carolina Press, 2014.

Blair, William, and Karen Younger, eds, *Lincoln's Proclamation: Emancipation Reconsidered*, Chapel Hill: University of North Carolina Press, 2009.

Blight, David, *Race and Reunion: The Civil War in American Memory*, Cambridge, Mass.: Belknap Press, 2012.

Blumenthal, Sidney, *A Self-Made Man: The Political Life of Abraham Lincoln, 1809–1849*, New York: Simon & Schuster, 2017.

Blumenthal, Sidney, *Wrestling with his Angel: The Political Life of Abraham Lincoln, 1849–1856*, New York: Simon & Schuster, 2018.

Blumenthal, Sidney, *All the Powers of the Earth: The Political Life of Abraham Lincoln, 1856–1860*, New York: Simon & Schuster, 2020.

Bodenhorn, Howard, *The History of Banking in Antebellum America*, Cambridge, Mass.: Harvard University Press, 2000.

Boggs, Colleen Glenney, *Patriotism by Proxy: The Civil War Draft and the Cultural Formation of Citizen Soldiers, 1863–1865*, New York: Oxford University Press, 2020.

Bogue, Allan, *The Congressman's Civil War*, New York: Cambridge University Press, 1989.

Bonekemper, Edward, *The Myth of the Lost Cause: Why the South Fought the Civil War and Why the North Won*, New York: Regnery History, 2015.

Boritt, Gabor, *The Gettysburg Gospel: The Lincoln Speech That Nobody Knows*, New York: Simon & Schuster, 2006.

Boritt, Gabor, ed., *Lincoln, The War President: The Gettysburg Lectures*, New York: Oxford University Press, 1992.

Boritt, Gabor, ed., *Lincoln's Generals*, Lincoln: University of Nebraska Press, 1994.

Brands, H.W., *Heirs of the Founders: The Epic Rivalry of Henry Clay, John Calhoun, and Daniel Websters, the Second Generation of American Giants*, New York: Doubleday, 2018.

Brands, H.W., *The Zealot and the Emancipator: John Brown, Abraham Lincoln, and the Struggle for America's Freedom*, New York: Doubleday, 2020.

Briggs, John, *Lincoln's Speeches Reconsidered*, Baltimore: Johns Hopkins University Press, 2005.

Bright, David, *Frederick Douglass' Civil War*, Baton Rouge: Louisiana State University Press, 1989.

Brodie, Fawn, *Thaddeus Stevens: Scourge of the South*, New York: W.W. Norton, 1966.

Brooks, Corey, *Liberty Power: Antislavery Third Parties and the Transformation of American Politics*, Chicago: University of Chicago Press, 2016.

Brown, Kent, *Meade at Gettysburg: A Study in Command*, Chapel Hill: University of North Carolina Press, 2021.

Bruce, Dickson, *Violence and Culture in the Antebellum South*, Austin: University of Texas Press, 1979.

Burin, Eric, *Slavery and the Peculiar Solution: A History of the American Colonization Society*, Gainesville: University of Florida Press, 2005.

Burlingame, Michael, *Abraham Lincoln: A Life*, 2 vols, Baltimore: Johns Hopkins University Press, 2013.

Burlingame, Michael, *An American Marriage: The Untold Story of Abraham Lincoln and Mary Todd*, New York: Pegasus, 2021.

Butchart, Ronald, *Northern Schools, Southern Blacks, and Reconstruction: Freedmen's Education, 1862–1875*, Westport: Praeger, 1980.

Bynum, Victoria, *Unruly Women: The Politics of Social and Sexual Control in the Old South*, Chapel Hill: University of North Carolina Press, 1992.

Calore, Paul, *Naval Campaigns of the Civil War*, Jefferson: McFarland and Company, 2001.

Campbell, Edward, and Kym Rice, eds, *A Woman's War: Southern Women, Civil War, and the Confederate Legacy*, Charlottesville: University of Virginia Press 1996..

Campbell, Joseph, *The Hero with a Thousand Faces*, New York: MJF Books, 1949.

Campbell, Stanley, *The Slave Catchers: Enforcement of the Fugitive Slave Act, 1860–1860*, Chapel Hill: University of North Carolina Press, 1970.

Carley, Kenneth, *The Dakota War of 1862: Minnesota's Other Civil War*, St Paul: Minnesota Historical Society Press, 1976.

Carmichael, Peter, *The War for the Common Soldiers: How Men Thought, Fought, and Survived in Civil War Armies*, Chapel Hill: University of North Carolina Press, 2018.

Carnes, Mark, and Clyde Griffin, eds, *Meanings for Manhood*, Chicago: University of Chicago Press, 1990.

Carter, Dan, *When the War Was Over: The Failure of Self-Reconstruction in the South, 1865–1867*, Baton Rouge: Louisiana State University Press, 1985.

Carwardine, Richard, *Lincoln: A Life of Purpose and Power*, New York: Vintage, 2007.

Cash, W.J., *Mind of the South*, New York: Vintage, 1991.

Cashin, Joan, ed., *The War Was You and Me: Civilians in the American Civil War*, Princeton: Princeton University Press, 2002.

Castel, Albert, *Decision in the West: The Atlanta Campaign of 1864*, Lawrence: University of Kansas Press, 1992.

Chernow, Ron, *Grant*, New York: Penguin, 2017.

Clark, John, *Railroads in the Civil War: The Impact of Management on Victory and Defeat*, Baton Rouge: Louisiana State University Press, 2004.

Clinton, Catherine, *The Plantation Mistress: Woman's World in the Old South*, New York: Pantheon books, 1982.

Clinton, Catherine, *Harriet Tubman: The Road to Freedom*, New York: Back Bay Books, 2005.

Clinton, Catherine and Nina Silber, eds, *Divided Houses: Gender and the Civil War*, New York: Oxford University Press, 1992.

Cochran, Thomas, *Frontiers of Change: Early American Industrialization*, New York: Oxford University Press, 1983.

Coddington, Edwin, *The Gettysburg Campaign: A Study in Command*, New York: Charles Scribners' Sons, 1968.

Connelly, Thomas, *The Marble Man: Robert E. Lee and His Image in American Society*, New York: Knopf, 1977.

Connelly, Thomas, and Barbara Bellows, *God and General Longstreet: The Lost Cause and the Southern Mind*, Baton Rouge: Louisiana State University Press, 1982.

Cook, Adrian, *The Armies of the Streets: The New York City Draft Riots of 1863*, Lexington: University of Kentucky Press, 1974.

Cooper, William, *Liberty and Slavery: Southern Politics to 1860*, New York: Knopf, 1982.

Cooper, William, *Jefferson Davis, American*, New York: Vintage, 2001.

Cornish, Dudley, *The Sable Arm: Negro Troops in the Union Army, 1861–1865*, New York: Longmans, Green, 1956.

Cornog, Evan, *The Birth of Empire: Dewitt Clinton and the American Experience*, New York: Oxford University Press, 2000.

Coski, John, *The Confederate Battle Flag: America's Most Embattled Emblem*, Cambridge, Mass.: Harvard University Press, 2005.

Cox, Karen, *Dixie's Daughters: The United Daughters of the Confederacy and the Preservation of Confederate Culture*, Gainesville: University of Florida Press, 2019.

Cox, Karen, *No Common Ground: Confederate Monuments and the Ongoing Fight for Racial Justice*, Chapel Hill: University of North Carolina Press, 2021.

Cozzens, Peter, *The Shipwreck of Their Hopes: The Battle for Chattanooga*, Champlain: University of Illinois Press, 1996.

Cozzens, Peter, *General John Pope: A Life for the Nation*, Urbana: University of Illinois Press, 2000.

Cozzens, Peter, *Shenandoah 1862: Stonewall Jackson's Valley Campaign*, Chapel Hill: University of North Carolina Press, 2008.

Crook, D.P., *The North, the South, and the Powers, 1861–1865*, New York: John Wiley, 1974.

Cullen, Jim. *The Civil War in Popular Culture: A Reusable Past*, Washington DC: Smithsonian, 1995.

Curtin, Philip, *The Atlantic Slave Trade: A Census*, Madison: University of Wisconsin Press, 1969.

Cutch, Ovid, *The History of Andersonville Prison*, Tallahassee: University Press of Florida, 2011.

Cutter, Barbara, *Domestic Devils, Battlefield Angels: The Radicalization of American Womanhood, 1830–1865*, Dekalb: Northern Illinois University Press, 2003.

Dannett, Sylvia, ed., *Noble Women of the North*, New York: Thomas Yoseloff, 1959.

Daughty, Robert, Ira Gruber, et al., *The American Civil War: The Emergence of Total Warfare*, Lexington, Mass.: D.C. Heath, 1996.

Davis, Burke, *To Appomattox: Nine April Days, 1865*, New York: Rinehart, 1959.

Davis, Burke, *Sherman's March*, New York: Random House, 1980.

Davis, David, *The Problem of Slavery in the Age of Revolution*, Ithaca: Cornell University Press, 1975.

Davis, Donald, *Stonewall Jackson: Lessons in Leadership*, New York: St Martin's Press, 2007.

Davis, Jefferson, *The Rise and Fall of the Confederate Government*, New York: D. Appleton and Company, 1881.

Davis, Stephen, *A Long and Bloody Task: The Atlanta Campaign from Dalton through Kennesaw Mountain to the Chattahoochee, May 5–July 18, 1864*, New York: Savas Beattie, 2016.

Davis, Stephen, *All the Fighting They Want: The Atlanta Campaign from Peachtree Creek to the City's Surrender, July 18–September 2, 1864*, New York: Savas Beattie, 2017.

Davis, William, *Jefferson Davis: The Man and His Hour*, New York: Lume Books, 2016.

Delfino, Susan, Michele Gillespie, and Louis Kyriakoukis, eds, *Southern Society and Its Transformation, 1790–1860*, Columbia: University of Missouri Press, 2011.

Dew, Charles, *Apostles of Disunion: Southern Secession Commissions and the Causes of the Civil War*, Charlottesville: University of Virginia Press, 2002.

Dobak, William, *Freedom by the Sword: The Official Army History of the U.S. Colored Troops in the Civil War, 1862 to 1867*, New York: Red and Black Publishers, 2020.

Dodd, Donald and Wynelle Dodd, *Historical Statistics of the South, 1790–1970*, Tuscaloosa: University of Alabama Press, 1973.

Donald, David, *Lincoln*, New York: Simon & Schuster, 1995.

Donald, David, ed., *Why the North Won the Civil War*, New York: Collier Books, 1960.

Douglas, Anne, *The Feminization of American Culture*, New York: Knopf, 1977.

Douglass, Frederick, *The Life and Times of Frederick Douglass*, New York: Dover Books, 2003.

Dowdey, Clifford, *Lee's Last Campaign: The Story of Lee and His Men against Grant, 1864*, Lincoln: University of Nebraska Press, 1993.

Dowdey, Clifford, *The Seven Days: The Emergence of Lee*, Lincoln: University of Nebraska Press, 1993.

Duffy, James, *Lincoln's Admiral: The Civil War Campaigns of David Farragut*, New York: Castle Books, 2008.

Durden, Robert, *The Gray and the Black: The Confederate Debate on Emancipation*, Baton Rouge: Louisiana State University Press, 1972.

Egerton, Douglas, *Year of Meteors: Stephen Douglas, Abraham Lincoln, and the Election that Brought on the Civil War*, New York: Bloomsbury Press, 2010.

Egnal, Marc, *Clash of Extremes: The Economic Origins of the Civil War*, New York: Hill and Wang, 2009.

Eisenhower, John, *Agent of Destiny: The Life and Times of General Winfield Scott*, New York: Free Press, 1997.

Ellis, Richard, *The Union at Risk: Jacksonian Democracy, States' Rights, and the Nullification Crisis*, New York: Oxford University Press, 1987.

Emerson, Jason, *The Madness of Mary Lincoln*, Carbondale: University of Southern Illinois Press, 2012.

Engs, Robert, and Randall Miller, eds, *The Birth of the Grand Old Party: The Republicans' First Generation*, Philadelphia: University of Pennsylvania Press, 2002.

Ericson, David, *The Debate Over Slavery: Antislavery and Proslavery Literature in Antebellum America*, New York: New York University Press, 2000.

Escott, Paul, *After Secession: Jefferson Davis and the Failure of Confederate Nationalism*, Baton Rouge: Louisiana State University Press, 1992.

Etcheson, Nicole, *Bleeding Kansas: Contested Liberty in the Civil War Era*, Lawrence: University Press of Kansas, 2004.

Fabs, Alice, *The Imagined Civil War: Popular Literature of the North and South, 1861–1865*, Chapel Hill: University of North Carolina Press, 2001.

Farwell, Byron, *Stonewall: A Biography of General Thomas J. Jackson*, New York: W.W. Norton, 1993.

Faust, Drew Gilpin, *The Ideology of Slavery: Pro-Slavery Thought in the Ante-Bellum South*, Baton Rouge: Louisiana State University Press, 1981.

Faust, Drew Gilpin, *A Sacred Circle: The Dilemma of the Intellectual in the Old South, 1840–1860*, Baton Rouge: Louisiana State University Press, 1981.

Faust, Drew Gilpin, *The Creation of Southern Nationalism: Ideology and Identity in the Civil War South*, Baton Rouge: Louisiana State University Press, 1989.

Faust, Drew Gilpin, *Mothers of Invention: Women of the Slaveholding South*, Chapel Hill: University of North Carolina Press, 1996.

Faust, Drew Gilpin, *This Republic of Suffering: Death and the American Civil War*, New York: Vintage, 2008.

Fehrenbacher, Don, *The Dred Scott Case: Its Significance in American Law and Politics*, New York: Oxford University Press, 2001.

Fellman, Michael, *Inside War: The Guerilla Conflict in Missouri during the Civil War*, New York: Oxford University Press, 1989.

Ferris, Norman, *Desperate Diplomacy: William H. Seward's Foreign Policy*, Nashville: University of Tennessee Press, 1976.

Filler, Louis, *The Crusade Against Slavery: Friends, Foes, and Reforms, 1820–1860*, New York: Routledge, 2017.

Finkelman, Paul, *Dred Scott v. Sandford: A Brief History with Documents*, Boston: Bedford-St Martin's Press, 1997.

Finkelman, Paul, *Defending Slavery: Proslavery Thought in the Old South*, Boston: Bedford-St Martin's Press, 2003.

Finkelman, Paul, *Supreme Injustice: Slavery in the Nation's Highest Court*, Cambridge, Mass.: Harvard University Press, 2018.

Finkelman, Paul, ed., *His Soul Goes Marching On: Responses to John Brown and the Harpers Ferry Raid*, Charlottesville: University of Virginia Press, 1995.

Firth, Raymond, *Symbols: Public and Private*, Ithaca: Cornell University Press, 1973.

Fishel, Edwin, *The Secret War for the Union: The Untold Story of Military Intelligence in the Civil War*, New York: Houghton Mifflin, 1996.

Flexner, James, *Steamboats Come True: America Inventors in Action*, Boston: Little Brown, 1978.

Flood, Charles, *Grant and Sherman: The Friendship that Won the Civil War*, New York: Harper Perennial, 2006.

Fogel, Robert, and Stanley Engerman, *Time on the Cross: The Economics of American Negro Slavery*, New York: W.W. Norton, 2013.

Foner, Eric, *Reconstruction: America's Unfinished Revolution, 1863–1877*, New York: Harper and Row, 1988.

Foner, Eric, *A Short History of Reconstruction*, New York: Harper and Row, 1990.

Foner, Eric, *Free Soil, Free Labor, Free Men: The Ideology of the Republican Party before the Civil War*, New York: Oxford University Press, 1995.

Foner, Eric, *Gateway to Freedom: The Hidden History of the Underground Railroad*, New York: W.W. Norton, 2015.

Foner, Eric, *The Second Founding: How the Civil War and Reconstruction Remade the Constitution*, New York: W.W. Norton, 2020.

Foner, Philip, ed., *Frederick Douglas on Slavery and the Civil War: Selections from His Writings*, Mineola: Dover, 2003.

Foote, Shelby, *The Civil War: A Narrative, From Fort Sumter to Perryville*, New York: Vintage, 1986.

Foote, Shelby, *The Civil War: A Narrative, From Fredericksburg to Meridian*, New York: Vintage, 1986.

Foote, Shelby, *The Civil War: A Narrative, From Red River to Appomattox*, New York: Vintage, 1986.

Forbes, Robert, *The Missouri Compromise and Its Aftermath: Slavery and the Meaning of America*, Chapel Hill: University of North Carolina Press, 2009.

Foreman, Amanda, *A World on Fire: Britain's Crucial Role in the American Civil War*, New York: Random House, 2012.

Forgie, George, *Patricide in the House Divided: A Psychological Interpretation of Lincoln and His Age*, New York: W.W. Norton, 1973.

Foster, Gaines, *Ghosts of the Confederacy: Defeat, the Lost Cause, and the Emergence of the New South*, New York: Oxford University Press, 1987.

Fox-Genovese, Elizabeth, *Within the Plantation Household: Black and White Women of the Old South*, Chapel Hill: University of North Carolina Press, 1988.

Fox-Genovese, Elizabeth, and Eugene Genovese, *The Mind of the Master Class: History and Faith in the Southern Slaveholders' World View*, New York: Cambridge University Press, 2005.

Freehling, William, *Prelude to Civil War: The Nullification Controversy in South Carolina, 1816–1836*, New York: Oxford University Press, 1965.

Freehling, William, *The Road to Disunion: Secessionists at Bay, 1776–1854*, New York: Oxford University Press, 1990.

Freehling, William, *The South vs. the South: How Anti-Confederate Southerners Shaped the Course of the Civil War*, New York: Oxford University Press, 2001.

Freehling, William, *The Road to Disunion: Secessionists Triumphant, 1854–1861*, New York: Oxford University Press, 2009.

Freeman, Douglas, *R.E. Lee: A Biography*, 4 vols, New York: Charles Scribners' Sons, 1933–5.

Freeman, Douglas, *Lee's Lieutenants: A Study in Command*, 3 vols, New York: Charles Scribners' Sons, 1942–4.

Freeman, Joanne, *Affairs of Honor: National Politics in the New Republic*, New Haven: Yale University Press, 2001.

Freemon, Frank, *Gangrene and Glory: Medical Care during the Civil War*, Urbana: University of Illinois Press, 1998.

Freidman, Lawrence, *Gregarious Saints: Self and Community in American Abolitionism, 1830–1870*, New York: Cambridge University Press, 1982.

Fuller, J.F.C., *Grant and Lee: A Study in Personality and Generalship*, Bloomington: University of Indiana Press, 1957.

Furgurson, Ernest, *Chancellorsville 1863: The Souls of the Brave*, New York: Alfred Knopf, 1992.

Furgurson, Ernest, *Freedom Rising: Washington in the Civil War*, New York: Alfred Knopf, 2004.

Gallagher, Gary, *The Fredericksburg Campaign*, Chapel Hill: University of North Carolina Press, 1995.

Gallagher, Gary, *The Confederate War: How Popular Will, Nationalism, and Military Strategy Could Not Stave Off Defeat*, Cambridge, Mass.: Harvard University Press, 1997.

Gallagher, Gary, *Lee and His Army in Confederate History*, Chapel Hill: University of North Carolina Press, 2006.

Gallagher, Gary, *The Richmond Campaign of 1862: The Peninsula and the Seven Days*, Chapel Hill: University of North Carolina Press, 2008.

Gallagher, Gary, and Alan Nolan, eds, *The Myth of the Lost Cause in Civil War History*, Bloomington: Indiana University Press, 2010.

Gallman, Matthew, *Northerners at War: Reflection on the Civil War Home Front*, Ohio: Kent University Press, 2010.

Gallman, Robert, and John Wallis, eds, *American Economic Growth and Standards of Living Before the Civil War*, Chicago: University of Chicago Press, 1992.

Gaston, Paul, *The New South Creed: A Study in Southern Mythmaking*, New York: Alfred Knopf, 1970.

Geary, James, *We Need Men: The Union Draft in the Civil War*, Chapel Hill: University of North Carolina Press, 1990.

Genovese, Eugene, *The Slaveholders' Dilemma: Freedom and Progress in Southern Conservative Thought*, Columbia: University of South Carolina Press, 1992.

Genovese, Eugene, *Fatal Self Deception: Slaveholding Paternalism in the Old South*, New York: Cambridge University Press, 2012.

Gienapp, William, *The Origins of the Republican Party, 1852–1856*, New York: Oxford University Press, 1987.

Giesberg, Judith Ann, *Civil War Sisterhood: The U.S. Sanitary Commission and Women's Politics in Transition*, Boston: Northeastern University Press, 2000.

Giesberg, Judith Ann, *Army at Home: Women and the Civil War on the Northern Front*, Chapel Hill: University of North Carolina Press, 2009.

Glatthaar, Joseph, *Forged in Battle: The Civil War Alliance of Black Soldiers and White Officers*, Baton Rouge: Louisiana State University Press, 1990.

Glatthaar, Joseph, *March to the Sea and Beyond: Sherman's Troops in the Savannah and Carolina Campaigns*, Baton Rouge: Louisiana State University Press, 1995.

Goldfield, David, *America Aflame: How the Civil War Created a Nation*, New York: Bloomsburg Press, 2011.

Goodheart, Adam, *1861: The Civil War Awakening*, New York: Vintage, 2012.

Goodwin, Doris Kearns, *Team of Rivals: The Political Genius of Abraham Lincoln*, New York: Simon & Schuster, 2006.

Gordon-Reed, Annette, *Andrew Johnson: The 17th President, 1865–1869*, New York: Time Life Books, 2011.

Goss, Thomas, *The War Within the Union High Command: Politics and Generalship during the Civil War*, Lawrence: University Press of Kansas, 2003.

Gott, Kenneth, *When the South Lost the Civil War: An Analysis of the Fort Henry-Fort Donelson Campaign, February 1862*, Mechanicsburg: Stackpole Books, 2003.

Grant, Susan-Mary, *North Over South: Northern Nationalism and American Identity in the Antebellum Era*, Lawrence: University Press of Kansas, 2000.

Grant, Ulysses, *Memoirs*, Princeton: Collectors Reprints, 1998.

Green, Michael, *Freedom, Union, and Power: Lincoln and His Party during the Civil War*, New York: Fordham University Press, 2004.

Greenberg, Amy, *Manifest Manhood and the Antebellum American Empire*, New York: Cambridge University Press, 2005.

Greene, Wilson, *The Final Battles of the Petersburg Campaign: Breaking the Backbone of the Rebellion*, Knoxville: University of Tennessee Press, 2012.

Greene, Wilson, *A Campaign of Giants: The Battle for Petersburg: From the Crossing of the James to the Crater*, Chapel Hill: University of North Carolina Press, 2018.

Griffith, Paddy, *Battle Tactics and the Civil War*, London: Crowood Press, 2014.

Grimsley, Mark, *The Hard Hand of War: Union Military Policies toward Southern Civilians, 1861–1865*, New York: Cambridge University Press, 1995.

Grimsted, David, *American Mobbing, 1828–1861: Toward Civil War*, New York: Oxford University Press, 1998.

Groom, Winston, *Shiloh, 1862*, Washington DC: National Geographic Society, 2013.

Grossman, Dave, *On Killing: The Psychological Cost of Learning to Kill*, Boston: Little, Brown, 1995.

Guelzo, Allen, *Lincoln and Douglas: The Debates That Defined America*, New York: Simon & Schuster, 2008.

Guelzo, Allen, *Gettysburg: The Last Invasion*, New York: Vintage, 2014.

Gwynne, S.C., *Rebel Yell: The Violence, Passion, and Redemption of Stonewall Jackson*, New York: Charles Scribner's Sons, 2015.

Hacker, Baron, *Astride Two Worlds: Technology and the American Civil War*, Washington DC: Smithsonian Institute Scholarly Press, 2016.

Hagedon, Ann, *Beyond the River: The Untold Story of the Heroes of the Underground Railroad*, New York: Simon & Schuster, 2004.

Hagerman, Edward, *The American Civil War and the Origins of Modern Warfare: Ideas, Organization, and Field Command*, Bloomington: Indiana University Press, 1988.

Hammond, Bray, *Sovereignty and an Empty Purse: Banks and Politics in the Civil War*, Princeton: Princeton University Press, 1970.

Hammond, Bray, *Banks and Politics in America from the Revolution to the Civil War*, Princeton: Princeton University Press, 1991.

Hansen, Harry, *The Civil War: A History*, New York: Signet, 2010.

Harris, Brayton, *Blue & Grey in Black and White: Newspapers in the Civil War*, Washington DC: Brassey's, 1999.

Harris, William, *With Charity for All: Lincoln and the Restoration of the Union*, Lexington: University Press of Kentucky, 1997.

Harrold, Stanley, *The Abolitionists and the South, 1831–1861*, Lexington: University Press of Kentucky, 1995.

Harsh, Joseph, *Confederate Tide Rising: Robert E. Lee and the Making of Southern Strategy, 1861–1862*, Kent: Kent State University Press, 1998.

Hart, Lindell, *Sherman: Soldier, Realist, American*, New York: Da Capo Press, 1993.

Hartley, Roger, *Monumental Harm: Reckoning with Jim Crow Era Confederate Monuments*, Columbia: University of South Carolina Press, 2021.

Hatch, Thom, *Black Kettle: The Cheyenne Chief Who Sought Peace But Found War*, New York: John Wiley, 2004.

Hattaway, Herman, and Archer Jones, *How the North Won: A Military History of the Civil War*, Urbana: University of Illinois Press, 1991.

Hearn, Charles, *Grey Raiders of the Sea: How Eight Confederate Warships Destroyed the Union's High Seas Commerce*, Baton Rouge: Louisiana State University Press, 1996.

Hearn, Chester, *Lincoln, the Cabinet, and the Generals*, Baton Rouge: Louisiana State University Press, 2010.

Hebert, Walter, *Fighting Joe Hooker*, Lincoln: University of Nebraska Press, 1999.

Hedrick, Joan, *Harriet Beecher Stowe: A Life*, New York: Oxford University Press, 1994.

Heleniak, Roman, and Lawrence Hewitt, eds, *The Confederate High Command*, Shippensburg: White Mane Publishing, 1990.

Hennessey, John, *Return to Bull Run: The Campaign and Battle of Second Manassas*, New York: Simon & Schuster, 1993.

Herndon, William, *The Herndon's Lincoln: The True Story of a Great Life*, Springfield: The Herndon's Lincoln Publishing Company, 1921.

Herrold, Stanley, *American Abolition: Its Direct Political Impact from Colonial Times to Reconstruction*, Charlottesville: University of Virginia Press, 2019.

Hess, Earl, *Liberty, Virtue, and Progress: Northerners and Their War for the Union*, New York: Fordham University Press, 1997.

Hess, Earl, *The Union Soldier in Battle: Enduring the Ordeal of Combat*, Lawrence: University Press of Kansas, 1997.

Hess, Earl, *Trench Warfare Under Grant and Lee: Field Fortifications in the Overland Campaign*, Chapel Hill: University of North Carolina Press, 2007.

Hess, Earl, *Into the Crater: The Mine Attack at Petersburg*, Columbia: University of South Carolina Press, 2010.

Hess, Earl, *Civil War Infantry Tactics: Training, Combat, and Small Unit Effectiveness*, Baton Rouge: Louisiana State University Press, 2015.

Hess, Earl, *Braxton Bragg: The Most Hatted Man of the Confederacy*, Chapel Hill: University of North Carolina Press, 2016.

Hess, Earl, *Civil War Logistics: A Study of Military Transportation*, Baton Rouge: Louisiana State University Press, 2017.

Hesseltine, William, *Lincoln and the War Governors*, New York: Alfred Knopf, 1955.

Hesseltine, William, *Civil War Prisons: A Study in War Psychology*, Columbus: Ohio State University Press, 1998.

Hesseltine, William, ed., *Civil War Prisons*, Kent: Kent State University Press, 1972.

Hietala, Thomas, *Manifest Design: American Exceptionalism and Empire*, Ithaca: Cornell University Press, 1985.

Hoke, Donald, *Ingenious Yankees: The Rise of the American System of Manufacturing in the Private Sector*, New York: Oxford University Press, 1990.

Holt, Michael, *The Rise and Fall of the American Whig Party: Jacksonian Politics and the Onset of Civil War*, New York: Oxford University Press, 2003.

Holt, Michael, *By One Vote: The Disputed Presidential Election of 1876*, Lawrence: University Press of Kansas, 2017.

Holt, Michael, *The Election of 1860: A Campaign Fraught with Consequence*, Lawrence: University Press of Kansas, 2017.

Holzer, Harold, ed., *The Lincoln–Douglas Debates: The First Complete, Unexpurgated Text*, New York: HarperCollins, 1993.

Holzer, Harold, *Lincoln at Cooper Union: The Speech That Made Him President*, New York: Simon & Schuster, 2004.

Holzer, Harold, *Lincoln and the Power of the Press*, New York: Simon & Schuster, 2014.

Hood, Stephen, *John Bell Hood: The Rise, Fall, and Resurrection of a Confederate General*, New York: Savas Beattie, 2013.

Horowitz, Tony, *Midnight Rising: John Brown and the Raid that Sparked the Civil War*, New York: Picador, 2012.

Horsman, Reginald, *Race and Manifest Destiny: The Origins of the American Racial Anglo-Saxonism*, Cambridge, Mass.: Harvard University Press, 1981.

Horton, James, and Lois Horton, *Slavery and the Making of America*, New York: Oxford University Press, 2005.

Horwitz, Tony, *Confederates in the Attic: Dispatches from the Unfinished Civil War*, New York: Pantheon, 1998.

Houndshell, John, *From the American System to Mass Production, 1800–1932*, Baltimore: Johns Hopkins University Press, 1984.

Howe, Daniel, *What Hath God Wrought: The Transformation of America, 1815–1848*, New York: Oxford University Press, 2007.

Howe, David, *The Political Culture of the American Whigs*, Chicago: University of Chicago Press, 1984.

Huntington, Tom, *Searching for George Gordon Meade: The Forgotten Hero of Gettysburg*, Mechanicsville: Stackpole Books, 2013.

Huston, James, *Calculating the Value of the Union: Slavery, Property Rights, and the Economic Origins of the Civil War*, Chapel Hill: University of North Carolina Press, 2003.

Hyman, Harold, *The Radical Republicans and Reconstruction, 1861–1870*, Indianapolis: Bobbs-Merrill, 1967.

Hysop, Stephen, *Atlas of the Civil War: A Complete Guide to the Tactics and Terrain of Battle*, Washington DC: National Geographic, 2009.

Janney, Caroline, ed., *Petersburg to Appomattox: The End of the War in Virginia*, Chapel Hill: University of North Carolina Press, 2018.

Jefferson, Thomas, *Notes on the State of Virginia*, Chapel Hill: University of North Carolina Press, 1955.

Jeffrey, Julie Roy, *The Great Silent Army of Abolitionism: Ordinary Women in the Antislavery Movement*, Chapel Hill: University of North Carolina Press, 1998.

Jenkins, Brian, *Britain and the War for the Union*, 2 vols, Montreal: McGill-Queens University Press, 1974, 1980.

Jeremy, David, *Transatlantic Industrial Revolution: The Diffusion of Textile Technology between Britain and America, 1790–1830s*, Cambridge, Mass.: MIT Press, 1981.

Jimerson, Randall, *The Private War: Popular Thought during the Sectional Conflict*, Baton Rouge: Louisiana State University Press, 1988.

Johnson, David, *Decided on the Battlefield: Grant, Sherman, Lincoln, and the Election of 1864*, New York: Prometheus, 2020.

Johnson, Reinhard, *The Liberty Party, 1840–1848: Antislavery Third Party Politics in the United States*, Baton Rouge: Louisiana State University Press, 2021.

Jones, Archer, *Civil War Command and Strategy: The Process of Victory and Defeat*, New York: Free Press, 1992.

Jones, Archer, *The Politics of Command: Factions and Ideas in Confederate Strategy*, Baton Rouge: Louisiana State University Press, 1998.

Jones, Howard, *Blue and Grey Diplomacy: A History of Union and Confederate Foreign Relations*, Chapel Hill: University of North Carolina Press, 2009.

Jones, Martha, *Birthright Citizenship: A History of Race and Rights in Antebellum America*, New York: Cambridge University Press, 2018.

Jones, Virgil, *The Civil War at Sea: The Blockaders*, New York: Holt, Rinehart, 1960.

Jones, Wilmer, *Generals in Blue and Gray: Davis's Generals*, Mechanicsville: Stackpole Books, 2006.

Jones, Wilmer, *Generals in Blue and Gray: Lincoln's Generals*, Mechanicsville: Stackpole Books, 2006.

Josephy, Alvin, *The Civil War in the American West*, New York: Alfred Knopf, 1992.

Jung, Carl, *Man and His Symbols*, New York: Dell Publishing, 1968.

Kahan, Paul, *The Bank War: Andrew Jackson, Nicolas Biddle, and the Fight for America's Finances*, Yardley: Westholme Publishing, 2015.

Kahan, Paul, *Amiable Scoundrel: Simon Cameron, Lincoln's Scandalous Secretary of War*, Lincoln: Potomac Books, 2020.

Kalmoe, Nathan, *With Ballots and Bullets: Partisanship and Violence in the Civil War*, New York: Cambridge University Press, 2020.

Kammen, *Mystic Cords of Memory: The Transformation of Tradition in American Culture*, New York: Alfred Knopf, 1991.

Kane, Harnett, *Spies for the Blue and Gray*, New York: Doubleday, 1954.

Kete, Mary Louise, *Sentimental Collaborations: Mourning and Middle-Class Identity in Nineteenth Century America*, Durham: Duke University Press, 2000.

Kimmel, Michael, *Manhood in America: A Cultural History*, New York: Free Press, 1995.

Kinchen, Kinchen, *Confederate Operations in Canada and the North*, North Quincy: Christopher Publishing House, 1970.

Klein, Maury, *Days of Defiance: Sumter, Secession, and the Coming of the Civil War*, New York: Vintage, 1999.

Klement, Frank, *Dark Lanterns: Secret Political Societies, Conspiracy, and Treason Trials in the Civil War*, Baton Rouge: Louisiana State University Press, 1984.

Klement, Frank, *The Limits of Dissent: Clement L. Vallandigham and the Civil War*, New York: Fordham University Press, 1999.

Koch, Adrienne, and William Peden, eds, *The Life and Selected Writings of Thomas Jefferson*, New York: Modern Library, 1998.

Koistenen, Paul, *Beating Plowshares into Swords: The Political Economy of American Warfare, 1606–1865*, Lawrence: University Press of Kansas, 1996.

Korda, Michael, *Clouds of Glory: The Life and Legend of Robert E. Lee*, New York: Harper Perennial, 2015.

Korman, Abraham, *The Psychology of Motivation*, Englewood Cliffs: Prentice Hall, 1974.

Kraditor, Aileen, *Means and Ends in American Abolitionism: Garrison and His Critics on Strategy and Tactics, 1834–1850*, New York: Pantheon Books, 1969.

Langer, Suzanne, *Philosophy in a New Key: A Study of the Symbolism of Reason, Rite, and Art*, Cambridge, Mass.: Harvard University Press, 1963.

Latzer, Barry, *The Myth of Overpunishment: A Defense of the America Justice System and a Proposal to Reduce Incarceration while Protecting the Public*, New York: Republic Books, 2022.

Lawson, Melinda, *Patriot Fires: Forging a New American Nationalism in the Civil War North*, Lawrence: University Press of Kansas, 2002.

Leonard, Elizabeth, *Yankee Women: Gender Battles in the Civil War*, New York: W.W. Norton, 1997.

Lerner, William, ed., *Historical Statistics of the United States, Colonial Times to 1970*, 2 vols, Washington DC: US Department, Bureau of the Census, 1975.

Levine, Bruce, *Half Slave and Half Free: The Roots of the Civil War*, New York: Hill and Wang, 2005.

Licht, Walter, *Industrializing America: The Nineteenth Century*, Baltimore: Johns Hopkins University Press, 1995.

Linderman, Gerald, *Embattled Courage: The Experience of Combat in the American Civil War*, New York: Free Press, 1989.

Lively, Robert, *Fiction Fights the Civil War: An Unfinished Chapter in the Literary History of the American People*, Chapel Hill: University of North Carolina Press, 1957.

Lonn, Ella, *Desertion during the Civil War*, Lincoln: University of Nebraska Press, 1998.

Lowance, Mason, ed., *A House Divided: The Antebellum Slavery Debates in America, 1776–1865*, Princeton: Princeton University Press, 2003.

Lowry, Thomas, *Confederate Heroines: 120 Southern Women Convicted by Union Military Justice*, Baton Rouge: Louisiana State University Press, 2006.

McCardell, John, *The Idea of a Southern Nation: Southern Nationalists and Southern Nationalism, 1830–1860*, New York: W.W. Norton, 1981.

McCarthy, Timothy, and John Stauffer, eds, *Prophets of Protest: Reconsidering the History of American Abolitionism*, New York: New Press, 2006.

McClintock, Russell, *Lincoln and the Decision for War: The Northern Response to Secession*, Chapel Hill: University of North Carolina Press, 2008.

MacCloskey, Monro, *Hallowed Ground: Our National Cemeteries*, New York: Richard Rosens Press, 1968.

McCurry, Stephanie, *Confederate Reckoning: Power and Politics in the Civil War South*, Cambridge, Mass.: Harvard University Press, 2010.

McDonough, James, *William Tecumseh Sherman: In the Service of My Country, A Life*, New York: W.W. Norton, 2017.

Mackay, Thomas, *Opposing Lincoln: Clement L. Vallandigham, Presidential Powe, and the Legal Battle over Dissent in Wartime*, Lawrence: University Press of Kansas, 2020.

McKenzie, John, *Uncertain Glory: Lee's Generalship Reexamined*, New York: Hippocrene Books, 1997.

McKitrick, Eric, *Andrew Johnson and Reconstruction*, Chicago: University of Chicago Press, 1960.

McKivigan, John, and Stanley Herrold, eds, *Antislavery Violence: Sectional, Racial, and Cultural Conflict in Antebellum America*, Knoxville: University of Tennessee Press, 1999.

McPherson, James, *Ordeal by Fire: The Civil War and Reconstruction*, New York: Alfred Knopf, 1982.

McPherson, James, *Battle Cry of Freedom: The Civil War Era*, New York: Oxford University Press, 1988.

McPherson, James, *What They Fought For, 1861–1865*, Baton Rouge: Louisiana State University Press, 1994.

McPherson, James, *'We Cannot Escape History': Lincoln and the Last Best Hope of Earth*, Urbana: University of Illinois Press, 1995.

McPherson, James, *For Cause and Comrades: Why Men Fought in the Civil War*, New York: Oxford University Press, 1997.

McPherson, James, *Crossroads of Freedom: Antietam*, New York: Oxford University Press, 2002.

McPherson, James, *The Negro's Civil War: How America's Blacks Felt and Acted during the War for Union*, New York: Vintage, 2003.

McPherson, James, *Tried by War: Abraham Lincoln as Commander in Chief*, New York: Penguin, 2009.

McPherson, James, *Embattled Rebel: Jefferson Davis as Commander in Chief*, New York: Penguin, 2014.

McPherson, James, and William Cooper, eds, *Writing the Civil War: The Quest to Understand*, Columbia: University of South Carolina Press, 1998.

McWhiney, Grady, and Perry Jamieson, *Attack and Die: Civil War Military Tactics and the Southern Heritage*, Tuscaloosa: University of Alabama Press 1984.

Magdol, Edward, *The Antislavery Rank and File: A Social Profile of the Abolitionist Constituency*, Westport: Greenwood Press, 1986.

Mahin, Dean, *One War at a Time: The International Dimensions of the American Civil War* Washington DC: Potomac Books, 1999.

Maltz, Earl, *Slavery and the Supreme Court, 1825–1861*, Lawrence: University of Kansas Press, 2009.

Mangual, Rafael, *Criminal (In)Justice: What the Rise for Decarceration and Depolicing Gets Wrong and Who It Hurts Most*, New York: Center Street Books, 2022.

Manning, Chandra, *What This Cruel War Was Over*, New York: Vintage, 2008.

Markle, Donald, *Spies and Spymasters of the Civil War*, New York: Hippocrene, 2004.

Martis, Kenneth, *Historical Atlas of Political Parties in the United States Congress, 1789–1989*, Englewood Cliffs: Prentice Hall, 1989.

Marvel, William, *Burnside*, Chapel Hill: University of North Carolina Press, 1991.

Marvel, William, *Andersonville: The Last Depot*, Chapel Hill: University of North Carolina Press, 1994.

Marvel, William, *Mr. Lincoln Goes to War*, Boston: Houghton Mifflin, 2006.

Marvel, William, *Lincoln's Autocrat: The Life of Edwin Stanton*, Chapel Hill: University of North Carolina Press, 2015.

Maurantonio, Nicole, *Confederate Exceptionalism: Civil War Myth and Memory in the Twenty-First Century*, Topeka: University Press of Kansas, 2019.

Maxfield, Derek, *Hellmira: The Union's Most Infamous Civil War Prison Camp*, New York: Savas Beattie, 2020.

Maxwell, William, *Lincoln's Fifth Wheel: The Political History of the United States Sanitary Commission*, New York: Longmans, Green, and Company, 1956.

May, Robert, *Manifest Destiny's Underworld: Filibustering in Antebellum America*, Chapel Hill: University of North Carolina Press, 2002.

Mayer, Henry, *All On Fire: William Lloyd Garrison and the Abolition of Slavery*, New York: W.W. Norton, 2008.

Mayr, Otto, and Robert Post, eds, *Yankee Enterprise: The Rise of the American System of Manufactures*, Washington DC: Smithsonian, 1982.

Meltzer, Milton, *Slavery: A World History*, New York: Da Capo Press, 1993.

Merrill, James, *Rebel Shore: The Story of Union Sea Power in the Civil War*, New York: Little, Brown, 1958.

Merritt, Keri Leigh, *Masterless Men: Poor Whites and Slavery in the Antebellum South*, New York: Cambridge University Press, 2017.

Meyer, David, *The Roots of America's Industrialization*, Baltimore: Johns Hopkins University Press, 2003.

Meyer, David, *Networked Machinists: High Technologies Industries in Antebellum America*, Baltimore: Johns Hopkins University Press, 2006.

Miller, Donald, *Vicksburg: Grant's Campaign that Broke the Confederacy*, New York: Simon & Schuster, 2020.

Miller, Randall, Harry Stout, and Charles Wilson, eds, *Religion and the American Civil War*, New York: Oxford University Press, 1998.

Miller, William, *President Lincoln: The Duty of a Statesman*, New York: Alfred Knopf, 2008.

Mitcham, Samuel, *Bust Hell Wide Open: The Life of Nathan Bedford Forrest*, New York: Regnery, 2019.

Mitchell, Elizabeth, *Lincoln's Lies: A True Caper through Fake News, Wall Street, and the White House*, New York: Counterpoint, 2020.

Mitchell, Reid, *Civil War Soldiers*, New York: Viking, 1988.

Monaghan, Jay, *Civil War on the Western Border, 1854–1865*, Lincoln: University of Nebraska Press, 1955.

Moore, John, *The Emergence of the Cotton Kingdom in the Old Southwest*, Baton Rouge: University of Louisiana Press, 1988.

Morris, Charles, *The Dawn of Innovation: The First American Industrial Revolution*, New York: Public Affairs, 2012.

Morris, Roy, *Sheridan: The Life and Wars of General Phil Sheridan*, New York: Vintage, 1993.

Morris, Roy, *Ambrose Bierce: Alone in Bad Company*, New York: Oxford University Press, 1995.

Morris, Roy, *Fraud of the Century: Rutherford B. Hayes, Samuel Tilden, and the Stolen Election of 1876*, New York: Simon & Schuster, 2004.

Morrison, Michael, *Slavery and the American West: The Eclipse of Manifest Destiny and the Coming of the Civil War*, Chapel Hill: University of North Carolina Press, 1997.

Moss, Elizabeth, *Domestic Novelists in the Old South: Defenders of Southern Culture*, Baton Rouge: Louisiana State University Press, 1992.

Mowery, David, *Morgan's Great Raid: The Remarkable Expedition from Kentucky to Ohio*, Charleston: History Press, 2013.

Murdock, Eugene, *Patriotism Limited 1862–1865: The Civil War Draft and the Bounty System*, Kent: Kent State University Press, 1967.

Murdock, Eugene, *One Million Men: The Civil War Draft in the North*, Madison: University of Wisconsin Press, 1971.

Myerson, Joel, and Daniel Shealy, eds, *The Journal of Louisa May Alcott*, Athens: University of Georgia Press, 1997.

Nash, Howard, *A Naval History of the Civil War*, New York: A.S. Barnes, 1972.

Neely, Mark, *The Fate of Liberty: Abraham Lincoln and Civil Liberties*, New York: Oxford University Press, 1991.

Neely, Mark, *Southern Rights: Political Prisoners and the Myth of Confederate Constitutionalism*, Charlottesville: University of Virginia Press, 1999.

Neely, Mark, *The Divided Union: Party Conflict in the Civil War North*, Cambridge, Mass.: Harvard University Press, 2002.

Neely, Mark, Harold Holzer, and Gabor Boritt, *The Confederate Image: Prints of the Lost Cause*, Chapel Hill: University of North Carolina Press, 1987.

Nelson, James, *Reign of Iron: The Story of the First Battling Ironclads: The Monitor and the Merrimack*, New York: William Morrow, 2004.

Nelson, Scott, and Carol Sheriff, *A People at War: Civilians and Soldiers in America's Civil War, 1854–1877*, New York: Oxford University Press, 2007.

Nester, William, *The Revolutionary Years, 1775–1789*, Washington DC: Potomac Books, 2011.

Nester, William, *The Hamiltonian Vision, 1789–1800: The Art of American Power during the Early Republic*, Washington DC: Potomac Books, 2012.

Nester, William, *The Age of Jackson and the Art of America Power, 1815–1848*, Washington DC: Potomac Books, 2013.

Nester, William, *The Age of Lincoln and the Art of American Power, 1848–1876*, Washington DC: Potomac Books, 2013.

Nester, William, *The Jeffersonian Vision, 1801–1815: The Art of American Power during the Early Republic*, Washington DC: Potomac Books, 2013.

Nester, William, *The Struggle for Power in Colonial America, 1607–1776*, New York: Lexington Books, 2017.

Nester, William, *Putin's Virtual War: Russia's Subversion and Conversion of America, Europe, and the World Beyond*, London: Frontline Books, 2019.

Nester, William, *The Old West's First Power Couples: The Fremonts, the Custers, and Their Epic Quest for Manifest Destiny*, Tucson: Rio Nuevo Publishers, 2020.

Newman, Richard, *The Transformation of American Abolitionism: Fighting Slavery in the Early Republic*, Chapel Hill: University of North Carolina Press, 2002.

Newson, Ryan, *Cut in Stone: Confederate Monuments and Theological Disruption*, Waco, Texas: Baylor University Press, 2020.

Nicoletti, Cynthia, *Secession on Trial: The Treason Prosecution of Jefferson Davis*, New York: Cambridge University Press, 2017.

Nolan, Alan, *Lee Reconsidered: General Robert E. Lee and Civil War History*, Chapel Hill: University of North Carolina Press, 1991.

Nolan, Alan, *Lee Reconsidered: General Robert E. Lee and Civil War History*, Chapel Hill: University of North Carolina Press, 2000.

Noll, Mark, *The Civil War as a Theological Crisis*, Chapel Hill: University of North Carolina Press, 2006.

North, Douglas, *The Economic Growth of the United States, 1790–1860*, Englewood Cliffs: Prentice Hall, 1961.

Northup, Solomon, *Twelve Years a Slave*, New York: Barnes and Noble, 2017.

Nosworthy, Brent, *The Bloody Crucible of Courage: Fighting Methods and Combat Experience of the Civil War*, New York: Carrol and Graf, 2003.

O'Brien, Michael, *Conjectures of Order: Intellectual Life and the American South*, 2 vols, Chapel Hill: University of North Carolina Press, 2004.

Onuf, Peter, *Nations, Markets, and War: Modern History and the American Civil War*, Charlottesville: University of Virginia Press, 2006.

Osterweis, Rollin, *The Myth of the Lost Cause, 1865–1900*, Hamden: Archon Books, 1973.

Owsley, Frank, *King Cotton Diplomacy: Foreign Relations of the Confederate States of America*, Tuscaloosa: University of Alabama Press, 2008.

Owsley, Ted, ed., *Black and White: Cultural Interaction in the Ante-Bellum South*, Oxford: University of Mississippi Press, 2008.

Packard, Jerrold, *American Nightmare: The History of Jim Crow*, New York: St Martin's Press, 2002.

Paludan, Philip, *The Presidency of Abraham Lincoln*, Lawrence: University Press of Kansas, 1994.

Panzer, Mary, *Mathew Brady and the Image of History*, Washington DC: Smithsonian Books, 2004.

Parsons, Elaine Frantz, *Ku Klux: The Birth of the Klan during Reconstruction* (Chapel Hill: University of North Carolina Press, 2019).

Perret, Geoffrey, *Lincoln's War: The Untold Story of America's Greatest President as Commander in Chief*, New York: Random House, 2004.

Perry, James, *The Bohemian Brigade: The Civil War Correspondents – Mostly Rough, Sometimes Ready*, New York: John Wiley, 2000.

Perry, Lewis, *Radical Abolitionists: Anarchy and Government of God in Antislavery Thought*, Ithaca: Cornell University Press, 1973.

Peterson, Lawrence, *Decisions of the Atlanta Campaign: The Twenty-one Central Decisions that Defined the Operation*, Chattanooga: University of Tennessee Press, 2019.

Pfarr, Gary, *Longstreet at Gettysburg: A Critical Assessment*, Jefferson: McFarland Publishing, 2019.

Phillips, Christopher, *Damned Yankee: The Life of General Nathaniel Lyon*, Baton Rouge: Louisiana State University Press, 1996.

Pierson, Michael, *Free Hearts, Free Homes: Gender and American Abolitionist Politics*, Chapel Hill: University of North Carolina Press, 2003.

Piston, William, *Lee's Tarnish General: James Longstreet and His Place in Southern History*, Athens: University of Georgia Press, 1990.

Pittenger, William, and James Bogle, *Daring and Suffering: A History of the Andrews Raid*, Nashville: Cumberland House, 1999.

Powell, David, *The Chattanooga Campaign – A Mad Irregular Battle: From the Crossing of the Tennessee River through the Second Day, August 22 to September 19, 1863*, New York: Savas Beattie, 2016.

Powell, David, *The Chattanooga Campaign – Glory or the Grave: The Breakthrough, the Union Collapse, and the Defense of Horseshoe Ridge, September 9, 1863*, New York: Savas Beattie, 2016.

Powell, David, *The Chattanooga Campaign – Barren Victory: The Retreat to Chattanooga, the Confederate Pursuit, and the Aftermath of Battle, September 21–October 20, 1864*, New York: Sava Beattie, 2016.

Powell, David, *The Spoils of Victory: Ulysses S. Grant at Chattanooga*, Carbondale: Southern Illinois Press, 2020.

Powell, David, and Eric Wittenberg, *Tullahoma: The Forgotten Campaign that Changed the Course of the War*, New York: Savas Beattie, 2010.

Pryor, Elizabeth, *Clara Barton: Professional Angel*, Philadelphia: University of Pennsylvania Press, 1987.

Pugh, David, *Sons of Liberty: The Masculine Mind in Nineteenth Century America*, Westport: Greenwood Press, 1983.

Quarles, Benjamin, *Allies for Freedom: Blacks and John Brown*, New York: Da Capo, 2001.

Rable, George, *But There Was No Peace: The Role of Violence in the Politics of Reconstruction*, Athens: University of Georgia Press, 1984.

Rable, George, *Civil Wars: Women and the Crisis of Southern Nationalism*, Urbana: University of Illinois Press, 1989.

Rable, George, *The Confederate Republic: A Revolution against Politics*, Chapel Hill: University of North Carolina Press, 2007.

Rael, Patrick, *Black Identity and Black Protest in the Antebellum North*, Chapel Hill: University of North Carolina Press, 2002.

Rafuse, Ethan, *McClellan's War: The Failure of Moderation in the Struggle for the Union*, Bloomington: University of Indiana Press, 2011.

Ramage, James, *Rebel Raider: The Life of General John Hunt Morgan*, Lexington: University of Kentucky Press, 1995.

Ramage, James, *Gray Ghost: The Life of Col. John Singleton Mosby*, Lexington: University of Kentucky Press, 1999.

Ransom, Roger, *Conflict and Compromise: The Political Economy of Slavery*, New York: Cambridge University Press, 1989.

Ratner, Lorman, and Dwight Teeter, *Fanatics and Fire-eaters: Newspapers and the Coming of the Civil War*, Champlain: University of Illinois Press, 2002.

Rawley, James, *Race and Politics: 'Bleeding Kansas' and the Coming of the Civil War*, Lincoln: University of Nebraska Press, 1979

Reader, John, *Africa: A Biography of the Continent*, New York: Vintage, 1999.

Reed, Rowena, *Combined Operations in the Civil War*, Annapolis: Naval Institute Press, 1978.

Reid, Brian, *The Origins of the American Civil War*, London: Longman, 1996.

Reid, Brian, *The Scourge of War: The Life of William Tecumseh Sherman*, New York: Oxford University Press, 2020.

Reynolds, David, *John Brown, Abolitionist: The Man Who Killed Slavery, Sparked the Civil War, and Seeded Civil Rights*, New York: Vintage, 2006.

Rhea, Gordon, *On to Petersburg: Grant and Lee, June 4–15, 1864*, Baton Rouge: Louisiana State University Press, 2017.

Richards, Leonard, *The Slave Power: The Free North and Southern Domination, 1780–1860*, Baton Rouge: Louisiana State University Press, 2000.

Richardson, Heather Cox, *The Greatest Nation of the Earth: Republican Economic Policies during the Civil War*, Cambridge, Mass.: Harvard University Press, 1997.

Risley, Ford, *Civil War Journalism*, New York: Praeger, 2012.

Robert, Alistair, *America's First Great Depression: Economic Crisis and Political Disorder after the Panic of 1837*, Ithaca: Cornell University Press, 2013.

Robertson, James, *Stonewall Jackson: The Man, the Soldier, the Legend*, New York: Macmillan, 1997.

Robertson, James, *Soldiers Blue and Gray*, Charleston: University of South Carolina Press, 1998,

Robinson, Armstead, *Bitter Fruits of Bondage: The Demise of Slavery and the Collapse of the Confederacy, 1861–1865*, Charlottesville: University of Virginia Press, 2005.

Robinson, Donald, *Slavery in the Structure of American Politic, 1765–1820s*, New York: W.W. Norton, 1979.

Root, Damon, *A Glorious Liberty: Frederick Douglass and the Fight for an Anti-Slavery Constitution*, Lincoln: Potomac Books, 2020.

Rubin, Anne Sarah, *A Shattered Nation: The Rise and Fall of the Confederacy*, Chapel Hill: University of North Carolina Press, 2005.

Russo, Peggy, and Paul Finkelman, eds, *Terrible Swift Sword: The Legacy of John Brown*, Athens: Ohio University Press, 2005.

Sachsman, David, *A Press Divided: Newspaper Coverage of the Civil War*, New York: Transaction Books, 2014.

Sachsman, David and George Borchard, *The Antebellum Press: Setting the Stage for the Civil War*, New York: Routledge, 2019.

Sachsman, David, Kittrell Rushing, and Roy Morris, *Memory and Myth: The Civil War in Fiction and Film from Uncle Tom's Cabin to Cold Mountain*, Richmond: Purdue University Press, 2007.

Sachsman, David, Kittrell Rushing, and Debra Reddin van Tryll, eds, *The Civil War and the Press*, New York: Routledge, 1999.

Sachsman, David, Kittrell Rushing, et al., *Words at War: The Civil War and American Journalism*, West Lafayette: Purdue University Press, 2008.

Sandburg, Carl, *Abraham Lincoln: The Prairie Years and the War Years*, New York: Mariner Books, 2002.

Sandefur, Timothy, *Frederick Douglass: Self-Made Man*, Washington DC: Cato Institute, 2018.

Saulaude, Steve, *France and the Civil War: A Diplomatic History*, Chapel Hill: University of North Carolina Press, 2019.

Savage, Kirk, *Standing Soldiers, Kneeling Slaves: Race, War, and Monument in Nineteenth Century America*, Princeton: Princeton University Press, 1997.

Scales, John, *Nathan Bedford Forrest, 1861–1865: The Battles and Campaigns of Confederate General*, New York: Savas Beattie, 2019.

Schecter, Barnet, *The Devil's Own Work: The Civil War Draft Riots and the Fight to Reconstruct America*, New York: Walker Books, 2007.

Schiff, Adam, ed., *The January 6 Report: Findings of the Selective Committee to Investigate the January 6 Attack on the United States Capitol*, New York: Random House, 2023.

Schmidt, Christopher, *Civil Rights in America: A History*, New York: Cambridge University Press, 2020.

Schultz, Duane, *Month of the Freezing Moon: The Sand Creek Massacre, November 1864*, New York: St Martin's Press, 1990.

Schutz, Wallace, and Walter Trenerry, *Abandoned by Lincoln: A Military Biography of General John Pope*, Urbana: University of Illinois Press, 1990.

Sears, Stephen, *To the Gates of Richmond: The Peninsula Campaign*, New York: Ticknor and Shields, 1992.

Sears, Stephen, *Chancellorsville*, New York: Mariner Books, 1998.

Sears, Stephen, *George B. McClellan: The Young Napoleon*, New York: Da Capo Press, 1999.

Sears, Stephen, *The Landscape Turned Red: The Battle of Antietam*, New York: Mariner Books, 2003.

Sears, Stephen, *Gettysburg*, New York: Mariner Books, 2004.

Sears, Stephen, *Lincoln's Lieutenants: The High Command of the Army of the Potomac*, Boston: Houghton Mifflin, 2017.

Seidule, Ty, *Robert E. Lee and Me: A Southerner's Reckoning with Lost Cause*, New York: St Martin's Press, 2021.

Selby, John, *Meade: The Price of Command*, Kent: Kent State University Press, 2018.

Sewall, Richard, *Ballots for Freedom: Antislavery Politics in the United States, 1837–1860*, New York: Oxford University Press, 1976.

Sheriff, Carol, *The Artificial River: The Erie Canal and the Paradox of Progress, 1817 to 1862*, New York: Oxford University Press, 1997.

Sherman, William Tecumseh, *The Memoirs of General W.T. Sherman*, New York: Library of America, 1990.

Silber, Nina, *Daughters of the Union: Northern Women Fight the Civil War*, Cambridge, Mass.: Harvard University Press, 2005.

Silbey, Joel, *A Respectable Minority: The Democratic Party in the Civil War Era, 1860–1868*, New York: W.W. Norton, 1977.

Simon, James, *Lincoln and Chief Justice Taney: Slavery, Secession, and the President's War Powers*, New York: Simon & Schuster, 2006.

Sinha, Manisha, *The Slave's Cause: A History of Abolition*, New Haven: Yale University Press, 2017.

Sklar, Karyn Kish, ed., *Women's Rights Emerges within the Antislavery Movement, 1830–1870: A Brief History with Documents*, Boston: Bedford-St Martin's Press, 2000.

Smith, Gene, *Lee and Grant: A Dual Biography*, New York: McGraw-Hill, 1984.

Smith, Jean, *Grant*, New York: Touchstone, 2001.

Smith, Timothy, *Grant Invades Tennessee: The 1862 Battles for Forts Henry and Donelson*, Lawrence: University Press of Kansas, 2016.

Smith, Timothy, *Shiloh: Conquer or Perish*, Lawrence: University Press of Kansas, 2016.

Snay, Michael, *Gospel of Disunion: Religion and Separatism in the Antebellum South*, New York: Cambridge University Press, 1993.

Snow, Richard, *Iron Dawn: The Monitor, the Merrimack, and the Civil War Sea Battle that Changed History*, New York: Scribner, 2016.

Sodergren, Steven, *The Army of the Potomac in the Overland and Petersburg Campaigns: Union Soldiers and Trench Warfare*, Baton Rouge: Louisiana State University Press, 2017.

Soley, James, *The Blockade and the Cruisers*, New York: Charles Scribner's Sons, 1885.

Soltow, Lee, *Men and Wealth in the United States, 1850–1870*, New Haven: Yale University Press, 1975.

Speer, Lonnie, *Portals to Hell: Military Prisons of the Civil War*, Lincoln: University of Nebraska Press, 2005.

Stampp, Kenneth, *The Peculiar Institute: Slavery in the Antebellum South*, New York: Vintage, 1989.

Stauffer, John, and Zoe Trodd, eds, *Meteor of War: The John Brown Story*, Maplecrest: Brandywine Press, 2004.

Steigmaier, Mark, *Texas, New Mexico, and the 1850 Compromise: Boundary Dispute and Sectional Crisis*, Kent: Kent State University Press, 1996.

Steiner, Paul, *Disease in the Civil War: Natural Biological Warfare in 1861–1865*, Springfield: C.C. Thomas, 1968.

Stern, Philip Van Doren, ed., *The Life and Writings of Abraham Lincoln*, New York: Modern Library, 1940.

Stewart, David, *Impeached!: The Trial of President Andrew Johnson and the Fight for Lincoln's Legacy*, New York: Simon & Schuster, 2009.

Stewart, James. *Holy Warriors: The Abolitionists and American Slavery*, New York: Hill and Wang, 1976.

Stoker, Donald, *The Grand Design: Strategy and the U.S. Civil War*, New York: Oxford University Press, 2010.

Stowe, Harriet Beecher, *Uncle Tom's Cabin*, New York: Barnes and Noble, 2012.

Studenski, Paul, and Herman Krooss, *The Financial History of the United States*, New York: Beard Books, 2003.

Summers, Mark, *The Plundering Generation: Corruption and the Crisis of the Union, 1849–1861*, New York: Oxford University Press, 1987.

Sutherland, Daniel, *The Emergence of Total Warfare: Civil War Campaigns and Commanders* Abilene, Texas: McWhiney Foundation Press, 1998.

Sutherland, Daniel, *A Savage Conflict: The Decisive Role of Guerrillas in the Civil War*, Chapel Hill: University of North Carolina Press, 2013.

Sutherland, Daniel, ed., *Guerillas, Unionists, and Violence on the Confederate Homefront*, Fayetteville: University of Arkansas Press, 1999.

Sword, Wiley, *Southern Invincibility: A History of the Confederate Heart*, New York: St Martin's Griffin, 2000.

Symonds, Craig, *Joseph E. Johnston: A Civil War Biography*, New York: W.W. Norton, 1993.

Symonds, Craig, *The Civil War at Sea*, New York: Oxford University Press, 2012.

Symonds, Craig, ed., *Union Combined Operations in the Civil War*, New York: Fordham University Press, 2010.

Tadman, Michael, *Speculators and Slaves: Masters, Traders, and Slaves in the Old South*, Madison: University of Wisconsin Press, 1998.

Tanner, Robert, *Stonewall in the Valley: Thomas J. 'Stonewall' Jackson's Shenandoah Valley Campaign, Spring 1862*, Mechanicsburg: Stackpole Books, 1996.

Tap, Bruce, *Over Lincoln's Shoulder: The Committee on the Conduct of the War*, Lawrence: University Press of Kansas, 1998.

Tate, Adam, *Conservatism and Southern Intellectuals, 1789–1861: Liberty, Tradition, and the Good Society*, Columbia: University of Missouri Press, 2005.

Taylor, George, *The Transportation Revolution, 1815–1860*, New York: Routledge, 1977.

Taylor, William, *Cavalier and Yankee: The Old South and American National Character*, New York: Braziller, 1957.

Thelen, David, ed., *Memory and American History*, Bloomington: University of Indiana Press, 1990.

Theoharris, Jeanne, *A More Beautiful and Terrible History: The Uses and Misuses of Civil Rights History*, New York: Beacon Press, 2019.

Thomas, Edison, *John Hunt Morgan and His Raiders*, Lexington: University of Kentucky Press, 1985.

Thomas, Emory, *The Confederacy as a Revolutionary Experience*, Columbia: University of South Carolina University Press, 1992.

Thomas, Emory, *Robert E. Lee: A Biography*, New York: W.W. Norton, 1997.

Thomas, Hugh, *The Slave Trade: The Story of the Atlantic Slave Trade, 1440–1870*, New York: Touchstone, 1997.

Tidwell, William, James Hall, and David Gaddy, *Come Retribution: The Confederate Secret Service and the Assassination of Lincoln*, Jackson: University Press of Mississippi, 1988.

Tise, Larry, *Proslavery: A History of the Defense of Slavery in America, 1701–1840*, Athens: University of Georgia Press, 1987.

Tomblin, Barbara Brooks, *The Civil War on the Mississippi: Union Sailors, Gunboat Captains, and the Campaign to Control the River*, Lexington: University Press of Kentucky, 2020.

Trefousse, Hans, *The Radical Republicans: Lincoln's Vanguard for Racial Justice*, New York: Alfred Knopf, 1969.

Trefousse, Hans, *Andrew Johnson*, New York: W.W. Norton, 1997.

Trelease, Allen, *White Terror: The Ku Klux Klan Conspiracy and Southern Reconstruction*, New York: Harper and Row, 1971.

Trudeau, Noah, *Gettysburg: A Testing of Courage*, New York: Perennial, 2002.

Trudeau, Noah, *Southern Storm: Sherman's March to the Sea and Beyond*, New York: Harper Perennial, 2009.

Tucker, Barbara, and Kenneth Tucker, *Industrializing Antebellum America: The Rise of Manufacturing Entrepreneurs in the Early Republic*, New York: Palgrave Macmillan, 2008.

Tucker, Spencer, *Blue and Grey Navies: The Civil War Afloat*, Annapolis: Naval Institute Press, 2013.

Tulloch, Hugh, *The Debate on the American Civil War Era*, Manchester: Manchester University Press, 1999.

Turner, George, *Victory Rode the Rails: The Strategic Place of Railroads in the Civil War*, New York: Bobbs-Merrill, 1953.

Unger, Irwin, *The Greenback Era: A Social and Political History of America*, Princeton: Princeton University Press, 1964.

United States, *Official Records of the Union and Confederate Navies in the War of the Rebellion*, 30 vols, Washington DC: Government Printing Office, 1894–1922.

United States, *War of the Rebellion: A Compilation of the Official Records of the Union and Confederate Armies*, 128 vols, Washington DC: Government Printing Office, 1880–1901.

Van Doren, Mark, ed., *The Portable Walt Whitman*, New York: Penguin, 1977.

Veron, Elizabeth, *Disunion!: The Coming of the American Civil War, 1789–1859*, Chapel Hill: University of North Carolina Press, 2008.

Veron, Elizabeth, *Appomattox: Victory, Defeat, and Freedom at the Civil War's End*, New York: Oxford University Press, 2013.

Vinovskis, Maris, ed., *Toward a Social History of the American Civil War*, New York: Cambridge University Press, 1990.

Walters, Ronald, *The Antislavery Appeal: American Abolitionism after 1830*, Baltimore: Johns Hopkins University Press, 1976.

Ward, Andrew, *The River Ran Red: The Fort Pillow Massacre in the American Civil War*, New York: Viking, 2005.

Waugh, John, *Reelecting Lincoln: The Battle for the 1864 Presidency*, New York: Da Capo Press, 2001.

Waugh, John, *On the Brink of Civil War: The Compromise of 1850 and How It Changed the Course of American History*, Wilmington: Scholarly Resources, 2003.

Waugh, John, *Lincoln and McClellan: The Troubled Partnership between a President and His General*, New York: St Martin's Griffin, 2011.

Weber, Jennifer, *Copperheads: The Rise and Fall of Lincoln's Opponents in the North*, New York: Oxford University Press, 2008.

Weigley, Russell, *A Great Civil War: A Military and Political History, 1861–1865*, Bloomington: University of Indiana Press, 2000.

Welles, Gideon, *The Diary of Gideon Welles, Secretary of the Navy*, Boston: Houghton Mifflin, 1911.

Wert, Jeffry, *From Winchester to Cedar Creek: The Shenandoah Campaign of 1864*, Carlisle: South Mountain Press, 1987.

Wert, Jeffry, *General James Longstreet: The Confederacy's Most Controversial Soldier*, New York: Simon & Schuster, 1994.

Wert, Jeffrey, *The Sword of Lincoln: The Army of the Potomac*, New York: Simon & Schuster, 2005.

West, Richard, *Mr. Lincoln's Navy*, New York: Longmans, Green, 1957.

Wheelan, Joseph, *Terrible Swift Sword: The Life of Philip H. Sheridan*, New York: Da Capo, 2012.

Wheelan, Joseph, *Their Last Full Measure: The Final Days of the Civil War*, New York: Da Capo, 2016.

Wheeler, Joseph, *Bloody Spring: Forty Days That Sealed the Confederacy's Fate*, New York: Da Capo, 2014.

White, Jonathan, *Emancipation, the Union Army, and the Reelection of Abraham Lincoln*, Baton Rouge: Louisiana State University Press, 2014.

Widener, Ralph, *Confederate Monuments: Enduring Symbols of the South and the War between the States*, Washington DC: Andromeda Associates, 1982.

Wilentz, Sean, *The Rise of American Democracy: Jefferson to Lincoln*, New York: W.W. Norton, 2005.

Wilentz, Sean, *No Property in Man: Slavery and Antislavery at the Nation's Founding* Cambridge, Mass.: Harvard University Press, 2019.

Wiley, Bell Irvin, *Confederate Women*, Westport: Praeger, 1975.

Williams, David, *A People's History of the Civil War*, New York: New Press, 2005.

Williams, Harry, *McClellan, Sherman, and Grant*, New Brunswick: Rutgers University Press, 1962.

Williams, Jack, *Dueling in the Old South: Vignettes of Social History*, College Station: Texas A & M University Press, 2000.

Wills, Gary, *Lincoln at Gettysburg: The Words That Remade America*, New York: Simon & Schuster, 1992.

Wilson, Charles, *Baptized in Blood: The Religion of the Lost Cause, 1865–1920*, Athens: University of Georgia Press, 1980.

Wilson, Edmund, *Patriotic Gore: Studies in the Literature of the American Civil War*, New York: W.W. Norton, 1994.

Wilson, Mark, *The Business of War: Military Mobilization and the State, 1861–1865*, Baltimore: Johns Hopkins University Press, 2006.

Wineapple, Brenda, *The Impeachers: The Trial of Andrew Johnson and the Dream of a Just Nation*, New York: Random House, 2020.

Winkle, Kenneth, *Lincoln's Citadel: The Civil War in Washington DC*, New York: W.W. Norton, 2013.

Wise, Stephen, *Lifeline of the Confederacy: Blockade Running during the Civil War*, Charleston: University of South Carolina Press, 1991.

Witt, John, *Lincoln's Code: The Laws of War in American History*, New York: Free Press, 2012.

Wittenberg, Eric, Edmund Sargus, and Penny Barrick, *Seceding from Secession: The Civil War, Secession, and the Creation of West Virginia*, New York: Savas Beattie, 2020.

Wolosky, Shira, *Emily Dickinson: A Voice of War*, New Haven: Yale University Press, 1984.

Wood, Betty, *Slavery in Colonial America, 1619 to 1776*, New York: Rowman and Littlefield, 2005.

Woodman, Harold, *King Cotton and His Retainers: Financing and Marketing the Cotton Crop of the South, 1800–1926*, New York: Beard Books, 2000.

Woodward, C. Vann, *The Origins of the New South, 1877–1913*, Baton Rouge: Louisiana State University Press, 1951.

Woodward, C. Van, *The Strange Career of Jim Crow*, New York: Oxford University Press, 1974.

Woodward, C. Van, *Reunion and Reaction: The Compromise of 1877 and the End of Reconstruction*, New York: Oxford University Press, 1991.

Woodward, C. Vann, ed., *Mary Chestnut's Civil War*, New Haven: Yale University Press, 1981.

Woodworth, Steven, *Jefferson Davis and His Generals: The Failure of Confederate Command in the West*, Lawrence: University Press of Kansas, 1990.

Woodworth, Steven, *Davis and Lee at War*, Lawrence: University Press of Kansas, 1995.

Woodworth, Steven, *Nothing But Victory: The Army of the Tennessee, 1861–1865*, New York: Alfred Knopf, 2005.

Wooster, Ralph, *The Secession Conventions of the South*, Princeton: Princeton University Press, 1962.

Wright, Gavin, *The Political Economy of the Cotton South: Households, Markets, and Wealth in the Nineteenth Century*, New York: W.W. Norton, 1978.

Wyatt-Brown, Bertram, *Southern Honor: Ethics and Behavior in the Old South*, New York: Oxford University Press, 1982.

Wyeth, John, *That Devil Forrest: A Life of General Nathan Bedford Forrest*, Baton Rouge: Louisiana State University Press, 1989.

Yellin, Jean Fagan, and John Van Horne, eds, *The Abolitionist Sisterhood: Women's Political Culture in Antebellum America*, Ithaca: Cornell University Press, 1994.

Young, Alfred, *Lee's Army during the Overland Campaign: A Numerical Study*, Baton Rouge: Louisiana States University Press, 2013.

Zelinsky, Wilbur, *Nation into State: The Shifting Symbolic Foundations of American Nationalism*, Chapel Hill: University of North Carolina Press, 1988.

Index